A Man publickly Whipped in the Sessions House Yard

THE MALEFACTOR's REGISTER;

OR, THE NEWGATE and TYBURN CALENDAR.

CONTAINING THE

AUTHENTIC LIVES, TRIALS, ACCOUNTS OF EXECUTIONS, AND DYING SPEECHES,

OF THE MOST NOTORIOUS

VIOLATORS OF THE LAWS OF THEIR COUNTRY;

WHO HAVE

Suffered DEATH, and other exemplary PUNISHMENTS, in *England*, *Scotland* and *Ireland*, from the Year 1700 to LADY-DAY 1779.

Together with

NUMEROUS TRIALS in EXTRAORDINARY CASES, where the Parties have been ACQUITTED.

This Work comprehends all the moſt material Paſſages in the SESSIONS-PAPERS for a long Series of Years, and complete NARRATIVES of all the Capital TRIALS for

BIGAMY,	HIGH-TREASON,	RIOTS,
BURGLARY,	MURDER,	STREET-ROBBERY,
FELONY,	PETIT-TREASON,	UNNATURAL CRIMES,
FORGERY,	PIRACY,	And various other
HIGHWAY-ROBBERY,	RAPES,	OFFENCES.

To which is added,

A correct Liſt of all the Capital Convictions at the Old Bailey, &c. ſince the Commencement of the preſent Century; which will be of the higheſt Uſe to refer to on many Occaſions.

The whole tending, by a general Diſplay of the Progreſs and Conſequence of Vice, to impreſs on the Mind proper Ideas of the Happineſs reſulting from a Life of ſtrict Honor and Integrity: and to convince Individuals of the ſuperior Excellence of thoſe Laws framed for the Protection of their Lives and Properties.

Such is the Folly, ſuch the Fate
Attendant on diſhoneſt Schemes,
That Villains ever find, too late,
An End to their deluſive Dreams.
We ſee—and oftimes they confeſs
With their departing Breath,
" The Paths of Honour lead to Peace,
The Ways of Vice—to Death."

Embelliſhed with a moſt elegant and ſuperb ſet of Copper Plates, engraved in a ſpirited Manner, from original Deſigns, by capital Artiſts.

VOL. V.

LONDON:

Printed, by Authority, for ALEXANDER HOGG, at No. 16, Paternoſter-Row.

Peter Conway & Michael Richardson, shooting Mr Venables and Mr Rogers, near Stepney Fields.

THE MALEFACTOR's REGISTER;

OR,

The NEWGATE and TYBURN CALENDAR.

A Narrative of the horrid Murder, committed by PETER CONWAY and MICHAEL RICHARDSON, on Mr. Venables, a Butcher in Whitechapel, and Mr. Rogers, a Carpenter; with an Account of their Execution, and being hung in Chains for the same.

FROM the best accounts we have been able to obtain of these unhappy men, we learn, that an inattention to their education laid the foundation of their ruin. They engaged in the paths of vice early in life, and having forfeited their characters by the irregularity of their conduct, their minds were gradually prepared for the commission of the most horrid of crimes. It was too frequently their practice to spend the greater part of the day in houses of ill fame, where they drank to such a degree as to qualify themselves for scenes of more than brutal enterprize during the night.

On Saturday the 26th of May, 1770, Richardson, Conway, and two men named Jackson and Fox, went to the shop of Mr. Robert Dun, in Princes-square, near Ratcliff-highway, and purchased a pair of pistols. The above-mentioned Jackson was afterwards an evidence against his accomplices: but we do not learn that Fox was ever taken into custody.

Having thus purchased the pistols, they left them at the house of an acquaintance, named Thomas; after which they all went to the lodgings of Conway, where they spent the night.

On the succeeding day (Sunday) they took a coach to Whitechapel, where they continued drinking till the dusk of the evening, when they went to Thomas's house for the pistols. Being unprovided with balls, they remained for a while in consultation what to substitute in their stead; and at length they cut a pewter-spoon in pieces, and loaded their pistols.

This being done, Conway and Richardson went together, and the other two accompanied them, but at a small distance, that they might not appear to be a gang of Ruffians. They met a gentleman's servant, whom they stopped; but, as he had no money, he was permitted to pass without farther molestation.

It happened that, in the afternoon, Mr. Venables, a Butcher in Whitechapel, had been walking to Stepney, with his neighbour, Mr. Rogers, a Carpenter; and they were returning to town when they were met by the villains abovementioned, which happened a few minutes after they had parted from the gentleman's servant.

Mr. Venables and Mr. Rogers had the appearance of men from whom a considerable booty might be be expected; whereupon Conway stopped the former, and demanded his money; but, instead of delivering it, Mr. Venables, who was a robust man, twice knocked down Richardson and Fox; and they had no sooner recovered their legs, than Richardson and Conway instantly fired their pistols, and the two unoffending passengers were killed on the spot.

These unprovoked murders being thus perpetrated, the villains did not stay to rob the parties; but, with the consciousness of guilt, hurried away towards Stepney, whence they went to Ratcliff-highway, and thence to Wapping, where they stopped a man, and robbed him of eighteen shillings and his watch.

This robbery being committed, they hastened to Darkhouse-lane, near Billingsgate, where they staid during the night; and the next morning, after breakfasting at a public house in Southwark, they parted, with a view of consulting their safety in flight.

The bodies of the deceased, being found in the road, were conveyed to the watch-house; and a surgeon being sent for, he examined the wounds, and found that they had been made by pieces of pewter.

On the following Wednesday Jackson was apprehended on suspicion of having been concerned in the commission of these horrid murders. On his examination he gave information who were his accomplices; on which he was admitted an evidence for the crown.

In a few days after Jackson was taken in custody, Conway went to the shop of Mr. Burtman, a pawnbroker in Jermyn-street; where he offered a watch in pledge. An advertisement in the news-paper, describing the person of Conway, having been read by Mr. Burtman, the latter imagined that he was the man thus described; on which he gave a hint to one of his servants to sit by Conway, while he (Burtman) examined the watch.

The servant, apprehending danger, whispered his master that it was probable he had pistols in his possession; on which a person was sent out, to request the attendance of the neighbours, with a view to prevent mischief. In the interim Conway, remarking that they whispered together, begged permission to retire to the vault; which he was readily allowed to do:—but on his return he was taken into custody, and a coach was called to convey him to Sir John Fielding's office in Bow-street.

As they were going thither, Mr. Burtman hinted a strong suspicion that Conway * was guilty of the murders; to which the latter made this remarkable and shocking answer; "D—— my eyes! though I am guilty (I mean not guilty) I could not shoot two men at once."

When he was brought to the house of the magistrate abovementioned, he was confronted with Jackson, when they mutually endeavoured to criminate each other; but the circumstances against Conway were so very suspicious, that Sir John Fileding did not hesitate to commit him to Newgate.

Richardson was likewise apprehended within five days after this commitment, and taken to Bow-street for examination; when the charge against him was so very strong, that he was likewise committed to Newgate, to abide the event of a trial by jury.

Jackson

---

* Some of the accounts give this man's name *Connaway*; but it is uncertain which is the true spelling.

Jackson having been admitted an evidence (as abovementioned), bills of indictment were preferred, at the next sessions at the Old Bailey, against Conway and Richardson, who were thereupon put on their trials for the murders of Mr. Venables and Mr. Rogers. Jackson's evidence against them was full and positive; and this being strongly supported by that of the person of whom they had purchased the pistols, aided by a variety of collateral circumstances, the jury did not hesitate to convict them; the consequence of which was, that they were condemned to die.

After conviction they were, as usual in such cases, lodged in the cells of Newgate; and we are sorry to say that their penitence did not seem proportioned to the dreadful crime they had committed; a crime of the blackest dye, and altogether unprovoked by those who fell victims to their inhuman barbarity.

On the Monday following they were conveyed to the place of execution; an incredible number of people attending the solemn procession, and preparing to see the exit of men who had distinguished themselves by the atrociousness of their crimes, and whose story had excited the public curiosity in a very high degree.

Unprepared as these men appeared to have been for the dreadful fate that awaited them, yet, when they saw how near and how certain it was, they seemed to be shocked to a degree beyond description; and appeared as solemn and sincere in their devotions as others who had suffered at the fatal tree.

After execution their bodies were cut down, and conveyed to Bow-common, where they were put in chains, and hung on a gibbet. It is hardly credible

ble to think what immense numbers of people went from London, to take a view of these malefactors while hanging in chains: to talk of a thousand, or ten thousand, would be saying nothing. Perhaps more than fifty thousand visited the spot within the first five days. On Sunday, particularly, the place resembled a crowded fair; and many people got money by selling liquors and other provisions to the assembled multitude. So great was the crowd, that the banks in the neighbourhood, and even the hedges, were broken down, that the mob might gratify their eager curiosity.

These malefactors suffered at Tyburn on the 19th of July, 1770.

In the case of these men the consciousness of guilt will appear in its most striking light; for after they had committed the murders, such was their terror, that they did not dare to reap the intended fruits of their illegal expedition; for we find that the murdered men were not robbed, but the guilty parties sought their safety in flight; so true is that scriptural expression, "the wicked fly, when no "man pursueth."

No account has ever reached us of what became of the accomplice Fox. It was presumed that he escaped out of the kingdom; but could he escape from his own conscience? from those terrors which must ever haunt the guilty mind? Alas! he could not. The attempt must have been vain; since he carried about with him the consciousness of being a murderer, and must have had a perpetual hell within his own breast.

The story before us will serve to enforce, in a very emphatic manner, that divine command, "Thou shalt do no murder." May all the readers of this narrative be instructed in the doctrines of
hu-

humanity! nor provoke the vengeance of that God, who, though he may be flow to punish, will not suffer his holy commands to be trampled under foot!

A Narrative of the Cafe of JOHN STRETTON, who was executed for robbing the Mail; with an Account of the Circumftance that led to his Detection.

THIS unhappy man was defcended of refpectable parents, who gave him a liberal education; nor did any circumftance arife to throw blame on his character, till the difcovery of the crime which coft him his life.

He was apprenticed to a grocer in London, and ferved his time with a degree of fidelity that would have done credit to any fervant; and he appeared to gain the general good opinion of thofe who were acquainted with him.

At the expiration of his apprenticefhip he went to live as a journeyman to a grocer in Bifhopfgate-ftreet, where he ftill maintained a fair character, and continued in this ftation feveral years, during which he married and had a daughter; but his wife died a confiderable time before the perpetration of the fact which rendered him a fatal victim to the violated laws of his country.

Mr. Stretton, having by his frugality accumulated a fum of money, opened a fhop in Bifhopfgate-ftreet on his own account, and had every reafonable profpect of fuccefs; for fo regular had been his

his conduct, and so irreproachable was his character, that not any person in his own way of business refused to give him credit to any reasonable amount.

Unhappily, however, he had not long embarked in trade, before his ruin ensued, from a cause which one would have thought very unlikely to produce it.

Having conceived a design of advancing himself in life by a second marriage, and a butcher in the neighbourhood being reputed worth a considerable sum of money, he paid his addresses to his daughter, who was so well pleased with him, that she did not hesitate to make a declaration in his favour; but the father, unwilling to part with any money, as a portion for his daughter, resolved not to give his consent, because Mr. Stretton was not in circumstances of independence.

In the mean time the lovers contrived frequent opportunities of seeing each other, and the young woman repeatedly informed Mr. Stretton with the determination of her father. Chagrined by this circumstance, and resolved to remove the objection which seemed to arise from his presumed poverty, he made the dreadful resolution of robbing the mail.

He had not, however, for some time an opportunity of carrying his intention into execution; for he was seized with a severe fit of illness, which confined him to his bed for some weeks, during which time he was frequently visited by the girl whom he had courted, and also by her mother, who was a warm friend to the proposed marriage.

At length he recovered his health in a very considerable degree; on which he resolved to compleat, if possible, the plan which had so long agitated his mind.

mind. In purfuance hereof he took an opportunity when his fhopman was in bed one Saturday night to quit the houfe, and go as far as the City-road, between Iflington and London, where he awaited the arrival of the Northern mail, which came oppofite Peerlefs-pool about two o'clock in the morning.

Stretton, obferving the poft-boy coming up, ftopped the mail, and took out fuch bags as he thought proper; after which he went into Moorfields, where he examined the contents of the bags, and taking out fuch bills and notes as he thought proper, left the bags behind him, and retired to his own houfe.

As foon as the robbery was made known at the Poft-office, the Poftmafter-general offered by advertifement, as is ufual on fuch occafions, a reward of two hundred pounds for the apprehenfion of the robber: but nothing tranfpired in the courfe of feveral weeks; and it is probable that the offender might have remained much longer undetected, but for the following circumftance.

Stretton ftill continued to pay his addreffes to the butcher's daughter; but her father, unwilling that fhe fhould marry a man in low or doubtful circumftances, was continually talking to Stretton on the fubject of money matters; till at length the latter was fo imprudent as to fhew him the draughts in his poffeffion, and even to fend a porter to Mr. Boldero's, the banker, for the acceptance of one of them, that no doubt might remain of their being good notes: but the porter had no fooner prefented the bill, than he was detained, and a peace-officer, and other perfons, were fent in fearch of Mr. Stretton, whom they found at his own houfe.

They enquired how he came to be possessed of the note in question; to which he replied, that he had taken it in the course of business from a person in Bond-street who was in his debt.

This story did not seem to be credited: however a coach was called; and the parties went together to Bond-street, in search of the person who was said to have paid the bill: but no such man could be found; on which the suspicions against Stretton being greatly strengthened, he was conveyed to the house of Sir John Fielding, who committed him to Newgate, to abide the event of a trial.

Objections being made by council to the putting him on his trial at the first and second sessions after his commitment, it was accordingly brought on at the third *.

When Mr. Stretton was put on his trial, full proof arose that the draughts and notes which had been taken out of the mail were found in his house, and, as he could give no probable account how they came into his possession, there was a strong presumptive, amounting almost to positive, proof that he had himself committed the robbery; for it appeared evident to the jury, that a tradesman, who had taken these bills and notes in the common course of business, could have accounted for the manner in which he became possessed of them, or at least of the greater part of them.

After a full deliberation on the case, the jury did not hesitate to pronounce him guilty, the con-

---

* It ought to be mentioned, to the credit of our Courts of justice, that the slightest argument, which has but the appearance of reason, is sufficient to influence the bench in favour of the prisoner.

fequence of which was, that he received fentence of death.

After conviction he was regular in his attendance on the offices of divine worfhip; but no arguments that were made ufe of could prevail on him to acknowledge his guilt; and he fteadily perfifted in a denial of the Juftice of his fentence. Notwithftanding this, he appeared exceedingly penitent for all the faults which he had ever committed; and declared that he expected falvation only through the merits of the Redeemer of mankind:—but with regard to robbing the mail, he infifted that he had never been guilty of it, and that he detefted the thought of fuch an execrable bafenefs, and was totally innocent of the crime alledged againft him.

Thefe declarations he repeatedly made; and on the morning of execution, when he was called down to the prefs-yard, to have his irons knocked off, he was urged by the ordinary of Newgate to make an explicit confeffion of the crime; but, far from doing fo, he ftill avowed his perfect innocence.

He was attended to the place of execution by immenfe crouds of people, who wifhed to hear the dying words of a man to be executed for fo capital a crime, for which he would never acknowledge the juftice of that verdict by which he had been condemned.

This unhappy man fuffered at Tyburn on the 1ft of Auguft, 1770.

Many people have thought it impoffible, and indeed humanity would fuppofe it fo, for any man to die with a lie in his mouth; but in the cafe of Stretton it will be very hard to form an opinion in his favour; for, if he did not obtain the notes and draughts by robbing the mail, how did he obtain them?—If he could have given an honeft account how he became possessed of them; if he could, as Shakespear emphatically phrases it, have delivered "a round unvarnished tale;" it would have been almost impossible that he should have been convicted; for the jurymen of this country, (to their honour be it recorded) are exceedingly tender of the lives of their fellow-citizens.

The presumption then, in this particular case, is very strong that the malefactor must have denied his crime from a species of pride altogether unwarrantable. We would not wish to be thought severe or uncharitable in our conjectures; but it is improbable that any man could have been possessed of the contents of a mail, which had been robbed, without knowing how they came into his possession.

His sending the draught to the banker's for acceptance is a proof of the most egregious folly; for he must have been morally certain that his messenger would be stopped, and that his own detection would inevitably ensue.

If we suppose that his love induced him to take this dangerous step; we should recollect that he had been married before, and was therefore the less likely to have been involved in a passion so violent as to tempt him to so dangerous an experiment.

Upon the whole, notwithstanding all appearances to the contrary, the presumption is very strong, that this man was in distressed circumstances, which he sought to repair by marriage; but finding his hopes at least postponed, he took the most dangerous method imaginable to repair his shattered fortunes.

It is astonishing that, during his sickness, he should not have had recollection enough to induce him

him to desist from carrying into execution the dangerous plan he had formed. In general, sickness is productive of thoughts more serious than those which attend us in perfect health :—but the whole of this unhappy man's conduct should teach us to pray continually for the assisting grace of God, that we may not be led into temptation, but delivered from all the evils that surround us; so that, after a short passage through this troublesome world, we may be received into the arms of eternal mercy!

A Narrative of the Trials of LUKE CANNON and JOHN SIDAY, who suffered for Burglary; with some Account of their Behaviour.

AT the sessions held at the Old Bailey in the month of February, 1771, Luke Cannon and John Siday were indicted for breaking and entering the dwelling house of the Honourable Edward Stratford about two o'clock in the morning of the 12th of January preceding, and stealing silver plate, gold rings, diamonds, and a variety of other valuable articles, to the amount of two thousand pounds.

It would be equally useless and tedious to recount the particulars of the indictment; for the things stolen were so very numerous, that the bare recital of them would fill some pages of this work.

Mary Brain, who had been a servant to Mr. Stratford at the time of the robbery, deposed, that Cannon had likewise lived with her Master, but had been discharged on the second of January; that

Siday came for some cloaths which Cannon had left behind him; but that the servants would not deliver them, as they conceived he had no authority to come thither. She said that there was an area before the window of the fore-kitchen, which she found to be fast at ten o'clock, and that the kitchen window-shutter was secure at eight o'clock; and likewise, that the robbers must have entered at the fore-kitchen.

Alexander Cornelius deposed, that he was a servant of Mr. Stratford; and that when he arose on the morning of the 12th of January, he found a press burst open which he had safely locked on the preceding night, and that the plate was gone: that he found the plate chest in the house keeper's room burst open; that the sash in the window of the area had been burst, and the cords were hanging to it; and that he observed many specks of wax about the hall, and some dirt which was not there on the preceding night. He said he had not been above ten or eleven days in Mr. Stratford's service, and was ignorant of what was lost out of the house-keeper's room.

Elizabeth Chamberlayne (the house-keeper) confirmed as much of Cornelius's evidence as came within her knowledge, and said that nothing was stolen from her room except the plate. She deposed that Cannon entered into Mr. Stratford's service at Bath; but she had never seen Siday till after he was taken into custody.

Mr. Stratford gave the particulars of his having been robbed, as far as he could be acquainted with them;—he said, that he had taken Cannon into his service at Bath, but discharged him on the second of January, on finding him much flushed with liquor,

quor, as he made it a rule never to keep a servant who was attached to the vice of drunkenness.

Moses Levi, a dealer in old cloaths, deposed, that Siday called him into his lodgings in Sea-coal-lane on the 21st of January, when Cannon was present, and that he bought of Siday some valuable cloaths, and 650 ounces of plate, paying for it upwards of one hundred and seventy pounds in cash and a note; and that he paid a part of the sum to Siday, and a part to Cannon; and farther, that he sold the plate to Jacob Jacobs, the son of Lazarus Jacobs. The testimony of the witness was positive that both the prisoners were present at the time he made the purchase.

There were a variety of corroborative circumstances, tending to prove the stealing and selling of the plate and other effects: but the affair was so clear to the jury, that they did not hesitate to find the prisoners guilty; in consequence of which they received sentence of death.

At the same time Lazarus Jacobs, Jacob Jacobs, and Michael Glannon, were tried for receiving the stolen effects; when Lazarus was acquitted, but Jacob Jacobs and Glannon were convicted, and sentenced to be transported for fourteen years, though they made very artful defences, and Glannon particularly brought many people to testify to his character:—but character will have little weight against positive evidence.

After conviction, the behaviour of Cannon and Siday was by no means adapted to their unhappy situation. They were attended, as usual in such cases, by the ordinary of Newgate, but paid little regard to his pious exhortations.

On the morning of execution Siday behaved in the most hardened manner; and of three others that

that were condemned to suffer, one of them struck the executioner when he was put into the cart.

Immense crowds of spectators attended these unhappy young men to the place of their fatal exit; for their crimes had been much the subject of public conversation. Siday, in particular, had been concerned with George Birch in breaking open the house of Mr. Greenfield, linen-draper, in Fleet-street, and robbing it of goods to the amount of more than thirteen hundred pounds.

When they arrived at the place of execution, Cannon said, that he had been a single man, a married man, an honest man, and a rogue, within a twelvemonth; and in which time he should suffer.

Luke Cannon and John Siday were executed at Tyburn on the 27th of February, 1771.

Of Cannon we have not been able to learn any farther particulars than what may be gathered from the course of the evidence above-recited. With regard to Siday, we are told, that he was born of respectable parents, well educated, and apprenticed to the very genteel profession of a printer. What use he made of these advantages is but too plainly seen in the preceding narrative.

An early attachment to bad company, an early introduction to the paths of vice, led with rapid and certain success to his ruin. Such ruin may be expected, and ought to be dreaded, by every youth, who dare not have the resolution of treading in the paths of virtue.

Yet, when we consider how much more easy it is to be honest than otherwise, how safe and how plain is the path of duty, one would wonder that any

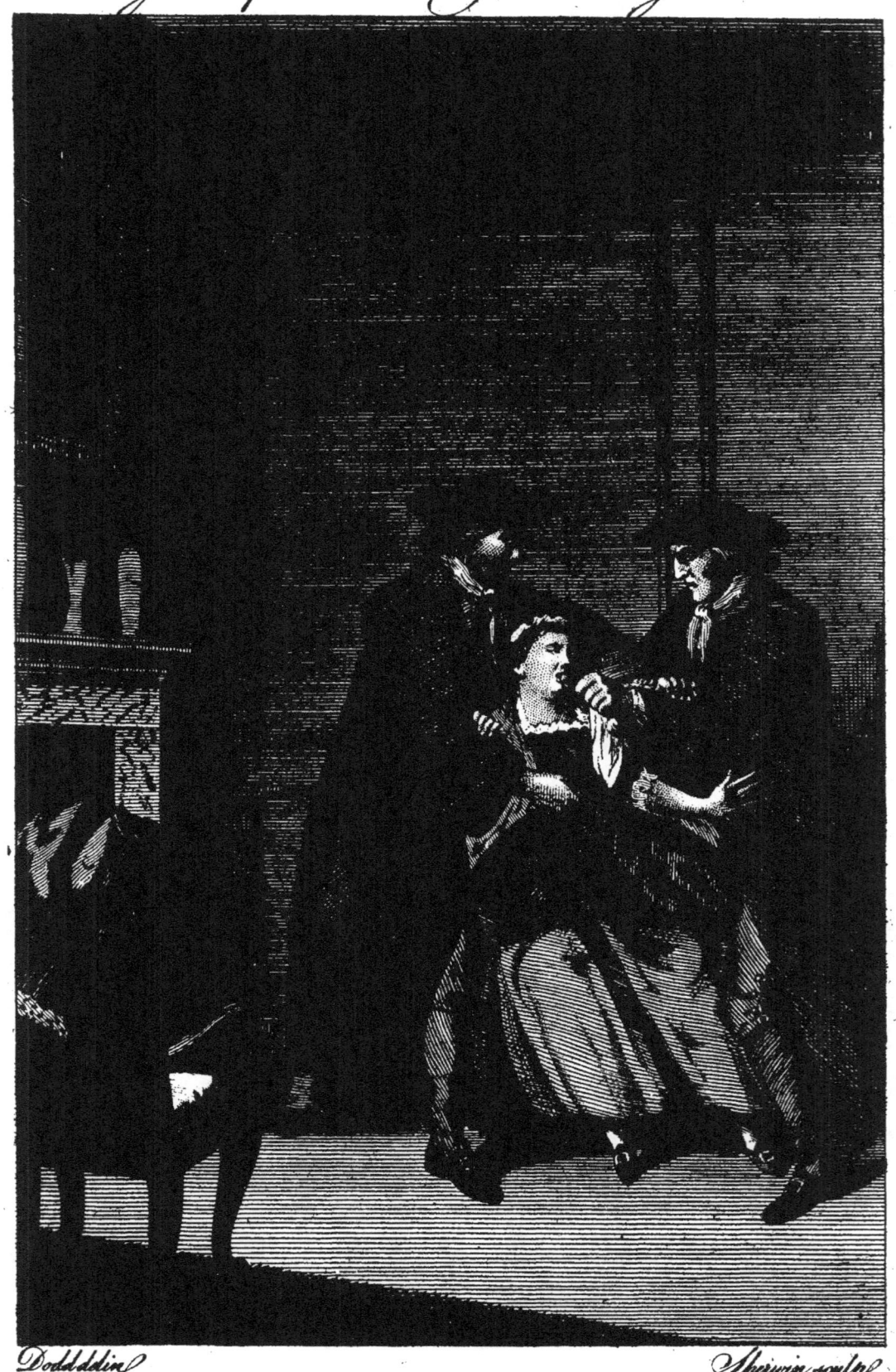

Engraved for The Malefactors Register.

LEVI WEIL *the Jew-Doctor, preventing* HYAM LAZARUS *from shooting* Mrs HUTCHINS *at Chelsea.*

any could be blind enough to deviate into the ways of error!

From a serious consideration of the case before us, youth should be taught that a steady and unremitting perseverance in the line of duty, whatever little inconveniencies may seem to attend them at the time, will infallibly tend to promote their welfare, temporal and eternal.

What person in his senses would condescend to to be a rogue, when it is so much his interest to be honest? To say nothing of higher considerations, the mere credit of living in reputation, and being spoken well of by all our neighbours, should be sufficient to put vice out of fashion!

In the case before us one excellent lesson is taught to servants: Mr. Stratford dischaged Cannon, because he found him in liquor.—The reason was a good one. The man who will disguise himself, so as not to have the command of his own intellects, can never be the faithful servant of any master.

A full and particular Account of the Cases of LEVI WEIL, ASHER WEIL, JACOB LAZARUS, and SOLOMON PORTER, who were convicted of, and executed for, Robbery and Murder.

THE circumstance of the robbery at Mrs. Hutchins's house at Chelsea, and the murder that was the consequence of this egregious violation of the laws, must be within the memory of almost all our readers: but as the affair was greatly the subject of public conversation at the time, and a whole body of people were insulted for the crimes of a few individuals, we think it proper to be as exact as possible in the recital of particulars.

The subjects of this shocking narrative were all of them Jews; and such were their proceedings, that it may be easily conceived that they were a disgrace to people of any persuasion.

Levi Weil had been educated in a rank above his accomplices. He had studied physic in the university of Leyden, where he was admitted to the degree of Doctor in that faculty; and then coming to England, he practised physic in London, with no inconsiderable degree of success, and was always known by the name of Doctor Weil: but so destitute was he of all principle, and such was the depravity of his heart, that he determined to engage in the dangerous practice of robbery; and, having formed this fatal resolution, he wrote to Amsterdam to some poor Jews, to come to England, and assist him in his intended depredations on the public; and at the same time informed them, that in England large sums were to be acquired by the practice of theft.

The inconsiderate men no sooner received Dr. Weil's letter, than they procured a passport from the English consul, and, embarking in the Harwich packet boat, arrived in England.

They lost no time in repairing to London; and immediately attending Dr. Weil, he informed them that his plan was, that they should go out in the day-time, and minutely survey such houses near London as might probably afford a good booty in the night.

In pursuance of this plan they robbed the house of a lady near Cheshunt in Hertfordshire, and likewise that of Mr. Barclay near Endfield, whence they carried off plate and cash to a considerable amount.

This

This courſe of life they continued for ſome time, always binding the ſervants in the houſes which they robbed, and leaving them in that ſituation till they might be relieved by any perſon who ſhould witneſs their diſtreſs ; and in the mean time the villains haſtened to London with their ill-acquired booty.—But we now proceed to relate the particulars of the dreadful crime which ended in the death of the four malefactors whoſe names are mentioned at the head of this narrative.

Mrs. Hutchins was a widow lady, who occupied a very conſiderable farm in the King's-road, Chelſea ; and the Jews having made artful enquiries into her circumſtances, and finding a probability of obtaining a valuable booty, they formed the reſolution of robbing her houſe.

In purſuance of this plan they went to Chelſea on the evening of the 11th of June, 1771; and having ſauntered in the fields till the clock had ſtruck ten, they then went to the houſe of Mrs. Hutchins, and knocking at the door, it was opened by a maid-ſervant.

The door was no ſooner opened, than eight Jews ruſhed into the houſe. At this time Mrs. Hutchins was in the parlour ; but, hearing the barking of her dog, ſhe ran forwards, to learn what occaſioned the diſturbance, when ſhe found that the girl's cap was torn by the villains, who were treating her with very unwarrantable ſeverity. Mrs. Hutchins would have aſſiſted the girl ; but Doctor Weil ſeized on her, and compelled her to ſit down in a chair ; after which he threw part of her cloaths over her head, to prevent her having a view of the houſe-breakers ; and he threatened to murder Mrs. Hutchins, if ſhe made any diſturbance.

Terrified into ſubmiſſion, ſhe promiſed to remain in her preſent ſituation ; and in the mean time five of the Jews went up stairs to a room where Joseph Slow, and William Stone, two men-servants of Mrs. Hutchins, were in bed together, and in a sound sleep. Doctor Weil gave Stone a violent blow on the breast, by which he was awakened; and Slow starting up at that instant, one of the villains cried out, "shoot him;" and a pistol was immediately fired, the ball from which took place in the body of Slow, who instantly exclaimed, "Lord have mercy on me! I am murdered, I am "murdered."

The villains now dragged the body of the wounded man towards the head of the stairs, which being observed by Stone, he made his escape out of the window; but, before he had effected his escape, he was fired at by one of the gang; though happily the shot did not take effect.

They now proceeded to plunder the house, and obtained a considerable booty in plate. After this they applied to Mrs. Hutchins for money. She gave them her watch; but still they insisted on money, which they said they came for, and would have, or they would destroy her. One of them struck her so forcibly on the mouth, as to loosen a tooth; on which, in the dread of still farther violence, she went up stairs with them, and gave them sixty-four guineas.

Having thus obtained all the booty they could, the villains quitted the house; on which Mrs. Hutchins went to see how her servants had fared in this horrid violation of law and humanity. She found two of the maid-servants bound together; and no sooner had she given them their liberty, than the wounded man approached her, and said, "How are you, Madam?—for I am dead."—These words were scarcely pronounced, when he dropped on the floor; and, having languished under the most excruciating pains till the afternoon of the following day, he then expired, leaving behind him a wife and two children to lament his loss.

The murderers, having effected a perfect escape, remained undiscovered for a considerable time, till Daniel Isaacs, one of the gang, became the means, in the hand of Providence, of discovering his accomplices. The case was this. Isaacs was one of those unhappy men who had been induced to come from Holland in consequence of Dr. Weil's letter; and being now reduced to circumstances of distress, he applied for assistance to the elders of the Jewish synagogue.

The treasurer of the synagogue, Mr. Myers,* refused Isaacs any immediate assistance, urging as a reason, that he had acted improperly in leaving his native country, Holland, where he might have probably obtained an honest livelihood, and coming to England, where he could not have an equal chance of living in credit.

The robbery and murder at Mrs. Hutchins's was no sooner known, than a reward was offered, from the Secretary of State's office, for the apprehension of the offenders; and this offer was seconded by that of a much more considerable reward from the city of London: on which, Isaacs, greatly reduced by poverty, and tempted by the prospect of the reward, went to Mr. Myers, whom he made acquainted with the whole of the shocking transaction.

Hereupon Mr. Myers took Isaacs to Sir John Fielding's office, where he was strictly examined,

---

* This Mr. Myers is still living (in January 1779), and, to his honour be it spoken, has been always as ready to promote the punishment of dishonest Jews, as to protect honest men of the same religion.

and

and admitted an evidence against his accomplices, fix of whom were soon apprehended; but the other made his escape, and it is supposed he went abroad, as he has not been heard of since.

At the sessions held at the Old Bailey in the month of December, 1771, Levi Weil, Asher Weil, Marcus Hartogh, Jacob Lazarus, Solomon Porter, Lazarus Harry, and Abraham Linevill (the party who had absconded), were indicted for the felony and murder above-mentioned; when the two of the name of Weil, with Jacob Lazarus, and Solomon Porter, were capitally convicted; and Marcus Hartogh, and Lazarus Harry, were acquitted.

These men, as is customary in all cases of murder, when it can be made convenient to the court, were tried on a Friday; and on the following day they were anathematized in the synagogue.

As their execution was to take place on the Monday following, one of their Rabbies went to them in the press-yard of Newgate, and delivered to each of them a Hebrew book; but declined attending them to the place of death, nor even prayed with them at the time of his visit.

They were attended to the place of execution by immense crowds of people, who were anxious to witness the exit of wretches whose crimes had been so much the object of public notice.

Having prayed together, and sung an hymn in the Hebrew language, they were launched into eternity. After the bodies had hung the customary time, that of Doctor Weil was delivered to the gentlemen of the Royal Academy, while those of his accomplices were conveyed to Surgeons'-hall to be dissected.

These victims to the violated laws suffered at Tyburn on the 9th of December, 1771.

Every

Every one who has read this narrative, will allow that the crime of the above-mentioned malefactors was of the first magnitude; and that the forfeit they paid was not too great for the offences they had committed;—burglary and murder equally unprovoked;—but their crime, conviction, and execution, gave rise to a scene of insult and inhumanity highly reproachful to the lower ranks of people in London: nor were those in superior stations wholly divested of it.

A Jew could scarcely pass the streets but he was upbraided with the words, "Hutchins" and "Chelsea," and many of them were pulled by the beards; while those, who ought to have taken the insulters into custody, stood calmly by, and triumphed in the insult.

All this might arise from what they thought to be, and perhaps might be, generous impulses: but shall any person of liberal breeding see a fellow subject insulted, in defiance of law and reason, and not endeavour to protect him? All the rights of humanity, as well as the laws of the land, forbid the supposition.

There is something wantonly cruel in affronting the whole body of a people, because a few individuals of that people have rendered themselves obnoxious by the atrocity of their guilt. As well might we affront an Englishman, because an Englishman may have suffered the sentence of the law, as a Jew, because that fatal sentence may have followed the crimes of some of his profession.

In this case, to put all considerations of good manners and decorum out of the question, christian charity ought to prevail; and we should no more quarrel with a man because he cannot coincide with us in sentiments, than we should for not being born with us at the same time and place with ourselves.

A true christian will pity and forgive the errors of a Jew:—he has the glorious light of the gospel to guide him; and devoutly ought he to be thankful for its superior influence! The Jews hope for a Messiah to come: we boast of the revelation already made; and surely our compassion ought to be extended to those whom we think less happy than ourselves:—This is the very essence of charity; and he, who cannot pity the man that he thinks in distress, is scarcely deserving of pity from others.

Christians ought to offer up their most ardent thanks to God who has bestowed on them the blessings of divine revelation; and well may they say, in the words of the poet,

> Lord, I ascribe it to thy grace,
> And not to chance, as others do,
> That I was born of *Christian* race,
> And not a *Heathen*, or a *Jew*.
>
> What would the ancient *Jewish* kings,
> And *Jewish* prophets, once have given,
> Could they have heard the glorious things,
> Which Christ reveal'd, and brought from
> (heaven!

After all, much must be allowed to the force of birth, and the prejudice of education; nor can the sincerest christian, firm as he thinks he treads on christian ground, be assured, that he should not have been a Jew, if he had been born of Jewish parents, and educated in that persuasion.

Humility, therefore, and devout reverence for the blessings of the gospel-revelation, are the great lessons

lessons to be drawn from this serious conclusion of a very melancholy tale; and we hope they will be properly attended to by all our readers!

A Narrative of the extraordinary Cases of EDWARD BIRCH, and MATTHEW MARTIN, who were hanged for Forgery; with some Account of their Behaviour after Conviction.

THE first mentioned of these malefactors, Birch, was the son of very respectable parents, and born at Hereford; and after having received a very liberal education, he served as a lieutenant in the militia during the late war.

Being concerned in a matter respecting a family estate, the right of which was litigating in the court of chancery, he came to London in the year 1766; and as his business obliged him to stay in town for a considerable time, and being of a scheming turn of mind, and possessed of some money, he determined to employ it in some manner that he thought would prove advantageous.

While he was deliberating on the best method of disposing of his money, he became acquainted with a person named Cobb, a mechanic of singular ingenuity, who had contrived a machine for the catching of fish in much greater numbers than by the usual methods.

Mr. Cobb was not in circumstances to carry his plan into execution, yet was exceedingly anxious to reap the fruits of his ingenuity. It is not therefore to be wondered at, that he readily embraced an offer of partnership with Birch, who was able to lay down the sum that might be wanted for the completion of the scheme. This being the situation of both parties, the partnership of course ensued, the terms of which were very advantageous to Birch.

Mr. Cobb having procured a patent to secure to him the sole emoluments to arise from his scheme, Birch advanced the money to pay for it, and a farther sum to fit out a vessel, which was sent to sea under the immediate direction of Cobb. This step was intended only as an effort of the success that was likely to attend the scheme; but as the first trial exceeded the most sanguine expectations of either party, Birch formed the ungenerous design of becoming sole proprietor of the patent.

With this view he found a pretence to quarrel with Cobb. The scheme did not take complete effect; but the partnership was dissolved on the following terms, viz. " that Birch should be al-
" lowed the use of Cobb's machine to fish with till
" such time as the money owing to him was paid,
" while Cobb was to carry on the fishery in what
" manner he thought proper." This agreement took place early in the year 1768, and Cobb being now reduced to very low circumstances, embarked for Denmark, where he continued many months.

Birch, in the mean time, flattered himself with the hope of obtaining a very considerable fortune by the new project; and at this time he married a girl, with whom he received a fortune of five hundred pounds. During Mr. Cobb's absence from England, Birch went to South Wales, where he engaged in the business of the fishery, which, for
some

some months, was attended with as great succefs as could have been expected.

In order to difpofe to advantage of the fifh thus taken, an agent was employed to fell them in London; and they were regularly fent up in machines conftructed for bringing them up with expedition, and without injury.

It happened that a quarrel arofe between Birch and the perfon who was his agent, refpecting the punctuality of payments; on which the latter was arrefted by Birch; but he inftantly gave bail to the action, and then prevailed on a rope-maker to arreft Mr. Birch.

Thefe matters were litigated with the utmoft warmth and imprudence on both fides; till at length Birch found himfelf fo embarraffed by the expences of law,* that he was obliged to take refuge in a prifon.

The bufinefs of his fifhery was now wholly neglected, and at length he determined to take the benefit of an infolvent act; and it is faid that he was perjured in this matter, fwearing that he was in Ireland at the time prefcribed by law, though he had not been out of this kingdom; but this we do not aver as a fact, unwilling to load the unfortunate, and the deceafed, with the imputation of crimes which poffibly they may never have committed: and we are the more diffident of admitting the alledged crime in this particular cafe, becaufe it is probable, that if Birch had been perjured, he would

---

* Surely no man in his fenfes would deliberately embark in law. How many inftances do we fee of the lawyers fwallowing up the whole property! It is better for a man to fubmit to an infult, than to be ftripped of all he has in the world, as is but too frequently the cafe.

have been prosecuted with the utmost severity of the law.

Be this as it may, he was now in circumstances of great distress, having no other support for himself and his wife than what arose from the casual bounty of his friends.

We are told, that for a year after he was cleared by the act for the relief of insolvent debtors, he was perpetually devising schemes to raise money, some of which were not the most laudable; and that at length he engaged in a forgery, not less extraordinary in the design, than fatal in its consequences.

It happened that Sir Andrew Chadwick, who was one of the band of gentlemen pensioners, was in possession of estates to a very considerable amount. Sir Andrew, having attained a very great age, had repeatedly drawn his will, at distant periods, but had not signed his name to any will that he had made, though there were many copies of what he intended to have done for his relations and immediate heirs at law.

Birch becoming acquainted with a woman who had found one of the wills in an old trunk that had been the property of Sir Andrew, the former seemed to think, on the perusal of it, that some emolument might arise from the possession of this paper.

In a short time afterwards Sir Andrew died; and no will regularly executed being found, a gentleman of Lancashire, who had married a niece of the deceased, took possession of his fortune, in defect of claim being made by any nearer relation.

In the mean time Birch made diligent enquiry after the relations of Sir Andrew, and at length
found

found that one of them, who lived in Ireland, had a better title to the estate than the person who was then in possession of it. With a view to make a private advantage, Birch made known his discovery to Matthew Martin, the other subject of this melancholy narrative. Martin was a watch-maker by profession, and in easy circumstances. He advanced a sum of money to enable Birch to go to Ireland, and find out the right heir to the estate.

Birch set out on this expedition; and having found more than one claimant, he returned to London, and made a new will in the name of the deceased, conveying the fortune to the Irish relations. This being done, Birch and Martin submitted the forged will to the inspection of an attorney; and it was agreed to commence an action for recovery, against the gentleman who was in possession of the estate.

It appeared, that the presumptive will had been dated in the year 1764; but some draughts of wills made since that time by Sir Andrew Chadwick being found among the papers of the deceased, a suspicion arose that a forgery had been committed in the business; on which Birch and Martin were taken into custody, and carried to Sir John Fielding's office, where Birch's behaviour was plausible in a very high degree; and he gave such an account of his becoming possessed of the will, as would have satisfied persons not aware of the knavery of mankind. Several persons attended at the office, ready to bail Birch and Martin; but the magistrate refused to accept of any bail, and committed the prisoners to Newgate.

In the interim between the commitment and the trial, one of the most extraordinary circumstances happened that was ever recorded in a work of this nature.

nature. A paper-maker who lived at Maidstone, being in town on his private business, fell into company with the attorney who was employed to carry on the prosecution; and the conversation happening to turn on the circumstances of the presumed forgery, he begged to have a sight of the will, which at this time being in the hands of Sir John Fielding, the attorney took him to the office of that magistrate, where the will was presented to him; and no sooner had he taken a view of it, than he declared, that in the year 1768, he had made the paper on which that very will was written.

The trial of the prisoners was brought on at the ensuing session of gaol delivery at the Old Bailey. The paper-maker above mentioned was an evidence, and the most material one, on the trial; for he proved, that the paper had a mark upon it, which he himself invented in the year 1768, and he positively swore, that the paper was of his own manufacture.

Though there were several collateral proofs of the fact, yet they would not have been of sufficient weight to convict the prisoners, but for this positive evidence of the paper-maker. Birch cross-examined the witnesses in such a manner as proved that he was a man of subtlety and address; but, notwithstanding all his artifices, both the prisoners were found guilty, after a trial which continued thirteen hours.

The council for the convicts moved an arrest of judgment on the last day of the sessions, founded on a point of law presumed to have arisen in their favour. No objection being made to this motion, the sentence was postponed till the final opinion of the learned judges had been taken on the case.

This case was learnedly argued before the judges (nine of whom were present) at Serjeants'-inn-hall, in Michaelmas term, 1771; when the reverend bench was unanimous in opinion, that the convicts were guilty of the crime alledged against them; in consequence of which they were condemned to die.

After sentence of death was passed on them, they behaved with a decent and devout resignation to their fate; for not entertaining the least hope of that pardon which could not reasonably be expected, they made every preparation for the awful change that was to await them.

On the day of execution they were fervent in their devotions at the fatal tree; and, after the customary ceremonies on such solemn occasions, they were turned off, and after hanging the usual time, their bodies were delivered to their friends, in order to be buried.

These unhappy men suffered at Tyburn on the 2d of January, 1772.

The intervention of Providence in the detection of guilt is most strongly exhibited in the case of these malefactors. Who could have conceived that the discovery of forgery should have arisen from a circumstance so apparently trifling as the writing a presumptive will on one sheet of paper rather than on another?—Yet so it happened. Little did the forger think, when he purchased the sheet of paper, that it was to be the immediate instrument of his own destruction!

We have had many opportunities, in the course of this work, of remarking on the horrid nature, and dangerous consequences, of forgery: but nothing has equalled the particularity of the cases of Birch and Martin, and perhaps such an instance
may

may not occur again for an age :—yet surely this ought to afford a lesson of the highest caution, never to be guilty of a crime which leads to such certain and absolute destruction.

One would think common considerations of honesty might prevent the commission of an act so detrimental to the commercial world; and yet forgeries are generally committed by persons in trade. What would the tradesman, who is daring enough to take up the pen to forge a bill, think of another who should take such a liberty with himself? He would be ready to execrate him as a villain. This consideration ought to be allowed to have its due influence. " Do unto others as you " would they should do unto you" is a precept of divine authority, and ought to be of perpetual force.

In the affair of the malefactors in question, their council started an objection, which left their case to the consideration of the judges. Very few cases have we known where the opinions of the judges differed from those of the juries of this country. In fact, the juries, according to the construction of our laws, and in the eye of reason, are the true judges of the fact, the essential declarers of the guilt or innocence of the party accused.

Notwithstanding this, we ought to think ourselves happy in the tender exertion of our legislative power. When one jury has found a man guilty, the slightest error, real or accidental, will entitle his case to the retrospection of a second, that of the venerable bench of judges, who cannot be supposed to be biassed by any interest, to be influenced by any consideration, to give their opinions in favour of either party, contrary to the established rules of right, and the known laws of the land.

Upon

Upon the whole, we have a claim to triumph in the protection afforded us by the laws; and those who wilfully transgress them, ought to be punished in the most exemplary manner.

A full and particular Account of the Case of ROBERT POWEL, who was hanged for Forgery; with such Reflections as naturally arise from the Subject.

THIS unhappy victim to the violated laws of his country was a native of Merioneth, in North Wales. His parents were poor people; but were distinguished by the honesty and regularity of their conduct. They educated him as well as their circumstances would permit them, and then sent him to London, in the hope that he might be able to advance himself in life.

Powel had not been long in town before he obtained the place of a shopman, in the service of a tradesman of reputation. In this station his behaviour was so unexceptionable, and there was so much of gracefulness in his person and manner, that his master soon raised his wages, and sought every opportunity of promoting his interest: indeed every person in the family was pleased with the decorum that appeared in all his behaviour; which was laid down as a rule of conduct that ought to be observed and copied by the other servants.

By an even and steady course of frugality Powel saved money enough to embark in business for himself; and, on the death of his master, he courted

courted the sister of Mr. Taylor Barrow, who held a place of some importance in the custom-house. Mr. Barrow, exclusive of his place, carried on a considerable business; and Mr. Powel, having engaged in trade, was as successful as the most sanguine of his friends could have wished him to be; and, in general, was looked upon to be a young man in a thriving way of business.

In fact, he was soon in very flourishing circumstances, and his success induced him, contrary to the advice of his friends, to take a large farm a few miles from the metropolis; which took up more of his time and attention, than it can be presumed a tradesman could spare from his business; so that the wonder will be less that ruin should ensue.

Having involved himself by undertaking too many concerns, he was reduced in circumstances, and determined on the commission of that forgery which cost him his life.

His brother-in-law, Mr. Taylor Barrow, was possessed of very considerable property in the East-India Stock. Powel being apprized of this, and knowing that Stock bore a very high price at that time, forged his name to an order for the selling out four hundred pounds.

This being done, he went to a coffee-house, and enquired for a broker. The master of the house recommended him to a Mr. Portis, who was largely concerned in the brokery business. Mr. Portis, being sent for, attended Powel to the East-India house in Leadenhall-street, where the latter declared that he was Taylor Barrow, the proprietor of the Stock, which he transferred by imitating the hand of his brother-in-law with so much art, that no suspicion arose of the forgery.

On

On the day the stock was transferred Portis sold it to a third person, and giving the produce to Powel, he immediately quitted his family, and went into Wales on a visit to his relations.

It was not long before a discovery was made of the forgery, and a large reward was offered for the apprehension of Powel; but Portis being totally unacquainted with his name, and none of his friends or relations conceiving that he could have been concerned in such a transaction, no suspicion of his guilt arose for a considerable time.

In the mean time, Portis exerted his utmost diligence to discover the offender; but all his endeavours proved fruitless, till a circumstance merely accidental occasioned his apprehension. Powel continued in Wales till he presumed the affair was forgotten in London, where he was received in the most affectionate manner by his relations, who had no idea of what had passed; for if they had, they would undoubtedly have advised him to consult his safety in flight.

Powel now lived on Dowgate-hill; and about a month after his return to London, he went to Cheapside on business, and after that to Lombard-street, when Mr. Portis met him near the Post-office.

Powel happened at this time to be dressed in the same cloaths that he wore when the forgery was committed; and Mr. Portis immediately recollected his person, but was unwilling to take him into custody till he was fully convinced that he was not mistaken in the man. Powel, observing that Portis regarded him with some attention, turned his face aside, from a consciousness of guilt, and to prevent the other from having a full knowledge of him.

Mr. Portis paffed him, but immediately turned back, and took a fecond, and afterwards a third view of him; when no doubt remaining in his mind that he was the real offender, he took him by the arm, and begged him to accompany him to the coffee-houfe, where they had firft met. Powel pretended not to have any knowledge of the other party; but Portis refolutely infifting that he fhould go with him, the latter complied with as much grace as he could, to prevent any difturbance happening in the ftreet.

They no fooner got to the coffee-houfe than the mafter and one of the waiters, at the defire of Portis, paid an attentive regard to Powel, and avered that he was the man who had afked for the broker to fell the ftock.

On this the prifoner was taken before the fitting alderman at Guildhall, and his perfon being pofitively fworn to, the magiftrate committed him to Newgate, in order to his being tried at the next feffions at the Old Bailey.

When the trial came on, the culprit produced a number of people to prove that he was in the country at the time the robbery was committed; but the jury, not being fatisfied with their teftimony, brought in their verdict that he was guilty.

When he was taken to the bar to receive fentence of death, his council moved, that the judgment might be poftponed, " on account of fome " informalities in the record;" and the court, ever attentive to the laws of humanity, acceded to the motion.

The confequence was, that in Michaelmas term, 1771, the cafe was learnedly argued before the judges, who were unanimoufly of opinion, that Powel had been guilty of the forgery; whereupon
sentence

sentence was passed that he should undergo the judgment awarded by law.

After condemnation, his behaviour was highly proper for a man in his unhappy situation. He was earnest and regular in his devotions, made every proper preparation for death, and resigned to his fate with the composure that became a christian, who placed his hopes on a better world than that, to a longer residence in which he had forfeited his title.

He was indulged with a mourning coach to the place of execution, where his conduct was such as proved him properly affected by his situation. He appeared sincere and ardent in his devotions; and after he was turned off, and his body had hung the usual time, it was delivered to his friends for interment.

Robert Powel suffered at Tyburn on the 2d of January, 1772.

In the case of this offender we see the almost absolute impossibility of concealing a guilty transaction. His name was unknown to Portis; his crime was a secret even from his relations; and he remained in Wales till he thought the affair was forgot; yet he had been but a short time in London before he found himself in Newgate, for the commission of that very crime which he flattered himself had been effectually concealed; and an ignominious death followed.

Mysterious are the ways of Providence, and past finding out. Who that reads this story will scruple to admire that divine wisdom and justice which cannot be comprehended?

If Powel could have been contented with his situation, he might have lived in credit and reputation. The keeping of farms near London has been
the

the ruin of many a tradesman.—A regular attention to one branch of business is generally productive of more profit than the embarking in a variety of schemes; and as such we would recommend it to all our Readers who are engaged in the mercantile line.

Particular Account of the many atrocious Villainies practised by JAMES BOLLAND, who, after a long Career of Wickedness, in which he experienced a Variety of Changes of Fortune, was executed for forging an Endorsement upon a Promissory Note.

THE father of this malefactor was a butcher, and he brought his son up to the same business. The youth gave early proofs of a profligate turn of mind, and constantly associated with worthless people of both sexes.

The term of his servitude being expired, Bolland opened a shop in the borough of Southwark; and his business afforded him a very favourable prospect of success; but through his irregularity and extravagance his trade gradually declined, and to free himself from some embarrassments that his misconduct had produced, he sold his effects.

Bolland's favourite associates for some years had been bailiffs, bailiff's followers, thief-takers, and the runners to the different prisons: and the natural cruelty of his disposition being encouraged by the example of the worthless people in whose company he spent the greatest part of his time, he resolved

James Bolland,
Executed for FORGERY.

solved to gain a maintenance by preying upon the distresses of his fellow-creatures.

Having procured himself to be appointed one of the officers to the sheriff of the county of Surry, he hired a house at the bottom of Falcon-court, facing St. George's church, Southwark; and, having fitted it up in the manner of a prison, it was soon inhabited by a number of unfortunate persons.

The people he arrested who were in indigent circumstances he took to gaol as soon as the law would permit; but such as were in a different situation were entertained at his house till all their money was spent, or they insisted upon going to prison, to avoid further imposition, or till the writs by which they were detained became returnable. The money he extorted from his guests by divers stratagems was so considerable, that he held the fees usually paid at lock-up houses as almost beneath his regard, and frequently distributed them among his followers and other servants.

Bolland was continually endeavouring to encourage card-playing in his house, and when his unfortunate guests had recourse to that diversion, for employing the tedious moments of confinement, he seldom failed to join in the game; and though he suffered no opportunity of cheating them, even in the most palpable manner, to escape him, they were obliged to submit to the insult and imposition; for if they ventured to expostulate on the unfairness of his proceedings, it was his custom to discharge a volley of blasphemous oaths, and to threaten that he would instantly take them to gaol, for daring to affront him in his own house.

Some of his prisoners hoping their affairs would be speedily compromised, and others who were not so happy as to entertain such favourable expectations, wishing to remain as long as possible without the walls of a prison; the insolence of the tyrant was frequently submitted to by men, who, had not their spirits been depressed by the weight of misfortunes, would have disdained to be made the dupes of such atrocious and palpable villainy.

Though the emoluments arising from the infamous practices of Bolland were very considerable, they were not equal to the expences of his profligate course of life. His wine-merchant and many other persons having demands upon him that he was unable to discharge, he procured a person to sue out a commission of bankruptcy against him; but before the commission took place he secreted his most valuable effects; and he farther defrauded his creditors, by giving notes and other securities to a number of people who had received no valuable considerations from him; and by means of these nominal creditors he obtained his certificate in a very short time.

Among a great number of frauds committed while he lived in the Borough was the following: he went into Oxfordshire, and there purchased a string of horses. Having paid for them, he expressed a desire of having a mare, which the owner positively refused to sell. However, the following morning Bolland took away the horses he had bought, and with them the mare, wholly unknown to the person whose property she was. The owner of the mare intended to prosecute Bolland for the felony; but he was dissuaded from that measure, and advised to draw a bill upon him for the value of the beast. Bolland accepted the bill, but he became a bankrupt before the time of payment arrived.

The

The infamous practices of Bolland had now rendered his character so notorious, that the attornies imagined that, if they continued to employ him, they should be reflected upon for encouraging so abandoned a villain; and such repeated and heavy complaints were made against him, that his business rapidly declined: but, instead of endeavouring to obtain better success by an amendment of his conduct, he seized every opportunity of practising extortion and defraud with greater rapacity, and became a still more abominable pest to society.

He resolved to move from Surry into the county of Middlesex, where he expected more frequent opportunities would occur for gratifying his avaricious and oppressive disposition. Notwithstanding the infamy that was justly annexed to the character of this accomplished villain, he procured persons to become his bondsmen, and made interest to be nominated one of the officers to the sheriff of Middlesex.

He opened a spunging-house in the Savoy; but it was some time before he had a prospect of success. He industriously sought every opportunity of joining in conversation with attornies, and by an artful insinuating conduct at length ingratiated himself into the favour of several of that fraternity, who were not very remarkable either for discernment or integrity; and his business gradually increased.

Bolland was an almost daily frequenter of places where billiards and other games were practised; and at one of these meetings he fell into company with a gentleman, who employed him to arrest the captain of a ship in the East India service for a debt of three hundred pounds, promising him a handsome compliment on condition of his recovering the money, or taking the prisoner into custody. Bolland assured his employer that he would use his utmost endeavours to serve the writ the next day.

The following morning the gentleman set out for the country, and in the course of the day Bolland arrested the captain, who immediately paid the debt and costs. In a short time the captain proceeded on his voyage; and the gentleman at whose suit he had been arrested coming to London soon afterwards, Bolland waited upon him, and said that, though he had made use of every stratagem he could possibly devise, the captain had eluded all his art, and got to sea; and, in order to enhance the promised gratuity, he pretended that his extraordinary vigilance to serve the writ had involved him in much trouble and some expence, for the truth of which he appealed to his followers, who readily supported all the falsities advanced by their wicked employer: and the gentleman being thus deceived, he made Bolland a handsome present.

Upon the return of the ship from the East Indies, another writ was taken out; but Bolland being gone to a horse-race, it was given to another officer. The bailiff went to Blackwall, and presently finding the captain, said he must either pay the three hundred pounds, or go with him to a place of security: but the captain shewing the officer Bolland's receipt for the money, he returned to town, and informed his employer that the debt was discharged previous to the captain's sailing for India.

A suit at law was now instituted against Bolland for the recovery of the three hundred pounds. Justice was so indisputably clear on the side of the plaintiff, that Bolland knew he must inevitably be

cast

cast if the matter came to trial; yet, at a considerable expence, he protracted a judicial decision of the case, imagining his adversary would give up his claim, rather than pursue him through all the delays and chicanery of the law.

The cause at length was brought to a hearing; and judgement being pronounced in favour of the plaintiff, Bolland, being surrendered by his bail, was taken in execution. He was conducted to a lock-up house, where he remained some time, and then moved himself by Habeas Corpus to the Fleet prison, from which place he was released by virtue of an act of insolvency.

Bolland, and a person with whom he had contracted an acquaintance in the Fleet, were enlarged nearly at the same time; and the latter soon after went into business, and found means to procure bondsmen for his companion, who was again appointed an officer to the sheriff of Middlesex.

Bolland now hired a large house in Great Shire-lane, near Temple-bar, but, that the outward appearance might not convey an intimation of the severe and tyrannical treatment that was to be exercised within, the windows were not, according to the general custom at spunging houses, secured with iron bars.

When prisoners came into the house, he informed them that it was his custom to charge six shillings per day for board and lodgings; adding, that the entertainment would be such as would give universal satisfaction, and that all trouble and disagreements concerning reckonings would be avoided: and such as refused to comply with these exorbitant terms were instantly conducted to gaol.

When Bolland's prisoners appeared inclinable to remove to the King's Bench or Fleet, he used every ry artifice he could suggest for detaining them in his house till they had exhausted the means of supplying his extravagant avarice: but when their money was expended, no entreaties could prevail upon the merciless villain to give them credit for the most trifling article, or to suffer them to continue another hour in his house. His common excuse for his rapacious and brutal conduct was, that he incurred very considerable expence by supporting a house for accommodating gentlemen, and such as wished to be treated consistently with that character must pay accordingly.

Notwithstanding the public infamy of Bolland's character, he transacted perhaps more than double the business of any man of the same profession.

Not satisfied with the great emoluments he derived from cruelly oppressing his unhappy prisoners, he had recourse to practices which, though not less iniquitous in themselves, were more calculated to bring him under the censure of the law. He defrauded a great number of tradesmen of property to a considerable amount; and among them was an upholsterer, of whom he obtained household furniture to the value of two hundred pounds, under false pretences.

Though Bolland was a married man, he was violently addicted to the company of abandoned women; and when his wife expostulated on the impropriety of his illicit connexions, he applied to her the most disgraceful epithets, accompanied with vollies of profane oaths, and frequently beat her in a barbarous manner.

His conversation proved the vulgarity of his breeding, and his whole behaviour marked him as a worthless and detestable character. These disqualifying circumstances however proved no impediment

diment to his being received on terms of familiarity by feveral women who were in the keeping of perfons of diftinction. But this will be no longer furprifing, when it is confidered that money is ever a fufficient recommendation to the favour of that abandoned part of the fex who fubfift on the wages of proftitution.

Bolland frequently took debtors into cuftody who had fought fhelter within the verge of the board of Green-cloth; and for an offence of this kind he was once called before the board, and ordered to pay the fum for which he had illegally detained the complaining party.

Bolland was connected with two men of infamous characters; one of whom was chiefly employed in difcovering perfons on whom the arts of villainy might be practifed with the moft fuccefs; and the other was an attorney by whofe affiftance Bolland was frequently relieved from embarraffments, and enabled to execute his villainous projects in fuch a manner as to evade the punifhment of the law.

Bolland and his two affociates abovementioned got poffeffion of a bill for thirty pounds that had been ftolen out of a gentleman's pocket. The bill was prefented for payment, which was refufed, the party on whom it was drawn alledging that it had been ftolen. Hereupon the attorney wrote to the gentleman, that an arreft would follow unlefs the bill was immediately difcharged. The anfwer fignified that, if an arreft was refolved upon, the writ might be left with an attorney in Chancery-lane, who would put in bail.

Mortified and difappointed by the fpirited repulfe they had received, and defpairing of obtaining cafh for the bill by means of threats, they de-

determined to arrest the gentleman, and take him to Bolland's house, where they supposed they could scarcely fail of extorting some money from him.

A messenger was dispatched to desire the gentleman's company at the King's-head-tavern in Bridges-street. He attended according to the appointment, and was arrested by Bolland; who, pretending to be desirous of acting with all possible lenity, told the gentleman that he would waive his power of taking him to a place of confinement, lest his reputation should be injured, on condition that he would give him proper security. Hereupon the gentleman deposited thirty pounds in Bolland's hands; but the note was still detained with a view of gaining further advantage.

The gentleman communicated all the circumstances that had come to his knowledge to his attorney, who moved the court of King's-bench for a rule. Bolland and his accomplices, however, determined still to contest the matter, though they were conscious that the cause must be decided in favour of their adversary.

When prisoners came into Bolland's house, he immediately employed his followers to make particular enquiries into the state of their pecuniary affairs, and the extent of their connexions; and according to the information he received, he suggested plans for deceiving his unhappy guests.

A young gentleman whose imprudencies had drawn upon him the displeasure of his friends, was arrested at the suit of his taylor, and confined in Bolland's house. His money being soon expended, and despairing of being able to effect a compromise with his creditor, he expressed a desire of being moved to the King's-bench or the Fleet. Bolland informed him that he must be taken to Newgate,
that

that being the gaol for the county; and that he could not be moved to either of the other prisons but by means of a writ of Habeas Corpus. The young gentleman was greatly alarmed at the idea of being confined in Newgate, which he supposed to be a place for the reception only of felons. Bolland, perceiving his anxiety, advised him to recall his resolution, saying that if he would follow his directions a method might still be adopted for relieving him from all his difficulties. Anxious to recover his liberty, the youth said, if Bolland would signify the means by which so desirable a purpose was to be obtained, he would gladly embrace the proposal, and ever consider him as his most generous benefactor. Hereupon Bolland informed him that he would immediately procure bail, and then recommend him to different tradesmen of whom he might obtain a chariot and horses, household furniture, and other effects, on credit; adding that he would find no difficulty in obtaining a fortune by marriage, before he would be called upon for the discharge of his debts.

The young man being released on the bail of two of Bolland's accomplices, a chariot was procured, and a house hired and furnished in a superb manner, and one of Bolland's followers assumed the character of a footman, from the double motive of assisting in the scheme of villainy, and reporting to his principal all the particulars of the conduct of the imprudent young man.

Reports were industriously propagated that the youth was heir to an immense fortune; and, by a variety of stratagems, effects to a considerable amount were obtained from different tradesmen, great part of which were deposited in Bolland's house,

house, by way of security to him for the bail he had procured.

Payment for the furniture and other effects being demanded, the creditors were for some time amused by a variety of plausible pretences: but at length they became exceedingly importunate for their money; and Bolland, now concluding that the young man could no longer be made subservient to his villainous stratagems, surrendered him in discharge of his bail, and caused him to be conveyed to Newgate.

The persons whom he had been seduced to defraud were no sooner acquainted with the imprisonment of the young adventurer than they lodged detainers against him. His unfortunate connexions having greatly exasperated his relations and friends, they refused to afford him any kind of assistance, and his situation became truly deplorable. His present distress, and the upbraidings of conscience for the impropriety of his conduct, overwhelmed him with affliction, which soon put a period to his life.

Bolland's character was now become so notorious, that he judged it prudent to alter his mode of proceeding for some time; and therefore he had recourse to the following practices.

In consideration of being handsomely gratified, he provided bail for persons who were under arrest; and, when he knew that the persons whom he himself arrested were not in desperate circumstances, he frequently released them, after exacting money from them, and the promise to surrender if they could not compromise matters with their creditors. He applied to these people to become bail for others, who paid him in proportion to the sums for which they were arrested; and, circumstanced as they

they were, it was seldom that he met a refusal; for, upon their making the least hesitation, he threatened to take them into custody, and convey them instantly to prison.

He provided genteel apparel for Jews and other men in desperate circumstances, and encouraged them to commit purjury, by bribing them to swear themselves house-keepers and men of property, in order that their bail might be admitted.

Having supplied two men of most profligate characters with genteel cloaths, they attended him to Westminster-hall, and there justified bail for sums to a considerable amount, though they were not possessed of property to the value of twenty shillings. After the business, these three infamous associates adjourned to a tavern in Covent-garden; and, while they were regaling themselves, some of Sir John Fielding's officers took the two men who had justified bail into custody, on a charge of highway robbery. They were convicted at the ensuing sessions at the Old Bailey; and soon afterwards Bolland, being a sheriff's officer, attended them to Tyburn, where they were hanged in the apparel that he had provided for them.

A publican in Cecil-street in the Strand, named Wilkinson, went into Lancashire in the year 1768, upon a visit to his relations, leaving the care of his house to a female servant. Upon the landlord's return, he found that two men had taken possession of his household goods and stock of liquors, under a warrant of distress. He asked by what authority they had made a seizure of his effects; and the reply was, that, if he presumed to dispute their authority, they would knock out his brains, or put him to death in some other manner.

Wilkinson made application to justice Kynaston, and made an affidavit that Bolland had no legal claim upon him. A warrant was granted for the recovery of Wilkinson's goods; but before it could be put into execution, the greatest part of them had been moved from the premises.

The following day Bolland caused Wilkinson to be arrested for five hundred and fifty pounds, which was falsely alledged to be a debt he had some time before contracted. The unfortunate Wilkinson, being unable to procure bail for so considerable a sum, moved himself to the King's-bench. The attorney employed by Wilkinson was an accomplice of Bolland's; and, under pretence of defending him against the machinations of that accomplished villain, he extorted from him his last shilling; and after the unhappy man had suffered a long imprisonment, in a most deplorable state of poverty, he was restored to liberty by virtue of an act of insolvency.

In the preceding part of this narrative we have mentioned that Bolland formed a connexion with a fellow-prisoner in the Fleet, through whose interest bondsmen were procured, when he a second time commenced officer to the sheriff of Middlesex. Learning some time after that this man had apartments elegantly furnished in the neighbourhood of Gray's-inn, he falsely swore a debt against him; and in conjunction with one of his accomplices, who was a lawyer, sued out a judgment, and obtained a warrant of distress for the seizure of his effects, which were conveyed to Bolland's house. The injured party applied to the court of King's-bench for redress; and attachments were issued against the delinquents; but before they could take effect, the attorney had absconded, and Bolland was

in

in cuftody, charged with the capital offence for which he fuffered; and therefore no redrefs was to be obtained.

A captain in the navy going a voyage, and not leaving his wife fufficiently provided with money, fhe contracted a debt to the amount of thirty pounds, for which fhe gave a note. The note not being paid when it became due, the creditor ordered Bolland to ferve a writ upon the unhappy woman. After fhe had remained fome days a prifoner in his houfe, he procured bail for her, on her paying him five guineas.

In a few days fhe was again taken into cuftody, Bolland urging, that, upon making enquiry into her affairs, the bail deemed themfelves not fecure, and had furrendered her, from motives of prudence. Terrified at the ideas of going to prifon, fhe paid him ten guineas for procuring bail a fecond time; but he infifted on having a bond to confefs judgment for the furniture of her houfe, as a collateral fecurity. Being ignorant of the nature of the fecurity propofed, fhe complied with the terms offered by the villain, who, on the following day, entered up judgment, and took poffeffion of her effects.

Upon difcovering that fhe had been made a dupe to the confummate art and villainy of Bolland, the unfortunate woman was driven nearly to diftraction, and, while in that ftate of mind, fhe attempted to fet fire to the houfe, in confequence of which a warrant was granted for apprehending her, and fhe was committed to Newgate.

In a fhort time the husband returned to England; and Bolland bribed an infamous woman to fwear a falfe debt againft him; in confequence of which he was arrefted, and being in confinement at the time of his wife's trial at the Old Bailey, he was deprived of that affistance he might have afforded her. She was convicted, and fentenced to fuffer death; but her caufe being efpoufed by a number of humane perfons, they drew up an authentic ftate of her cafe, which was prefented to the king, who was gracioufly pleafed to grant her an unconditional pardon.

Bolland formed a connexion with a proftitute, towards whom a failor, then abroad, entertained a ftrong attachment. Upon the failor's return, he gave three hundred pounds into the care of the woman, propofing at the fame time to efpoufe her, and faying he meant to take a public houfe in Wapping. The woman communicated the failor's propofal to Bolland, and they formed a plan of defrauding him of his money. By Bolland's direction fhe intimated to him that three hundred pounds was not a fum fufficient to carry on the trade of a publican with a profpect of fuccefs, and advifed him to leave the money he had already acquired to her care, and make another voyage. The unfufpecting feaman complied; and in a fhort time after he had failed, Bolland got the three hundred pounds into his poffeffion, and applied it to his own ufe.

Bolland's behaviour to the woman was for fome time exceedingly kind; but he at length procured a fellow to charge her with a falfe debt; and being taken to prifon, fhe furvived only a fhort time, during which fhe laboured under the fevereft afflictions of poverty and difeafe.

The failor, having completed his voyage, no fooner landed in England than he haftened to the houfe where his miftrefs had refided; and having learnt the particulars of her conduct, vexation and difappointment had fuch an effect upon his mind, that the recovery of his reafon was for a long time judged to be doubtful.

Bolland being ordered by an attorney in the city to ferve a writ on a colonel in his Majefty's fervice for one hundred pounds, he arrefted the gentleman the next day, and was paid the debt and cofts: but, inftead of delivering the money for the plaintiff's ufe, he declared that he had not ferved the writ. The attorney, however, foon learning that the debt was difcharged, commenced a fuit againft the fheriffs; and the perfons who had become fureties for Bolland were compelled to pay the hundred pounds, with full cofts,

The colonel had neglected to take Bolland's receipt; and of this circumftance the villain determined to avail himfelf. He a fecond time arrefted the gentleman for a hundred pounds: the action was bailed; and a trial enfued, in the courfe of which a witnefs fwore that he was prefent when the colonel paid Bolland a hundred pounds, and cofts, in difcharge of the writ. Hereupon the jury pronounced in favour of the colonel.

Though Bolland's character was notorious throughout the kingdom, he might perhaps have continued his depredations much longer, had not many of his moft infamous practices been expofed in the news-papers, by the perfon whom we have already mentioned his having contracted an acquaintance with in the Fleet; and whofe effects he feized in the neighbourhood of Gray's-inn, under a warrant of diftrefs, obtained by fwearing to a falfe debt.

When the fheriffs were informed of Bolland's villainy, they were highly exafperated againft him, and fufpended him from acting as their officer,
and

and assigned the bail-bonds as security, by which the parties he had injured might obtain some recompence.

Bolland's avarice was so excessive, and his inclination to villainy so strong, that his being deprived of the power of following his usual practices, proved the source of much uneasiness. He was advised to act under the Marshalsea court; but he rejected the proposal, alledging, that a compliance would *degrade* his character, after having long moved in so superior a line of life.

The office of upper city marshal becoming vacant by the decease of Osmond Cook, Esquire, Bolland determined to dispose of part of his infamously acquired property in the purchase thereof. The place being put up for sale by auction, he became the purchaser for two thousand four hundred pounds. Having paid the deposit money, which was lodged in the chamberlain's office, he anxiously waited for the approbation of the court of aldermen, which was only wanting to give him that power over the citizens which he was predetermined to abuse.

A letter was addressed to the lord Mayor and court of aldermen, exhibiting Bolland's character in all its horrid deformity; and proper enquiries being made, the facts appeared to be well founded; in consequence of which the court of aldermen refused him the place, and ordered the chamberlain to return the deposit money.

He declared that he would commence a suit at law against the court of aldermen for the recovery of damages; and when the recorder communicated to him the very strong reasons that had induced the court to deem him unqualified for the place of city marshal,

marshal, he behaved in a manner extremely reprehensible.

To contest the matter with the city he found not likely to produce him any advantage; and one of the serjeants at mace at that time resigning his office, he formed the resolution of purchasing his place, which was denied him, though he offered a sum considerably above the usual price.

The deposit-money still remained in the chamberlain's office, under an attachment taken out by his sureties, on account of their bail-bonds being assigned over for the benefit of the persons who had suffered through his iniquitous proceedings.

A man named Jesson had discounted a note for Bolland; some time after which they casually met at the George and Vulture tavern in Cornhill, when the former desired the note might be redeemed. The other said he then happened to be short of cash, but produced a note of hand for an hundred pounds, given by Mr. Bradshaw, offering to take up the other note, if Jesson would take Bradshaw's security, and return the overplus. To this Jesson agreed; and while he was counting the money, Bolland endorsed the note; which being observed by the other, he said he had no doubt as to the responsibility of Bradshaw, but that Bolland's name would render the note unnegotiable. Hereupon Bolland took a knife, and erazed all the letters of his surname excepting the first, and in their room inserted *anks*; after which he delivered the note to Jesson.

On the following day Jesson requested a person named Cardineaux, to discount the note he had received from Bolland; and Cardineaux paid him fifteen pounds ten shillings on account, desiring him to call the next day for the balance.

The next Saturday Cardineaux, Jeffon, and Bolland, met at a tavern in Queen-ftreet; when Cardineaux queftioning Bolland refpecting *Banks*, the name endorfed upon the note, he faid Banks was a victualler in the neighbourhood of Rathbone-place, in an extenfive and reputable way of bufinefs. Cardineaux, faying he was fully fatisfied, paid Jeffon the balance in his favour in fome fmall notes, and a draught upon his banker.

Cardineaux, having occafion for cafh, carried the note to his banker, who difcounted it; and foon after Bradfhaw was declared a bankrupt. Cardineaux now applied to Jeffon, defiring that, as Bradfhaw had failed, he would provide money to take up the note when it became due: Jeffon had recourfe to Bolland; but he refufed to take up the note, and even denied that Jeffon had received it of him.

Cardineaux, Jeffon, and Bolland, met at the Edinburgh coffee-houfe the next day, when the former introduced a converfation refpecting Bradfhaw's note; in the courfe of which Bolland faid, that his endorfement did not appear upon the note, and that it had not paffed through his hands. Upon this Cardineaux faid Jeffon had mentioned his having altered the endorfement from Bolland to Banks; and Bolland then defired all difputes might fubfide, and promifed that the note fhould be difcharged when it became due.

The note was delivered to a perfon named Morris, who fhewed it to a gentleman of the law, and related to him the particulars of Bolland's conduct, in confequence of which a profecution was refolved on.

Bolland being apprehended, a man was fent, in the name of Banks, to carry the money to Cardineaux, who gave a receipt for it, telling him that the

the note he had to redeem was in the poffeffion of Morris, and would be detained in order to be produced at the Old Bailey as evidence againft Bolland.

The prifoner being brought to trial, his council exerted their utmoft abilities to prove that he had not committed forgery; but the jury found him guilty of the indictment. When fentence of death had been pronounced againft him, the recorder pathetically exhorted him to employ the fhort time he had to live in preparing for eternity, and not to deceive himfelf in the expectation of a pardon, which there was not the flighteft reafon to fuppofe would be granted.

His behaviour in Newgate was decent, and he was treated with great humanity by the keeper of that prifon, who, upon his complaint of being incommoded by the great weight of his iron, ordered it to be changed for one lighter. After condemnation he was daily attended by the ordinary, to whom he acknowledged that he had been guilty of great wickednefs: but he endeavoured to excufe himfelf on the fcore of impofing upon the perfons he arrefted, urging that the fums he received he confidered as fees which men of his profeffion had a right to expect in acknowledgment of civility fhewn to prifoners.

He continued to entertain ftrong hopes of a pardon, even till the time of learning that the warrant was iffued for his execution; but for obtaining it he purfued meafures exceedingly improper. He caufed a paper to be prefented to the king, wherein he falfely reprefented his cafe, and alledged that he was innocent of the fact for which he was condemned to fuffer death. This falfe ftate of his cafe he publifhed in the news-papers; and procured copies

copies of it to be distributed among the ministers of state, representatives in parliament, and other persons of influence.

Copies of the different papers that Bolland had circulated were submitted to the consideration of lord North; and when the recorder made a report to his Majesty of the convicts under sentence of death in Newgate, he was very particularly examined as to the evidence adduced on the trial of Bolland; and his answers were so clear and satisfactory, that Bolland was included in the warrant for execution.

He attended divine service in the chapel the morning of his execution, and received the sacrament with an appearance of earnest devotion. He was accompanied to the fatal spot by a methodist preacher, and his behaviour was decent and composed. He acknowledged that he had been guilty of innumerable sins, but declared that the fact for which he was to die was not committed with a view to defraud. Observing Mr. Wilkinson (whom he had ruined in the manner we have already related) among the crowd, he desired he would approach the cart, and begged his forgiveness, which was cordially granted; soon after which he suffered the sentence of the law.

The body of this malefactor was taken to Highgate in a hearse; and in the evening carried to an undertaker's in Prince's-street, Drury-lane, whence it was conveyed to Bunhill-fields for interment.

James Bolland was executed at Tyburn on the 18th of March, 1772.

Every generous breast will rise with indignation on the perusal of this narrative. To oppress those already sinking under the weight of misfortunes, is a species of villainy of the most enormous kind. Bolland was guilty of innumerable crimes for which no punishment that the law had power to inflict would have been too severe; and suffered at length for a fact which (though a daring insult to the law) was perhaps (according to his dying declaration) not committed with an injurious intention. Hence, however, we may learn the danger of violating those institutions that are formed for the protection of individuals, and the good order of society. Be it remembered, that such actions as will not bear the test of conscience, must prove offensive to that Almighty Being, before whose dread tribunal we must all appear, to receive the award that Infinite Wisdom shall apportion to our virtues and demerits.

A full Account of the Life, extraordinary Proceedings, Trial, Conviction, and Execution, of JONATHAN BRITAIN, who was hanged for Forgery.

THE case of Britain was so extraordinary in itself, and so much the subject of public conversation, that we shall be the more particular in laying a full and complete narrative of it before our readers.

This offender was a native of a village near Thirsk, in the county of York. His parents were poor people, not able to give him a liberal education: but they sent him to school for some time, till he had learned to read and write, and had made himself master of the common rules of arithmetic; but it was not in their power to advance him farther in learning: however, having a natural propenſity to the acquirement of knowledge, he, without the aſſiſtance of a maſter, made a great proficience in the ſciences of aſtronomy and algebra; and qualified himſelf to teach the mathematics to young gentlemen.

Having had the misfortune to break his arm when a boy, and a weakneſs continuing in it for a conſiderable time afterwards, his parents ſent him to York to an attorney, whom he was to ſerve as an errand-boy; but he had not been long in this ſtation before his maſter diſcovered ſuch uncommon marks of genius and ability in him, that he articled him as a clerk, and took him into his office.

Happy would it have been for Britain, if he could have been contented in this creditable ſituation; but an impatience of reſtraint induced him to leave a maſter who had behaved to him with ſo much civility.

He had not, however, been long out of place, when the maſter of a public academy employed him as a teacher of the mathematics, for which his own ſtudies had well qualified him; and he was promoted to be principal uſher in the ſchool.

In this ſituation he was as reſtleſs as in the former; and therefore quitted it, and entered as a ſoldier in the tenth regiment of dragoons. As he was a man of remarkably fine appearance, as his behaviour was graceful in a high degree, and his accompliſhments greatly ſuperior to the generality of thoſe in his rank of life, he was taken great notice of by his officers; who paid ſuch attention to him as very much flattered his vanity, and inducing him to rival his ſuperiors in point of expence, his circumſtances were ſoon greatly reduced,

and

and he had recourse to the art of chicane to support his extravagance.

In these reduced circumstances he committed a variety of frauds, most of them of so artful contrivance as to elude all possibility of detection. He had a custom of introducing himself into the company of persons who had no suspicion of deceit, and then he would so far insinuate himself into their good opinion, as to take undue advantage of their unsuspecting honesty.

The following will serve as one proof of this disposition. A gentleman named Peachy having informed Britain that he had a law-suit depending, the latter told him that he was an attorney, and under that pretence defrauded him of forty pounds. But no sum that he could obtain by his irregularity was equal to the support of his unbounded extravagance.

Soon after this he married the young widow of a serjeant in the same regiment in which he served, and deserting from the army, he repaired with his wife to Bristol, where soon becoming reduced to circumstances of absolute distress, he made application to a gentleman who kept an academy in that city, desiring to be employed in teaching the mathematics. The gentleman was in no want of an assistant at that time, but he engaged him for a while, in mere pity to his distressed situation; and afterwards recommended him to a gentleman, who had a considerable property in the West India islands, as a proper person to be overseer of his plantations.

This was an engagement too flattering to be rejected by a person in Britain's circumstances, and he accordingly embraced it; and articles were drawn up between him and his intended employer;
but

but when these articles were ready to be signed by Britain, his wife prevailed on him not to put his hand to them, the consequence of which was, that he lost his engagement, and the friendship of his intended employer.

This very imprudent refusal reduced him to great distress; for the master of the academy was now no longer his friend. Thus situated, he enlisted as a soldier in two different regiments on the same day, though he was at that very time a deserter from a third: but a gentleman, compassionating his situation, paid money to release him from both these engagements.

After this he became an usher to another academy in Bristol; and his next employment was that of a land-surveyor, at a place called Wrinton, in Somersetshire. His several engagements took place with rapid succession after each other; and in his last situation he might have been exceedingly happy, had not an extravagant and restless disposition defeated all his better prospects. He could not settle in any regular employment, for his expences were always more than proportioned to his income.

Reduced to circumstances of great distress, he was tempted to the commission of forgery, a crime that scarce ever leaves the perpetrator even a chance of escape. Having forged several drafts, he passed them at Bristol, and then repaired to London, in fear of detection. On his arrival in the metropolis, he wrote several letters to the king, intimating that he had been concerned in setting fire to the dockyard at Portsmouth.

No regard being paid to these letters to his Majesty, he wrote to the Lord Mayor, declaring that he was ready to surrender himself, and make a discovery

covery of his accomplices, on the condition that his pardon should be promised in an advertisement in the London Gazette.

No immediate notice was taken of this letter, on which this extraordinary man went into Saint James's Park, with a pistol concealed under his coat, and copies of some threatening letters in his pocket; in this manner he followed the King from the Queen's palace to St. James's, not, as it was presumed, with a view to injure his Sovereign, but to give an air of plausibility to the tale which he intended to invent respecting the fire at Portsmouth.

At length a pardon to any accomplice was advertised in the Gazette; on which Britain went to Reading, to meet his wife, in consequence of a previous agreement; but on the very evening of his arrival in that town he offered some forged drafts in payment, the consequence of which was that he was apprehended, and lodged in gaol.

During his imprisonment at Reading, he wrote a number of letters, which he contrived to transmit to distant parts of the kingdom; the contents of which intimated that he should be rescued, and many persons gave credit to the insinuations contained in these letters; but the whole turned out to be only a species of fraud and forgery.

There was something so remarkable in Britain's proceedings, that the under secretaries of state went to Reading to examine him; but they could make nothing of his tale, the whole of which served only to convince them that he had no real discovery to make: in consequence of which they left him, for the law to decide on his other offences.

Disappointed

Disappointed in this scheme, Britain had recourse to another, if possible more extraordinary. He wrote letters, which he caused to be inserted in some of the news-papers, in which he charged Lord Mansfield, and the Earls of Halifax and Faulconbridge, together with other persons of rank, with having been bribed by the court of France, " to encou-
" rage the setting fire to the dock-yard at Ports-
" mouth."

Improbable as this story was, many people gave a temporary attention to it, and some even affected to believe it; but it was too absurd to obtain credit for any considerable time. It was a little unlucky for Britain's device, that he charged Lord Faulconbridge with being of the Roman Catholic persuasion, though the contrary was known to be the fact. The absurdity of this story soon caused it to be treated with the contempt that it deserved.

At the next assizes for the county of Berks a bill of indictment for forgery was preferred against Britain, but thrown out by the grand jury, on what they considered as defective evidence; and his discharge would have ensued of course, but that three detainers were lodged against him, which kept him in prison at Reading till he was removed to Bristol by a writ of Habeas Corpus.

The keeper of the prison at Reading having shewed very few signs of lenity towards him, he expressed himself agreeably surprized by the superior humanity of the master of the gaol at Bristol, whose kindness appeared to have a very visible effect on the mind of the prisoner.

Britain was now visited by numbers of people, who from motives of curiosity wished to enquire into the validity of the tale he had invented respecting the fire: but they could make no satisfactory

tory discoveries: they saw that the whole tale was a lie; yet they contributed to his immediate support in a manner so liberal as to do honour to their humanity.

On the commencement of the sessions he was arraigned on several indictments for forgery; but being put to the bar, he refused to plead, and held in his hand the Gazette which contained the offer of pardon, insisting that he had "given informa-" tion against his accomplices who had set fire to " the dock-yard at Portsmouth."

On this he was informed by the recorder that he could take no notice of the proclamation inserted in the Gazette: but Britain, instead of paying attention to this declaration, threw the Gazette upon the table where the clerk sat, and declared that a scheme was formed to deprive him of life contrary to the due course of law.

Hereupon the recorder mentioned a late act of parliament, by which he would be deemed guilty, if he refused to plead to the indictment: but the magistrate did not chuse to proceed on the trial without being in possession of the act in question; on which a special messenger was sent to London, to procure the act if it could be had in print, or otherwise to bring an attested copy of it from the Record-office.

The messenger returning with the act of parliament in print at the end of two days, Britain was again brought to his trial, when he pleaded not guilty to the indictment. The recorder would have allowed him council, but he refused all such kind of assistance, and determined to plead for himself. He cross-examined the witnesses in a manner that gave sufficient testimony of his abilities; but the evidence against him was such as not to admit of a doubt of his guilt; in consequence of which he was capitally convicted and sentenced to die.

Before the passing the dreadful sentence of the law, the recorder addressed him in the most pathetic terms, informed him that he had no reason to expect an interposition of the royal mercy, and entreated him to make every possible preparation for the ignominious fate that awaited him.

After this unhappy man had received sentence of death, he seemed to abandon himself to despair, and was, in all respects, in a most horrid state of mind. A gentleman of Bristol, being made acquainted with his very unhappy situation, wrote a letter to him, of which the following is a faithful abridgement.

In the first place he represented that his own anxiety to promote his eternal happiness gave rise to that letter, which being dictated by motives of the purest and most disinterested regard, he hoped that all due attention would be paid to its contents. The writer then proceeded in the following manner: " You have now passed your trial, and every
" chance for life is over — You are sentenced to
" die — to die! O my God how soon! In three
" short weeks you must bid adieu to this life, a-
" midst the solemnities of a public execution. Then
" the secrets of the invisible world will be made
" known to you, and you must commence an exist-
" ence in everlasting and inconceivable torments,
" or eternal glory.— You are sensible, Mr. Bri-
" tain, that there is a God, and that he will ar-
" raign you at his tribunal for all your sins against
" him; and that there will be no possibility of es-
" caping his wrath, if you depart hence without
" ob-

" obtaining his mercy. Let this one thing en-
" gage your attention day and night."

After thefe commendable advices and exhortations the letter-writer proceeds as follows:—" You
" have brought upon yourfelf the abhorrence of
" your fellow-creatures, and procured a fcanda-
" lous death. — You are laden with fetters — in
" prifon — and left to all the bitternefs of reflec-
" tion! — Your crimes are many, and heinous
" againft God and man.—Your poor foul is deep-
" ly wounded with your fins, and your heart, I
" hope, finks within you! Ah poor unhappy Bri-
" tain! fee your fad condition; your foul expofed to
" endlefs mifery! What will or can you do?"

After this folemn and pathetic addrefs, the writer reprefented to him the fuperior excellency of the Chriftian religion, as it is developed in the holy fcriptures: he advifed him not to flatter himfelf with the hope of that pardon which he had no reafon to expect, and entreated him to apply himfelf to reading and prayer, and to keep only religious company, as the moft proper methods of preparing himfelf for the awful ftate that awaited him.

This benevolent writer concluded his letter in the following terms: — " Let me advife you to
" keep yourfelf from idle company; be as much
" alone as poffible; converfe about nothing that
" does not concern your better part; — think
" how fhort your time is; confider the important
" bufinefs you fhould be engaged in, and fet about
" it in the fear of God, and with a firm refolution;
" and, as the ftrongeft motive to all this, ponder
" upon eternity, think of its duration! May its
" miferies alarm your fears and diligence, and its
" glories excite your defires."

The accounts transmitted to us say that Britain had been educated in the Roman Catholic persuasion: and indeed this appears to have been the fact; for, in answer to the letter abovementioned, he sent to the writer, informing him, that he would have no concern with any one of his faith:—but this resolution did not hold him long; since, soon after dispatching his messenger, he sent a letter to the gentleman, of which the following is a copy.

Sir,—" Sorry I am to think that I rejected you,
" (God's servant) this morning. My soul is
" troubled, my spirits fail, my conscience tells me
" I have done amiss. Oh! for Christ's sake, for-
" give my stubbornness, forget my naughty answer,
" and come and administer comfort to a poor af-
" flicted soul, whose appearance must be before
" the Lord in a short time.—My case is desperate;
" my time is short; and my sins are many, many in-
" deed! The grief and horrors of a poor afflicted
" soul are not easily conceived; and every tem-
" poral advantage seems only to encrease my mi-
" sery. Your compliance with my request will, I
" hope, through the blessing of God, afford me
" some relief."

The gentleman had no sooner received this letter than he attended the unhappy man, with a sincere wish to afford him all the consolation in his power. Britain received him in a very proper manner, paying all respect to his person and function: but said he was concerned that he had requested his company, as he was resolved, for the short remainder of his life, to adhere to the doctrines of the church of Rome. The reasons he alledged for this perseverance were, that the Protestants were enthusiasts, and that no confidence could be placed in the clergy of that church.

The

The benevolent visitor easily comprehended that Britain was greatly distressed in his mind, and used every argument in his power to console him. He begged that he would mention the objections that he had to his visiting him, and hoped he might give such answers as might be satisfactory to the unhappy man.

Britain expressed his thanks in a handsome manner, but begged to decline the proposed visits, saying, that he was resolved to pursue his own scheme. The visitor demanding what this scheme was, the unhappy man answered " morality."

A conference now ensued on the subject of morality, in which the gentleman endeavoured to convince Britain that his time in this life would be too short to form himself to the first habits of morality; and that, if he could do so, it was impossible for him to atone for the sins of his past life.

The gentleman further urged the necessity of an immediate and unfeigned repentance, without which he could not expect the mercy of God.

He took pains to explain to him the nature of the gospel dispensation, and quoted the following and other texts for his encouragement. " Who-
" soever cometh unto me, I will in no wise cast
" out:—Seek, and ye shall find; ask, and it shall
" be given."

Britain seemed to be attentive to these pious exhortations, but not to be convinced by them. In particular he said, that when he attempted to pray, he was so confused in his mind, and felt such remorse of conscience for the enormities of his past life, that he knew not how to sustain the load of affliction with which he was oppressed. His benevolent friend now told him that he had paid the visit with the most disinterested wish to promote his
hap-

happiness, and desired him to think how that might be most effectually promoted, and the peace of his mind restored; adding, with a generous benevolence of mind, "I would rather see you die "a good Papist than not to be of any religion what-"ever." He even went farther than this; he advised him to send for a priest, if he thought his own arguments had no weight.

This amazed Britain, who had no idea that a Protestant could be influenced by such liberality of sentiment, and would fain have entered into debate on the comparative merits of the Protestant and Popish faith; but this the gentleman wished to decline, observing that the short remains of his life ought to be spent in the practice of devotion.

In answer hereto, Britain said that the matter was of the highest consequence to him, for he believed in the doctrine of purgatory, and in the propriety of an invocation to saints; whereas the Protestants, unreasonably as he conceived, were averse to both. Britain's words were as follow:
" You will not pray to departed saints, and yet
" you solicit the prayers of each other, and you
" know that you are neither so pure or holy as
" they. Your objections to purgatory are still
" weaker, for they contradict that passage in the
" holy scripture, where the apostle Peter estab-
" lisheth it, 1st Peter, chap. III. ver. 19. I
" should be glad to know what you have to say to
" these particulars."

In reply hereto, the gentleman remarked that St. Paul, in his epistle to Timothy, enjoined us to pray for each other, when he directs that " prayers
" and supplications should be made for all men;"
" but (said he) for poor fallen men to assume
" the office of a mediator, it is condemned in scrip-
" ture,

" ture, where we are told that there is but one
" mediator between God and man, the man Chrift
" Jefus."

The gentleman farther remarked on the reafonablenefs of our praying for each other, as it was a proof of the pity that we entertained for our mutual frailties, and tended to conciliate that affection which is the honour of our nature. He likewife obferved, that though we might pray for our fellow-creatures, we could not effectually ferve them without their own affifting endeavours; and therefore it was ridiculous for a perfon to neglect his own duty, in the confidence of a bleffing to be granted in confequence of the prayers of others. The gentleman's farther remarks are comprized in the following words:

" You fee how this duty, properly explained,
" is confiftent with reafon and the authority of
" fcripture; whereas the addreffes that are made
" to departed fouls are hazardous and dangerous.
" They are hazardous, as departed fouls may be in
" fome region diftant from our atmofphere; or,
" if it could be afcertained that they are conver-
" fant with mortals, yet they cannot every where
" be attentive to the petitions which are prefented
" to them, unlefs we admit of their omniprefence,
" which would be to commence Heathens, and
" rob God of one of his moft glorious attributes.
" Add to all this, that the fcriptures altogether dif-
" countenance it, and direct us to truft only in
" God. It is, therefore, much fafer to truft in his
" power and goodnefs, who is the fame, yefterday,
" to-day, and for ever, than to rely on the me-
" diation of thofe, who have obtained an inheri-
" tance in heaven thro' the merits of Chrift.

" Your

"Your notions of purgatory are altogether un-
"scriptural, as the very text you bring in proof
"of it shall evince. St. Peter is there speaking
"of the spirit which quickened, or raised
"Christ from the dead, and assures us, that by
"the same spirit he went in the days of Noah,
"long before he assumed our nature, and preached
"unto the spirits in prison, meaning either the
"spirits imprisoned in the body, or fast bound in
"trespasses and sins.

"That this must be the sense of the text will
"appear quite clear, when we recollect, that in
"the day of judgment men will be tried for the
"deeds done in the body, consequently when the
"spirit returns to God, every thing remains fixed
"till the great re-union, when the final sentence
"will be given, according to the deeds done in
"the body, whether they be good or evil.

"Now, though I oppose purgatory, yet I ad-
"mit of an intermediate state; and I believe that
"happy spirits in that state are waiting for the
"consummation of glory. But this cannot afford
"you any benefit, if you quit this world without
"the necessary qualification for it, I mean peace
"with God."

When the gentleman had concluded what he had to say, he proposed to pray with the unhappy convict, which was consented to after some hesitation; but yet Britain behaved with the utmost decency, and they parted as soon as the devotions were ended.

The benevolent friend visited the unfortunate man on the following day, agreeable to his own desire, and was happy to find him more composed in mind than he had been, though he was not yet resigned to the deplorable fate that awaited him,

nor

nor convinced of his errors by the arguments that had been used.

The subject of their discourse on this occasion was the necessity of obtaining the favour of God, to prevent the certainty of eternal punishment. Britain seemed pleased with this subject, observing that it made him look with horror on the sins of his past life, and fitted his mind to pray for the pardon of his crimes.

The kind visitor now enquired if the Roman catholic priest should be admitted. Britain expressed his desire to have one conversation with him on the important subject. The gentleman said that the visit should be made if it was at his earnest request; but when he visited the convict on the following day, and found that his view was to obtain absolution for his sins, he represented to him the absurdity of a practice that could tend only " to fill the mind " with a false confidence, and make people believe " that they are objects of the divine favour, when " they are enemies to God, and strangers to the " truth of the everlasting gospel."

The unhappy convict now begged an explanation of the following words in the gospel of St. John, chap. xx. ver. 23. " Whose-soever sins ye " remit, they are remitted unto them ; and whose- " soever sins ye retain, they are retained."

To this the gentleman replied, that the preaching the remission of sins to those who repented, and believed in Jesus Christ, was a duty enforced on the Apostles, but that it was not in their power to remit sins, which could be only the consequence of repentance, and faith in Christ. He added, that the Apostles were said to retain sins when the auditors of their doctrine neither believed nor repented; but that the remission of the sins of an impenitent

penitent unbeliever was never once mentioned in the New Testament.

This answer did not satisfy Britain; on which his generous friend said farther, that "supposing the "Apostles had an absolute power to forgive sins, "yet he could not, with the least shadow of reason, "say that one of their priests had the same power, "unless he could give such proofs thereof as the "Apostles did."

He farther urged that it would be an insult offered to Almighty God for one sinner to pretend to pardon another, the forgiveness of sins being a power lodged only with the supreme Being.

Britain acknowledged that there was some force in these arguments; yet such was the prejudice of education that he would not yield to their weight. His friend having left him, he was visited by the Romish priest, the keeper of the prison being present. Nothing material passed at this visit, other than a promise of a second on the succeeding Monday, when it was agreed that the priest should take his confession.

The two following days being Saturday and Sunday, Britain was visited by his friend, who found him much disturbed in mind, and anxious for the visit of the priest, to absolve him from his sins. On this the humane visitor exerted himself more than ever to explain the sacred doctrines of christianity; so that Britain at length began to have a clear conception of what had hitherto been matter of doubt and obscurity.

When the Romish priest came on the Monday morning, Britain declined accepting his visit; and, when the friend who had been so anxious to serve his most essential interests waited on him some hours afterwards, he was amazed at the happy change

change of difposition that had taken place in the mind of the convict.

Henceforward Britain appeared not to dread the inevitable ftroke of death. He employed his time in the moft exemplary devotion, being continually reading or finging divine hymns; and confeffed the juftice of the fentence by which he had been condemned, faying that it would be the happy means of promoting his eternal felicity.

An undertaker coming to take meafure of him to make his coffin *, he evinced no kind of concern; and on the fight of it he furveyed it with the utmoft calmnefs, and even with a fmiling countenance, as that of a man who had got above the fear of death.

On the day before he was executed he received the facrament with every mark of unfeigned penitence and devotion; expreffed the utmoft hope of pardon through the merits of the Redeemer of mankind, and appeared highly grateful for the benefit of the gofpel revelation.

On the evening preceding his death his ever generous friend vifited him, and begged that he would endeavour to compofe himfelf to fleep, as a refrefhment to his difturbed mind; but he replied in the following remarkable words: — "God for-
" bid! — I have fpent many nights, as well as
" days, to the difhonour of God, and deftruction
" of my foul; but this, my laft night, fhall be
" fpent in praifing that God, from whom alone I
" expect to find mercy."

---

* One would think the ceremony of meafuring a man on fo folemn an occafion might be difpenfed with. How eafy would it be for a friend to give intimation of his height and fize, and for a coffin to be provided accordingly?

Britain having injured a particular person, desired to see him, to beg his pardon:—the other attended, but treated him in the most insulting manner; yet the prisoner bore his insults in a way becoming his unhappy situation.

Britain took a solemn leave of his fellow-prisoners on the morning of his execution, telling them that he must prepare for his approaching dissolution. At this time he was visited by his friend so often mentioned, who seemed generously determined to attend him to the last fatal moment. When his irons were knocked off in the lodge of the prison, and his arms bound back with a halter, as is customary on these solemn occasions, he surveyed himself in a looking-glass, and said, "Britain! thou wast "never so happily arrayed in all thy life."

A short time before his execution he signed a paper, importing that what he had said respecting the fire at Portsmouth was mere invention of his own, with a view to screen himself from punishment for the various crimes that he had committed.

Britain's zealous friend attended the clergyman who went with him to the place of execution, where the malefactor made a long speech to the surrounding multitude, concluding his address in the following terms: "Let the righteous rejoice; "let the sinner take warning, young or old, the "young especially;—see what sin has done for "poor Britain! and see in me what God can do "for poor sinners! Let this encourage you to re- "turn to him."

The friends of the malefactor having prayed with him, and taken a last solemn farewel of him, he was left to his own private devotions, and then turned off, on a signal given which had been agreed on between him and the executioner.

Jonathan Britain was hanged at Bristol on the 15th of May, 1772.

After the very particular account given of this malefactor, it cannot be necessary to make any tedious remarks on his case. People of common sense will judge of him as a madman, rendered so by the enormity of his crimes; and will pity him in proportion as they may deem him an object of compassion.

The generosity of the gentleman who attended him in the last stages of his life is worthy of the highest praise; but that gentleman does not seem to have adverted to the doubtfulness attending a presumed sudden conviction from one religious faith to another. — But it is time to quit this subject. Let all our hopes center in the expectation of that eternal felicity, in which there is no distinction of religion, when we shall all join in the praises of that God who is equally the protector of the devout of all denominations.

An Account of the Cases of SAMUEL ROBERTS and THOMAS BACCHUS, who were hanged for High Treason, in counterfeiting the current Coin of this Realm.

THE first mentioned of these malefactors was a native of Shrewsbury. He was descended of parents of very fair character, but in circumstances rather contracted; however, they gave him what education was in their power, and then apprenticed him to a baker.

After the expiration of the term of his apprenticeship, he repaired to the metropolis, and laboured as a journeyman with different masters for a considerable time, still supporting the character of an industrious and honest man. Some friends, observing the goodness of his disposition, advanced him money, with which he took a shop in Grays-inn-lane, and met with such success in business as rewarded his assiduity.

At length, very unhappily for himself, he became acquainted with the father of Bacchus, from the casual meeting him at a public house. Soon after their acquaintance the old man advised him to remove into Southwark, where he said an excellent house and shop offered for his accommodation. Roberts being married, and having four children, listened to this advice, in the hope of making a better provision for his family.

A very short time after his residence in Southwark, the elder Bacchus and his son, with some other people who were coiners, told Roberts that they would be ready to assist him with money on any emergency. It happened that, some little time afterwards, Roberts wanted some money to make up a bill due for flour, on which he mentioned the affair to the elder Bacchus, and he was immediately furnished with the requisite sum.

This circumstance had not long taken place, when the younger Bacchus informed Roberts that his father was out of town, and begged his assistance in coining, on the condition of which he should be amply supplied with such money as he might want.

Roberts hesitated for a while to comply with a scheme big with such evident destruction; but the prospect of gain becoming at length too strong for

his

his more virtuous resolutions, he fatally consented, and ruin was the consequence. The nature of the partnership, for such it may be deemed, was this: Bacchus was generally the immediate coiner of the counterfeit money, which Roberts put off to unsuspecting people. They had imitated a variety of gold and silver coin, which was so well executed that it could hardly be distinguished from the real money made at the Tower; yet the adulteration was so great, that, in many pieces, the intrinsic value was not a fourth of the nominal.

Great part of this counterfeit money was put off at country-fairs, where the agents employed to dispose of it (for there were others besides Roberts) appeared as horse-dealers, and found several country tradesmen ready enough to traffic with them for this false coin.

The coiners used to sell this money by weight to the countrymen, who circulated it in the course of their connexions; so that the evil spread wide, to the injury of many an unfortunate individual.

In the interim Bacchus and Roberts lived in a very handsome manner on the profits of their iniquitous trade. Their neighbours could not conceive how they procured a subsistence; and it is possible that they might have continued their practices a considerable time longer, but that one of their accomplices gave such hints as led to the ready means of detecting them.

Some constables being employed to search the house, they found Bacchus, with all the implements proper for coining, in the act of making counterfeit money, while Roberts was assisting him in this unlawful transaction; on which both the parties were taken into custody, and being carried

before

before Sir John Fielding, that magistrate committed them to Newgate.

It may be now proper to mention that Bacchus was a native of the town of Stafford, and was, at a very early age, initiated into the art of coining by his father, who seems purposely to have trained him to the gallows. The younger Bacchus never followed any business but coining, except occasionally dealing in smuggled goods when he happened to have a considerable sum of money in his possession.

The prisoners remained in Newgate several months before they were brought to trial; but at length they were convicted on the clearest evidence, and sentenced to die.

The behaviour of Roberts after conviction was exceedingly well adapted to his unhappy situation. He was regular and devout in his attendance on religious duties, employed much time in reading books of devotion, and was regardful of the instructions given him by the ordinary of Newgate. On learning that the warrant for his execution was arrived, his seriousness and penitence appeared to be augmented, and he looked forward to eternity in the humble hope of the divine pardon.

Nor was the behaviour of Bacchus less regular, penitent, and devout. He made a decent preparation for his approaching death. The father of Bacchus had retired into the country, whence he sent his son a letter after condemnation, of which the following is a copy:

My dear Child,

I send you these few lines to comfort you; I should have sent you some money before, but I hope, my dear child, you will forgive me, as you hope

hope to be forgiven in heaven. There you will find a better father than you have found in me. Be as happy as you can;—you are going to happiness, and leave me behind to be miserable. I hope you will die happy, because you know you are innocent. Thou art now going, I shall soon follow thee. I hope you will meet your dear mother in heaven. As we shall soon part in this world, may my prayers be heard for you in heaven!

From your loving father till death,

WILLIAM BACCHUS.

P. S. My dear love to Roberts; and tell him, if it should be in my power to serve his family, I will, I shall think it a pleasure. May heaven receive you both!

The unhappy convicts received the holy sacrament on the morning of execution, and behaved in a manner suitable to their calamitous circumstances. They were drawn to the gallows on a sledge, as is usual in the case of coiners. They warned the multitude not to follow their evil example, and acknowledged the justice of that sentence by which they had been condemned to an ignominious death.

After the customary exercises of devotion, the prisoners underwent the final sentence of the law; and when the bodies had hung the usual time, they were delivered to their relations, in order that the bodies might be deposited with the parent earth.

Samuel Roberts and Thomas Bacchus were hanged at Tyburn on the 21st of May, 1772.

In the course of these volumes we have had frequent occasions to expatiate on the cases of coiners:—but there is something singular in the affair before us. We see that the counterfeit money was sold by weight to people in the country, who could be mean enough to make such purchases from avaricious motives, though they must know that their neighbours would be ultimately defrauded.

The younger Bacchus, though a professed coiner, appears to have been in some measure an object of pity. His father had trained him to the business from his early youth: but surely that father ought to be the general object of execration. It is difficult to form an idea of the aggravated guilt of that man who can wilfully train his own child to destruction. The paternal and the filial duty ought to be mutual: a failure on either side is usually fatal to the happiness of one of the parties.

An Account of the Case of RICHARD MORGAN, who was executed for privately stealing Goods from his Master; with a Narrative of his Behaviour after Conviction.

THIS malefactor was a native of Ellesmere in Shropshire, descended of poor parents, whose virtuous characters were the greatest part of their possession. They bestowed on him as good an education as their circumstances would admit, and were careful to instruct him in the duties of religion. When he grew towards years of maturity, he entered into the service of a farmer in the neighbourhood, with whom he lived near three years with an unblemished reputation.

After this he engaged to serve other farmers in different parts of England, continuing to labour as a husbandman till he became almost two and twenty years

years of age, and then repaired to London, in order to obtain a subsistence by his honest endeavours.

He had not been long in town, before he entered into the service of Mr. Hotchkin, a capital linen-draper near Smithfield-bars. His principal business was to carry out parcels, and his behaviour was such, for a considerable time, as entitled him to the approbation of his master.

At length he was unfortunate enough to become acquainted with the servant of a distiller in the neighbourhood, who introduced him into a set of company which led to his ruin. Morgan had been hitherto remarkable for his sobriety; but a fatal change soon took place. The distiller's servant was one of a low alehouse club, of which Morgan became a member; and each of the company paid four-pence halfpenny for his evening's expences in beer and tobacco.

It was in this club that the first taint appears to have been given to Morgan's morals. Some of the company, who were chiefly porters, used to boast how considerably they defrauded their masters, and even mentioned the names of the parties to whom they sold the stolen effects.

For some time Morgan appeared shocked at the idea of obtaining money by such a violation of the laws of duty and integrity; and actually absented himself from the club; but at length the servant of the distiller prevailed on him to rejoin the company, which he did, but with a reserve in his own mind, that he would not be concerned in any of their iniquitous transactions.

These good resolutions, however, did not last any considerable time; for his companions, wishing him to enter into their practices, artfully took him to the houſe of the man who received the ſtolen goods, where he ſaw ſuch various articles which porters had ſtolen from their maſters, and remained undetected, that he was but too eaſily induced to commence the illicit practice.

His mind being thus prepared for acts of diſhoneſty, he ſoon began to purloin his maſter's effects, which he ſtole in conſiderable quantities; and as Mr. Hotchkin had a very large ſtock, and dealt in the wholeſale trade, the articles could not be eaſily miſſed, ſo that he had opportunity of continuing his depredations for a conſiderable ſpace of time; and indeed, when the articles were at length miſſed, no one ſuſpected Morgan to be the thief, as his character had been hitherto irreproachable, and his behaviour ſuch as to entitle him to general reſpect.

His cuſtom was to convey the ſtolen goods to a ſtable in Durham-yard, Chick-lane, where they were depoſited till the uſual purchaſer came, and bought them, and carried them off.

Morgan's practices in this way were ſo conſiderable, that his companions of the club began to look on him as a proper agent for diſpoſing of ſuch goods as ſhould be ſtolen by others; but this plan was defeated almoſt as ſoon as it was formed.

Mr. Hotchkin at length diſcovering that he had been robbed, and that the depredations had been frequently renewed, and obſerving that not any perſon had broken into his houſe, he concluded, that the robber muſt be one who lived in the family.

In conſequence hereof a perſon was appointed to watch the motions of Morgan; and on his going out he was followed to a houſe, whence he took ſeveral

veral parcels to an inn, to be carried by the Birmingham waggon.

Enquiry being made into the affair, it was discovered that Morgan had a considerable quantity of goods destined for the same place; and these being examined were found to be the property of Mr. Hotchkin, whose marks were on the several pieces; on which the offender was taken into custody, and carried before a magistrate. On his examination he denied the having been guilty of the crime alledged against him; but as the presumptive evidence was too strong to allow of his being dismissed, he was committed to Newgate, till the ensuing sessions at the Old Bailey, that his guilt or innocence might abide the award of a jury.

On his trial the evidence against him was so conclusive, that no hesitation could be made to find him guilty, and judgment of death passed of course.

After conviction he acknowledged to the Ordinary of Newgate the justice of his sentence, and owned that he had defrauded his master of goods to a considerable amount. He was constant and regular in his devotions, both in the chapel and in his cell; nor did he seem to entertain a hope of that mercy which he had no right to expect.

When he was told that his name was included in the warrant for execution, he received the dreadful news with great composure; and confessed that he had merited the shocking fate that awaited him. He behaved even with pious resignation, and acknowledged that faith in the merits of Christ by which poor sinners are to expect salvation.

He was visited after conviction by a number of people who had known him in the former part of life, and who kindly assisted him in his solemn preparations for eternity.

He

He received the sacrament on the morning of his death, and repeated the declarations he had formerly made of his guilt. At the fatal tree he addressed himself to the surrounding multitude, earnestly desiring servants not to defraud their employers. He prayed in the most earnest manner, and so audibly as to be heard by great numbers who attended his fatal exit.—After the body had hung the customary time, it was delivered to his friends, in order to its being buried as they might think proper.

Richard Morgan suffered at Tyburn on the 27th of May, 1772.

From the case of this unfortunate man persons in a dependent situation should principally learn two things, viz. never to injure their masters; and by all means to avoid any connexion with low company at alehouses, as the keeping such company may insensibly involve them in expences which may lead to the commitment of acts of dishonesty.

Honest countrymen are generally too fond of repairing to London, in the vain hope of making that fortune which very few of them ever acquire; and perhaps those who do might be more happy in their native fields, undisturbed with the cares of the busy world.

It is not every man that grows rich that becomes happy of course; and perhaps the contrary is more generally the case.

Upon the whole, we should learn resignation to the will of Providence, and be taught the great doctrine of being content in any station in which we may be placed.

Life's but a *short chace*; the *game* CONTENT,
Which most *pursued*, is most *compell'd* to fly;
And

And he that mounts him on the swiftest hope,
Shall often run his courser to a stand;
While the poor peasant, on some distant hill,
Undanger'd, and at ease, views all the sport,
And sees CONTENT take shelter in his COTTAGE.
SHAKESPEAR.

The Case of PETER M'CLOUD, *who was hanged for House-breaking before he had attained the Age of Sixteen.*

THIS ill-fated youth was the son of a poor man at Shields, near Newcastle, who brought him to London while he was quite a child; and the father dying in a short time, left the boy to the care, or, perhaps more properly speaking, to the neglect of his mother, who was a woman of very doubtful character, and said to encourage young lads in the practice of theft.

M'Cloud had been connected with a lad named Younger, who had been concerned with him in a variety of irregular practices. At length M'Cloud engaged himself on board one of the colliers trading to Newcastle; and while he was absent, Younger accused his mother of having been the receiver of stolen goods, the consequence of which was that she was apprehended, and brought to trial, but was discharged in defect of evidence.

M'Cloud returning from his voyage, and learning in what manner his mother had been treated by Younger, he made the most solemn vow of taking vengeance on him, whatever might be the consequence of such a proceeding.

That

That he might effect the ruin of his old companion in iniquity, he surrendered himself to a magistrate, and gave information, that himself and Younger had been concerned in a robbery; on which the latter was soon taken into custody, and committed to Newgate, M'Cloud being admitted an evidence for the crown against his presumed accomplice: but at the ensuing sessions M'Cloud was incapable of giving any thing like evidence against his companion, who was of course acquitted, and the scheme of revenge was consequently frustrated.

It is no less astonishing than true, that, notwithstanding what had passed, these young fellows soon renewed their former connexion; so that whatever degree of malice might have harboured in the breast of M'Cloud, he seemed to have forgot it in the wish to recommence his depredations on the public with his former accomplice in iniquity.

They now joined, with five or six other boys, in the practice of picking pockets, in which, for some time, they met with too much success; but their thefts were of the lowest kind, being principally confined to the stealing of handkerchiefs, in the practice of which they were frequently detected, but dismissed after receiving the discipline of the horse-pond. These young thieves were harboured at houses of ill fame in the neighbourhood of Salt-petre-bank.

One would have imagined that such repeated punishments as were inflicted on these boys might have deterred them from continuing their iniquitous practices: M'Cloud in particular had been so often dragged through horse-ponds, and exposed to the derision of the public, that he seemed to have lost all sense of shame, and his paltry gains by theft consoled him for the ignominy that attended it. He was

was three times tried at the Old Bailey for different offences, and had repeatedly the good fortune to escape, which ought to have warned him to discontinue his depredations on the public.

At length, after a series of practice in the picking of pockets, the gang of young villains determined to commence house-breakers, for which they were qualified, not so much by their strength, as by their artifice. They furnished themselves with a variety of tools proper for the wrenching doors and window-shutters. Occasionally they used to climb over roofs, enter at the garret-windows of houses, and descend to the lower rooms to commit their robberies; and at other times they would enter through any small opening that had been casually left unguarded. When one or two of the smallest of them had got into a house, they used to go down stairs, and open the door for their associates. Sometimes only a part of the gang went in, and the rest waited to prevent detection from the arrival of any casual passenger.

It is almost incredible to think how many houses were robbed of very valuable effects by this little confederacy of villains; but their depredations were chiefly confined to Ratcliff Highway and its neighbourhood, where a great number of persons were sufferers by their villainies.

At length three of the gang, of whom M'Cloud was one, repaired to Poplar, where they broke open the house of Joseph Hankey, Esquire, in the dead of the night. The family were all asleep; but the barking of a dog awaking one of the servants, he alarmed the rest, and begged them to oppose the intruders. Two of the thieves made an immediate escape; but M'Cloud was apprehended, and lodged in the watch-house.

On the following day he was carried before a magistrate, who committed him to Newgate, and at the next sessions held at the Old Bailey he was brought to trial, capitally convicted, and sentenced to die.*

For some time after conviction M'Cloud appeared hardened in a very high degree, nor paid any attention to the exhortations of the ordinary of Newgate; but, when he learnt that he was one of the convicts ordered for execution, a total alteration was visible in the whole of his conduct and behaviour. He apologized to the ordinary for the indifference with which he had heretofore treated him. It happened at this time that Younger was in Newgate under sentence of transportation; and M'Cloud sending for him, begged his pardon for the injury that he had formerly attempted.

The unhappy convict continued in a serious disposition for the remainder of his life, and on the morning of his death he received the sacrament, in company with the other malefactors who were to die with him.

When he arrived at the fatal tree, he requested a person to beg that his mother would not unreasonably grieve at his death; as he had hopes that he was departing to the regions of eternal glory.

Peter M'Cloud suffered at Tyburn on the 27th of May, 1772.

---

* It has been thought hard, by some persons, that the mere breaking into a house whence nothing is stolen should cost a man his life; but it ought to be considered that the intent, in the eye of reason, constitutes the crime; that the man who breaks a house means to rob it; and that the punishment should follow of course.

There is something very shocking in the revenge of M'Cloud, which could instigate him to swear against Younger a fact that was never committed; but there is, if possible, a still greater depravity of heart, evidenced in his joining his former accomplice, the very one whose life he had so lately attempted to take away.

Let us hope that this malefactor, old as he was in sin, yet young in years, may have met with that mercy the hope of which seemed to inspire his departing moments: but let no one be tempted to follow his example: let young people, in particular, learn that the slightest deviation from the path of duty may lead to the most ignominious fate: but let not this be the *only* consideration: let them consider that there is more of criminality in breaking the laws of God, than in infringing those that are merely of human institution; and may they regulate their conduct by the inferences they will draw from these considerations!

A full and particular Account of JOSEPH GUYANT, and JOSEPH ALLPRESS, who were hanged for robbing the Mail, and afterwards hung in chains; with a Narrative of their Lives and Behaviour.

THE first mentioned of these offenders was a native of Essex, descended from honest but poor parents, who gave him as good an education as consisted with their circumstances, and then bound him apprentice to a smith, with whom he served his time with fidelity, after which he laboured as a journeyman in his own profession.

Quitting the county of Essex, he repaired to Edmonton, near London, where he married and commenced business on his own account. For a considerable time he was as successful in trade as could be reasonably expected, but at length sustained a loss to which he attributed all his future misfortunes.

Guyant, having been out receiving money from several people who employed him, was stopped on his return to his own house by two footpads, who robbed him of above sixty pounds, and then bound him to a tree. This loss was a matter of great importance to him; but it was still aggravated by the consequences that followed it: for, as the robbery happened in the day time, he was advised to sue the county, to indemnify him for the loss; but failing to adduce the necessary proofs, he lost his suit, and was involved in still farther difficulties by the consequence.

The expence of the suit being considerable, Guyant was arrested, and sought refuge in a prison. In consequence of a subscription among his friends, he removed himself to the Fleet, where he continued till an act for the relief of insolvent debtors enabled him to obtain his liberty.

He had at this time a family which was in want of the necessaries of life; but, during his imprisonment, he had acquired such a habit of idleness that he was still less disposed to provide for them than before. It will be now proper that we say something of Joseph Allpress, the person concerned with Guyant in robbing the mail.

Allpress was a native of St. Ive's in Huntingdonshire, and, like his accomplice, had served his apprenticeship

prenticeship to a smith. After his time was expired, he laboured a considerable time in draining the fens in the Isle of Ely, and then his ill fortune led him to Edmonton, where he contracted an acquaintance with Guyant, which ended in the most fatal consequences; for Guyant, having now lost all relish for a life of industry, persuaded the other to be concerned with him in deer-stealing.

This proposal was but too well relished by Allpress, who, without reflecting on the dangerous tendency of such a practice, embarked in the scheme with Guyant, and they robbed the parks of several gentlemen in the neighbourhood.

Encouraged by what they deemed success, because they remained undetected, they broke into the church at Edmonton, and carried off some of the communion plate; but it was not known who were the offenders till after they were convicted of robbing the mail.

A very little time had passed after the sacrilege, when Guyant proposed to Allpress the fatal scheme which ended in the destruction of them both; intimating, at the same time, that their fortunes might be made by the putting off the bank-notes. Allpress declared that he had never seen a bank-note in his life, and confessed that he was very illiterate; but, overborne by the persuasions of the other, he at length agreed to be concerned in robbing the mail.

This shocking resolution being made, they lost no time in the attempt to carry it into execution, the first step to which was the preparing an ax, hardened to such a degree as to cut iron.

Having thus resolved on their plan, they waited in the road, at a place called Houndsfield, for the arrival of the northern mail. At length the post-boy

boy arrived, and had with him a perſon named John Thomas, to whom he had given a lift on the road. Guyant ſtopped the horſes of the mail-cart, and threatened inſtant deſtruction to Thomas and the driver, unleſs they immediately got down.

This threat was too terrible not to be complied with; on which the poſt-boy was ordered to drive his carriage into an adjacent field, and Thomas was compelled to attend him. The robbers now bound the other parties to a tree, and then demanded the key of the mail-cart; but finding that it was not in poſſeſſion of the driver, they took the cart acroſs the field, broke it open with their ax, and then took out ſome of the bags, and buried a number of the notes in the earth *.

The driver of the mail-cart, and his companion, remained bound to the tree till morning, when the latter happily freed himſelf, and then gave liberty to the other.

On ſearching for the horſes, they found them grazing in the field, and diſcovered that the cart had been broken as above-mentioned. The poſt-boy inſtantly drove to London, and gave proper notice of the injury that had been done.

The ſecretary of the general poſt office immediately advertiſed a reward of two hundred pounds for the diſcovery of the offenders; but nothing tranſpired for ſome months, till at length Allpreſs ventured to London, to procure the acceptance of ſome of the ſtolen drafts; the worſt ſcheme that could poſſibly have been deviſed; for the payment

---

* This circumſtance-firſt appeared on the examination of the priſoners at Sir John Fielding's, when the writer of this account was preſent, and ſaw the notes, diſcoloured by laying in the ground.

of these drafts being previously stopped, Allpress was taken into custody, and being carried before Sir John Fielding, he immediately confessed the fact; on which he was committed to prison, and some officers of justice sent in search of Guyant, who soon found him, and discovered several bags in a yard behind his house, in which were a number of letters which had been stolen from the mail.

Both offenders were lodged in Tothill-fields bridewell, and at the proper time removed to Newgate, in preparation for their trials at the Old Bailey; where they were convicted on the fullest evidence, and received sentence of death.

After conviction, and indeed long before it, they exhibited the truest penitence that perhaps was ever observed by illiterate men in their unhappy situation. They were exceedingly attentive to the instructions of the ordinary of Newgate, and made the devoutest preparations for their fatal exit.

On the morning of execution they received the sacrament with every mark of the sincerest contrition, and made a solemn declaration of their hope of eternal bliss through the merits of the redeemer of mankind.

On their way to the place of execution they behaved with the utmost decency, and, when arrived at the fatal spot, Guyant was so weak that it was necessary for two men to support him while the executioner fixed the halter round his neck; yet he was fervent in his devotions notwithstanding his weakness.

Both the malefactors begged the spectators to take warning by their fatal exit, and, having finished their devotions, suffered the sentence of the law, after which their bodies were cut down, and
carried

carried to Finchley-common, where they were hung in chains.

Joseph Guyant and Joseph Allpress were hanged at Tyburn on the 8th of July, 1772.

In the case of the malefactors before us, we see a remarkable instance of the progressive nature of vice. Guyant and Allpress were first deer-stealers, then guilty of sacrilege, and at length ventured on the horrid plan of robbing the mail. Those who do not see, in this instance, the absurdity of encouraging the first emotions to vice, will not be convinced by any arguments that we can offer. We shall therefore drop the subject, to make a remark which is new in a work of this kind.

When these unhappy men were examined at the public-office in Bow street, there appeared a degree of contrition in their countenances and behaviour, that no language can describe. They begged it as a favour of Sir John Fielding that they might be re-committed to Tothill-fields bridewell; alledging, as a reason, that the devotions at that place were more regularly performed than at other prisons; and this we have good reason to believe to be the fact. The governor of that prison is a religious man, and laudably exerts himself in the instruction and edification of the unhappy people who fall under his care. This is a rare instance, which cannot be sufficiently applauded; and we trust, that Mr. Smith (the governor) will pardon the liberty we have now taken * in mentioning his name on an occasion which is intended, and ought, to do him honour.

Happy would it be if every keeper of a prison was equally zealous to promote the eternal welfare

---

* In February, 1779.

of the unhappy persons committed to his care! But while we say this, we must in common justice remark, that the prisons throughout England were never managed with a stricter regard to the laws of decency and regularity than at present.

Particulars respecting JOHN ADSHEAD, and BENJAMIN ALSWORTH, who were hanged for House-breaking; with an Account of their Lives and Connexions.

THE former of these malefactors was a native of Northamptonshire, and trained up to the business of husbandry, which he followed till he approached nearly to manhood, when he repaired to London, and lived in the service of different persons in quality of a footman.

By an attention to the rules of frugality he became possessed of a sum of money, ten guineas of which he gave to a person to instruct him in the art of a gunsmith; and, having acquired the knowledge of the art, he for some time laboured industriously to support himself; but getting into bad company, he was prevailed on to commence the dangerous practice of house-breaking; but being at length too well known in London, he was afraid of being discovered, and therefore repaired to Bristol, to commit his depredations in that city.

Soon after he arrived at Bristol he broke into the house of a watchmaker, and carried off effects to the amount of 150£. These he conveyed to London, where he disposed of them, and with the produce took a public-house in Princes-street, Drury-lane;

lane; but no success attending him in this situation, he quitted business, and re-commenced the practice of house-breaking, which ended in his destruction, as will be seen in the course of this narrative.

Alsworth (the other criminal) was a native of Birmingham, and followed the profession of gun-making. After practising his trade some time, he repaired to London, and enlisting in the army, became a drummer in the 85th regiment of foot. He served in Portugal during the last war, in the reign of King George the Second, and was likewise present at the siege of Belleisle; but when the peace came on he returned to his original profession.

During his military life his behaviour was consistent with his duty. On his return to England he married a young woman, who bore him two children; but happening to become acquainted with Adshead, his ruin soon followed. These men were frequently in company; and Alsworth, observing that Adshead dressed in a stile of gentility which he presumed to be above his circumstances, asked how he afforded to make such an appearance; to which the other replied, that an uncle, who was lately dead, had left him several articles of considerable value.

Their intimacy now daily increased; and Alsworth's children being indisposed, and himself deficient of employment, he asked the other to lend him three or four guineas, which he would not fail to return on a happier change in his circumstances.

Adshead said that he was not then in possession of so much money, but, if the other would take his advice, he would instruct him how to " obtain a " hundred pounds in an hour."

Alsworth thought he spoke jestingly, but begged to know his real meaning; on which the other

confessed

confessed that he subsisted by house-breaking, and invited his acquaintance to come to his lodgings that evening. This invitation was complied with: a copartnership in iniquity was agreed on, and they committed several burglaries: but that, of which we are now about to relate the particulars, brought them to their fatal end.

About one o'clock in the morning of the 18th of May, 1772, they broke into the house of Mrs. Bellamy, a widow lady in Newman-street, Oxford-road, whence they carried off silk, wearing apparel, and other effects, to a considerable amount.

They packed the goods in two parcels, and proceeded towards Tottenham-court-road, where they were observed by two watchmen, who followed them towards Russel-street, Bloomsbury, where they were noticed by another watchman belonging to the parish of St. Giles, who seized on Alsworth; on which the other threw down his parcel and ran off, but was soon taken into custody.

Being conveyed to the watch-house, they were searched by the constable of the night, who likewise examined the parcels of stolen goods. On the following morning they were carried before justice Cox, to whom they asserted that the things were their own property, and that they were removing them from their lodgings, to prevent their landlord seizing on them for rent.

This story did not seem to be at all plausible; and, as they refused to give an account of their place of residence, a well-grounded suspicion arose that they were thieves; on which they were committed for re-examination when the persons who had been robbed could be found.

When Mrs. Bellamy's family arose in the morning, the servants discovered that the house had been robbed as abovementioned. Hereupon handbills were instantly printed *, and circulated through London; the consequence of which was that justice Cox sent for Mrs. Bellamy and her servants, and the prisoners being brought to a re-examination, the stolen effects were identified, and the two men were committed to Newgate for trial.

At the sessions held at the Old Bailey in the month of June, 1772, the prisoners were indicted for breaking and entering the dwelling-house of Mary Bellamy, widow, and stealing a gauze sack and petticoat with silk and gold flowers, three silk sacks and petticoats, a brocaded silk night-gown, a chased gold outside watch-case, and a variety of other valuable articles, the property of Mrs. Bellamy and her daughter.

Adshead pleaded guilty to the indictment, begging for mercy on account of his youth; and the evidence against the other accomplice was so conclusive, that the jury could not hesitate to convict him, in consequence of which they both received sentence of death.

After conviction their behaviour was very various. On some occasions they appeared hardened in a very high degree, and at others were free to confess the crime of which they had been guilty: but, when they found that their names were included in the warrant for execution, their behaviour was more regular, consistent, and penitent; and the ordinary of Newgate, forming a favourable opinion

---

* The immediate circulation of hand-bills is the readiest method of detecting thieves. This has been proved in a thousand instances that have occurred at the public-office in Bow-street. Thieves generally carry stolen goods immediately to the pawnbrokers: but, when they do not, the bills frequently fall into the hands of peace-officers, and a discovery follows of course.

of their sincerity, administered the sacrament to them, and gave them such advice as he deemed proper in their unhappy situation: he cautioned them not to trust to their own penitence, but to rely on the merits of Christ for eternal salvation.

On the day appointed for their execution the ordinary attended them early in the morning, renewed his good advice, and besought them to fix their minds on a better world than that to which they were so soon to bid a final adieu. On being put into the cart they shed many tears, and lifted up their eyes to heaven in the hope of that mercy whence alone, in their situation, it could be expected.

At the fatal tree they confessed that they were guilty of the crime of which they had been convicted, and cautioned their auditors never to be guilty of a similar violation of the laws of justice. An immense concourse of people attended this execution; and when the bodies had hung the usual time, they were delivered to the friends of the deceased, in order for interment.

John Adshead and Benjamin Alsworth suffered at Tyburn on the 8th of July, 1772.

The reflections arising from the case of these men can but little deviate from those we have made on that of former housebreakers; but we see that a copartnership in iniquity is no bar to the inevitable consequences of guilt. Adshead's confession of his crime amounted to little less than an accusation of his accomplice, since they were both taken into custody almost immediately after the commission of the fact.

Upon consideration of the whole matter, it will appear evident that nothing can so effectually secure our peace of mind, as a strict adherence to the laws of honesty, and a regular and constant attendance on the duties of religion.

An Account of the Case of ROBERT JONES, *who was tried for, and convicted of, the Crime of Sodomy; with some Particulars respecting his conditional Pardon.*

IT is painful to recite a narrative of this kind, wherein it is almost impossible to avoid some little degree of indelicacy; but our promise in our advertisements for this work renders it necessary for us to give an account of all those trials which have been remarkable enough to engage the particular attention of the public.

At the sessions held at the Old Bailey in the month of July, 1772, Robert Jones was indicted for feloniously making an assault on Francis Henry Hay, an infant of the age of thirteen years, and committing the crime mentioned at the head of this narrative.

The evidence given on the trial (for we would be as concise in a tale of this kind as possible) was simply this. That young Hay lived with his uncle, who was a jeweller in Parliament-street; that the prisoner, who used to deal at the shop, met him in St. Martin's-lane, and told him he had a buckle to mend; that he told him to come to his lodgings in St. Martin's-court; that the boy went more than once; that Jones actually perpetrated the fact for which he was indicted, and gave him some halfpence to keep the affair secret.

It appeared farther, in evidence, that the boy declined going to Mr. Jones's with a shirt-buckle which he had bespoke, seeming to be ashamed of what had formerly passed; and that the child was indisposed in his health.

This gave rise to a suspicion that something improper had been transacted; the consequence of which was, that Mr. Jones was taken into custody, and brought to trial.

The character of the boy, as far as we are able to judge, was very fair; the court repeatedly questioned his friends as to his veracity; and they deposed that he was accustomed to tell the truth.

Mr. Jones called some witnesses to prove his attachment to women; and they deposed, among other things in his favour, that they did not think him capable of being guilty of such a crime as was alledged against him; but that his character was of a very different complexion.

The jury, however, gave credit to the evidence that had been adduced against the prisoner, and gave a verdict of guilty, in consequence of which he received judgment of death.

Mr. Jones was a lieutenant in the army, and generally known by the name of Capt. Jones. It would seem almost incredible to those who may not remember the particulars of this case, if we were to mention how much it became the subject of public discussion. The news-papers were, for a time, crouded with an account of the affair of Capt. Jones. A letter or paragraph reprobated him one day as a devil; and on the next he was represented as a man of honour and a gentleman. Girls of the town published letters in his favour, which though, in a case of this kind, they could not be answered, were severely censured by writers on the other side of the question. The contest, in short, was inexpressibly violent; and, while some were most eagerly and daily seeking his destruction, others were as eager to plead in his behalf.

There is nothing in his trial that seems to militate in his favour, nor any thing to destroy the credibility of the evidence against him. There seems not to have been any motive of malice in the prosecution, nor any sinister end to answer by the conviction of the culprit.—His prosecutors were persons of reputation:—his jury was composed of men of honour and conscience, and there can be no doubt but that they gave a verdict conformable to the oath that they had taken.

Be all this as it may, the utmost interest was exerted in his favour; and such representations were made to the King, that his Majesty was pleased to grant him his pardon, on the condition of his transporting himself for the term of his natural life.

In consequence hereof he quitted Newgate privately, and embarked for some foreign shore. What became of him afterwards we have never learnt, nor can the reader be solicitous to know. If he is alive and conscious of his guilt, we hope he has had time to repent. At any rate the memory of himself and his crime ought to be buried in oblivion.

On this occasion the words of the poet, with a slight alteration, may be properly applied:

Perish the wretches, wherefoe'er they're found,
Who propagate this vice on British ground;
A vice that, spite of sense and reason, reigns,
And poisons genial love, and manhood stains!

The Case of WILLIAM GRIFFITHS, who was hanged for robbing the Reverend Dr. Dodd on the Highway near Tottenham-court-road, with an Account of his Behaviour after Conviction, and of his Execution.

THIS malefactor was a native of Shropshire, and followed the business of husbandry till he had attained his eighteenth year, when he engaged in a naval life, and remained near three years in the East Indies. The ship was paid off on his return to England; and Griffiths, receiving a considerable sum for wages, spent his money, as sailors too generally do, in no very reputable company, at public houses in Wapping, and adjacent parts.

By his connexions with men and women of abandoned character, his money was soon spent, and he began to think of going to sea for a supply; and happy might it have been for him if he had done so: but David Evans and Timothy Johnson, two of his newly-acquired associates, and men of very abandoned character, advised him to be concerned with them in committing robberies on the highway; and this triple association of thieves did actually commit a variety of depredations on the public, treating those they attacked with great inhumanity, but never obtaining any thing considerable by their lawless pursuits.

One of their robberies was the following. Having strolled into the fields in the neighbourhood of London, they wandered about till near eight o'clock in the evening, when they stopped a single-horse chaise, in which were a Mrs. Constable, the wife of a surgeon of Highgate, and her servant-maid.

maid. Mrs. Constable was driving the chaise; and the robbers had no sooner ordered them to stop, than one of them fired a pistol, the ball from which touched the cloaths of the parties, but did not do any farther mischief. Mrs. Constable was greatly terrified, and gave them what money she had in her purse; but, not content with this, they searched her pockets, and took out some other articles; but a carriage coming up at the time, they ran off with the utmost precipitation.

They were taken into custody for this offence within a very few days, and conducted to Sir John Fielding's office in Bow-street, where Evans was admitted an evidence against his accomplices. He deposed positively to the fact, and signed the information which he had given against them; yet when they were brought to trial at the ensuing sessions at the Old Bailey, he absolutely denied all that he had previously asserted, declaring that neither Johnson nor Griffiths were in his company at the time of the commission of the robbery.

On this testimony it was absolutely necessary for the jury to acquit the prisoners; but Evans was told from the Bench, that he had behaved in a most scandalous manner, and was ordered back to Newgate, to take his trial for perjury.

Griffiths had no sooner experienced this narrow escape from the most ignominious death, than he returned to the company of several of his old acquaintance, who used to assemble at a house of ill fame in Tothill-street, Westminster, and soon had again recourse to the highway, for a supply of money to support his extravagances.

His reign, however, was now very short, for he soon committed the fact which terminated in an ignominious death, of which we shall proceed to re-

late

late the particulars. The Rev. Dr. Dodd* and his lady were returning from a visit they had been making to a gentleman at St. Alban's, but were detained on the way at Barnet, because a post-chaise could not be immediately procured.

Night was hastily approaching when they left Barnet; but they proceeded unmolested till they came near the turnpike at the extremity of Tottenham-court-road, when three men called to the driver of the carriage, and threatened his instant destruction if he did not stop. The post-boy did not hesitate to obey such a summons; but no sooner was the carriage stopped than a pistol was fired, the ball from which went through the front glass of the chaise; but did not take any effect to the injury of the parties in it, though it terrified them in a very high degree, as they apprehended that the most fatal consequences might ensue.

While the Doctor was waiting at Barnet for the chaise, it occurred to him that there might be danger on the road; whereupon he concealed most of his money, except two guineas which he put in his purse, with a bill of exchange.

Soon after the pistol was fired, Griffiths opened the door of the chaise; on which the Doctor begged him to behave with civility, on account of the presence of the lady. He then delivered the purse, with its contents, and likewise gave the robber some loose silver. Griffiths, having received the booty, decamped with the utmost precipitation.

Dr. Dodd lost no time in repairing to Sir John Fielding's office, where he and his lady gave so

---

* Our readers will see, in the course of this work, that Dr. Dodd himself was tried and executed for forgery; a crime little to have been apprehended from a gentleman of his profession!

full a description of the person of the principal robber, that it was easily conjectured that Griffiths must have been the party; but who had been his associates in the business has never yet transpired.

In consequence of this information, Griffiths was soon taken into custody; but on his examination before Sir John Fielding, Dr. Dodd hesitated to swear positively to his person; but Mrs. Dodd, who had regarded him with more attention, positively declared on oath that he was the person who had committed the robbery.

Hereupon the magistrate committed Griffiths to Newgate, and a bill of indictment being found against him by the grand jury, he was called down to trial at the next sessions at the Old Bailey, when the following was the substance of the evidence against him.

Dr. Dodd declared, that it was with great reluctance he came into a court of justice on such an occasion, which he said he would not have done, if the robbery had not been attended with circumstances of an aggravating kind; but that the firing of the pistol was a crime of so horrid a nature, that his regard to the safety of others had induced him to commence a prosecution so abhorrent to the feelings of his own mind; but the Doctor would not swear to the identity of the prisoner's person.

On the contrary, Mrs. Dodd swore that he was the actual person that had committed the robbery; and declared that he had confessed his guilt when before Sir John Fielding. This evidence was deemed so conclusive, that the jury did not hesitate to find him guilty, in consequence of which he received sentence of death.

After conviction he behaved for some time in such a manner as was by no means proper for his melancholy

melancholy situation; and he refused to attend divine service in the chapel: but after the arrival of the warrant for his execution, his conduct appeared to be totally changed, and he wept almost incessantly. He acknowledged the utmost readiness to listen to the instructions of the Ordinary of Newgate, and made a ready confession of many robberies in which he had been concerned, owning that he had been long deserving of the dreadful fate that then awaited him.

Among other things which he confessed was, that he was the person who fired the pistol at Mrs. Constable; and that he prevailed on a woman of his acquaintance to persuade Evans to take a false oath on the trial, the consequence of which was the acquittal of himself and Johnson.

He owned that his attachment to the company of women of abandoned character contributed in a great degree to his destruction, as his extravagance in the support of them induced him to think of having recourse to the highway for a supply, the consequence of which would be an ignominious death.

The rest of his behaviour was by no means inconsistent with his calamitous situation; and the ordinary of Newgate, conceiving that he was a sincere penitent, did not hesitate to administer to him the sacrament of the Lord's supper.

When the fatal day of execution arrived, he attended service in the chapel of Newgate, where his behaviour was such as to justify the ideas that had been formed of the sincerity of his repentance. Being brought down into the press-yard, his irons were knocked off, and he was put into the cart to be conveyed to the fatal tree, on which occasion he wept, as penetrated with the utmost contrition for his past crimes; and at the place of execution he cautioned the attending multitude in general, and youth in particular, to take warning by his unhappy fate.

William Griffiths was hanged at Tyburn on the 20th of January, 1773.

In the case of this malefactor we plainly see the fatal consequences of an attachment to bad company, which naturally leads to ignominy, destruction, and death. The man, who can harden his mind so far as to fire a pistol at an unoffending traveller, is not deserving of any pity.

Dr. Dodd's tender caution in hesitating to swear to the prisoner furnishes a proof of the humanity of his mind. Indeed he was a man of humane feelings, notwithstanding what happened afterwards to tarnish his own character. He was the patron of charities public and private: but this will more fully appear hereafter, when we come to treat of his own melancholy story.

From all that has been said let us remember that punishment is the natural consequence of vice, and that the only sure path to happiness is through the road of virtue.

Narrative of the Case of Joseph Cooper, who was hanged for Housebreaking; with some Particulars of his Behaviour after Conviction, and at the Time of Execution.

THIS malefactor was the son of honest but poor parents, who were unable to educate him as they could have wished; and his father dying

ing before he was seven years of age, his mother, who was a poor washerwoman, was left the sole protector of him in the helpless state of infancy.

The mother procured his admission into a charity-school, where he continued till he was fourteen years of age, when Mr. Beaumont, a capital cutler in Redcross-street, took him as an apprentice, in mere compassion to his destitute situation of life.

Mr. Beaumont was a man in a very extensive way of business; so that the youth had an opportunity of becoming a compleat master of his profession; and such was his diligence and good behaviour for a considerable time, that perhaps no lad in such a situation as he was ever acquired a better character, or was more esteemed by the neighbours and others who had connexions with his master,

Mr. Beaumont, observing his diligent and obliging behaviour, treated him with the utmost kindness, with a view to inspire him with a resolution of continuing in the practice of that duty which was so likely to be productive of his present and future happiness.

Unhappily, however, for Cooper, this gentle treatment had not its desired effect, as will be seen in the sequel of this story; yet he served out his apprenticeship with fidelity, and afterwards lived some time with his master as a journeyman. Mr. Beaumont still continued to treat him with his usual kindness, and so generous was his behaviour towards him, that the least attention to his own interest would most probably have preserved him from ruin, and enabled him to have made a very creditable figure in life.

Unhappily for himself, Cooper got acquainted with a number of young fellows of dissolute character, who frequented a public-house in Golden-lane, where they spent their time in scenes of riot and dissipation, equally calculated to destroy their health of body and peace of mind.

Cooper's former principles of virtue were all unhinged by an association with such obnoxious companions, and his mind was soon contaminated with ideas that led with rapid and certain progress to his destruction.

At length, through the instigation of his companions, he frequented houses of ill fame, which introduced him to the company of women of abandoned character, one of whom he became intimately acquainted with, and cohabited with her at a house of infamous character in Denmark-court in the Strand.

In a conversation between Cooper and his girl, the latter advised him to rob his late master, as the readiest way to raise a supply to support their present extravagance; and this scheme was thought the more practicable, as Cooper, having lived several years in the house, knew all the avenues to it, and every part of which he was well acquainted with.

Cooper at first appeared to be shocked at the simple idea of so basely injuring a man who had protected him in the early part of life, and had, on all occasions, proved himself such a disinterested friend; and he actually, for some time, refused to have any concern in such an ungenerous transaction: at length the arguments of the girl prevailed, and he resolved on the commission of the crime which terminated in his destruction.

It was Mr. Beaumont's custom to spend his evening at a public house in Old-street; and on his return home he carefully locked his doors, and observed that every other place of possible entrance was made fast, in order to prevent the admission of robbers: yet his vigilance proved fruitless; for Cooper, whom of all men he would have least suspected, proved the ungenerous infringer on the property of his benefactor.

Mr. Beaumont having seen his house secure one night, retired to rest; but about two on the following morning he was awakened by a noise that seemed to arise from the trampling of feet on the stairs.

Terrified in a high degree by this unexpected visit, he was for some time afraid of venturing out of his bed; but at length, hearing that some person had gone out of his chamber, and shut the door, he got up, and discovered that his bureau had been broken open, and a hundred guineas stolen from it. He likewise observed that the lock of the chamber-door, and the chain which confined it, had been forced open by means of a chiffel.

As it was presumed that the person who had committed the robbery could not be at any great distance, Mr. Beaumont alarmed the watchmen, who made an immediate pursuit; and though they did not overtake the robber, they presumed that they were near him, from hearing the trampling of feet hastily moving in the street, as those of a person flying from a pursuer.

The circumstances attending this robbery made it almost evident that the person who committed it must have been intimately acquainted with the avenues of the house; and Mr. Beaumont was induced to suspect that Cooper was the thief, from what he had

had then lately heard of the abandoned course of his life.

Hereupon Mr. Beaumont sent for a constable, and at seven o'clock the following morning Cooper was taken into custody at the house where he resided in Denmark-court in the Strand.

He at first denied having had any concern in the robbery, but being conveyed to his master's house, the precise money lost, except one guinea, was found on him. Mr. Beaumont sent for a neighbour, named Dyson, to advise with him how to act, and expressed, with tears, his aversion to the thought of prosecuting him.

Mr. Dyson told him it would be unsafe to discharge him; on which he was conveyed to the Compter, and on his examination before the sitting alderman such strong evidence of his guilt appeared, that he was committed to Newgate, for trial at the next Old Bailey sessions.

On his trial the master deposed against him with the most generous reluctance, and begged that, if it were possible, his punishment might be mitigated to any thing short of that of death. Cooper, by way of defence, recounted an absurd tale, hinting that the prosecution was undertaken from revengeful motives, on account of a quarrel which had taken place when he quitted Mr. Beaumont's service.

After a fair and candid trial the jury brought in a verdict of guilty, but joined in recommending him as an object of the royal clemency; and Mr. Beaumont signed a petition in behalf of the wretched convict; but, after the report was made to the king, he was included among those who were ordered for execution.

A confinement in the cells of Newgate brought this unhappy youth to a due consideration of the enormity

enormity of his crime, of which he appeared sincerely to repent, and confessed the justice of his sentence to the clergyman who directed him in his devotions.

He behaved in the most contrite manner at the fatal tree, where he again confessed that he had merited that public and ignominious death which the law had awarded for his crimes.

Joseph Cooper was hanged at Tyburn on the 30th of June, 1773.

In the fate of this malefactor we see the just punishment due to the crime of ingratitude. The robbing a master, who had treated him with such unusual kindness, was a proof that an assoication with bad company will so corrupt the mind, as to make it capable of the deepest baseness.

Hence, then, young people should learn to abstain from all evil associations, and to connect themselves only with the sober, the virtuous, the religious; and they may be assured that peace of mind will follow this conduct.

A full Relation of the Life, Trial, Behaviour, and Execution, of JOHN LENNARD, who was hanged for committing the horrid Crime of a Rape.

THIS offender was one of the lowest and most abandoned of the human race. He had been taught to read and write, which was all his education; but was too idle to think of any reputable employment, and even from his childhood discovered the most brutal and barbarous disposition.

Having a low, as well as a most savage turn of mind, he made himself acquainted with some bailiffs, who used to employ him to seize the goods of unfortunate people who were indebted in trifling sums; and in this capacity he gave such singular proofs of hardness of heart, that an officer of the Marshalsea court employed him as his follower.

In this station he was so exceedingly vigilant, active, and penetrating, that it was almost impossible for any man who had a writ out against him to escape him. He used to dress himself in a variety of disguises, to carry on his schemes, and seldom failed to render the unfortunate still more miserable.

Lennard's employer was a native of Dumfries in Scotland, and carried a pack of linen round the country for many years; but being greatly involved in debt to several linen-drapers, he was arrested, and lodged in the Marshalsea prison, whence he obtained his liberty under an act of insolvency, after which he commenced the very reputable profession of a Marshal's-court officer.

If he wanted a villain to assist him in his business, he could not have made choice of one more complete than Lennard, whose heart was formed of the most flinty materials, and whose head was as keen to contrive, as his hand ready to execute. A proof of the truth of this assertion will arise from the following horrid narrative.

At Reading in Berkshire lived a tradesman, who had been so unfortunate in his commercial connexions, that for two years together he secreted himself in his own house, Sundays excepted. This unhappy man had seven children, and his wife attended the shop, to support the infants; while the husband anxiously waited the arrival of a friend who had

made

made a large fortune in the East Indies, and who, he made no doubt, would assist him with money to discharge his just obligations to his creditors.

At this time the unhappy tradesman had a woman servant, who had heretofore lived in a scandalous intimacy with the bailiff and his follower. This woman informed her old associates what she had learnt of the East India story; on which Lennard formed a scheme that would ever mark his character with infamy, if that had been his only violation of the laws of humanity.

The bailiff had no conception that any advantage could be made of the base woman's intelligence; but Lennard, begging that the matter might be left to him, went to Reading, and sending for the woman, told her that his design was to return to London, and send her master a letter in a fictitious name, informing him that his friend was returned from the East Indies, and wished to see him.

On his return, the creditors were told that the tradesman might be arrested; on which a writ was taken out, and delivered to the bailiffs; and a letter was written, informing the tradesman that his friend was returned to England, and, having learnt that his circumstances were embarrassed, would send a gentleman to meet him at Hammersmith, and attend him to London in all possible privacy.

The devoted victim to this infernal plan, unsuspicious of what might happen, took place in the coach; and when it came to Hammersmith, Lennard and his master were in waiting, and told him they attended him at the request of his friend, who was returned to England very rich; and there being room for them, they got into the coach, and drove to Piccadilly.

Lennard

Lennard now defired the coachman to ſtop while they drank a glaſs of wine; and inviting the tradeſman into a public houſe, they preſented their writ, and conveyed their priſoner to a ſpunging-houſe near Covent-garden.

The dexterity of Lennard now became the general ſubject of converſation and praiſe among the bailiffs of London and Weſtminſter; and the villain who contrived the plan was extolled as the moſt ingenious of his profeſſion. His fame now ſpread at a rapid rate; and he ſoon afterwards engaged as follower to an officer under the ſheriff of Middleſex, who had been a linen-draper in Piccadilly, but had failed in trade. Lennard now got conſiderable ſums of money by his rapacity and extortion; but he was no ſooner in poſſeſſion of it, than he ſpent his ill-acquired gains among women of the town, two of whom he contributed greatly to ſupport :—but we come now to ſpeak of the atrocious crime which brought him to a ſhameful end.

An execution having been ſerved on the goods of Mr. Brailsford, a gentleman in Petty-France, Weſtminſter, Lennard, and two other fellows, named Guy and Groves, were put into poſſeſſion. This execution was ſerved on the 14th of June, 1773, and on the following day the crime was perpetrated.

Miſs Anne Boſs, a young lady of virtue and prudence, lodged in Mr. Brailsford's houſe; and when his misfortunes came on, that gentleman left his children in the care of the young lady.

Miſs Boſs going up ſtairs to dreſs herſelf, in order to pay a viſit to a lady in the neighbourhood, ſhe was followed by Lennard, whom ſhe was aſtoniſhed to ſee enter her chamber, where he perpetrated

petrated the rape, with every circumstance of horrid aggravation.

In the interim she alarmed the neighbourhood; but Lennard having by this time left her, she went down into the yard, where she fainted away, and continued some time in a state of insensibility. Some of the neighbours now came to the door, and insisted on being admitted; but Lennard drew a sword, and threatened instant destruction to the first who should presume to enter.

A foreign gentleman who lodged at the next house, having observed the unhappy situation of Miss Boss, recommended an immediate application to a Magistrate; but, as the hour grew late, it was resolved to wait till the morning before any such step should be taken *.

In the interim Mr. Houseman of Berkhamstead, an acquaintance of Mr. Brailsford, being in London, went to the house of his friend, late on the same night; where finding Lennard in possession of the effects, he begged to speak with Miss Boss; but the villain kicked him out of the house, instead of complying with his request.

On the following morning the neighbours applied to Sir John Fielding, who immediately sent several constables to take into custody the three men in the possession of the house.

Being conveyed to Bow-street, Miss Boss gave positive testimony against Lennard for the rape, on which he and his companions were committed to Newgate.

---

* It was strange that any hesitation should be made respecting the hour in a case of this nature. Any hour of the night would have been equal at Bow-street, and immediate steps would have been taken to secure the offender.

At

At the next seffions at the Old Bailey Lennard was capitally convicted, and received sentence of death; and Guy and Groves, being found guilty of a misdemeanour, were adjudged to be burnt in the hand and imprisoned.

Lennard's behaviour after conviction was insensible and brutal in a high degree; nor could he be induced to perform any office of religion, notwithstanding his deplorable situation: nor at the place of death was his behaviour more becoming; he died as little lamented as perhaps any one that ever suffered at the fatal tree.

John Lennard was hanged at Tyburn on the 12th of August, 1773.

It is a common saying, when a man is known for an egregious villain, that "hanging is too good "for him;" and surely if this could ever be applied with truth, it must have been to this malefactor: yet his brethren of the order of bailiffs did not seem to think so; for they made a subscription for his funeral; whereas his carcase ought to have been given to the fowls of the air.

The life of this man seems to have been one chain of guilt from the cradle to the gallows: but it is time to have done with so execrable a subject; and we trust it cannot be necessary to warn any one from following his example; a dreadful example to present and future times!

A Particular Account of the Cafe of WILLIAM FIELD, otherwife GREEN, who was hanged for a Highway-robbery, after a long Reign of Iniquity.

THIS malefactor was an accomplice of the notorious Hawke the highwayman, of whom we fhall have occafion to fpeak in the courfe of this work.

Field went by a variety of names, fo that it would be difficult to diftinguifh which was the true one; but this is the name by which he was examined at Bow-ftreet, tried, and convicted.

Not having learnt any trade, he entered into the fervice of a gentleman, with whom he lived three years, but was at length difcharged, on account of his character: however, he foon got a new place on a falfe recommendation; but his extravagance and ill hours induced this mafter likewife to difcharge him.

Being reduced to great poverty, the confequence of his vices, he refolved on commencing highwayman; and, having hired horfes at livery ftables, he committed fuch a variety of robberies, that he foon became the fubject of public converfation.

The money he acquired by his lawlefs depredations he fquandered among men and women of abandoned character; but at length he was fought after by the officers of juftice, who carried him before a magiftrate, by whom he was committed to Newgate

He was tried at the next feffions at the Old Bailey: when the profecutor gave his teftimony against him in so favourable a manner, that though the jury found him guilty, they recommended him to the royal mercy. The consequence was, that he was reprieved for transportation in the year 1770.

On his arrival in North America he was sold to slavery; but, soon finding means to escape with other slaves to New York, they embarked on board a vessel bound for Pool, and landed in England.

Field hastening to London engaged with Hawke in the practice of robbing on the highway; and making large booties, he assumed the character of a gentleman; and courting a girl who lived servant with a man of fortune, she consented to accept him for a husband.

For some months after his marriage, he committed highway-robberies about twice a week; but his wife had no suspicion of the life he led, conceiving him to be a man in good circumstances.

It is said that in five months he collected ten thousand pounds, in Bills of exchange and cash; but this we believe is beyond the truth; though he frequently committed four or five robberies on a night, sometimes on Finchley Common, and often on Shooter's-hill, Blackheath, and other places in that neighbourhood; till being closely pursued, he effected a difficult escape to town. After this he frequented Putney-common and its adjacencies, whence he brought considerable booties to London.

Field, Hawke, and another, having robbed some coaches, dined and made merry at a public house at Barnes; and staying till it was near night, they crossed Kew bridge, and went to Acton, where they slept, being afraid of coming to London.

Notice having been given at Sir John Fielding's office, persons were sent out on different roads, and the

the offenders being taken were conveyed, handcuffed, to Tothill-fields bridewell. On a subsequent day they were examined, and a great number of robberies being sworn against Hawke and Field, they were remanded to prison, whence the former made his escape in a few days.

Though Field had returned from transportation, it was thought proper to indict him at the Surry assizes for the subsequent robberies; when he would have pleaded guilty, but Lord Chief Baron Smythe advised him to put himself on his trial; and when the jury had given a verdict against him, the judge pronounced sentence, after addressing him in the most pathetic manner.

Being conveyed to the New-gaol in Southwark, he was attended by the Reverend Mr. Dyer, to whom he acknowledged that the robberies he had been charged with were far short of those he had committed, and he appeared very penitent for his crimes. At the place of his death he warned young people to avoid bad company, as it was the certain road to destruction.

William Field was hanged at Kennington Common on the 1st of September, 1773.

The fate of this offender should serve as a lesson of caution to gentlemen's servants. He lost two places through the badness of his character; and being reduced to poverty, he was tempted to turn highwayman. His success for awhile was extraordinary; but this led him, with only the greater rapidity, to the gallows. Nothing more need be said on this subject; this wretched man brought destruction on his own head!

The remarkable Case of Lieutenant General WILLIAM GANSEL, who was tried at the Old Bailey for feloniously firing a Pistol at JOHN HYDE, a Sheriff's Officer, while attempting to arrest him under the Authority of a Special Capias.

GENERAL GANSEL having greatly impaired his fortune by a life of gaiety, had been several years under great pecuniary embarrassments, from which he was using his utmost endeavours to extricate himself at the time when the transaction happened which gave rise to the trial, of which it is our present business to relate the particulars.

In the forenoon of the 26th of August, 1773, Mr. Lee, an eminent surgeon, applied to John Hyde to arrest General Gansel for a debt of an hundred and thirty-four pounds. They went to the proper office, and obtained a special capias; after which the officer applied to his brother, Thomas Hyde, Henry Feltus, William Sleigh, and Richard Reeves, to assist in the intended capture.

Between two and three in the afternoon Mr. Lee met the bailiff and his assistants, and, accompanied by John Hyde, went to the house of Mr. Mayo, in Craven-street, Strand, the other men being appointed to wait at some distance. The street door being open, they went into the parlour, and Mr. Lee asked Mrs. Mayo whether General Gansel lodged in her house. Being answered in the affirmative, Hyde went into the street, and having beckoned for his companions to come up, attempted to go towards the general's apartments; but on the stairs he was opposed by two boys, who were brothers, and servants to the general. At this time the other

other bailiffs entered the passage, and John Hyde having struck a knife from the hand of one of the boys with a walking-stick, and thrown it out of the window, he and his brother were soon overpowered and bolted in the yard.

John Hyde deposed, that, when the boys were in the yard, he proceeded towards the second floor, and observing the general, with whose person he was well acquainted, upon the landing-place, hastened towards him, and placed his knee between the chamber-door and the wainscot, and endeavoured to force into the room, when the general discharged a pistol, the ball from which passed through the upper pannel of the door towards the hinge, and struck the wainscot on the stair-case; that he then got into the room, and, clapping the general on the shoulder, said, "Sir, you are my prisoner;" when the general, with his left arm over his right shoulder, pointed another pistol at his face; but that by suddenly stooping his head, he fortunately escaped the ball, which passed through the hat of Henry Feltus; that the general was then with much difficulty forced down stairs, and put into a hackney coach, which conveyed him to a lock-up house kept by a sheriff's officer, named Armstrong, whence he was soon afterwards removed to Newgate.

Feltus produced the hat through which the ball of the second pistol had passed: but neither his evidence not that of Thomas Hyde, Sleigh, or Reeves, materially differed from that of the first witness.

The general said, that though he was not wholly unused to speak in public, his ill state of health and other circumstances had given rise to an apprehension that he might be incapable on the present occasion to do justice to his cause in an extempore address,

address, and he had therefore reduced his defence to writing.

He then read the defence, which, among other matters, set forth, that being informed by his servants, Henry and James, that the house was surrounded by armed ruffians, and presently after hearing a violent uproar at the head of the stairs, he locked himself into his chamber, against the door of which he placed an elbow-chair, and the uproar encreasing, he fired off a pistol pointed to the upper part of the door, with a view of deterring the assailants, who soon broke into the room, the forcing the door throwing him down, and the second pistol going off without design, while he was falling. He said that, from a perusal of Blackstone's Commentaries, he was taught to believe that an Englishman's house is his castle, and that a room hired for a certain time was to be considered as his castle; that he paid for his apartments by the year; and that he had occupied them eight and thirty years, sixteen years of which Mr. Mayo had been his landlord; and that he conceived he had an undoubted right of defending himself in his own habitation. In the course of his address the prisoner mentioned several persons whom he desired might be examined on his behalf.

Several witnesses swore that the bolt of the lock belonging to the general's chamber-door had been strained, and the screws of the receiver of the bolt forced out of the wood; and they likewise deposed that, from a very particular examination, they were confident the ball must have took a different direction, had the pistol been fired when the door was open, adding that, when the door was open only three inches, they perceived that the impression made by the ball on the wainscot of the stair-case was

was not nearly in a right line with the hole in the pannel in the door, but that when the door was perfectly closed there was an exact correspondence between the hole through which the ball passed and the mark where it afterwards struck the wainscot.

Mrs. Mayo swore, that from the time the transaction happened the premises had not been seen by any person but in her presence, and that no alterations whatever had been made.

The above is a faithful abstract of the evidence adduced for and against the prisoner on an indictment for feloniously shooting at John Hyde; the first count charging him with firing off a pistol held in his right, and the second with firing at the same man another pistol held in his left hand. After the jury had remained out of court some time, they brought in their verdict, " not guilty."

The general was arraigned on two other indictments; one for feloniously shooting at Thomas Hyde; and the other for feloniously shooting at Henry Feltus: but the counsel for the prosecution informed the court, that " as the general was ac-
" quitted on the merits, he should waive proceed-
" ing on the two last indictments."

General Ganfel was tried at the sessions house in the Old Bailey on Wednesday the 8th of September, 1773.

It was imagined that the principal matter for the decision of the court would have been, Whether the law would justify a man in opposing a forcible entry into his place of habitation, and how far the character, office, and authority of the assailants were to be considered in mitigation of a violent attack: but the question took a turn very different from what was expected.

The

The evidence of John Hyde and his associates set forth, that the door was partly open when the general fired; but the contrary appeared from the depositions of other witnesses. It does not seem that the first pistol was pointed immediately at any person; for the hole in the door was considerably higher than the head of the tallest man; and it is very probable that the second pistol went off while the general was falling. Thus the matter seems to have been understood by the jury.

Nothing but the last extremity of danger can justify the use of fire-arms, or other desperate weapons. There is something extremely shocking in the idea of taking away the life of a fellow-creature, when he is unprepared for eternity.

Let our readers remember, that if it should prove their misfortune to labour under injury and oppression, the most eligible means of obtaining redress will be by an application to the legislative power.

Genuine Memoirs of the famous WILLIAM COX, who was executed for stealing Bank Notes and Cash to the Amount of more than four hundred Pounds, the Property of Mr. JOHN KENDRICK.

THE father of the unfortunate youth, who is the subject of this narrative, was a ribbon-weaver, and lived in Holywell-lane, near Shoreditch. His mother was esteemed honest and industrious, and was considered as the only person of the family deserving that character. At a very early time of life young Cox was initiated into the arts of thieving by his own father, who was in America, under

WILLIAM COX,
in the Press Yard, Newgate.

sentence of transportation, at the time of his son's execution.

The following is an account of the first felonious transaction in which this unhappy young man was engaged: the father and son passing through Grosvenor-street, the former observed a silver tankard in a window, and attempted to steal it; but being prevented by the iron rails of the area, he lifted the boy over them, ordering him to take the tankard, which he immediately handed to his father, and was then lifted again into the street.

Soon after the above adventure young Cox commenced pick-pocket, and in a short time he was reckoned the most expert of that fraternity. Being committed to Clerkenwell bridewell, he was reduced to a most miserable degree of poverty: but he no sooner obtained his liberty, than he procured decent apparel, and he was from that time remarkably clean and neat in his appearance.

Cox lived some years at the house of his uncle West, in Feathers-court, High Holborn, who encouraged him to pursue those illegal courses which led to his destruction.

He got unperceived into a grocer's, the corner of Long-lane, in Aldersgate-street, and stole a silver-hilted sword from a room on the first floor: returning through the shop with his booty, he was asked some questions; on which he said he had been playing with master Billy, which he had informed himself was the name of the grocer's son: but on going out of the shop the sword struck against the steps, and he was taken into custody, and brought to trial, but it was his fortune to escape conviction.

Being provided with a tame sparrow, he let the bird fly into a window of a house in Hanover-street, and the door happening to be open, he went in, and concealed plate to a considerable amount. Hearing some person walking towards the room, he sought refuge in the area, where being perceived by an elderly gentlewoman, who was the only person in the house, he burst into tears, and saying his sparrow had flown into the window, begged he might be allowed to catch it. The old lady complied; and he soon found an opportunity of decamping with his booty.

It was the common practice of Cox to play at marbles and other games with young gentlemen before the doors of their parents, and he seldom suffered an opportunity to escape of getting into, and robbing the houses. He had a very remarkably boyish appearance; and on a variety of occasions that circumstance greatly assisted him in the pursuit of his felonious designs.

Cox was connected with a notorious thief, who called himself Captain Davis; and by means of the most artful stratagems that could be suggested, these accomplices perpetrated a surprising number of robberies. Davis was at length apprehended, and sentenced to suffer death; but he was reprieved on condition of transportation.

About the middle of the summer 1773, the apartments of Mr. Kendrick in Oxford-street were privately entered, and a bureau was opened, and three bank-notes, of a hundred pounds each, and a hundred and thirty guineas, and a silver watch, were stolen thereout. Soon after Mr. Kendrick's robbery, Cox and William Claxton went together to Reading in Berkshire, and there purchased three horses, for which Claxton paid with one of the notes stolen from Mr. Kendrick, receiving in part of change a fifty pounds bank-note, which he afterwards changed at the bank for notes of smaller value,

value, two of which were found in the possession of West, Cox's uncle. On the first examination of these offenders at the public office in Bow-street, which was on Wednesday, the eleventh day of August, West said he received the notes of his wife, on the day preceding that of her decease, which was about the time of Mr. Kendrick's robbery: but on the following Wednesday he assured the magistrates that the notes had been in his possession three years. In contradiction to this it was proved that the notes had not been many days issued from the bank.

Mr. Knapp and Mr. White of Reading appeared, and the fifty pounds note, given in part of change of that of an hundred, was regularly traced from the hands of Claxton to the bank, where he had changed it for others of smaller value. West was discharged, the receiving of notes, which are the produce of other notes feloniously obtained, not coming under the description of the law: and Claxton was admitted an evidence against Cox, who was committed for trial at the ensuing sessions at the Old Bailey.

The evidence against Cox was wholly circumstantial: but it was of such a nature as to be almost as strong as positive proof; and on that evidence he was convicted at the sessions at the Old Bailey in September, 1773.

While under sentence of death he seemed not to be remarkably shocked at the idea of the dreadful fate that awaited him: he was chearful among his companions; but yet he appeared not wholly regardless of the necessary preparations for eternity.

William Cox was executed at Tyburn on the 27th of October, 1773.

Cox was by no means addicted to drunkenness. At the public houses he frequented he seldom staid long at a time, it being his usual custom to drink a small glass of liquor at the bar, for which he generally paid a shilling. For some years he had kept a little black mare, on which he rode to the races within a moderate distance of London, where he was generally very successful in making bets. He long cohabited with a woman who was equally famous for her dexterity in shoplifting, and being the sister of so accomplished a villain, and so dangerous a pest to society, as William Claxton.

It was the peculiar misfortune of Cox to be instructed in the arts of villainy by his own father at a time of life when he was incapable of distinguishing between right and wrong. The most important part of a parent's duty is to inspire his offspring with an ardent love of virtue. If any of our readers should be so peculiarly unfortunate as to be countenanced in vicious courses by their parents, let them disclaim all filial obedience, and seek support and protection from that Almighty Power whose favour will ever be extended to such as live in a strict adherence to his divine commands.

Particulars relating to WILLIAM HAWKE, who was executed for a robbery on the Highway.

THIS offender was born at Uxbridge in the county of Middlesex. Soon after the decease of his father he came to London, and hired himself to draw beer at a public house upon Saffron-hill. Contracting an acquaintance with some abandoned

Hawke *robs* Capt. Cunningham & Mr. Hart *on the* Highway *near* Knightsbridge.

abandoned people who frequented an alehouse in St. Giles's, he was persuaded to join them in committing depredations upon the public.

Hawke at length commenced highwayman, and became an accomplice of James Field, the particulars of whose life we have already mentioned. Field and Hawke were transported to America; and returning to England nearly at the same period, they again became associates in committing robberies upon the highway. Hawke and Field being apprehended together, the former escaped from Tothill-fields bridewell, and got to France; but the other suffered the sentence of the law.

Upon his return to England he committed a surprising number of most daring robberies; and several months elapsed before the thief-takers knew him to be the man by whom the roads about London were so dangerously infested.

Information being given to Mr. Smith, the keeper of Tothill-fields bridewell, that Hawke's wife had been to Uxbridge on a party of pleasure, he sought the driver of the coach in which she was conveyed, and learnt from him that Hawke lodged in Shoe-lane. The following morning Mr. Smith, Mr. Bond, Mr. Leigh, and some other persons in the service of Sir John Fielding, went to Shoe-lane. Bond going up two pair of stairs, entered the front room, and there discovering Hawke slumbering in bed, threw himself across the highwayman, who, twisting the sheet round Bond's head, reached at a pistol that was under the pillow, at which instant Smith entered, and caught hold of his hand. With much difficulty Hawke was secured; and being put into a coach, he said that his misfortunes were in some measure alleviated by the consideration that no life was lost, for he was

provided

provided with several loaded pistols, and had formed the resolution of firing upon every man who should attempt to take him into custody.

Being conveyed to the public office in Bow-street, a great number of persons were bound to prosecute, and he was committed to Newgate.

At the next sessions at the Old Bailey he was arraigned on an indictment for robbing Mr. Hart of a small sum of money; and the following are the most remarkable circumstances adduced in evidence: Mr. Hart and Captain Cunningham were stopped in the Fulham stage, a little beyond Knightsbridge, by the prisoner, who demanded their money: the captain refused to resign his property; and Hawke threatened to fire, and pointing his pistol at the captain, he said, " fire away and be damned!" on which the robber discharged his pistol, and the ball passed between the captain's shoulder and his coat. Mr. Hart then delivered a few shillings; and Captain Cunningham, getting out of the coach in the interim, seized the bridle of the highwayman's horse, when he discharged a second pistol. He then remounted, but did not ride away for some minutes, during which interval the captain employed himself in picking up stones and throwing them at him. At the time of Hawke's trial Captain Cunningham was abroad, but Mr. Hart's evidence was so positive, clear, and circumstantial, that no doubt remained as to the guilt of the prisoner, who was therefore sentenced to be executed.

While Hawke was under sentence of death, in Newgate, his behaviour was such as may be called decent, rather than penitential. While his irons were knocking off on the morning of execution, one of his acquaintance addressed him thus: " How " do you do, Billy? will you have some flowers?"

William Hawke, in the Press Yard New--gate

Hereupon Hawke said, "I am pretty well, I thank you. How is Harry Wright*? he has been ill of late, I hear." And then, while the man held the nosegay, he picked out a flower, and with great compoſure placed it in a button-hole of his coat.

When the cart was preparing to be driven from under the gallows, he threw off both his ſhoes; and when he found it move, he collected his utmoſt ſtrength, and leaped up, ſo that his neck was inſtantly diſlocated.

William Hawke was executed at Tyburn on the 1ſt of July, 1774.

The behaviour of this malefactor at the place of execution ſeemed to evince, that his mind was too much occupied by the deſire of meeting his fate with reſolution. A becoming fortitude is to be preſerved even in the moment of entering upon eternity; but that fortitude muſt ariſe from a conſciouſneſs of unfeigned repentance, and be accompanied by the pleaſing hope of obtaining pardon at the dread tribunal of the Almighty.

The Caſes of CHARLES MILLS and JOHN PUGH, who were executed for a Robbery on the King's Highway, commonly called a Footpad Robbery.

THESE offenders were born of poor parents, and received little or no education. In the winter they acted as porters on the wharfs of the Thames, and in the ſummer employed themſelves as haymakers; but at length aſſociating with aban-

---
* One of the turnkeys of Tothill-fields bridewell.

doned company of both sexes, who lived in Chick-lane, and such places, they lost those fair characters they had hitherto supported.

Distressed in circumstances by their own vices, they determined to supply their wants by robbery; but their appearance being too mean to permit them to think of hiring horses, they determined to commence footpads; and committed a number of robberies in the fields north of London, frequently ill-treating those whom they robbed. Their success for some time was trifling, but being sufficient to furnish them with several offensive weapons, their depredations became more frequent, and their booties were spent, as those of thieves generally are, in the company of abandoned women.

They commonly met at an alehouse in Tottenham-court-road, and, having flushed themselves with liquor, sallied forth to assault the unoffending passenger. We now proceed to mention the fact, the commission of which cost them their lives.

On the 10th of August, 1774, they met, according to custom, at the alehouse, and having drank themselves into spirits to undertake daring exploits, they went into the fields near Primrose-hill, between London and Hampstead, when a violent shower of rain falling, they took shelter under a hedge. In the interim a gentleman named Gilson, who had been reading in a book as he strolled over the fields, came to the same spot, to avoid the violence of the shower.

When the rain abated, Mr. Gilson was going away; but the villains threatened his instant death if he hesitated to deliver his money. In the mean time Mills rifled his pockets, where finding only a few shillings, the robbers blasphemed in a horrid manner; and Mr. Gilson, apprehensive of fatal consequences,

sequences, then delivered his watch, with a guinea and some silver, which he had till then concealed.

Ten days afterwards Mr. Gilson was again near the same spot, and sitting down to read, observed the identical robbers approaching him. Knowing them well, he applied to a man-servant belonging to farmer Wellings, to assist him in taking them into custody. The man hesitated, as doubting if the gentleman had been really robbed; but Mr. Wellings, being informed of the affair, directed two men to go in search of the footpads, who were soon taken, conveyed before a magistrate, and lodged in Newgate.

At the next Old Bailey sessions they were capitally convicted, and sentenced to die. After conviction, they sent to some of their former companions in iniquity; but not one would attend them. For a short time they entertained hopes of being respited; but these hopes soon vanished.

Pugh behaved penitently; but Mills much more so, answering explicitly all the questions that were asked him, confessing his guilt, and wishing for life, only in the hope of making reparation to those who had been sufferers by his crimes.

They were admitted to the sacrament on the morning of their execution; and, when their irons were knocked off, Pugh seemed almost abandoned to despondency, and at the place of Execution he acknowledged the justice of his sentence. Mills acknowledged that he had committed many other robberies, the result of his attachment to women of abandoned character.

Charles Mills and John Pugh were hanged at Tyburn on the 7th of November, 1774.

The most remarkable circumstance in the case of these malefactors is, that, after conviction, their former abandoned acquaintance would not visit them. Thus were they left in the utmost distress in the hour of the greatest extremity!

Hence young people should learn the extreme ill consequence of keeping bad company; and that the true way to be happy, is to associate with those who have more wisdom and virtue than themselves.

A full and particular Account of the Life and extraordinary Transactions of JOHN RANN, *otherwise Sixteen-Strings Jack, who was hanged for a Robbery on the Highway.*

JOHN RANN was born at a village a few miles from Bath, of honest parents who were in low circumstances, and incapable of giving him any kind of education. For some time he obtained a livelihood by vending goods, which he drove round the city and adjacent country on an ass.

A lady of distinction, who happened to be at Bath, took Rann into her service when he was about twelve years of age; and his behaviour was such, that he became the favourite of his mistress and fellow-servants.

At length he came to London, and got employment as a helper in the stables at Brooke's mews, in which station he bore a good character. He then became the driver of a post-chaise, after which he was servant to an officer; and in both these stations he was well spoken of.

About four years before his execution, he was coachman to a gentleman of fortune near Portman-square; and it was at this period that he dressed in
the

the manner which gave rife to the appellation of Sixteen-ftrings Jack, by wearing breeches with eight ftrings at each knee.

After living in the fervice of feveral noblemen, he loft his character, and turned pick-pocket, in company with three fellows, named Jones, Clayton, and Colledge, the latter of whom (a mere boy) obtained the name of *Eight-ftrings Jack*.

At the feffions held at the Old Bailey in April, 1774, Rann, Clayton, and one Shepherd, were tried for robbing Mr. William Somers on the highway, and acquitted for want of evidence. They were again tried for robbing Mr. Langford, but acquitted for the fame reafon.

For fome time paft, Rann had kept company with a young woman named Roche, who, having been apprenticed to a millener, and being feduced by an officer of the guards, was reduced to obtain bread by the cafual wages of proftitution; and, at length affociating with highwaymen, received fuch valuable effects as they took on the road.

On the 30th of May, Rann was taken into cuftody, and, being brought to Bow-ftreet on the following Wednefday, was charged with robbing John Devall Efquire, near the nine-mile ftone on the Hounflow-road, of his watch and money. This watch he had given to Mifs Roche, who had delivered it to Catherine Smith, who offered it in pledge to Mr. Hallam, a pawnbroker, who, fufpecting that it was not honeftly obtained, caufed all the parties to be taken into cuftody.

Mifs Roche was now charged with receiving the watch, knowing it to have been ftolen; and Mifs Smith, being fworn, depofed that, on the day Mr. Devall was robbed, Roche told her that " fhe ex-
" pected Rann to bring her fome money in the
" evening;"

"evening;" that he accordingly came about ten at night, and, having retired some time with Miss Roche, she, on her return, owned that she had received a watch and five guineas from him, which he said he had taken from a gentleman on the highway; that she, Miss Smith, carried the watch to pawn to Mr. Hallam, at the request of Miss Roche.

Sir John Fielding asked Rann if he would offer any thing in his defence; on which the latter said, "I know no more of the matter than you do, nor "half so much neither." On this occasion Rann was dressed in a manner above his stile of life and his circumstances. He had a bundle of flowers in the breast of his coat, almost as large as a broom; and his irons were tied up with a number of blue ribbands.

For the offence abovementioned, Rann was tried at the sessions held at the Old Bailey in July, 1774, and acquitted.

Two or three days after this acquittal, Rann engaged to sup with a girl at her lodgings in Bow-street, but not being punctual to his appointment, the girl went to bed, and Rann, not being able to obtain admittance at the door, attempted to get in at the window on the first floor, and had nearly accomplished his purpose when he was taken into custody by the watchman.

For this burglarious attempt he was examined at Bow-street on the 27th of July, when the girl, whose apartments he had attempted to break open, declared that he could not have had any felonious intention, as he knew that he would have been a welcome guest, and have been readily admitted, if she had not fallen asleep. On this he was dismissed, after Sir John Fielding had cautioned him to leave

his

his dangerous profession, and seek for some more honest means of support.

On the Sunday following, Rann appeared at Bagnigge-wells, " dressed in a scarlet coat, tambour " waistcoat, white silk stockings, laced hat, &c. and " publicly declared himself to be a highwayman. " Having drank pretty freely, he became extremely " quarrelsome; and several scuffles ensued, in one " of which he lost a ring from his finger, and when " he discovered his loss, he said it was but an hun- " dred guineas gone, which one evening's *work* " would replace. He became at length so trou- " blesome, that part of the company agreed to " turn him out of the house; but they met with so " obstinate a resistance, that they were obliged to " give up their design, when a number of young " fellows, possessed of more spirit than discretion, " attacked this magnanimous hero, and actually " forced him through the window into the road." Rann was not much injured by this severe treatment; but he complained bitterly against those who could so affront a *gentleman* of his character.

Rann being arrested for a debt of 50£. which he was unable to pay, was confined in the Marshalsea prison, where he was visited by a number of men and women of bad character, some of whom paid his debt, and procured his discharge.

At another time, Rann being with two companions at an alehouse in Tottenham-court-road, two sheriff's officers arrested Rann, who, not having money to pay the rent, deposited his watch in the hands of the bailiffs, and his associates advanced three guineas, which together made more than the amount of the debt; and as a balance was to be returned to Rann when the watch should be redeemed, he told the bailiffs that, if they would lend him

five

five shillings, he would treat them with a crown bowl of punch. This they readily did; and while they were drinking, Rann said to the officers, "You have not treated me like a gentleman. "When Sir John Fielding's people come after me, "they use me genteelly; they only hold up a fin- "ger, beckon me, and I follow them as quietly as "a lamb."

When the bailiffs were gone, Rann and his companions rode off; but our hero, soon returning, stopped at the turnpike, and asked if he had been wanted. "No," (said the tollman). "Why, (replied the other), "I am Sixteen-strings Jack, the "famous highwayman — have any of Sir John "Fielding's people been this way?"—"Yes, (said the man) "some of them are but just gone "through." Rann replied, "If you see them "again, tell them I am gone towards London;" and then rode off with the utmost unconcern.

Soon afterwards, Rann appeared at Barnet races, dressed in a most elegant sporting stile, his waistcoat being blue sattin trimmed with silver; and he was followed by hundreds of people, who were eager to gratify their curiosity by the sight of a man who had been so much the object of public conversation.

A very short time before Rann was capitally convicted, he attended a public execution at Tyburn, and, getting within the ring formed by the constables round the gallows, desired that he might be permitted to stand there, "for (said he) perhaps "it is very proper that I should be a spectator on "this occasion."

On the 26th of September, 1774, Rann and William Collier went on the Uxbridge road, with a view to commit robberies on the highway; and on the

the Wednesday following they were examined at the public office in Bow-street, when Dr. William Bell, chaplain to the princess Amelia, deposed, that between three and four o'clock in the afternnoon of Monday the 26th of September, as he was riding near Ealing, he observed two men, rather of a mean appearance, who rode past him; and that he remarked they had suspicious looks; yet neither at that time, nor for some little time afterwards, had he any idea of being robbed; that soon afterwards one of them, which he believed was Rann, crossed the head of his horse, and, demanding his money, said "Give it me, and take no notice, or "I'll blow your brains out." On this the doctor gave him one shilling and six-pence, which was all the silver he had, and likewise a common watch in a tortoise-shell case.

On the evening of the day on which the robbery was committed, Eleanor Roche (who was kept by Rann) and her maid-servant carried a watch to pledge with Mr. Cordy, pawnbroker in Oxford-road, who, suspecting that it had not been honestly acquired, stopped it, and applied to Mr. Grignion, watchmaker in Russel-street, Covent-garden, who had made the watch for Dr. Bell.

Mr. Clarke swore, that, on going to Miss Roche's lodgings on the Monday night, he found two pair of boots wet and dirty, which had evidently been worn that day; and Mr. Haliburton swore that he waited at Miss Roche's lodgings till Rann and Collier came thither, in consequence of which they were taken into custody.

On the 5th of October, John Rann, William Collier, Eleanor Roche, and Christian Stewart (servant to Roche) were brought to Bow-street, when Dr. Bell deposed in substance, as he had done the preceding

preceding week: and William Hills (servant to the princess Amelia) swore that he saw Rann (whom he well knew) ascend the hill at Acton about twenty minutes before the robbery was committed; a circumstance which perfectly agreed with Dr. Bell's account of the time that he was robbed.

Hereupon John Rann and William Collier were committed to Newgate, to take their trials for the highway robbery; Miss Roche was sent to Clerkenwell bridewell, and Christian Stewart (her servant) to Tothill-fields bridewell, to be tried as accessaries after the fact.

The evidence given on this trial was, in substance, the same as that which had been given at Bow-street; but, some favourable circumstances appearing in behalf of Collier, he was recommended to mercy, and afterwards respited during the king's pleasure. Miss Roche was sentenced to be transported for fourteen years, her servant was acquitted, and Rann was left for execution.

When Rann was brought down to take his trial, he was dressed in a new suit of pea-green cloth, his hat was bound round with silver strings, he wore a ruffled shirt, and his behaviour evidenced the utmost unconcern.

Rann was so confident of being acquitted, that he had ordered a genteel supper to be provided for the entertainment of his particular friends and associates on the joyful acquittal: but their intended mirth was turned into mourning; and the madness of guilty joy, to the sullen melancholy of equally guilty grief.

When Rann received his sentence, he attempted to force a smile, but it was evident that his mind was racked with pains that no language can express.

After conviction the behaviour of this malefactor was, for some time, very improper for one in his unhappy circumstances. On Sunday the 23d of October, he had seven girls to dine with him. The company were remarkably chearful, nor was Rann less joyous than his companions.

His conduct was expressive of great unconcern till the time that the warrant for his execution arrived; after which he began to be somewhat serious in his preparation for a future state.

On the morning of execution he received the sacrament in the chapel of the prison, and at the fatal tree behaved with great decency, but did not appear so much affected by his approaching fate as some printed accounts have represented him. When he came near the fatal tree, he turned round and looked at it as an object which he had long expected to see; but not as on one that he dreaded, as might reasonably have been expected.

After the customary devotions he was turned off, and, having hung the usual time, his body was delivered to his friends for interment.

John Rann was executed at Tyburn on the 30th of November, 1774.

Rann's general character was that of a bold, ignorant, fellow. He was fond of boasting of his exploits in all companies, without regard to his personal safety. He was exceedingly apt to be quarrelsome when in liquor, and fond of fighting with almost any man he might meet in the street.

Miss Roche was a girl, who, having been early seduced from the paths of virtue, had lived with different men in very various ranks of life, till she at length came into the knowledge of Rann.

From the fate of this unhappy youth, let others be taught never to embark in an illicit connexion with women of ill fame. It is the ready and certain path to destruction, from which nothing can so effectually guard young men as a steady adherence to the rules of virtue and religion*.

Narrative of the Trial, Conviction, and Execution, of Amos Merritt, who was hanged for breaking into and robbing the House of Mr. Ellicott.

AT the sessions held at the Old Bailey in the month of December, 1774, Amos Merritt was indicted for breaking and entering the dwelling house of Edward Ellicott, early in the morning of the 26th of October, and robbing it of plate, a gold watch, and other valuable articles to a large amount.

Mr. Ellicott deposed that he lived in Hornsey-lane, near Highgate; that he was awakened by his wife, who enquired what noise was in the house,

---

* Rann's attachment to women of ill fame was by no means extraordinary for a man in his situation. The debauched mind has no idea of the purity of real love; and it is to be lamented that we have so few books in our language calculated to inspire and direct this laudable passion. There is, however, one little pamphlet called " The Lover's New Guide," which exceeds any thing of the kind that has been written in the English, or any other language. It contains very interesting letters on the subjects of love, courtship, and marriage; with dialogues, cards of compliment, and poems on the same important subjects; and, in fact, a variety of that kind of writing which is calculated to teach the passions to move at the command of virtue. Young persons cannot purchase, or parents present, a more admirable production as a *guide* in the most important concerns of human life.

which

which he thought proceeded from the servants moving the tables in the passage; but this Mrs. Ellicott thought could not be, from the hour of the night; and ringing the bell, both of them jumped out of bed; when the first words heard were, "Come up directly;" and then somebody said, "D— your bloods! we will murder every soul in "the house." Mrs. Ellicott said, " Lord bless "me, the door is open;" and running to the door, pushed it close. Mr. Ellicott gave immediate assistance; and a person who was without, who he believed, from his voice, was the prisoner, said, "D— you, if you do not open the door, I will "murder every one of you."

The rest of the evidence was to the following effect.—The villains attempted to force open the door, putting a hanger with a scabbard between that and the post; but Mr. Ellicott, who is a powerful man, kept them out by mere strength, and having fastened the door with a drop-bolt, which went into the flooring, he ran to the window, and called out " Thieves!" In the mean time Mrs. Ellicott, by perpetual ringing of the bell, had alarmed the servants, who ran into the street after the thieves, who had by this time got off with the property.

Notice being given at Sir John Fielding's, Merritt and his accomplices were taken into custody on suspicion, and, after an examination at Bow-street, were committed to Newgate.

At the trial, the evidence was deemed so satisfactory, that the jury did not hesitate to find Merritt guilty, in consequence of which he received sentence of death.

There is nothing so extraordinary in the case of the burglary committed by Amos Merritt as to have induced us to infert it in this collection, but on account of some singular circumstances in the conduct of the culprit, which we now proceed to recite.

On the 19th of August, 1754, three convicts, one named Madan, were carried to Tyburn, to be executed pursuant to their sentence; when Amos Merritt addressed himself to the under-sheriff, declaring that Madan was innocent of the crime for which he was about to suffer; for that he himself was the guilty person. Mr. Reynolds, the under-sheriff, desired that he would look at the prisoner, and declare the same in an audible voice. He then insisted that the man was innocent, but declined acknowledging his own guilt.

Hereupon Merritt was taken into custody, and Mr. Reynolds was dispatched by the sheriffs to the office of the Secretary of State, where he obtained a respite for Madan. On his return the execution of the other convicts took place; and Madan was reconducted to Newgate, amidst the applause of surrounding multitudes. Immediately after this transaction, Merritt acknowledged before Justice Addington, at Bow-street, that he was the person who committed the robbery for which Madan had been convicted.

On the 2d of November, 1774, John Miller, who, with Amos Merritt, and John Cafs, had been apprehended for breaking open the house of Mr. Ellicott, made a full confession of that atrocious attempt, and declared that Amos Merritt, himself, and three others not then taken, were the guilty persons, and that Cafs was innocent. On this, two of the villains were apprehended in Whitechapel; but as they were on the way towards prison they were rescued, the constables terribly wounded, and

and the prisoners carried off in triumph by their associates.

On the 10th of January, 1775, Amos Merritt was hanged at Tyburn for the offence abovementioned.

Merrit had been an old, and was a very hardened offender. We do not hear of any thing particular in his behaviour after conviction; and, as he had lived a life of guilt, he died unlamented: and, indeed, the considerate part of mankind seemed thankful that a period was put to the life of a man whose conduct had long been nothing less than a continued breach of the peace.

From the example of Merritt, let youth be taught that those who practise the ways of vice have no chance of escaping the stroke of justice. It will certainly overtake them at an earlier or later period, and an ignominious death must be the forfeit to the violated laws of their country.

The Case of JOHN BOLTON, who was tried and condemned for Murder, but laid violent Hands on himself before the Sentence of the Law could take Place.

THIS unhappy man was reputably descended, and well educated. He served for some time in the army during the late war, and was distinguished by his gallant behaviour; but was dismissed from the military line of life in consequence of the peace of 1763.

While he was in the army, and on a recruiting party in Yorkshire, he became acquainted with a young lady, who possessing a moderate estate in her

her own right, he married her after he quitted the service, and turned farmer.

By this marriage he had six children, some of whom were living at the time of his death. In this station he continued happily for about ten years, when the event took place which ended in his destruction.

Near Mr. Bolton's place of residence was the village of Ackworth, in which was a house where the poor of several parishes were maintained by contract. From this house, in the year 1768, he took as apprentices, a boy, named Emanuel Bowes, and a girl of ten years old, called Elizabeth Rainbow. The girl grew up in his service, and was remarkable for her beauty; a circumstance very unfortunate for herself, as it induced Mr. Bolton to seduce her, the consequence of which was that a pregnancy ensued.

When Bolton was assured that the girl was with child, he went to York, and purchased a medicine, in order to procure an abortion; which medicine being administered to the young woman, she was thrown into violent convulsions; but the strength of her constitution effectually combating the potion, she advanced in her pregnancy without any appearance of having received the least injury.

Bolton, alarmed lest his intercourse with the girl should be known to his wife and family, formed the shocking resolution of murdering her who had fallen a victim to his seductive artifices: but no opportunity offered of perpetrating the horrid deed till Sunday the 21st of August, 1774.

On this day Mrs. Bolton took one of her children on a visit to a lady who lived at two miles distance; and there being no persons in the house but Emanuel Bowes, the young girl who had been seduced,

seduced, and a child of six years old, who was sick in bed, Bolton considered this as the proper time for perpetrating the crime on which he had previously resolved. He therefore sent the boy to fetch a cow-doctor, to look at a beast that was presumed to be disordered. The boy returning in about two hours, and finding the door fast, went to an adjoining field, and put a horse to grass; after which he knocked at the door, and his master letting him in, told him, that "Elizabeth Rainbow had run away, and left most of her cloaths behind her."

The boy was surprized at this intelligence, and some near neighbours said that the girl had not left the house that day; and a woman, who had been to the house to pay for milk, declared that she had given the money to Rainbow, on account of the absence of her mistress.

Mrs. Bolton, returning at seven at night, observed that her husband appeared to be very uneasy, and enquired into the cause of it; to which he only answered, that the girl had gone away, and left her cloaths on a table in the dining-room. Whether Mrs. Bolton was, or was not, suspicious of her husband's criminal connexion with Rainbow is a matter of doubt; but it seems probable that she was, as a violent quarrel ensued on this occasion.

About ten days after this affair happened, the neighbours being suspicious that murder had been committed, one of them, who was a constable, went to a magistrate, who granted a warrant for the apprehension of Bolton. The latter, having heard that a warrant was issued, went to the justice, and told him, that the report intended to prejudice him was circulated with a malicious view to injure

injure his character. On this the justice told Bolton to attend him in the afternoon, when the constable would be present; instead of which Bolton went home, and, packing up some plate, set off for York, whither he was followed by the constable, who apprehended him, and carrying him before a justice of the peace, he was lodged in prison.

On the trial, which came on at the ensuing assizes, the following circumstances were discovered; viz. that when Bolton had sent the boy for the cow-doctor, he took the girl into the cellar, and strangled her with a cord which he drew round her neck, placing a fife within the cord so as to twist it to a proper tightness.

On the Monday after this affair, he directed Emanuel Bowes to wheel several barrows filled with rubbish into the cellar, as it had been overflowed with water, which furnished him with a very plausible pretence for the concealment of his guilt, which he presumed would now remain undiscovered.

At length the body of the deceased was found under the rubbish in the cellar; and the coroner's inquest, being summoned on the occasion, gave a verdict of wilful murder; on which Mr. Bolton was committed to the castle of York.

The evidence on his trial was deemed so conclusive, that the jury did not hesitate to find him guilty, in consequence of which he received sentence of death. During his trial he behaved with uncommon effrontry; and when the judge had passed sentence on him, he turned to the court and declared his innocence.

On the following day a clergyman went to him, with a charitable view to prepare his mind to enable

able him to support himself with decency in the arduous trial he had to undergo, and to prepare for the awful event that was so soon to await him.

Still, however, he persisted that he was innocent of the alledged crime; and when the officers of justice went the next morning to convey him to the place of execution, they found that, by hanging himself, he had put a period to his own existence.

This event of self-murder happened in the castle of York on the 29th of March, 1775.

There is no language in which to express our proper sense of the crimes of this unhappy man. He was first guilty of seducing a young woman from the path of virtue; he then murdered her in the fear of detection; and at length laid violent hands on himself. Such a complication of guilt must make the heart shudder; and, we trust, it cannot be necessary to write a single word to deter our readers from the commission of any of these offences.

The Case of Miss JANE BUTTERFIELD, who was tried for the wilful Murder of WILLIAM SCAWEN, Esq; and acquitted.

IN pursuance of our promise to the public of inserting trials in extraordinary cases in consequence of which the parties had been acquitted, we give the following, which is very remarkable, as the presumption of guilt is the least that could possibly be imagined.

At the assizes at Croydon for the county of Surry, on the 19th of August, 1775, Jane Butterfield was

was indicted for the wilful murder of William Scawen, Esq;

The short story of this unhappy affair is as follows: Miss Butterfield was, at fourteen years of age, seduced from her father by a woman employed by Mr. Scawen, who too soon brought the young lady to a compliance with his wishes. The seduction was followed by very disagreeable consequences: the father reprobated his daughter; and his death was hastened, as she herself acknowledged, by the grief he felt for her unhappy departure from the paths of virtue.

Mr. Scawen did not appear less affected than herself at this deplorable event: he did every thing in his power to calm the mind of the young lady; promised to supply to her the place of her late parent, and faithfully discharged that duty, by taking the utmost care of her education, and studying to oblige her in every possible instance. He even, as she says, " faithfully supplied a parent's " duty; he was by nature generous, and that ge- " nerosity, with regard to herself, was unbounded."

Impelled by notions of gratitude, Miss Butterfield presumed that she could not be thought to have acted ungratefully by her benefactor. Her attachment to the deceased was faithful, and her care of him unremitted: she administered to his wants and infirmities, and in all respects fulfilled the tender offices of a wife, as much as if she had owed them to him under that sacred tie; and she was so diligent in her attendance, that her life was repeatedly endangered from excessive fatigue.

Mr. Scawen had been for a long time in a debilitated habit, and for the last six years could not arise or sit down without assistance; and such was the vitiated state of his body, " that he was
" obliged

"obliged to have the assistance of Mr. Cæsar Haw-
"kins, the surgeon, who applied causticks to his
"head, which was swelled to a degree almost in-
"credible."

At this time Mr. Scawen reposed such confidence in Miss Butterfield, that he would not permit any person but herself to apply the proper dressings. So violent was his disorder, that he remained blind near two years, but at length recovered his sight; and his other infirmities were greatly relieved: yet his habit of body became weaker, and those who visited him foresaw that he could not exist for any considerable time.

Mr. Scawen had consulted regular physicians till he was tired out of the hope of that relief which could not be obtained. He then had recourse to quackery, and had a perfect laboratory in his house, filled with variety of medicines, to which he had frequent recourse for the relief of his real or imaginary complaints. His closet was stocked with Ward's and Maredant's Drops, and other medicines advertised for the cure of all complaints.

Miss Butterfield constantly advised Mr. Scawen against quackery, nor ever administered any thing to him that she conceived prejudicial to his health, or that he was disinclined to take.

In the course of the trial, the strength of the evidence against Miss Butterfield rested with Mr. Edmund Sanxay, a surgeon, who deposed, that he had been acquainted with the deceased about fifty years; that he put himself under his care; that he was much emaciated; that he said he was but just recovered from a salivation which he had been thrown into by taking quack medicines for the rheumatism; that Mr. Sanxay recommended a regimen, which was obferved for two days only; when Mr. Scawen came to him, and told him, that in a decoction of farfaparilla, which had been given him, he found a *braffy* tafte, and that it made him very fick; that he had been frequently feverifh and fick at ftomach; that his mouth began to be fore; and that he apprehended he was going into another falivation.

After this Mr. Scawen was removed to Mr. Sanxay's houfe on the 20th of June, 1775, and died there on the 8th of July following. Mr. Sanxay declared his opinion, that Mr. Scawen did not die a natural death; but that a falivation produced by mercury was the caufe of this event.

On the contrary, feveral furgeons, and other perfons of refpectable character, gave fuch evidence as would induce a candid mind to believe that Mr. Scawen did not die by poifon, but in confequence of his debilitated habit of body, and his prepofterous attachment to quack medicines, in fearch of that relief which was not to be reafonably expected from them.

The confequence was, that the jury, after retiring about ten minutes, brought in a verdict of "Not guilty;" and Mifs Butterfield immediately fet out for London in a poft-chaife that had been previoufly provided.

We have been the fhorter in our narrative of this affair, becaufe there did not appear to be any juft ground of fufpicion of the alledged crime. What were the motives of this profecution it would not be decent in us to fay. It has been intimated that Mr. Scawen had made a will greatly in favour of Mifs Butterfield, and that this urged the fuit againft her.—Be this as it may, the generous public

will

will congratulate her, as her friends did, on her honourable acquittal!

The fatal consequences of seduction will appear evident on the consideration of this case. Miss Butterfield's father lost his life in consequence of his daughter's being drawn aside from the paths of virtue. Let this furnish a lesson of caution to men, never to be guilty of a crime with respect to the other sex, for which all their future tenderness can make no adequate compensation.

Particulars relating to REGINALD TUCKER, who was executed for the Murder of his Wife.

THIS offender was a native of Hervish, near Langport in Somersetshire. While he was in a state of infancy his father died, and he was maintained by his mother till he was about fourteen years old, when she apprenticed him to a bellows-maker in the city of Wells. He was of a morose and quarrelsome temper; but he proved an industrious servant, and continued with his master about five years, when he inlisted as a foot-soldier. Being wounded at the battle of Culloden, he was pronounced incapable of further service, and discharged; soon after which he was admitted an out pensioner of Greenwich hospital.

He went to Ansford in Somersetshire, and for some time resided with his mother, who kept an inn in that town, and occasionally worked at his business; but he was universally detested on account of his violent, disobliging, and oppressive disposition,

disposition, which involved him in several lawsuits.

He married in the year 1750, and the money he received with his wife enabled him to open a shop in the Strand, where his ingenuity in his business procured him great success; and he obtained the premium offered by the society for the encouragement of arts, for inventing a ventilator on a new construction. A short time after he had received the premium, all his effects were destroyed by fire; but the money he received from the insurance office was supposed to be greater than the value of his goods. A rich jew lodged in Tucker's house, and at the time of the fire he lost a considerable sum of money, which Tucker was strongly suspected of having secreted; and the suspicion was greatly strengthened when it was discovered that, shortly after the accident, he went to Ansford, and purchased an estate that produced thirty pounds per annum.

At Ansford he commenced farmer, but that employment not proving so advantageous as he expected, he lett the farm at a high rent, and moved to a small house adjacent. Tucker had a son and a daughter, of whom he was exceedingly fond, but he treated his wife with shocking barbarity; and, to avoid the effects of his brutal fury, she was often under the necessity of seeking refuge among her neighbours.

His son being deceased, Tucker's family in the year 1775 consisted only of himself, his wife, and daughter. On the 8th of June, the young woman went to visit a person at about a mile distant from Ansford; and presently after her departure, her father desired to have some pork roasted for dinner, and that, as he and his wife had appointed to spend

the

the afternoon at the house of a neighbouring farmer, it might be ready before twelve o'clock.

He employed himself in the garden till near twelve o'clock, and then his wife called him to dinner. He complained that the pork was not good, overturned the table, and beat his wife in a cruel manner. The unhappy woman made some resistance; on which Tucker took up a large hammer, and struck her with it two or three times on the back part of her head, which fractured her skull, and occasioned some blood to spring up against the cieling. He then hid the fatal instrument, with which he had perpetrated the horrid crime, in the grate, and having changed his cloaths, went to the farmer's house where he had engaged to spend the afternoon. The perturbation of his mind was observed with concern and surprize by the whole family; but they entertained not the least suspicion of the melancholy cause from whence it arose.

He returned about seven o'clock in the evening, and, after having several times knocked at the door, requested the assistance of some of his neighbours in breaking open one of the windows, pretending at the same time great surprize that he could not procure admittance. When the house was entered, the sight of the deceased created much consternation; and the husband appeared to be not less concerned and astonished than the rest.

The abovementioned melancholy circumstance being communicated to the coroner, a jury was summoned to meet on the following day, when they brought in a verdict of " Wilful Murder, " against persons unknown." In the evening several persons waited upon the coroner, and mentioned many reasons for believing Tucker to have committed

mitted the murder; in consequence of which his house was searched the next day, and, the cloaths he wore at the time of perpetrating the horrid fact being found, it appeared that endeavours had been used to wash out the blood, the stains of which were still clearly discernible. He was taken into custody on suspicion of the murder, and committed to gaol in preparation for his trial at the ensuing assizes at Wells.

Tucker suborned witnesses to appear in his behalf, and two of them were guilty of perjury on his trial; and he had recourse to other stratagems, with a view of avoiding the punishment that was due to his enormous crime; but the evidence against him, though of a circumstantial nature, was so strong that the jury were fully convinced of his guilt, and he was therefore sentenced to suffer death.

Tucker heard his sentence pronounced with great composure; and being conveyed back to prison, through the interest of his friends, he was frequently visited by two clergymen, and he prepared for the dreadful fate that awaited him in a manner that seemed to prove him perfectly resigned and penitent.

Reginald Tucker was executed at Wells in Somersetshire on the 25th of August, 1775.

The case of this unhappy man affords a striking instance of the dangerous effects of indulging violent passions. The disagreement preceding the murder arose from a circumstance of a very trifling nature. Whether the meat was really bad, or whether he only imagined it to be so, is of little consequence; in either case there was no cause for Tucker's displeasure against his wife. When we suffer our passions to gain the ascendency over reason,

son, we know not to what fatal extremes we may be hurried; and when we perceive the conduct of others to be really deserving censure, we should by mild remonstrance endeavour to prevent future errors of a similar nature, constantly remembering that the most unexceptionable characters cannot, in some instances, bear the test of strict enquiry, since "perfection is not the attribute of man."

Account of the Trials and Convictions of ROBERT PERREAU, and DANIEL PERREAU, for Forgery, attended with very extraordinary Circumstances.

IN order to preserve, as near as possible, the chronological disposition of this work, we insert the following in this place, though the brothers Perreau were not executed till a considerable time after conviction, nor till after the acquittal of Mrs. Rudd; but it is necessary that their trials should precede that of Mrs. Rudd, as the former were in some measure productive of the latter.

On the 10th of March, 1775, discovery was made of a series of forgeries, said to have been carried on for a length of time by Robert and Daniel Perreau, twin brothers; the one an apothecary of great practice, and the other living in the stile of a gentleman.

The above parties, together with Mrs. Margaret Caroline Rudd, who lived with Daniel Perreau as his wife, and who was deemed to have been a principal agent in the forgeries, were taken into custody, and carried before the bench of magistrates in Bow-street, where the crowd attending to hear their examination was so great, that it became necessary to adjourn to the Guildhall, Westminster.

The evidence there adduced tended to prove that the parties had raised considerable sums by bonds forged in the name of the well known agent, William Adair, Esquire, which they imposed on several gentlemen of fortune, as collateral securities with their own notes, for the payment of the said sums.

This transaction was discovered by the following means. Robert Perreau, whose character had been hitherto unimpeachable, applied to Mr. Drummond, the banker, to lend him 5000*l.* and offered a bond for 7500*l.* which he said Mr. Adair had given to his brother, as a security for the payment.

It will now be proper to remark, that, in order to give colour to the validity of these bonds, it had been artfully suggested, that Mrs. Rudd had near connexions with Mr. Adair; and it was even insinuated, that she was his natural daughter: but Mr. Drummond, to whom Mr. Adair's writing was familiar, had no sooner looked at the signature, than he doubted its authenticity, and very politely asked Robert Perreau, if he had seen Mr. Adair sign it? The latter said he had not, but had no doubt but it was authentic, from the nature of the connexion that subsisted.

To this Mr. Drummond said, that he could not advance such a sum without consulting his brother, and desired Perreau to leave the bond, promising to return it the next morning, or advance on it the sum required.

Mr. Perreau made no scruple to leave the bond, and call in the morning. In the interim Mr. Drummond examined the bond with greater attention; and Mr. Stephens, secretary of the Admiralty, happening to call, his opinion was demanded; when comparing the signature of the bond with letters he had lately received from Mr. Adair, he was firmly convinced that it was forged.

When Perreau came, Mr. Drummond spoke more freely than he had done before, and told him that he imagined he had been imposed on; but begged that, to remove all doubt, he would go with him to Mr. Adair, and get that gentleman to acknowledge the validity of the bond; on which the money should be advanced.

Perreau made not the least objection. They went together; and Mr. Adair was asked if the bond was his. He declared it was not; but Perreau smiled, and said he jested.

Mr. Adair told him that it was no jesting matter, and that it was his duty to clear up the affair. Perreau said, " if that was the case, he had been " sent on a fine errand!" He desired to have the bond, and said he would make the necessary enquiries: but this was refused, and it was thought a point of prudence to watch the motions of Robert Perreau, till Daniel and his pretended wife were produced.

Soon after he returned home, the three parties went into a coach; and, if Mrs. Rudd's testimony may be credited, she took with her what money and valuables she could conveniently carry; and said, that the brothers had taken her money, gold watch, and jewels, into their possession; but no reason was assigned for their doing so.

Their escape, however, if such was intended, was prevented; for an information being laid against them, they were apprehended, carried before Sir John Fielding, and examined at the Guildhall, Westminster, as above-mentioned. The facts already

ready mentioned were attested by Mr. Adair, Mr. Drummond, and other persons; and Sir Thomas Frankland charged them with obtaining from him 4000*l.* on the first application, which they honestly repaid before the money became due; afterwards 5000*l.* and then 4000*l.* on similar bonds, all signed with the name of Mr. Adair.

Mr. Watson, a money-scrivener, said that he had drawn eight bonds, all of them ordered by one or other of the brothers; but he hesitated to fix on either, on account of their great personal resemblance; but being pressed to make a positive declaration, he fixed on Daniel as his employer.

Dr. Brooke charged the brothers with obtaining from him fifteen bonds of the bank of Air, each of the value of 100*l.* upon the security of a forged bond for 3100*l.*

On the strength of this evidence the brothers were committed, the one to New Prison, and the other to Clerkenwell Bridewell; and Mrs. Rudd was admitted an evidence for the crown.

On her future examination she declared that she was the daughter of a nobleman in Scotland; that, when young, she married an officer in the army, named Rudd, against the consent of her friends; that her fortune was considerable; that, on a disagreement with her husband, they resolved to part; that she made a reserve of money, jewels, and effects, to the amount of 13,000*l.* all of which she gave to Daniel Perreau, whom she said she loved with the tenderness of a wife; " that she had three " children by him; that he had returned her kind- " ness in every respect till lately, when having been " unfortunate in gaming in the alley, he had be- " come uneasy, peevish, and much altered to her; " that he cruelly constrained her to sign the bond
" now

" now in queſtion, by holding a knife to her throat,
" and ſwearing that he would murder her if ſhe
" did not comply; that, being ſtruck with remorſe,
" ſhe had acquainted Mr. Adair with what ſhe had
" done, and that ſhe was now willing to declare
" every tranſaction with which ſhe was acquainted,
" whenever ſhe ſhould be called upon by law ſo
" to do."

At the ſeſſions held at the Old Bailey in June, 1775, Robert Perreau, Eſquire, was indicted for forging a bond for the payment of 7500*l*. in the name of William Adair, Eſquire, and alſo for feloniouſly uttering and publiſhing the ſaid bond, knowing it to be forged, with intention to defraud Robert and Henry Drummond, Eſquires.

After what we have mentioned above reſpecting this tranſaction, we ſhall be as conciſe as poſſible in the recital of the evidence. Henry Drummond, Eſquire, depoſed, that Robert Perreau requeſted the loan of 1,400*l*. having made a purchaſe in Suffolk or Norfolk to the amount of 12,000*l*. He ſaid he had a houſe in Harley-ſtreet, Cavendiſh-ſquare, which coſt 4000*l*. the deeds of which houſe he would leave as a ſecurity. Theſe he did leave, and promiſing to return in ten days, the money was paid him. He came ſome time afterwards, and apologized for not having kept his appointment; and ſaid he then came to borrow 5000*l*. on the bond, out of which he would pay the 1,400*l*. abovementioned.

Mr. Drummond and his brother doubting the validity of the bond, Perreau ſaid there were family-connexions between him and Mr. Adair, who had money of his in his hands, for which he paid intereſt.

A great

A great part of what Mr. Drummond delivered in evidence has been already given in the former part of this narrative. Mr. Drummond going with the prisoner to Mr. Adair's, Mrs. Daniel Perreau (Mrs. Rudd) was sent for, when Robert asked her, if she had not given the bond to him. She owned that she had, took the whole on herself, and acknowledged that she had forged the bond.

The counsel for the prisoner asking Mr. Drummond if he was certain that the prisoner said it was *his* money that Mr. Adair paid interest for, he answered in the affirmative. He declared likewise, that Mr. Perreau did not make the least objection to leaving the bond with him, nor shewed any reluctance in going with him to Mr. Adair's house.

He likewise said that Mrs. Rudd took the whole on herself, begged them, " for God's sake to have " mercy on an innocent man;" and that she said no injury was intended to any person, and that all would be paid; and that she acknowledged delivering the bond to the prisoner.

The counsel demanding if Mr. Drummond and Mr. Adair, after hearing what Mrs. Rudd said, had not expressed themselves as considering the prisoner as her dupe; the answer was, " We both " expressed ourselves to that effect. A constable " had been sent for, and we discharged him."

The identity of the bond was proved by Mr. Wheatley, Clerk to Messieurs Drummond.—The evidence of Mr. Robert Drummond was not, in any very essential point, different from that of his brother. He deposed, that when Mrs. Rudd had acknowledged that she forged the bond, he expressed his doubt, the hand-writing being so different from that of a woman, and said nothing would convince him of it but her shewing, on a piece of paper, that she could write that sort of hand. He said he did not mean to ensnare her, and would immediately throw the writing into the fire. Mrs. Rudd instantly wrote William Adair, or part of the name, so very like the signature of the bond, that it satisfied him, and he burnt the paper. Robert Perreau then said, that " he hoped that the information she had given sufficiently acquitted him;" but he was told that he had better not inquire into that; and on this occasion he shewed the first sign of anxiety.

Sir Thomas Frankland deposed, that the prisoner brought him two bonds at different times, one to Daniel Perreau for 6000£. and the other to himself (Robert) for 5300£. that for 5300£. on which he lent him 4000£. was to be repaid on the 26th of March, with the three days grace; the other was due on the 8th of March *.

Mr. Wilson declared that he filled up the bond at the desire of the prisoner; and produced his instructions for so doing. He likewise acknowledged that he had filled up other bonds for the prisoner.

That the hand-writing at the bottom of the bond was not the hand writing of William Adair was proved by Scroope Ogilvie and James Adair, esquires. Mr. James Adair was now questioned by counsel respecting a private interview he had with Mrs. Rudd, but the court doubted if this might be allowed as evidence. After some observations made by the counsel for the prisoner, a letter was read,

---

* The intent of this evidence seems to have been, to shew that the money to be borrowed of Mr. Drummond was designed to repay the money actually borrowed of Sir Thomas; and that there was no intention of defrauding either of them.

which he presumed had been sent him by William Adair, esquire, but which appeared to have been written by Mrs. Rudd, but it was scarcely intelligible.

The prisoner now proceeded to make his defence in the following terms:—" My Lords, and
" gentlemen of the jury; If I had been wanting
" in that fortitude which is the result of innocence,
" or had found any hesitation in submitting my
" proceedings to the strictest scrutiny, I need not
" at this day have stood before my country, or
" set my life upon the issue of a legal trial. Sup-
" ported by the consciousness of my integrity, I
" have forced that transaction to light, which
" might else have been suppressed, and I have vo-
" luntarily sought that imprisonment which guilt
" never invites, and even innocence has been known
" to fly from; ardently looking forward to this
" hour, as the sure, though painful, means of vin-
" dicating a character, not distinguished, indeed,
" for its importance, but hitherto maintained
" without a blemish. There are many respectable
" witnesses at hand (and many more, I persuade
" myself, would be found, if it had been necessa-
" ry to summon them upon a point of such notori-
" ety), who will inform your Lordships and the
" court, how I have appeared to them to act;
" what trust has been reposed in me, and what
" credit I had in their opinions, for my diligence,
" honesty, and punctuality. In truth, my Lords,
" I am bold to say that few men, in my line of life,
" have carried on their business with a fairer cha-
" racter, not many with better success. I have
" followed no pleasures, nor launched into any
" expences: there is not a man living who can
" charge me with neglect or dissipation. The
" ho-

"honest profits of my trade have afforded me a
"comfortable support, and furnished me with
"the means of maintaining, in a decent sort, a
"worthy wife, and three promising children,
"upon whom I was labouring to bestow the pro-
"perest education in my power: in short, we were
"as happy as afflucence and innocence could make
"us, till this affliction came upon us by surprize,
"and I was made the dupe of a transaction from
"whose* criminality, I call God, the searcher of
"all human hearts, to witness, I am now as free
"as I was at the day of my birth.— My Lords,
"and gentlemen of the jury, men who are un-
"practised in deceit will be apt to credit others
"for a sincerity which they themselves possess.
"The most undesigning characters have at all
"times been the dupe of craft and subtilty. A
"plain story, with the indulgence of the court, I
"will relate, which will furnish strong instances
"of credulity on one part, and at the same time
"will exhibit a train of such consummate artifices
"on the other, as are not to be equalled in the
"annals of iniquity; and which might have ex-
"torted an equal confidence from a much more
"enlightened understanding than I can claim."

Having said thus much, the unhappy man proceeded to relate a variety of circumstances relative to the imposition practised on him by Mrs. Rudd, of which the following are the most remarkable.

---

* If Mr. Perreau had spoken English, he would have said
" from the criminality of which;" but we presume this must
have been a mistake of the short-hand-writer; as the other parts
of his defence do not appear deficient in point of grammar.

He said that she was constantly conversing about the Interest she had with Mr. W. Adair; and that Mr. Adair had, by his interest with the king, obtained the promise of a baronetage for Daniel Perreau, and was about procuring him a seat in parliament. That Mr. Adair had promised to open a bank, and take the brothers Perreau into partnership with him: that the prisoner received many letters signed William Adair, which he had no doubt came from that gentleman; in which were promises of giving them a considerable part of his fortune during his life, and that he was to allow Daniel Perreau £. 2,400 a year for his houshold expences, and £. 600 a year for Mrs. Rudd's pin money. That Mr. Daniel Perreau purchased a house in Harley-street for £. 4000, which money Mr. William Adair was to give them. That, when Daniel Perreau was pressed by the person he bought the house of for the money, the prisoner understood that they applied to Mr. William Adair, and that his answer was that he had lent the king £. 70,000, and had purchased a house in Pall Mall, at £. 7000, in which to carry on the banking business, and therefore could not spare the £. 4000 at that time.

The prisoner now related a variety of circumstances, which would tempt an ingenuous mind to suppose him innocent, and that the guilt of the transaction rested with Mrs. Rudd. The unfortunate man then proceeded in his defence in the following terms:

"My lords, and gentlemen of the jury, I
"have now faithfully laid before you such circum-
"stances as have occurred to my memory, as
"necessary for your information, in order as they
"happened during my acquaintance with Mrs.
"Rudd,

"Rudd, under the character of my brother's
"wife. Many have been the sufferers by artifices
"and impostors, but never man appeared, I be-
"lieve, in this, or any other tribunal, upon whom
"so many engines were set at work to interest his
"credulity. It will not escape the notice of this
"splendid * court, that my compassion was first
"engaged by the story of Mrs. Rudd's sufferings,
"before my belief was invited to her representa-
"tions. Let me have credit with you for yielding
"up by pity in the first instance, and you cannot
"wonder I did not withhold my credulity after-
"wards. It is in this natural, this necessary con-
"sequence, I rest my defence. I was led from
"error to error by such insensible degrees, that
"every step I took strengthened my infatuation.
"When Mr. Drummond first hesitated at the
"hand-writing at the foot of the bond, if it
"did not so alarm me as to shake my belief in this
"artful woman, let it be considered that I had
"been prevailed upon to negociate other bonds
"of hers, depositing them in the hands of
"bankers who had never spied any defect, or
"raised the least objection. These bonds have
"been regularly and punctually paid in due time.
"The letters sent to me, as if from William Adair,
"critically agreed with the hand-writing of the
"bond. Mr. Adair did not keep money at Mr.
"Drummond's; opportunities of comparing his
"hand-writing for many years had not occurred,
"and the hesitation upon his part appeared to me
"no more than the exceptions and minute pre-

---

* *Splendid* is an awkward word on this occasion: perhaps *awful* would have been more proper.

"cautions

"cautions of a banker, which could not so sud-
"denly overturn the explicit belief that I had an-
"nexed to all that was told me in Harley-street.
"Can any greater proof be given than my own
"proposal to Mr. Drummond of leaving the bond
"in his hands till he had satisfied his credulity?
"Can your lordships, or gentlemen of the jury,
"for a moment suspect, that any man would be
"guilty of such a crime, whose proceedings were
"so fair and open? that single circumstance, I
"am satisfied, will afford my total exculpation.
"The resort to Mr. Adair was as easy to Mr.
"Drummond, as to the books in his compting-
"house; it does not come within the bounds of
"common sense, much less does it fall within the
"possibility of guilt, that any man living should
"voluntarily, with his eyes open, take a step so
"directly and absolutely centering in his certain
"destruction. But this circumstance, strong as it
"is, is not all my case. I bless God, the pro-
"tector of innocence, that, in my defence, proofs
"arise upon proofs: the least of them, I trust,
"will be thought incompatible with guilt. It
"should seem impossible that a guilty person would
"propose to Mr. Drummond to retain the bond
"for the satisfaction of his scruples; but that the
"same person should, after so long a time for
"consideration had passed after my leaving the
"bond, which was full twenty-four hours, openly,
"and in the face of day, enter the shop of
"Mr. Drummond, and demand if he had satis-
"fied all his scruples, unless a man from mere
"desperation had been weary of his life, and
"sought a dissolution; this, I humbly apprehend,
"would be an absolute impossibility: but, my
"lords, and gentlemen of the jury, I had nei-
"ther in my breast the principle of guilt, nor
"had

"had I that desperate loathing of existence as
"should bring a shameful condemnation on my
"head. It is true I have invited this trial; but
"it is equally true I have done it in the consci-
"ousness of my integrity, because I could not
"otherwise go through the remainder of my days
"with comfort and satisfaction, unless I had the
"verdict of my countrymen for my acquittal, and
"rested my innocence upon the purest testimony
"I could have on this side the grave. It is plain
"I had an opportunity of withdrawing myself.
"How many men are there, with the clearest
"intentions, yet from the apprehension of
"being made the talk of the public, and,
"above all, the dread of imprisonment, and the
"terror of a trial, would have thought themselves
"happy to have caught at any opportunity of
"saving themselves from such a series of dis-
"tress? greater confidence can no man be in, of
"the integrity of his case, and the justice of
"his country. When it was found necessary
"to the designs of Mrs. Rudd, that I and my
"family should be made the dupes of her con-
"nexions with the house of Adair, it may well
"be believed that nothing but the *strongest inter-
"dictions* could prevent my endeavours to obtain
"an interview. In fact, this point was laboured
"with consummate artifice, and nothing less than
"ruin to my brother and his affairs was denoun-
"ced upon my breaking this injunction. It was
"part of the same error to believe her in this also.
"A respectable witness has told you, and I do
"not controvert his evidence, that my confidence
"in her assertion, and *in the testimonials that she
"exhibited under the hand*, as I believed, *of Mr.
"Adair*, were such, in my mistaken judgement, as
"to be equal to the evidence of my own senses,
"pressed

"pressed by the forms of business to say to Mr.
"Drummond that I had seen Mr. Adair myself;
"but I neither went to Mr. Adair, nor disclosed
"those pressing motives which prevented me.
"No less free to confess my faults, than I am
"confident to assert my innocence, I seek no pal-
"liation for this circumstance, except my temp-
"tation and my failings; and I trust it will rather
"be a matter of surprize, that, in the course of
"a negotiation, through the whole of which I
"was acted upon by the most artful of impostors,
"that this only deviation was to be found: and
"yet this very circumstance carries with it a clear-
"er conviction of my being the dupe of Mrs.
"Rudd's intrigues, than any I have to offer in
"my defence; and if my subsequent proceedings,
"and the alacrity I shewed in going with Mr.
"Drummond to Mr. Adair, together with my
"conduct before this gentleman, is, as I appre-
"hend it is, absolutely irreconcileable with a con-
"sciousness of guilt, the circumstances abovemen-
"tioned will serve to shew with what a degree of
"credulity the artifices of Mrs. Rudd had fur-
"nished me.—Upon the whole, if, in the above
"detail, no circumstances are discovered in which
"an innocent man, under the like delusion with
"myself, might not have acted as I have acted,
"and, at the same time, if there be very many
"particulars in which no guilty man would have
"conducted himself as I have conducted myself,
"I should be wanting in respect to your Lordships
"and the jury, if I doubted the justice of their
"verdict, and which is inseparable from it, my
"honourable accquittal."

The prisoner now proceeded to call his witnesses, the substance of whose evidence we shall give in
the

the most concise manner. George Kinder, deposed, that Mrs. Perreau * told him "that she was a "near relation of Mr. James Adair; that he looked "upon her as his child, had promised to make "her fortune, and with that view had recommended "her to Mr. William Adair, a near relation, and "intimate friend of his, who had promised to set "her husband and the prisoner up in the bank- "ing business." He likewise deposed, that the said Mr. Daniel Perreau was to be made a baronet, and described how she would act when she became a lady. This witness deposed, that Mrs. Rudd often pretended that Mr. William Adair had called to see her, but that he never had seen that gentleman on any visit.

John Moody, a livery-servant of Daniel Perreau, deposed, that his mistress wrote two very different hands, in one of which she wrote letters to his master, as from Mr. William Adair, and in the other the ordinary business of the family; that the letters written in the name of William Adair were pretended to have been left in his master's absence; that his mistress ordered him to give them to his master, and pretend that Mr. Adair had been with his mistress for a longer or shorter time, as circumstances required. This witness likewise proved that the hand at the foot of the bond and that of his mistress's fictitious writing were precisely the same †: that she used different pens, ink, and paper, in writing her common and fictitious letters; and that she sometimes gave the

---

* The only name by which he knew Mrs. Rudd.

† If this evidence was credited, was it not conclusive against Mrs. Rudd, and in favour of the Perreaus?

witness half a crown, when he had delivered a letter to her satisfaction. He said he had seen her go two or three times to Mr. J. Adair's, but never to William's; and that Mr. J. Adair once visited his mistress on her lying in.

Susanna Perreau (the prisoner's sister) deposed to the having seen a note delivered to Daniel Perreau, by Mrs. Rudd, for £.19,000 drawn as by William Adair, on Mr. Croft, the banker, in favour of Daniel Perreau.

Elizabeth Perkins swore that, a week before the forgery was discovered, her mistress gave her a letter to bring back to her in a quarter of an hour, and say it was brought by Mr. Coverley, who had been servant to Daniel Perreau: that she gave her mistress this letter, and her master instantly broke the seal.

Daniel Perreau declared that the purport of this letter was " that Mr. Adair desired her to apply
" to his brother, the prisoner, to procure him
" £.5000 upon his (Adair's) bond, in the same
" manner as he had done before; that Mr. Adair
" was unwilling to have it appear that the money
" was raised for him, and therefore desired to have
" the bond lodged with some confidential friend, that
" would not require an assignment of it; that his
" brother, on being made acquainted with his re-
" quest, shewed a vast deal of reluctancy, and
" said it was a very unpleasant work; but under-
" took it with a view of obliging Mr. William
" Adair."

The counsel for the prosecution demanding, " if
" he did not disclaim all knowledge of the affair
" before Mr. Adair," he said, he denied ever having seen the bond before, nor had he a perfect knowledge of it till he saw it in the hands of Mr. Adair.

David

David Caſſady, who aſſiſted Mr. R. Perreau as an apothecary, depoſed, that he lived much within the profits of his profeſſion, and that it was reported he was going into the banking buſineſs.

John Leigh, clerk to Sir John Fielding, ſwore to the priſoner's coming voluntarily to the office, and giving information that a forgery had been committed *, on which Mrs. Rudd was apprehended. Mr. Leigh was aſked, if ſhe "ever charged "the priſoner with any knowledge of the tranſ- "action till the juſtices were hearing evidence to "prove her confeſſion of the fact." Mr. Leigh anſwered, that he did not recollect that circumſtance, but that on her firſt examination ſhe did not accuſe the priſoner.

Mr. Perreau now called ſeveral perſons of rank to his character. Lady Lyttleton being aſked, if ſhe thought him capable of ſuch a crime, *ſuppoſed ſhe could have done it as ſoon herſelf.* Sir John Moore, Sir John Chapman, General Rebow, Capt. Ellis, Capt. Burgoyne, and other gentlemen, ſpoke moſt highly to the character of the priſoner; yet the jury found him guilty.

After this copious account of the trial of Robert, a very ſhort abſtract of that of the other brother may ſuffice, eſpecially as that of Mrs. Rudd is to follow.

Daniel Perreau was indicted for forging and counterfeiting a bond, in the name of William Adair, for £.3,300, to defraud the ſaid William Adair; and for uttering the ſame, knowing it to be forged, with intent to defraud Thomas Brooke,

---

* Surely this evidence ought to have had great weight with the jury.

doctor of physic. Mr. Scroope Ogilvie, who had been clerk to Mr. William Adair nine or ten years, proved the forgery; and Dr. Brooke proved the uttering of the forged bond.

By way of defence, the prisoner declared that Mrs. Rudd had given him the bond as a true one; that he believed it genuine, authentic and valid; and protested, by all his hopes of happiness in this life and in a future, that he had never conceived an idea of any thing so base as the defrauding any man of his property. He added, " I ad-" jure the Almighty so to assist me in my present " dangerous situation, as I speak here before " you" *.

Mr. Daniel Perreau called several persons to prove the artifices which Mrs. Rudd had practised to deceive him. Many persons of fortune and credit appeared to his character; and spoke of his conduct previous to the fatal event in terms of the highest approbation; but the jury brought in a verdict of guilty; and the unfortunate brothers received sentence of death, but were not executed till January 1776, because though Mrs. Rudd had been admitted an evidence, yet the judges committed her as a principal, as will be seen more at large in the account of the subsequent trial.

After conviction, the behaviour of the brothers was, in every respect, proper for their unhappy situation. Great interest was made to obtain a pardon for them, particularly for Robert, in whose favour 78 bankers and merchants of London signed

---

* This is an odd phrase; but so it is recorded by the shorthand-writer. Perhaps the word *truth* should have been inserted instead of *here*.

a pea petition to the king; the newspapers were filled with paragraphs, evidently written by disinterested persons, in favour of men whom they thought dupes to the designs of an artful woman: but all this availed nothing.

On the day of execution the brothers were favoured with a mourning coach, and it was thought that 30,000 people attended. They were both dressed in mourning, and behaved with the most christian resolution. When they quitted the coach and got into the cart, they bowed respectfully to the sheriffs, who waved their hands as a final adieu.

After the customary devotions, they crossed their hands, joining the four together, and in this manner were launched into eternity. They had not hung more than half a minute when their hands dropped asunder, and they appeared to die without pain.

Each of them delivered a paper to the ordinary of Newgate, which declared their innocence, and ascribed the blame of the whole transaction to the artifices of Mrs. Rudd; and, indeed, thousands of people gave credit to their assertions, and a great majority of the public thought Robert wholly innocent.

Daniel Perreau and Robert Perreau were executed at Tyburn on the 17th of January, 1776.

On the Sunday following the bodies were carried from the house of Robert in Golden-square, and, after the usual solemnities, deposited in the vault of Saint Martin's Church. The coffins were covered with black cloth and nails, and a black plate on each, inscribing their names, the day of their death, and their ages (42), being twin brothers. They were carried in separate hearses, their friends attending in mourning coaches. The croud was so great, that the company could with difficulty get into the church; but at length the ceremony was decently performed, and the mob dispersed.

A few reflections naturally arise on this occasion. There was great guilt somewhere, but where it lay the public will determine. One would imagine that, if Robert Perreau had been guilty, he would not have returned to Drummond's, nor went to Adair's, after being suspected. Charity will suppose that he fell a victim to his friendship for his brother, and lost his life through the telling of a lye; a strong argument for a strict adherence to truth in all we say.

A very ingenious writer on this subject says, "Upon a dispassionate review of the above trial, is it not possible that the plausible promises of an artful impostor, aided by the vain hope of being made rich and great by her pretended connexions, may have operated on a credulous, though otherwise sensible, mind; like as a gypsey's tale is frequently found to do on weak and unsuspecting women? If so, it will naturally account for the absurdity of the prisoner's pretending an acquaintance with Mr. William Adair, whom he had never seen, and was stricty enjoined not to see, and for all the fallacious pretences that followed."

After this quotation, we shall say no more on this business, but proceed to the trial of Mrs. Rudd.

An

Mrs MARGARET CAROLINE RUDD on her TRIAL at the New Sessions House, in the Old Bailey.

An Account of the Trial and Acquittal of MARGARET CAROLINE RUDD, on a Charge of Forgery.

ON the 16th of September, 1775, Mrs. Rudd was put to the bar at the Old Bailey, to be tried for forgery; but the counsel for the prisoner pleading that, as she had been already admitted an evidence for the crown, it was unprecedented to detain her for trial, and the judges differing in opinion on the point of law, she was remanded to prison, till the opinion of the judges could be taken on a subject of so much importance.

On the 8th of December, 1775, Margaret Caroline Rudd was indicted for feloniously forging a bond, purporting to be signed by William Adair, and for feloniously uttering and publishing the same.

Having been brought to the bar in September sessions, to plead to the said indictment, and her counsel contending that she ought not to be tried, as she had acknowledged herself an accomplice, and had been admitted an evidence by the magistrates; and the judges "differing in opinion on "the point of law: reference was had to the opi- "nion of all the judges, that the matter might be "finally settled, how far, under what circumstan- "ces, and in what manner, an accomplice, received "as a witness, ought to be entitled to favour and "mercy."

Mr. justice Aston now addressed the prisoner, informing her that eleven of the judges had met (the chief justice of the Common Pleas being indisposed), " and were unanimous in opinion, that, " in cases not within any statute, an accomplice,
" who

"who fully discloses the joint guilt of himself and his companions, and is admitted by justices of the peace as a witness, and who appears to have acted a fair and ingenuous part in the disclosure of all the circumstances of the cases in which he has been concerned, ought not to be prosecuted for the offences so by him confessed, but cannot by law plead this in bar of any indictment, but merely as an equitable claim to mercy from the crown: and nine of the judges were of opinion, that all the circumstances relative to this claim *ought* to be laid before the court, to enable the judges to exercise their discretion, whether the trial should proceed or not. With respect to the case before them, the same nine judges were of opinion, that if the matter stood singly upon the two informations of the prisoner, compared with the indictments against her, she ought to have been tried upon all, or any of them, for from her informations she is no accomplice: she exhibits a charge against Robert and Daniel Perrean, the first soliciting her to imitate the handwriting of William Adair, the other forcing her to execute the forgery under the threat of death. Her two informations are contradictory: if she has suppressed the truth, she has no equitable claim to favour; and if she has told the truth, and the whole truth, she cannot be convicted. As to the indictments preferred against her by Sir Thomas Frankland, as her informations before the justices have no relation to his charges, she can claim no sort of advantage from these informations."

The trial was now proceeded on. The principal evidences were, the wife of Robert Perreau, and John Moody a servant to Daniel. The first endeavoured

voured to prove that the bond was published, the latter that it was forged. Sir Thomas Frankland proved that he had lent money on the bond. It was objected by the counsel for the prisoner, that Mrs. Perreau was an incompetent witness, as she would be interested in the event; but the court over-ruled this objection.

Mrs. Perreau deposed, that, on the 24th of December, she saw Mrs. Rudd deliver a bond to her husband, which he laid on the table while he brushed his coat; that it was for £.5,300 payable to Robert Perreau, and signed William Adair; and that it was witnessed in the names of Arthur Jones and Thomas Start, or Hart. Mrs. Perreau being asked when she again saw the bond, said it was brought to her on the 8th of March (the day after her husband was convicted), when she selected it from other bonds delivered to him on the 24th of December. She made her mark on it, and deposed that, when it was delivered to Mr. Perreau, Mrs. Rudd said, " Mr. Adair would be very much " obliged to Mr. Perreau to try to raise upon that " bond the sum of £.4000 of Sir Thomas Frank- " land."

Serjeant Davy cross-examined Mrs. Perreau. She acknowledged that till the 24th of December she had never seen a bond in her life, and that, on her first sight of that in question, she had no suspicion " that any thing was wrong." Being asked how she could recollect, at the distance of three months, the names, the sum, and the several circumstances respecting the bond, she said, " I have the " happiness to have a good memory." Being asked if she had not examined the other bonds at the same time, she said, she had. It was demanded if her memory had retained the date or sum in any other paper produced to her. She replied, "I do not remember."

John Moody, who had been servant with Mrs. Rudd, deposed that his mistress wrote two different hands, a common and a feigned one; that in her common hand she noted the usual business of the house; but that, when she wrote letters as coming from William Adair, she wrote her feigned hand. A bond signed William Adair was now shewn him; and he said, "the name appears to be the same "hand the letters were wrote in, which I gave to "Daniel Perreau, as coming from Mr. William "Adair, and which I saw Mrs. Rudd write the di- "rections of." He was asked if he thought Mr. Adair's name was of the prisoner's writing. He replied, "I believe it is her hand-writing."

On his cross-examination he owned that he had never seen Mrs. Rudd write Mr. Adair's name.*

Thus stood the evidence. Sir Thomas Frankland proved the lending Robert Perreau £.4000 on the bond in question, and that he had given him "a draught for £.3890, deducting the discount of "£.5000 formerly lent, with the discount of the "money then borrowed, and 15l. 10s. for a lottery "ticket: that he had since received, among other "things, jewels to the value of £.2800, with wo- "men's wearing apparel, &c. which might, for "what he knew, be the prisoner's, but were sold "to him by the two Perreaus by a bill of sale.

Christian Hart deposed, that she had received a paper from the prisoner, tending to prove that

---

* No doubt this was true.—If she wrote it at all, she had too much art to let a servant be witness of such a transaction

there was a combination against her life to have been concerted at the house of this witness, by Sir Thomas Frankland and the friends of the Perreaus. Our readers will give what credit they please to this evidence.

It was now demanded of Mrs. Rudd, what she would say in her defence. She addressed the jury in a short, but sensible speech, and concluded in these words, "Gentlemen, ye are honest men, and " I am safe in your hands."

The jury, after a short consultation, gave their verdict in the following singular, and perhaps unprecedented words: " *According to the evidence be-* " *fore us,* NOT GUILTY.

The verdict was no sooner given, than Mrs. Rudd quitted the court, and retired to the house of a friend at the west end of the town.

There is a mystery in the story of the brothers Perreau, and Mrs. Rudd, that no person but the latter can clear up. We are told that she is yet living *; but we hope that, before she quits this world, she will discover the secrets of a transaction concerning which the public opinion has been so much divided. The Perreaus were guilty, or they were not; and it is only from Mrs. Rudd the truth can be known. A declaration of the fact, if she *was* guilty, could not now affect her, as she was acquitted by the laws of her country.

---

* In March, 1779.

An authentic Account of the Proceedings in the House of Peers on the Trial of ELIZABETH DUTCHESS of KINGSTON, for Bigamy.

ABOUT nine o'clock in the morning of Monday the 15th of April, 1776, the peeresses, foreign ambassadors, &c. concluded the ceremony of assuming their respective places in Westminster hall: and at half past ten her majesty, accompanied by the prince of Wales, the bishop of Osnaburgh, two other young princes, and the princess royal, and attended by lord and lady Holdernesse, lord Hinchinbroke, and others of the nobility, entered the hall from the duke of Newcastle's house in New Palace Yard, and took her seat in the centre of his grace's gallery.

The procession came into the hall in the following order at a quarter past eleven: the eldest sons of peers, preceded by the domestics of the lord high steward, masters in chancery, king's serjeants and judges, barons, bishops, viscounts, earls, marquisses and dukes; the serjeant at arms, the lord high steward with black rod on his right, and garter on his left; the lord president, and the lord privy-seal. The barons proceeded to their seats next the bar, the junior barons taking the left hand seat next the bar, and the other barons following in that order till the seats were filled in the front of the court. The archbishops and bishops occupied the side benches on the right, and the dukes the benches extending from the throne to the table.

The persons who composed the court having taken their seats with the usual formalities, the lord high steward directed the clerk of the crown to
read

read the *certiorari*, the return thereof, the caption of the indictment, the indictment itself, and other official papers; which being done, the serjeant at arms made proclamation for the usher of the black rod to place the prisoner at the bar.

The dutchess then came forward, attended by Mrs. Egerton, Mrs. Barrington, and Miss Chudleigh, three of the ladies of her bedchamber, and her chaplain, physician, and apothecary; and as she approached the bar she made three reverences, and then dropped on her knees, when the lord high steward said, "Madam, you may rise." Having risen, she curtsied to the lord high steward and the house of peers; and her compliments were returned.

Proclamation being made for silence, the lord high steward mentioned to the prisoner the fatal consequences attending the crime of which she stood indicted, signifying that, however alarming and awful her present circumstances, she might derive great consolation from considering that she was to be tried by the most liberal, candid, and august assembly in the universe.

The dutchess then read a paper, setting forth that she was guiltless of the offence alledged against her, and that the agitation of her mind arose, not from the consciousness of guilt, but from the painful circumstance of being called before so awful a tribunal on a criminal accusation; begging, therefore, that if she was deficient in the observance of any ceremonial points, her failure might not be understood as proceeding from wilful disrespect, but be attributed to the unfortunate peculiarity of her situation. It was added in the paper that she had travelled from Rome in so dangerous a state of health, that it was necessary for her to be conveyed in a litter; and that she was perfectly satisfied that she should have a fair trial, since the determination respecting her cause, on which materially depended her honor and fortune, would proceed from the most unprejudiced and august assembly in the world.

The lord high steward desired the lady to give attention while she was arraigned on an indictment for bigamy. Proclamation for silence being made, the dutchess (who had been permitted to sit) arose, and read a paper, representing to the court that she was advised by her counsel to plead the sentence of the ecclesiastical court in the year 1769, as a bar to her being tried on the present indictment. The lord high steward informed her that she must plead to the indictment; in consequence of which she was arraigned; and, being asked by the clerk of the crown whether she was guilty of the felony with which she stood charged, she answered with great firmness, "Not guilty, my lords." The clerk of the crown then asking her how she would be tried, she said, " by God and her peers;" on which the clerk said, " God send your ladyship a " good deliverance."

The serjeant at arms made proclamation for all persons who had evidence to produce against the prisoner to appear. The lord high steward requested, that, as his seat was so distant from the bar, he might be allowed, for the convenience of hearing, to go to the table; to which the court readily acquiesced.

Mr. Dunning, in a concise speech, opened the pleadings in support of the prosecution. He was followed by Mr. Thurloe, the attorney general, who learnedly animadverted on the plea advanced by the prisoner, and said that, being counsel for the

the prosecution, it became his duty to declare his opinion on the case in question, which was, that he could not discover any reasonable foundation for the plea urged by the prisoner; and he desired that, if there were reasons sufficient to support it, they might be produced by the counsel on the opposite side.

Lord Mansfield moved, that a proper officer from Doctors Commons might read the sentence of the ecclesiastical court. Hereupon the attorney general said that it would be necessary for all the allegations, replications, &c. on which the sentence was founded, to be read; and the clerk of the crown read the allegations, and was proceeding with the replications, when Lord Mansfield observed, that it would not be necessary to read the latter papers, since the counsel, in the course of their pleadings, would introduce the material arguments therein contained.

Mr. Wallace rose to reply to the attorney general, and in an eloquent strain of forcible argument endeavoured to prove the determination of the ecclesiastical court to be conclusive. Mr. Wallace was followed by Mr. Mansfield, who displayed great ingenuity and learning in support of the same doctrine.

Doctor Calvert, a civilian, spoke nearly for the space of two hours, and produced many precedents to prove the sentence of the consistory court to be definitive and irrevocable. The same ground of argument was pursued by Doctor Wynne, another civilian, who also quoted several cases in point in behalf of the Dutchess; and on the conclusion of this gentleman's speech the court was adjourned on the motion of Lord Gower.

The business of the second day was opened by the lord high steward, who desired the counsel for her Grace to reply to the arguments advanced on the preceding day against evidence being admitted in support of the prosecution.

The attorney general entered upon a minute examination of the pleadings on the other side, and endeavoured to confute the arguments of the counsel and civilians, and to prove that the cases they had quoted were ill-applied, and undeserving authority. This gentleman spoke about an hour and twenty minutes.

The solicitor general then arose, and delivered a learned and elaborate speech, wherein he was extremely severe on the consistory court, saying he could not allow authority to that doctrine which puts the decisions of that court above the cognizance of the temporal ones. He said, that if the sentences of the ecclesiastical court were to be deemed conclusive, persons addicted to indulge a disposition to variety might each, by the exercise of industry and ingenious collusion, gratify his passions with seventy-five wives before attaining his thirtieth year. His witty and humorous allusions frequently provoked a general laugh at the expence of Doctors Commons; and he concluded with giving it as his opinion that the supreme court of legislature was invested with an indisputable power of reversing the decisions of the consistory courts. Mr. Dunning spoke next, strongly supporting the arguments of the solicitor general, and producing several authorities from the law-books in justification of his opinion, that the plea could not be admitted as a bar against calling evidence to prove the criminality of the prisoner.

Doctor

Doctor Harris, a civilian, rose in behalf of the prosecution; and, taking an extensive view of the pleadings of the Doctors Calvert and Wynne, exerted his utmost power to prove them nugatory.

Lord Talbot then addressed the court, observing, that as the matter in agitation was of the utmost importance both to the noble prisoner, and the right honourable court in general, the pleadings on both sides could not be weighed with too minute an attention; and lest the memory should be encumbered (candidly acknowledging that he had already heard more than he believed his mind would retain) he moved for the court to adjourn to the chamber of parliament. Hereupon the lord high steward came from the table to the throne, and requested to be informed whether it was the pleasure of the house to adjourn; and the question being put, it passed in the affirmative.

On Friday the 19th of April Mr. Wallace was called upon by the lord high steward to reply in behalf of the prisoner. Lord Ravensworth then begged he might propose a question to the counsel at the bar. His lordship's question was, " Is the " sentence of the ecclesiastical court in this case " final and conclusive, or is it not?" Upon this Lord Mansfield said, " If the noble lord means—Is " there any precedent for reversing the sentence of " the ecclesiastical court? the answer must cer- " tainly be in the negative. As to any other " meaning, the question is in debate among the " counsel at the bar, and has been so these three " days."

Mr. Wallace then largely expatiated in support of his former cases, and pleaded powerfully in refutation of the arguments advanced by the counsel on the opposite side, producing many other cases in point,

point, and urging that they were incontrovertible. The next speaker was Doctor Calvert, who pleaded very ably in support of the power of the ecclesiastical court: he concluded with insisting that the sentence of the consistory court was indisputably a legal plea in bar of evidence being produced against the prisoner.

It being intimated that the counsel for the Dutchess had concluded their replies, a motion was made by Lord Gower for adjourning to the parliament chamber, and for allowing her Grace permission to retire to her apartment till the peers should return into court; upon which the lord high steward adjourned the court about half past three o'clock.

The peers having taken their seats in the parliament chamber, Lord Camden proposed the following questions to the judges:—" Whether it was "their opinion that the court had power to call "evidence in support of the prosecution? or whe- "ther they deemed the sentence of the ecclesiasti- "cal court conclusive and irrevocable? and whe- "ther the prosecutor could or could not proceed "in this court against the prisoner for obtaining "the decision of the consistory court by collusion "and fraud?" The opinion of the judges was, "That in either case the prosecutor was authorised "to enter into evidence in support of the indict- "ment on which the prisoner stood arraigned."

In consequence of the above determination, the house, after having withdrawn for about half an hour, returned into court; and the lord high steward informed the attorney general, that he was directed by their lordships to order him to proceed with the trial.

Mr. Attorney then explained the nature of the evidence he meant to produce, and recapitulated a
great

great number of facts and circumstances from the year 1742, previous to the supposed marriage of her Grace with Mr. Hervey, to the time of her marriage with the late Duke of Kingston.

The solicitor general rose to examine the witnesses, and Anne Craddock being called to the bar, the Duke of Richmond observed that it would be proper for her to stand at a greater distance from the prisoner, and, after some debate on this head, Mr. Quarme, deputy usher of the black rod, was placed between them. One of the clerks of the house put the questions from the counsel, and delivered the answers of the witness with an audible voice.

The evidence of Anne Craddock was to the following purpose:—I have known her Grace the Dutchess of Kingston ever since the year 1742; at which time she came on a visit to Mr. Merrill's, at Launceston in Hampshire, during the Winchester races. At that time I lived in the family of Mrs. Hanmer, Miss Chudleigh's aunt, who was then on a visit at Mr. Merrill's, where Mr. Hervey and Miss Chudleigh first met, and soon conceived a mutual attachment towards each other. They were privately married one evening about eleven o'clock in Launceston church, in the presence of Mr. Mountney, Mrs. Hanmer, the Reverend Mr. Ames, the rector, who performed the ceremony, and myself. I was ordered out of the church, to entice Mr. Merrill's servants out of the way. I saw the bride and bridegroom put to bed together; and Mrs. Hanmer obliged them to rise again: they went to bed together the night following. In a few days Mr. Hervey was under the necessity of going to Portsmouth, in order to embark on board Sir John

Danvers's fleet, in which he was a lieutenant; and being ordered to call him at five o'clock in the morning, I went into the bed chamber at the appointed hour, and found him and his lady sleeping in bed together, and was unwilling to disturb them, thinking the delay of an hour or two would not be of any consequence. My husband, to whom I was not married till after the time I have mentioned, accompanied Mr. Hervey in the capacity of his servant. When Mr. Hervey returned from the Mediterranean, his lady and he lived together. I then thought her in a state of pregnancy. Some months after, Mr. Hervey went again to sea, and during his absence, I was informed that the lady was brought to bed. She herself told me she had a little boy at nurse, and that his features greatly resembled those of Mr. Hervey.

The Duke of Grafton asked the witness, whether she had seen the child? and she answered in the negative. His Grace also asked, whether, as the ceremony was performed at night, there were any lights in the church? In reply to which she said, Mr. Mountney had a wax light fixed to the crown of his hat. In reply to questions proposed by Lord Hillsborough, the witness acknowledged that she had received a letter from Mr. Fossard, of Piccadilly, containing a promise of a sinecure place, on condition of her appearing to give evidence against the lady at the bar, and expressing that if she thought proper she might shew the letter to Mr. Hervey.

On Saturday the 20th of April Anne Craddock was further examined. The Lords Derby, Hillsborough, Buckinghamshire, and others, questioning her whether she had not been promised a reward by the prosecutor on condition of her giving evidence to convict the prisoner; her answers were evasive, but she was at length brought to acknowledge that pecuniary offers had been made to induce her to give evidence in support of the prosecution.

Mrs. Sophia Pettiplace, sister to Lord Howe, was next examined; but her evidence was of no consequence. She lived with her Grace at the time when her supposed marriage took place with Mr. Hervey, but was not present at the ceremony; and she only believed that the Dutchess had mentioned the circumstance to her.

Cæsar Hawkins, Esquire, deposed, that he had been acquainted with the Dutchess several years, he believed not less than thirty. He had heard of a marriage between Mr. Hervey and the lady at the bar, which circumstance was afterwards mentioned to him by both parties, previous to Mr. Hervey's last going to sea. By the desire of her Grace he was in the room when the issue of the marriage was born, and once saw the child. He was sent for by Mr. Hervey soon after his return from sea, and desired by him to wait upon the lady, with proposals for procuring a divorce, which he accordingly did; when her Grace declared herself absolutely determined against listening to such terms; and he knew that many messages passed on the subject. Her Grace some time after informed him, at his own house, that she had instituted a jactitation suit against Mr. Hervey in Doctors Commons. On another visit she appeared very grave, and desiring him to retire into another apartment, said she was exceedingly unhappy in consequence of an oath, which she had long dreaded, having been tendered to her at Doctors Commons to disavow her marriage, which she would not do for ten thousand worlds. Upon another visit, a short time after, she informed him, that a sentence had passed in her favour at Doctors Commons, which would be irrevocable, unless Mr. Hervey pursued certain measures within a limited time, which she did not apprehend he would do. Hereupon he enquired how she got over the oath; and her reply was, that the circumstance of her marriage was so blended with falsities that she could easily reconcile the matter to her conscience; since the ceremony was a business of so scrambling and shabby a nature, that she could as safely swear she was *not*, as that she *was* married.

Judith Philips being called, swore, that she was the widow of the Reverend Mr. Ames; that she remembered when her late husband performed the marriage ceremony between Mr. Hervey and the prisoner; that she was not present, but derived her information from her husband; that some time after the marriage the lady desired her to prevail upon her husband to grant a certificate, which she said she believed her husband would not refuse; that Mr. Merrill, who accompanied the lady, advised her to consult his attorney from Worcester; that in compliance with the attorney's advice a register-book was purchased, and the marriage inserted therein, with some late burials in the parish. The book was here produced, and the witness swore to the writing of her late husband.

The writing of the reverend Mr. Ames was proved by the reverend Mr. Inchin, and the reverend Mr. Dennis; and the entry of a caveat to the duke's will was proved by a clerk from Doctor's Commons. The book in which the marriage of the duke of Kingston with the lady at the bar was registered on the 8th of March, 1769, was produced by the reverend Mr. Trebeck of St. Marga-

Margaret's, Westminster; and the reverend Mr. Samuel Harpur, of the Museum, swore, that he performed the marriage ceremony between the parties on the day mentioned in the book produced by Mr. Trebeck.

Monday the 22d of April, after the attorney-general had declared the evidence in behalf of the prosecution to be concluded, the lord high steward called upon the prisoner for her defence, which she read; and the following are the most material arguments it contained to invalidate the evidence adduced by the prosecutor:—she appealed to the Searcher of all hearts, that she never considered herself as legally married to Mr. Hervey; she said that she considered herself as a single woman, and as such was addressed by the late duke of Kingston; that, influenced by a legitimate attachment to his grace, she instituted a suit in the ecclesiastical court, where her supposed marriage with Mr. Hervey was declared null and void; but, anxious for every conscientious as well as legal sanction, she submitted an authentic state of her case to the archbishop of Canterbury, who, in the most decisive and unreserved manner, declared that she was at liberty to marry, and afterwards granted, and delivered to doctor Collier, a special licence for her marriage with the late duke of Kingston. She said that, on her marriage, she experienced every mark of gracious esteem from their majesties, and her late royal mistress, the princess dowager of Wales, and was publicly recognized as dutchess of Kingston. Under such respectable sanctions and virtuous motives for the conduct she pursued, strengthened by a decision that had been esteemed conclusive and irrevocable for the space of seven centuries, if their lordships should deem her

her guilty, on any rigid principle of law, she hoped, nay, she was conscious, they would attribute her failure as proceeding from a mistaken judgment and erroneous advice, and not censure her for intentional guilt.

She bestowed the highest encomiums on the deceased duke, and solemnly assured the court, that she had in no one instance abused her ascendency over him; and that, so far from endeavouring to engross his possessions, she had declared herself amply provided for by that fortune for life which he was extremely anxious to bequeath in perpetuity. As to the neglect of the duke's eldest nephew, she said it was entirely the consequence of his disrespectful behaviour to her; and she was not dissatisfied at a preference to another nephew, whose respect and attention to her had been such as the duke judged to be her due, in consequence of her advancement to the honour of being the wife of his uncle.

The lord high steward desired Mr. Wallace to proceed with the evidence. The advocate stated the nature of the evidence he meant to produce to prove that Anne Craddock had asserted to different people that she had no recollection of the marriage between Mr. Hervey and the lady at the bar; and that she placed a reliance on a promise of having a provision made for her in consequence of the evidence she was to give on the present trial; and, to invalidate the depositions of Judith Phillips, he ordered the clerk to read a letter, wherein she supplicated her grace to exert her influence to prevent her husband's discharge from the duke's service, and observed, that Mrs. Phillips had, on the preceding day, swore, that her husband was not dismissed, but voluntarily quitted his station in the household of his grace.

Mr.

Mr. Wallace called Mr. Berkley, Lord Bristol's attorney, who said his lordship told him he was desirous of obtaining a divorce, and directed him to Anne Craddock, saying she was the only person then living who was present at his marriage; and that, a short time previous to the commencement of the jactitation suit, he waited upon Anne Craddock, who informed him that her memory was bad, and that she could remember nothing perfectly in relation to the marriage, which must have been a long time before.

Anne Pritchard deposed that about three months had elapsed since being informed by Mrs. Craddock that she expected to be provided for soon after the trial, and of being enabled to procure a place in the custom-house for one of her relations.

The lord high steward addressed himself to the court; saying, that their lordships had heard the evidence on both sides, and that the importance and solemnity of the occasion required that they should severally pronounce their opinions in the absence of the prisoner, observing that the junior baron was to speak first.—Their lordships declared the prisoner to be guilty.

Proclamation being made for the usher of the Black-rod to bring the prisoner to the bar, she no sooner appeared than the lord high steward informed her that the lords had maturely considered the evidence adduced against her, and likewise all that had been advanced in her favour, and had pronounced her guilty of the felony for which she was indicted. He then requested whether she had any thing to urge against judgment being pronounced. Hereupon the lady delivered a paper containing the following words, to be read by the clerk:

"I

"I plead the privilege of the Peerage."

After this the lord high steward informed her grace, that the lords had considered the plea, and agreed to allow it; adding words to this effect, "Madam, you will be discharged on paying the usual fees."

The lady appeared to be perfectly composed and recollected during the greatest part of her long and important trial; but when sentence was pronounced she fainted, and was carried out of Court.

Sentence was pronounced upon Elizabeth Dutchess of Kingston on Monday the 22d of April, 1776.

Some years subsequent to the transaction on which the above trial was founded, the legislature made ample provision against every species of clandestine and collusive marriages; and therefore we shall, contrary to our usual practice, wave the introduction of concluding remarks, since there can be no necessity for dissuasives against crimes that can be no longer committed.

A Narrative of the singular Cases of BENJAMIN BATES and JOHN GREEN, who were convicted of Burglary, repeatedly respited, and at length pardoned.

AT the sessions held at the Old Bailey in the month of May, 1776, Benjamin Bates and John Green were indicted for breaking and entering the dwelling house of James Penleaze esq; on the night of the 20th of April preceding, and stealing

stealing a variety of valuable articles, principally plate, to the amount of between four and five hundred pounds.

Mrs. Penleaze swore that the windows were constantly barred and keyed every night; that the house was broke open; that she heard somebody trying to open the chamber-door; that she alarmed her husband; but the door was forced open, and four men immediately entered the room, one of whom had a dark lanthorn in his hand, and another a bit of gauze over his mouth, tied behind his head; that two of them got on the bed, and came almost close to her; that one of these men was Green, of whom she had a perfect view; that Bates was on Mr. Penleaze's side of the bed; that the other two went, one on each side, to the head of the bed, one of whom held a pistol to her head, and the other held a cutlass before her; and that four pistols were held to the heads of her and her husband; that they said "they came for money, " and would have it;" and that " they would not " have notes, but *only* money."

She farther deposed, that they asked what money was in the house. Mr. Penleaze directed them to a slab in the next room; but this deponent, recollecting that their valuable effects were in that room, directed them to another, in the hope that some person would come to their relief. Three of them went out of the room, and one of them staid behind, guarding her with a pistol and cutlass at her head.

On their demanding where the money lay, Mr. Penleaze said on the slab in the room on the right hand, and that his son had received a small sum on the preceding day, which he had not accounted for. The thieves enquiring where the son slept, were directed up one pair of stairs higher; on which two of them quitted the room, but did not go into that of young Mr. Penleaze, but returned and just looked into the chamber of the parents.

The door of the study was soon afterwards broke open, and Mrs. Penleaze heard the rattling of plate, as if it was packing up. The prisoners were soon afterwards apprehended, and carried before Justice Wilmot, who committed them for trial.

Mr. Penleaze swore to his house being broke open, and to his loss; but, as he was near-sighted, he would not swear to the parties, though he believed Bates had presented a pistol to his head as he lay in bed.

There was some collateral evidence of a servant, and another woman, respecting this affair; and the jury gave a verdict of guilty against the prisoners, though a number of persons appeared to testify to the goodness of their characters.

We do not mean, by what has been here said, to censure the verdict of the jury: undoubtedly they thought the evidence before them sufficient to convict the prisoners; but this short tale is inserted, to shew the fallibility of all human evidence: for Bates and Green were not the men who committed this robbery, as will appear in the sequel.

The writer of this narrative happened by mere accident to fall into company with one of the peace-officers employed by the keeper of Clerkenwell Bridewell. The situation of Bates and Green was mentioned, and, for reasons then adduced, supposed to be a very hard one. The writer was struck with the circumstance, and inserted various paragraphs in the News-papers in favour of the unfortunate men. The consequence was, that they were respited from time to time. When one respite

spite was nearly expired, another was solicited for; and at length Bates and Green received his Majesty's free pardon, but not till a person who was executed in the country had confessed that himself and some accomplices were guilty of the robbery at the house of Mr. Penleaze, and that the convicted parties were innocent.

There cannot be a doubt but Mrs. Penleaze believed herself certain of the parties against whom she swore; but it is certain that she was mistaken. The parties accused were of the fairest character, and Bates in particular remarkable for the singular inoffensiveness of his disposition. The inferences to be drawn from this story are, that persons giving evidence should be extremely cautious in swearing to the identity of a prisoner; and juries should be equally cautious of yielding implicit belief to evidence, however positive, unless it be attended with collateral proof of guilt in the party accused.

On this occasion Britons have cause to triumph in the LIBERTY OF THE PRESS. If News-papers had not been printed in this country, the lives of two honest men would have been sacrificed to the rigour of the laws, yet no party concerned have been the least to blame. The ways of Providence are mysterious; casual circumstances frequently produce great effects; and a life may be saved or lost by an accident apparently beneath the notice of a common observer.

Account of the Trial of BARNARD CHRISTIAN de NASSAW DEITZ, for a Misdemeanour.

AT the sessions held at the Old Bailey in December 1776, the prisoner abovementioned was indicted for causing to be engraved and cut in metzotinto, on a plate of copper, a blank promissory note, containing the word *twenty* in white letters, on a black ground, he not being an officer, workman, servant or agent, of the governor and company of the bank of England.

Mr. Joshua Long deposed that he was a copper-plate-printer in St. Martin's le Grand; that the prisoner came to him to engrave a copper-plate; that he gave him directions how it should be engraved; that he first said he wanted a 10£. and then a 20£. expressed.

Deitz gave Mr. Long some fine thin paper, cut to the size proper to print off the intended engraving; and Mr. Long carried it to Mr. Terry, engraver in Pater-noster Row.

Mr. Terry proved that Mr. Long brought him the plate to engrave, and that it was calculated to print white letters on a black ground.

The prisoner, who was a man of great artifice, demanded if he had ever given him any orders. Mr. Terry replied in the negative, and declared that he never saw the prisoner till he was in custody.

The prisoner then said, " If Mr. Long had it " executed in another place, am I answerable for " a trespass in the city of London *? Mr. Terry

---

* It should be remarked that St. Martin's le Grand is part of the Liberty of Westminster.

" had no orders from me: I have been detained
" four months, and never admitted to trial; I have
" obtained the high favour this day to be tried;
" I am not guilty now of what is laid to my charge,
" though I have been detained four months."

Deitz attempted by other artifices to prepossess the jury in his favour; but they delivered a verdict that he was guilty, and he was sentenced to a short imprisonment.

It will now be necessary, though a little out of chronological order, to relate the particulars of Deitz's second trial.

On the sessions held at the Old Bailey in September, 1777, he was indicted for defrauding John Van Roy, by false pretences, of 116 pounds of human hair, to the value of 90£.—The history of this affair is as follows. Mr. Van Roy was a Dutchman who bought up human hair in Holland for sale in England. Deitz went to his lodgings near Holborn, with a man who called himself Prince, and they said they wanted a hundred weight of hair, to send to a merchant at Marlborough. They called a second time, bringing with them a man whom they pretended was the King's hair-dresser, and had made the first wig his majesty wore. By a variety of artifices they prevailed on Van Roy to take the hair with them in a coach to Pemberton Row near Fleet-street, where the goods were laid down in a room where a clerk was sitting at a desk, on which were several books and papers.

A bottle of wine was called for; but the Dutchman, very cautious, refused to drink of it, but accepted of some porter. The agreement had been for ready money: and Prince produced a draught for 100£. on John Smith, a banker in Lombard-street.

street. Van Roy doubted if the note was good, and shewing it to Deitz, the latter said " it is as " good as the bank of England,"

Van Roy had not cash enough about him to give the ballance; but said he would go home for it; but he immediately hastened to Lombard-street, to find the banker, and learn if the note was good; but no such banker could be found. He now went to a friend, and told him what had happened; and on their going together to Pemberton Row, the purchasers and the goods were vanished.

The prisoner made a very artful defence, and cross-examined the prosecutor with the dexterity of a pleader: but as he was an old offender, well known, and the evidence was clear, the jury did not hesitate to find him guilty, and he was sentenced to three years labour at ballast-heaving, and he is now * on board one of the ballast-lighters off Woolwich.

We have the rather mentioned this case, because Deitz was one of the most artful and dangerous impostors about town; of superior abilities, deep contrivance, and consummate cunning; yet all his artifices could not screen him from the justice of his country, nor prevent a fate so ignominious that a man of common sensibility would blush to think of it.

We hope it is unnecessary to caution our younger readers to beware of treading in the steps of this dangerous man; and shall therefore dismiss the subject.

---

* In March 1779.

New Newgate Calendar Or Malefactor's Register.

Dr. DODD and JOSEPH HARRIS, *at the place of Execution.*

The extraordinary Case, Trial, Conviction, and Execution, of Dr. WILLIAM DODD, for Forgery.

ON the 8th of February, 1777, the reverend "Dr. Dodd, and Mr. Robertson, a broker, "were charged before the lord mayor, by Henry "Fletcher, and Samuel Peach, Esquires, with "forging and uttering as true a counterfeit bond, "purporting to be the bond of the earl of Ches- "terfield," for the payment of £.4,200, with an intent to defraud, &c.

The history of this affair is as follows. Dr. Dodd being in want of cash to pay his Tradesmen's bills, and having been preceptor to the earl of Chesterfield, he pretended that his lordship had an urgent occasion to borrow £.4000, but did not chuse to be his own agent, and begged that the matter might be secretly and expeditiously conducted. The doctor employed Mr. Robertson, a broker, to whom he presented a bond, not filled up or signed, that he might find a person who would advance the requisite sum to a young nobleman who had lately come of age. After applying to several persons who refused the business, because they were not to be present when the bond was executed, Mr. Robertson, absolutely confiding in the doctor's honour, applied to Messrs. Fletcher and Peach, who agreed to lend the money. Mr. Robertson returned the bond to the doctor, in order to its being executed; and on the following day the doctor produced it as executed, and witnessed by himself.

When Mr. Robertson was examined before the lord mayor, he said, "I, knowing Mr. Fletcher "to

"to be a particular man, and one of those who
"would object to one subscribing witness only,
"put my name under the doctor's. I then went
"and received the money, which I paid into the
"hands of Dr. Dodd, £. 3000 in notes of Sir
"Charles Raymond and Company, the remaining
"£. 1200 in bank-notes."

The money being thus in the doctor's possession, he gave Mr. Robertson a *hundred pounds* * for his trouble, and paid some of his own debts with a part of the remainder: but it does not appear but that he intended to replace the money, and pay off the bond in a short time, without the knowledge of any Person but the broker, and the gentlemen of whom the money had been borrowed. It happened, however, that the bond being left with Mr. Manly (attorney for Messrs. Fletcher and Peach), he observed, in the condition of the bond,
"a very remarkable blot in the first letter E, in
"the word SEVEN, which did not seem to be the
"effect of chance, but done with design. He
"thought it remarkable, but did not suspect a for-
"gery; yet he shewed Mr. Fletcher the bond
"and blot, and advised him to have a clean
"bond filled up, and carried to lord Chesterfield
"for execution."

Mr. Fletcher consented; and Mr. Manly went on the following day to his lordship, who, having previous notice of the intended business, asked him if he had called about the bond. Mr. Manly said he had; and his lordship answered, "I have burnt
"the bond."

---

*Was not this a handsome consideration for transacting such a business?

This appeared very extraordinary; but was soon explained, by lord Chesterfield's saying he thought the gentleman called about a bond for 500 £. which he had given some years before, and had taken up and burnt.

When Mr. Manly produced the bond in question, lord Chesterfield was surprized, and immediately disowned it. Upon this Mr. Manly went directly to Mr. Fletcher, to consult what steps to take. Mr. Fletcher, a Mr. Innis, and Mr. Manly, went to Guildhall, to prefer an information respecting the forgery against the broker and Dr. Dodd. Mr. Robertson was taken into custody, and with Fletcher, Innis, Manly, and two of the lord mayor's officers, went to the house of Dr. Dodd in Argyle-street. They opened the business; Dr. Dodd was very much struck and affected. Manly told him, if he would return the money, it would be the only means of saving him. He instantly returned six notes of 400 £. each, making 3000 £. He drew on his banker for 500 £. The broker returned 100 £. The doctor gave a second draught on his banker for 200 £. and a judgement on his goods for the remaining 400 £. which judgement was carried immediately into execution *.

All this was done by the doctor in full reliance on the honour of the parties that the bond should be returned to him cancelled: but notwithstanding this restitution, he was taken before the lord mayor, and charged as abovementioned, when his defence was expressed in the following terms: " I " had no intention to defraud my lord Chesterfield,

---

* After this full restitution, does there not appear a kind of cruelty in trying Dr. Dodd at all? But justice *must* be done.

"or the gentleman who advanced the money. I hope
"that the satisfaction I have made in returning the
"money will atone for the offence. I was pressed
"exceedingly for 300 £. to pay some bills due to
"tradesmen. I took this step as a temporary re-
"source: I should have repaid it in half a year.
"My lord Chesterfield cannot but have some ten-
"derness for me, as my pupil: I love him, and he
"knows it. There is nobody wishes to prosecute.
"I am sure my lord Chesterfield don't want my
"life: I hope he will shew clemency to me.
"Mercy should triumph over justice."

This defence was not allowed to have any weight; and the Doctor was committed to the Compter, in preparation for his trial.

On the 19th of February, 1777, Doctor Dodd, being put to the bar at the Old Bailey, addressed the court in the following terms:—" My lords, I
"I am informed that the bill of indictment against
"me has been found on the evidence of Mr. Ro-
"bertson, who was taken out of Newgate, with-
"out any authority or leave from your lordships,
"for the purpose of procuring the bill to be
"found. Mr. Robertson is a subscribing witness
"to the bond, and, as I conceive, would be swear-
"ing to exculpate himself, if he should be admit-
"ted as a witness against me; and as the bill has
"been found upon his evidence, which was sur-
"reptitiously obtained, I submit to your lordships
"that I ought not to be compelled to plead on this
"indictment, and upon this question I beg to be
"heard by my counsel. My lords, I beg leave
"also further to observe to your lordships, that
"the gentlemen on the other side of the question
"are bound over to prosecute Mr. Robertson."

It is now proper to remark, that, " previous to
" the arguments of the counsel, an order which
" had been surreptitiously obtained from an officer
" of the court, dated Wednesday, February the
" 19th, and directed to the keeper of Newgate,
" commanding him to carry Lewis Robertson to
" Hicks's-hall, in order to his giving evidence be-
" fore the grand inquest on the present bill of in-
" dictment; likewise a resolution of the court, re-
" probating the said order; and also the recog-
" nizance entered into by Mr. Manly, Mr. Peach,
" Mr. Innis, and the right hon. the earl of Ches-
" terfield, to prosecute and give evidence against
" Dr. Dodd and Lewis Robertson for the said
" forgery; should be read; and the clerk of the
" arraigns was directed to inform the court whether
" the name Lewis Robertson was indorsed as a wit-
" ness on the back of the indictment, which was
" answered in the affirmative."

The counsel now proceeded in their arguments for and against the prisoner. Mr. Howarth, one of Dr. Dodd's advocates, contended that not any person ought " to plead or answer to an indictment,
" if it appears upon the face of that indictment
" that the evidence upon which the bill was found
" was not legal or competent to have been adduced
" before the grand jury."

Mr. Cowper, of counsel on the same side, followed this idea, and hoped that Dr. Dodd might not be called on to plead to the bill of indictment, and that the bill might be quashed.

Mr. Buller, who was likewise retained for Dr. Dodd, spoke as follows; and his arguments are so ingenious, that we think it our duty to transcribe them literally:—" My lords, I am of counsel on
" the same side with Mr. Howarth and Mr. Cow-
" per.

"per. It is the established law of this land, that
"no man shall be put upon his trial for any
"offence, unless there be a bill first properly
"found by a grand jury: I say *properly* found;
"for if there be any objection whatsoever to the
"finding the indictment, and the most familiar
"that are to be found in our books are those that
"go to the objection of the grand jury; for in-
"stance, where only one person of the grand jury
"has been incompetent, where only eleven of the
"jury have found the bill, that therefore it shall
"not be tried. I take it the objections go uni-
"versally. I am aware that the objections I have
"been alluding to, and which are particularly
"stated in Lord Hale, go to the grand jury only;
"but I will beg leave to consider whether the rea-
"son that governs the one does not govern the
"other. Another case put by my Lord Hale is
"this: if one of the grand jury is outlawed,
"these objections go to the persons of the grand
"jury: I am aware that that is not the present
"objection; but I will beg leave, with your lord-
"ships' permission, to consider whether this does
"not fall within the same reason; for I cannot
"conceive that the law, which is so peculiarly
"watchful over the personal qualifications of the
"grand jury, should not be equally attentive to
"the evidence which is laid before them, and
"upon which they are to decide the fate of the
"bill which is offered to their consideration. I
"take it to be as essential to the finding of the bill,
"that the evidence offered to the grand jury
"should be such as the law allows, as it is when
"the indictment afterwards comes to be tried be-
"fore your lordships; and if that rule holds, I
"trust I shall have very little difficulty in con-
"vincing

"vincing your lordships that this bill has been
"improperly found. My lords, the prosecutor
"has thought it so material to admit Mr. Robert-
"son a witness in this cause, that though, in my
"humble apprehension, he stands in a much more
"criminal light than the prisoner at the bar, yet
"they have thought fit to bargain with him, to let
"him off from a capital felony of the most dan-
"gerous sort to society, the most peculiarly so
"from his situation in life, of any man that can be
"charged with such an offence. Mr. Robertson
"stands in this business as a sworn broker of the
"city of London: as such it was his peculiar duty
"to preserve good faith between man and man;
"he is bargained with by the prosecutor to be let
"off in a case where he stands upon the appear-
"ance against him, now as the most criminal, for
"the purpose of procuring evidence against the
"prisoner at the bar. My lords, if that evidence
"be improper, there remains but one thing more
"to be enquired into; that is, whether your
"lordships can say that that evidence has not had
"an improper effect when it was admitted before
"the grand jury: it is not improbable that the
"bill might be found wholly upon his evidence,
"if I have a right to assume that as a fact, because
"the prosecutor has thought it material and abso-
"lutely necessary to produce him before the
"grand jury, why then your lordships sitting here
"cannot say but this indictment may have been
"found upon his evidence only: if it be so, is
"Robertson a person whose evidence ought to
"have been received? If I am right in saying
"that the same evidence, and the same evidence
"only, is legal before a grand jury, which is legal
"upon a trial, I apprehend the case which was
"mentione

"mentioned yesterday in Lord Hale, folio 303, is
"decisive upon this point. My lords, there are
"more passages in that folio book; the first was
"the case mentioned yesterday of 'Henry Trew,
"was indicted for a burglary, and (by the advice
"of Keeling, chief justice; Brown, justice; and
"Wilde, recorder) Perrin was sworn a witness
"against Trew as to the burglary, which he con-
"fessed, but was not indicted for the other felony.'
"Here he was admitted because he confessed him-
"self guilty. The passage before that in Lord
"Hale seems to me still stronger:—'If two de-
"fendants be charged with a crime, one shall not
"be examined against the other to convict him of
"an offence, unless the party examined confess
"himself guilty.'—" Now, has Robertson con-
"fessed himself guilty? No, he has not; then
"there is an express authority by Lord Hale,
"that not having done it he is no witness, he does
"not stand in that predicament which Lord Hale
"states the man to be there. He says that they
"were both charged with the crime; that is the
"case here; the prisoner and Robertson were
"both committed for the same crime; he stands
"now charged with that crime, and he has not
"pleaded guilty; therefore upon this authority
"I take it to be clear, that he cannot be admitted
"a witness upon the trial; and if not, I must
"leave it to the ingenuity of the learned counsel
"to shew why a man, who the law says shall not
"be a witness upon the trial, shall be admitted a
"witness to find the bill upon, against a man
"whom there is no other evidence to affect."

Mr. Mansfield, and the other counsel employed for the prosecution, replied to these arguments in a manner that did honour to their ingenuity and pro-

fessional

feffional knowledge. It would greatly exceed our limits to give their arguments at length; and it will therefore be sufficient to say, that it was agreed on all hands that the trial should be proceeded on; the question respecting the competency of Robertson's evidence being reserved for the opinion of the twelve judges.

Hereupon Dr. Dodd was indicted for forging a bond, for the payment of 4,200£. with intent to defraud, &c. as mentioned at the head of this article.

As we have already recited the leading particulars of this business, it will be unneceffary to be more minute; but only to say, that when the evidence was gone through, the court told the doctor that was the time for him to make his defence; on which he spoke as follows:

" My lords, and gentlemen of the jury;—Upon
" the evidence which has been this day produced
" against me, I find it very difficult to address your
" lordships: there is no man in the world who has
" a deeper sense of the heinous nature of the
" crime, for which I stand indicted, than myself.
" I view it, my lords, in all its extent of malig-
" nancy towards a commercial state, like ours;
" but, my lords, I humbly apprehend, though no
" lawyer, that the moral turpitude and malignancy
" of the crime always, both in the eye of the law
" of reason, and of religion *, consists in the in-
" tention. I am informed, my lords, that the act
" of parliament on this head runs perpetually in

---

* This is a strange phrase; it is what an Irishman would call "*both* all *three*;" but it is thus printed; and if Dr. Dodd made use of it, his situation must be allowed for.

" this

"this ſtile, *with an intention to defraud.* Such an
"intention, my lords, and gentlemen of the jury, I
"believe, has not been attempted to be proved
"upon me, and the conſequences that have hap-
"pened, which have appeared before you, ſuf-
"ficiently prove that a perfect and ample reſtitu-
"tion has been made. I leave it, my lords, to
"you, and the gentlemen of the jury, to conſider,
"that if an unhappy man ever deviates from the
"law of right, yet, if in the ſingle firſt moment
"of recollection, he does all that he can to make
"a full and perfect amends, what, my lords, and
"gentlemen of the jury, can God and man deſire
"further? My lords, there are a variety of little
"circumſtances, too tedious to trouble you with,
"with reſpect to this matter. Were I to give a
"looſe to my feelings, I have many things to ſay
"which I am ſure you would feel with reſpect to
"me: but, my lords, as it appears on all hands, as
"it appears, gentlemen of the jury, in every view,
"that no injury, intentional or real, has been
"done to any man upon the face of the earth, I
"hope that therefore you will conſider the caſe
"in its true ſtate of clemency. I muſt obſerve to
"your lordſhips, that though I have met with all
"candour in this court, yet I have been purſued
"with exceſſive cruelty; I have been proſecuted
"after the moſt expreſs engagements, after the
"moſt ſolemn aſſurances, after the moſt deluſive,
"ſoothing arguments of Mr. Manley; I have
"been proſecuted with a cruelty ſcarcely to be
"paralleled: a perſon, avowedly criminal in the
"ſame indictment with myſelf, has been brought
"forth as a capital witneſs againſt me; a fact, I
"believe, totally unexampled. My lords, op-
"preſſed as I am with infamy, loaded as I am

"with

"with distress, sunk under this cruel prosecution, your lordships, and the gentlemen of the jury, cannot think life a matter of any value to me: no, my lords, I solemnly protest, that death of all blessings would be the most pleasant to me after this pain. I have yet, my lords, ties which call upon me; ties which render me desirous even to continue this miserable existence:—I have a wife, my lords, who for twenty-seven years has lived an unparalleled example of conjugal attachment and fidelity, and whose behaviour during this trying scene would draw tears of approbation, I am sure, even from the most inhuman. My lords, I have creditors, honest men, who will lose much by my death: I hope, for the sake of justice towards them, some mercy will be shewn to me. If, upon the whole, these considerations at all avail with you, my lords, and you gentlemen of the jury; if, upon the most partial survey of matters, not the slightest intention of injury can appear to any one; and I solemnly declare it was in my power to replace it in three months; of this I assured Mr. Robertson frequently; and had his solemn assurances that no man should be privy to it but Mr Fletcher and himself, and, if no injury was done to any man upon earth; I then hope, I trust, I fully confide myself in the tenderness, humanity, and protection of my country."

The discerning reader will easily see, by the defence, that Dr. Dodd was not a man of superior abilities; and the defence itself appears to be little else than a confession of guilt.

The jury retired for about ten minutes, and then returned with a verdict, that "The prisoner was GUILTY;" but at the same time presented a petition, humbly recommending the convict to the royal mercy *.

On the first day of the sessions held at the Old Bailey in May, 1777, Dr. Dodd, being put to the bar, was addressed by Mr. Justice Aston in the following terms:

"Doctor William Dodd,

"When you was brought up in last February
" sessions, to plead to an indictment found by the
" grand jury of Middlesex for forgery, before you
" pleaded, or the trial was proceeded upon, a
" question was submitted to the court by you,
" with the advice of your counsel, which was re-
" served for the opinion of the judges; that is,
" whether you was bound to plead to, and ought
" to be tried upon that indictment, as the name of
" Lewis Robertson, committed for the same for-
" gery, appeared to be indorsed as a witness upon
" the bill of indictment, and that he had been
" taken before the grand jury to be examined as
" a witness by means of an order directed to the
" keeper of Newgate, which had been improperly
" obtained, on the 19th of February, and which
" was afterwards vacated by the court.

" The judges have met, and have fully consider-
" ed the whole matter of this objection; and they

---

* It seems highly probable that this petition was previously prepared by the friends of Dr. Dodd; for an absence of ten minutes was insufficient to agree on a verdict, and prepare the petition.

"are unanimously of opinion, that the necessity of some proper authority to carry a witness who happened to be in custody before the grand jury to give evidence, regards the justification of the gaoler only; but that no objection lies upon that account in the mouth of the party indicted, for in respect of him the finding of the bill is right, and according to law.

"Whether a private prosecutor, by using an accomplice in or out of custody as a witness, gives such a witness a plea not to be prosecuted, or can entitle himself, the prosecutor, to have his recognizance discharged, is a matter very fit for consideration under all the circumstances of the particular case, when that question shall arise; but it is a matter in which the party indicted has no concern, nor can he make any legal objection to the producing such a person as a witness, for the accomplice is, against him, a legal and competent witness, and so was Lewis Robertson upon the bill of indictment preferred against you.

"The judges, therefore, are of opinion, that the proceedings upon that indictment against you were legally had, and that you was thereupon duly convicted according to law. Of this opinion I thought it most proper thus early to apprize you, that you may be prepared for the consequence of it at the close of the sessions."

To this address Dr. Dodd replied in the following terms: "My lord, I humbly thank your lordship, and the rest of the learned judges, for the consideration you have been pleased to give to the objections made by my counsel on that awful day of my trial; and I rest fully satisfied,

"my lord, in the justice of your lordship's
"opinion."

On the last day of the sessions Dr. Dodd was again put to the bar, when the clerk of the arraigns said, "Dr. William Dodd, you stand con‑
"victed of forgery; what have you to say why
"this court should not give you judgement to die
"according to law?"

Hereupon Dr. Dodd addressed the court in the following terms. "My lord, I now stand before
"you a dreadful example of human infirmity. I
"entered upon public life with the expectations
"common to young men whose education has
"been liberal, and whose abilities have been flat‑
"tered; and when I became a clergyman, I con‑
"sidered myself as not impairing the dignity of
"the order. I was not an idle, nor, I hope, an
"useless minister: I taught the truths of christi‑
"anity with the zeal of conviction, and the autho‑
"rity of innocence. My labours were approved;
"my pulpit became popular; and, I have reason
"to believe, that of those who heard me some
"have been preserved from sin, and some have
"been reclaimed. Condescend, my lord, to think,
"if these considerations aggravate my crime, how
"much they must embitter my punishment!

"Being distinguished and elevated by the con‑
"fidence of mankind, I had too much confidence
"in myself, and thinking my integrity, what
"others thought it, established in sincerity, and
"fortified by religion, I did not consider the dan‑
"ger of vanity, nor suspect the deceitfulness of
"my own heart. The day of conflict came, in
"which temptation seized and overwhelmed me!
"I committed the crime, which I entreat your
"lordship

" lordship to believe that my conscience hourly
" represents to me in its full bulk of mischief and
" malignity. Many have been overpowered by
" temptation, who are now among the penitent in
" heaven!

" To an act now waiting the decision of vindic-
" tive justice, I will not presume to oppose the
" counterbalance of almost thirty years, (a great
" part of the life of man) passed in exciting and
" exercising charity; in relieving such distresses
" as I now feel; in administering those consola-
" tions which I now want. I will not otherwise
" extenuate my offence, than by declaring, what I
" hope will appear to many, and what many cir-
" cumstances make probable, that I did not intend
" finally to defraud: nor will it become me to
" apportion my own punishment, by alledging,
" that my sufferings have been not much less than
" my guilt. I have fallen from reputation which
" ought to have made me cautious, and from a
" fortune which ought to have given me content.
" I am sunk at once into poverty and scorn: my
" name and my crime fill the ballads in the
" streets; the sport of the thoughtless, and the
" triumph of the wicked!

" It may seem strange, my lord, that, remember-
" ing what I have lately been, I should still wish
" to continue what I am:—but contempt of
" death, how speciously soever it may mingle with
" heathen virtues, has nothing in it suitable to
" christian penitence.

" Many motives impel me to beg earnestly for
" life. I feel the natural horror of a violent
" death, the universal dread of untimely dissolu-
" tion. I am desirous to recompence the injury

" I have

"I have done to the clergy, to the world, and to
"religion; and to efface the scandal of my crime,
"by the example of my repentance:—but, above
"all, I wish to die with thoughts more composed,
"and calmer preparation.

"The gloom and confusion of a prison, the
"anxiety of a trial, the horrors of suspence, and
"the inevitable vicissitudes of passion, leave not
"the mind in a due disposition for the holy exer-
"cises of prayer, and self-examination. Let not
"a little life be denied me, in which I may, by
"meditation and contrition, prepare myself to
"stand at the tribunal of Omnipotence, and support
"the presence of that judge, who shall distribute
"to all according to their works; who will re-
"ceive and pardon the repenting sinner; and
"from whom the merciful shall obtain mercy.

"For these reasons, my lords, amidst shame and
"misery, I yet wish to live; and most humbly im-
"plore, that I may be recommended by your
"lordship to the clemency of his Majesty."

The RECORDER now proceeded to pass sentence in the following terms:—"Dr. William Dodd;
"you have been convicted of the offence of pub-
"lishing a forged and counterfeit bond, knowing
"it to be forged and counterfeited; and you have
"had the advantage which the laws of this country
"afford to every man in that situation, a fair, an
"impartial, and an attentive trial.

"The jury, to whose justice you appealed, have
"found you guilty; their verdict has undergone
"the consideration of the learned judges, and
"they found no ground to impeach the justice of
"that verdict; you yourself have admitted the
"justice of it; and now the very painful duty that
"the

" the neceffity of the law impofes upon the court,
" to pronounce the fentence of that law againft
" you, remains only to be performed.

" You appear to entertain a very proper fenfe
" of the enormity of the offence which you have
" committed; you appear too in a ftate of con-
" trition of mind, and I doubt not have duly re-
" flected how far the dangerous tendency of the
" offence you have been guilty of is encreafed by
" the influence of example, in being committed by
" a perfon of your character, and of the facred
" function of which you are a member. Thefe
" fentiments feem to be yours; I would wifh to
" cultivate fuch fentiments; but I would not wifh
" to add to the anguifh of a perfon in your fitu-
" ation by dwelling upon it.

" Your application for mercy muft be made
" elfewhere; it would be cruel in the court to
" flatter you; there is a power of difpenfing mercy
" where you may apply. Your own good fenfe,
" and the contrition you exprefs, will induce you
" to leffen the influence of the example by publifh-
" ing your hearty and fincere deteftation of the
" offence of which you are convicted; and that
" you will not attempt to palliate or extenuate,
" which would indeed add to the degree of the
" influence of a crime of this kind being com-
" mitted by a perfon of your character and known
" abilities; I would therefore warn you againft
" any thing of that kind. Now, having faid this,
" I am obliged to pronounce the fentence of the
" law, which is—That you Dr. William Dodd be
" carried from hence to the place from whence
" you came; that from thence you are to be car-
" ried to the place of execution, where you are to
" be

"be hanged by the neck until you are dead."—To this Dr. Dodd replied, "Lord Jesus, receive my soul!"

We will now proceed to an account of the execution of Dr. Dodd, then relate some farther particulars respecting him, and conclude with remarks proper to the occasion.

This unhappy clergyman was attended to the place of execution, in a mourning coach, by the Rev. Mr. Villette, ordinary of Newgate, and the Rev. Mr. Dobey. Another criminal, named Joseph Harris, was executed at the same time. It is impossible to give an idea of the immense crouds of people that thronged the streets from Newgate to Tyburn. When the prisoners arrived at the fatal tree, and were placed in the cart, Dr. Dodd exhorted his fellow-sufferer in so generous a manner as testified that he had not forgot the duty of a clergyman, and was very fervent in the exercise of his own devotions. Just before the parties were turned off, Dr. Dodd whispered to the executioner. What he said cannot be known; but it was observed that the man had no sooner driven away the cart, than he ran immediately under the gibbet, and took hold of the doctor's legs, as if to steady the body; and the unhappy man appeared to die without pain; but the groans, prayers, and tears, of thousands attended his exit.

Dr. Dodd was executed on the 27th of June, 1777.

Thus perished all that was mortal of William Dodd, doctor of divinity, late prebendary of Brecon, and chaplain in ordinary to his Majesty. This man, with all his faults, was not without his virtues; he was the promoter of many charities, and the

the inſtitutor of ſome of them. The Magdalen hoſpital, the ſociety for the relief of poor debtors, and that for the recovery of perſons apparently drowned, will, we truſt, be perpetual monuments to his credit: but it is our duty not to conceal or diſguiſe his faults, the principal of which appear to have been vanity, and a turn for extravagance, which ruined his circumſtances, and urged him to commit the crime which coſt him his life.

After conviction, the exertions made to ſave Dr. Dodd were perhaps beyond all example in any country. The news-papers were filled with letters, and paragraphs in his favour. Individuals of all ranks and degrees exerted themſelves in his behalf: pariſh officers went, in mourning, from houſe to houſe, to procure ſubſcriptions to a petition to the king; and this petition, which, with the names, filled 23 ſheets of parchment, was actually preſented. Even more than this:—the lord mayor and common council went in a body to St. James's, to ſolicit mercy for the convict. But all this availed nothing: it was neceſſary to make an example of a man who had ſet but too bad an one to others; and who, from the faireſt proſpect of riſing to the higheſt honours of the church, ſunk to the loweſt degree of abaſement.

Surely this tale will be a leſſon againſt extravagance, and will teach us to be content in the ſtation of life in which Providence hath placed us. The fate of this unhappy man furniſhes, likewiſe, the ſtrongeſt argument againſt the crime of forgery; for if all the intereſt that was exerted to ſave Dr. Dodd could have no weight, no one hereafter guilty of it ought to expect a pardon. If, then, any one ſhould be tempted to the commiſſion of it, let him reflect on this cafe; let him, moral and religious confiderations apart, ftay the hafty hand, and let him retract the rafh refolution.

We fhall conclude this narrative with an extract from an addrefs which Dr. Dodd made, after conviction, to his fellow prifoners, as we deem it well worthy the public attention.—" There is al-
" ways," fays the doctor, " a danger left men,
" freſh from a trial in which life has been loſt,
" fhould remember with refentment and malignity
" the profecutor, the witneffes, or the judges.
" It is indeed fcarcely poffible, with all the pre-
" judices of an intereft fo weighty, and fo affecting,
" that the convict fhould think otherwife than
" that he has been treated, in fome part of the
" procefs, with unneceffary feverity. In this opi-
" nion he is perhaps fingular, and therefore pro-
" bably miftaken: but there is no time for dif-
" quifition; we muft try to find the fhorteft way
" to peace. It is eafier to forgive than to reafon
" right. He that has been injurioufly or unnecef-
" farily harraffed, has one opportunity more of
" proving his fincerity, by forgiving the wrong,
" and praying for his enemy.

" It is the duty of a penitent to repair, as far
" as he has the power, the injury he has done.
" What we can do is commonly nothing more
" than to leave the world an example of contri-
" tion. On the dreadful day, when the fentence
" of the law has its full force, fome will be found
" to have affected a fhamelefs bravery, or negli-
" gent intrepidity. Such is not the proper beha-
" viour of a convicted criminal. To rejoice in
" tortures is the privilege of a martyr; to meet
" death with intrepidity is the right only of in-
" nocence,

"nocence, if in any human being innocence could
"be found. Of him whose life is shortened by
"his crimes, the last duties are humility and self-
"abasement. We owe to God sincere repentance;
"we owe to man the appearance of repentance.
"Men have died with a steadfast denial of crimes,
"of which it is very difficult to suppose them in-
"nocent. By what equivocation or reserve they
"may have reconciled their consciences to false-
"hood it is impossible to know: but if they thought
"that, when they were to die, they paid their legal
"forfeit, and that the world had no farther de-
"mand upon them; that therefore they might,
"by keeping their own secrets, try to leave
"behind them a disputable reputation; and that
"the falshood was harmless because none were
"injured; they had very little considered the
"nature of society. One of the principal parts of
"national felicity arises from a wise and impartial
"administration of justice. Every man reposes
"upon the tribunals of his country the stability
"of possession, and the serenity of life. He there-
"fore who unjustly exposes the courts of judica-
"ture to suspicion, either of partiality or error,
"not only does an injury to those who dispense
"the laws, but diminishes the public confidence
"in the laws themselves, and shakes the founda-
"tion of public tranquillity.

"For my own part, I confess, with deepest com-
"punction, the crime which has brought me to
"this place; and admit the justice of my sentence,
"while I am sinking under its severity."

An authentic Account of JAMES HILL, otherwife JOHN HIND, otherwife JAMES HIND, otherwife JAMES ACKSAN, commonly called JOHN the PAINTER, who was executed for fetting fire to the Rope-houfe belonging to his Majefty's Dock Yard at Portfmouth.

ABOUT four o'clock in the afternoon of the 7th of December, 1776, a fire broke out in the Rope-houfe of Portfmouth dock, which entirely confumed that building. The fire was wholly attributed to accident; but on the 15th of January the following difcovery was made, which inconteftably proved that the building had been deftroyed by defign.

Three men being employed in the hemp-houfe, they found a tin machine, fomewhat refembling a tea cannifter, and near the fame fpot a wooden box containing various kinds of combuftibles. This circumftance being communicated to the commiffioner of the dock, and circulated among the public, feveral vague and indefinite fufpicions fell upon a man who had been lurking about the dock-yard, whofe furname was not known, but who had been diftinguifhed by the appellation of John the Painter, and had been a journeyman to Mr. Golding, a painter at Titchfield.

In confequence of advertifements in the News-papers, offering a reward of 50*l*. for apprehending John the Painter, he was fecured a Odiham. On the 7th of February the prifoner was examined at Sir John Fielding's office in Bow-ftreet, where John Baldwin, who had exercifed the trade of a
painter

painter in different parts of America, attended by the direction of Lord Temple, who imagined that the parties might know each other. Baldwin declared he had not the least knowledge of the prisoner, who then bowed to him, and soon after requested that he would favour him with a visit in New-prison. Baldwin attended him in the afternoon, and on the following days till the 15th, and their conversations were on general subjects relating to the affairs of America; but on the 15th, and the subsequent days till the 24th, the prisoner's discourse with Baldwin operated very materially towards his conviction, as it was brought in corroboration of a variety of evidence on trial. He asked Baldwin whether he was acquainted with Mr. Dean, and, being answered in the negative, exclaimed, "What not Mr. Dean, Silas Dean, employed by the congress? He is a fine fellow. I believe Benjamin Franklin is employed on the same errand." He said he had taken a view of most of the dock yards and fortifications about England, the number of Ships in the navy, and observed their weight of metal and their number of men, and had been to France two or three times to inform Silas Dean of his discoveries; and that Dean gave him bills to the amount of 300£. and letters of recommendation to a merchant in the city, which he had burnt, lest they should lead to a discovery. He informed Baldwin that he instructed a tin-man's apprentice at Canterbury to make him a tin cannister, which he carried to Portsmouth, where he hired a lodging at one Mrs. Boxall's, and tried his preparations for setting fire to the dock yard.

After recounting the manner of preparing matches and combustibles, he said that on the 6th of the preceding December he got into the hemp-house, and having placed a candle in a wooden box and a tin cannister over it, and sprinkled turpentine over some of the hemp, he proceeded to the rope-house, where he placed a bottle of turpentine among a quantity of loose hemp, which he sprinkled with turpentine, and having laid matches, made of paper painted over with powdered charcoal and gunpowder diluted with water, and other combustibles about the place, he returned to his lodgings. The next day he hired lodgings in two other houses to which he intended to set fire, that the engines might not be all employed together in quenching the conflagration at the dock. On this day he again went to the hemp-house, intending to set it on fire, which he however was unable to effect, owing to a halfpenny-worth of common house matches * that he had bought not being sufficiently dry. This disappointment, he said, rendered him exceedingly uneasy, and that he went from the hemp-house to the rope-house, and set fire to the matches he had placed there. He said his uneasiness was increased because he could not return to the lodging where he had left a bundle containing an Ovid's Metamorphoses, a treatise on war and making fire works, a Justin, a pistol, and a French passport, in which his real name was inserted.

When he had set fire to the rope-house he proceeded towards London, deeply regretting his

---

* The matches he had formed for firing the combustibles were so contrived as to continue burning for twenty four hours; so that by cutting them into proper lengths he provided for his escape, knowing the precise time when the fire would reach the combustibles.

failure in attempting to fire the other building, and was strongly inclined to fire into the windows of the woman who had sold him the bad matches. He jumped into a cart, and gave the woman who drove it sixpence, to induce her to drive quick; and, when he had passed the centinels, observed the fire to have made so rapid a progress, that the " ele-" ment seemed in a blaze." About ten the next morning he arrived at Kingston, where he remained till the dusk of the evening, and proceeded to London in the stage.

Soon after his arrival, he waited upon the gentleman in the city, and informed him of having been under the necessity of burning the bills upon, and letters to, him from Silas Dean. The gentleman behaved to him with shyness, but appointed to meet him at a coffee-house. At the coffee-house the gentleman seemed to be doubtful as to the story told by Acksan, who therefore went away displeased, and as soon as he reached Hammersmith wrote to the merchant, saying he was going to Bristol, and that the " handy works" he meant to perform there would be soon known to the public.

Soon after his arrival at Bristol, he set fire to several houses, which all were burning with great rapidity at one time, and the flames were not extinguished till damage was sustained to the amount of fifteen thousand pounds. He also set fire to combustibles that he had placed among a number of oil barrels upon the quay, but happily without effect. He related to Baldwin a great number of other circumstances, which were confirmed by a variety of evidence on the trial.

James Russel produced a tin case and a wooden box made to fit each other, containing combustibles,

bles, which he swore he found in the hemp-house at Portsmouth.

William Tench, apprentice to a tinman at Canterbury, deposed, that about a month or six weeks before Christmas he made the tin case produced by Russel, by the order and under the immediate inspection of the prisoner.

Elizabeth Boxall swore that the prisoner lodged at her house on the night preceding that on which the fire happened, and that in the morning she perceived a violent smell of sulphur, and going into the prisoner's room complained that she was fearful he would set fire to her house; that he left a bundle, which she opened and found to contain a tin case; and being shewn the cannister produced by Russel, she believed it to be the same.

Mrs. Cole swore that the prisoner took a lodging at her house, and left there a bundle * containing some books and other things, which she delivered to Mr. Jeffrey, clerk to the commissioner of the dock.

John Fisher, servant to Mr. Tuck, tinman at Canterbury, deposed, that about six or seven weeks before Christmas the prisoner came to his master's shop, and gave orders for two tin cases, but that, not being finished at the time he had appointed to call for them, they were left on his master's hands. Fisher produced one of the cases, which was found to correspond with that found in the hemp-house.

William Baldy and William Weston swore, that they saw and conversed with the prisoner in the hemp-house at Portsmouth on the 7th of December.

---

* This bundle contained the books, the French passport, &c. which the prisoner mentioned to Baldwin.

Anne

Anne Hopkins deposed that about four, or half past four, of the day on which the fire happened at Portsmouth-dock, the prisoner overtook her near the Flying-bull at Cosham, and saying he was going to Petersfield, and feared he should be benighted, desired she would allow him to ride part of the way in her cart, and gave her sixpence in order that she might drive quick; and that, when she came within sight of her house, he leaped out of the cart, and took the road leading to London.

Anne Gentle swore, that on the day before the fire at Portsmouth the prisoner bought a half-penny worth of matches at her shop on Portsmouth Common; and John Hillingdon swore that, as far as he could judge from human probability, the prisoner was the man to whom he sold two ounces of spirits of turpentine, and a quarter of a pound of salt-petre, either three or four days before or after the 20th of November.

Mary Bishop deposed, that some time between Michaelmas and Christmas the prisoner came to her house in Canterbury, and asked whether she could procure a wooden thing to be made for him. Being shewn the wooden box found with the tin case in the hemp-house, she said she saw a thing like it brought to the prisoner by Mr. Ormisham's apprentice, who was since dead.

John Dobby, who apprehended the prisoner, declared that he found in his custody the following articles; a snuff-box containing tinder, a small powder horn with gunpowder, a striking tinder-box primed, a phial half full of spirits of turpentine, a parcel of matches, and some other things not of a suspicious nature.

Thomas Mason, a painter near Bristol, swore that the day after Christmas day the prisoner came to his house and asked leave to grind a small quantity of charcoal; that he directed him to his colour-stone, on which he worked about two hours in grinding a piece of charcoal about the size of two of his fingers.

The bundle left by the prisoner at Mrs. Cole's was then produced; and the clerk informed the court that it contained a loaded pistol, a French passport, and some books, the titles of which he read.

The Court then informed the prisoner that the evidence against him was closed, and called upon him for his defence. He called no witnesses, but addressed the court two or three times, and proposed some questions to Baldwin, but he said nothing tending to invalidate the charge against him.

The judge then summed up the evidence in the most clear, circumstantial, and candid manner that can be imagined; and the jury pronounced him guilty; in consequence of which, the judge addressed him in a manner truly pathetic, reminding him of the shocking enormity of his crime, which was of such a nature as would not admit the possibility of his sentence being reversed, and exhorting him to exert his utmost endeavours that the eternity he was to enter upon in a few days might prove " an " eternity of bliss instead of misery." The prisoner said he entertained " no hopes of pardon, but " was willing to die, more so than to live."

This malefactor was tried at Winchester-castle on Thursday the 6th of March, 1777, before the right honourable Sir William Henry Ashurst, Knt. and Sir Beaumon Hotham, Knt.

James Acklan was executed at Portsmouth on the 10th of March, 1777.

During

New Newgate Calendar or Malefactor's Register.

View of the JUSTITIA HULK, with the Convicts at Work, near Woolwich.

During a residence of some years in America, Ackfan imbibed principles incompatible with the interests of this country. His case affords a striking instance of the extravagant lengths to which people may be transported by party zeal. Not influenced by private malignancy, or avaricious motives, he formed the desperate resolution of committing a crime of such horrid enormity as not to admit the possiblity of any kind of aggravation; and this resolution he, in some degree, effected. Had his diabolical purpose been attended with the full success he expected, long ere this Great Britain would, in all probability, have lost her national importance, and been reduced to a state of the most abject slavery to foreign and despotic powers.

Though Ackfan aimed at involving every individual of these kingdoms in immediate and general destruction, christian charity should induce us to hope that he followed the advice of the learned judge in endeavouring to make the eternity that awaited him " an eternity of bliss instead of mi-
" sery."

Particulars of the Examination, Commitment, and Trial, of DAVID BROWN DIGNAN, who was convicted of a Fraud, and sentenced to labour on the Thames.

ON Wednesday the 13th of March, 1777, this offender was brought to the office in Bow-street, when Mr. John Clark deposed, that between the 18th of June, and the 8th of July preceding, he paid the prisoner £1002 1 0 as a gratuity for invest-

investing him with the office of clerk of the minutes in his majesty's custm-house in Dublin; that the abovementioned sum was paid at different times in cash and drafts; and that the drafts were duly honoured by the parties on whom they were drawn. Mr. Clark produced a stamped paper bearing the signature of lord Weymouth, and countersigned Thomas Daw, which he deposed to have received from the prisoner as a legal warrant appointing him to the office in question. Mr. Daw proved that the signature of lord Weymouth and his own name were counterfeited; and it evidently appeared that the seals had been taken from some instrument, and affixed to the pretended warrant.

Dignan was charged with a similar offence by Mr. Brown, from whom he obtained £1000, under pretence of causing him to be appointed writer of the London Gazette. Mr. Brown produced a warrant bearing the similar marks of imposition with those exhibited in the former charge:—this gentleman likewise produced a letter, given to him by the prisoner, ordering Mr. Harrison, the printer of the Gazette, to act under the direction of Mr. Brown; and likewise an oath of qualification taken by him in presence of the prisoner.

After a very deliberate consideration of these circumstances, the magistrates were of opinion that Dignan's offence was not within the description of the laws respecting forgery: he was therefore committed to Tothill-fields bridewell, to take his trial for the frauds.

The prisoner, by way of defence, said that, on suspicion of his having been guilty of high treason, his papers had been seized, and were in the possession of Sir Alexander Leith; adding that some writings among them would fully exculpate him

him from the charges adduced against him. Sir Alexander ordered his trunk to be brought into the office, and all such papers as were not considered as matter of evidence were returned to him.

On the 5th of April, 1777, David Brown Dignan was indicted at Guildhall, Westminster, for defrauding Mr. Clarke of £700*, under pretence of appointing him clerk of the minutes in the customhouse, at Dublin, by means of a forged warrant pretended to be signed by lord Weymouth and Mr. Daw. The evidence against him was in substance what we have already related; and the jury found him guilty, without leaving the court.

The magistrates hesitated a long time on what punishment should be inflicted on so atrocious an offender; and at length sentenced him to work five years on the river Thames.

Dignan had carried on a still more atrocious traffic than that for which he was convicted. Not long before he was detected, he called at the house of lord Suffolk, requesting an interview on business of an important nature. His lordship admitted him to a private audience; when Mr. Dignan disclosed his purpose to the following effect: he said that he had unhappily engaged in a conspiracy, with some gentlemen of rank and fortune, to shoot the King; and he had the audacity to mention the names of several gentlemen of rank and fortune, particularly the Duke of Richmond, the Earl of Shelburne, and the Aldermen Sawbridge and Lee, &c. as being among the number of the conspirators.

---

* Mr. Clark's charge was for £1002 1 0; but indictments are seldom laid to the full amount of the injury sustained.

He even went farther than this: he talked of the time and place where the suppofed treafonable confultations were held. He pretended that the ftings of confcience had occafioned a remorfe in his mind; and that he had made fo ample a confeffion, as the only atonement in his power for having engaged in fo villainous a confpiracy.

Lord Suffolk with great prudence urged him to make oath of the particulars; but this Dignan declined, faying " that, as the fcheme was not yet " ripe for execution, no inconvenience could " therefore enfue from the delay. The confpira- " tors (he faid) were to meet that evening; and " the next morning he would wait on his lordfhip, " to give him information of every particular " which paffed at the meeting."

Dignan returned to lord Suffolk at the appointed time, when he was urged to make a full difclofure of the affair. He then defired a procraftination of one day only; and faid that on the next he would fwear to every particular he had related.

Juftly fufpicious that Dignan had no good intention, his lordfhip had employed perfons to watch his motions; but he was traced only to the ftews of debauchery: and the gentlemen charged with the confpiracy were likewife furrounded, unknown to themfelves, by a group of obfervers.

From the characters of the gentlemen accufed, and that of the accufer, and from all the circumftances that had paffed, lord Suffolk was convinced that the former were totally innocent, and that the latter was a villain. When, therefore, Dignan waited on his lordfhip for the laft time, the fecretary was prefent. The fcoundrel was charged with his baseness in explicit terms. He appeared to be confounded; his voice faultered, he turned pale, and was evidently self-convicted.

On Wednesday the 23d of April, 1777, Mr. Smith, governor of Tothill-fields bridewell, requested the advice of the magistrates at Bow-street, as to the disposal of Dignan. He said he had received an order for removing the prisoner to the ballast-lighter, pursuant to the sentence passed on him by the magistrates of Middlesex and Westminster at the Guildhall; but that the solicitor in a prosecution cognizable by the magistrates usually presiding at Hicks's Hall, had given him notice to detain the prisoner in custody till an Habeas Corpus should be procured to bring him for trial before the last mentioned magistrates. The bench agreed in opinion, that as Tothill-fields bridewell was a county gaol, the Middlesex magistrates would have been justifiable in claiming the appearance of the prisoner without the authority of an Habeas Corpus; and they commissioned Mr. Smith to remove Dignan on the first opportunity.

Mr. Smith said that on the same evening or the next morning he would endeavour to get rid of such a troublesome guest, who had suggested a variety of stratagems to obtain his liberty; adding, that on the Saturday morning preceding he had offered to bribe an attendant in the prison with a bank note of ten pounds, to favour his escape in a large chest.

No time was now lost in conveying Dignan on board the ballast-lighter. Being possessed of plenty of money, and having high notions of gentility, he went to Woolwich in a post-chaise, with his Negro-servant behind, expecting that his money would procure every indulgence in his favour, and

and that his servant would be still admitted to attend him; but in this he was egregiously mistaken;—the keepers of the lighter would not permit the Negro to come on board; and Dignan was immediately put to the duty of the wheelbarrow.

On Monday the 5th of May Dignan sent a forged draft for 500£. for acceptance to Mr. Drummond, Banker, at Charing-cross, who, discovering the imposition, carried the publishers before Sir John Fielding; but they were discharged; and it was intended to procure an Habeas Corpus to remove Dignan to London for examination.

This plan, however, was soon seen through; for on consideration it seemed evident that Dignan, by sending the forged draft from on board the lighter, preferred death to his situation *; so that no farther steps were taken in the affair; and Mr. Dignan yet † remains a victim to the equitable laws of his country.

This man had been genteelly born and educated; and his vices, his contrivances, his unwarrantable artifices alone, reduced him to a situation which the meanest beggar would not envy.—It is unnecessary to caution our young readers from treading in his steps; because whoever should do so would infallibly meet with the most disgraceful punishment, and general detestation.

---

* Is not this a kind of proof of the excellence of the plan for punishment by ballast-heaving?

† In March 1779.

An Account of the Trial of RALPH CUTLER, who was charged with having committed a Rape, and acquitted.

AT the sessions held at the Old Bailey in September, 1777, Ralph Cutler was indicted for committing a rape on Mary the wife of Thomas Bradley, on the 16th of July preceding.

Mrs. Bradley lived in Red Lion Alley, Cowcross: her husband was what she called an auctioneer and appraiser; but his principal business was keeping possession of effects in houses under commissions of bankrupt.

Mrs. Bradley used to frequent the Merlin's Cave, a reputable public house in Spa-fields, Clerkenwell, where, as it appears, she became acquainted with Mr. Cutler; and it is probable that their connexion was of a very intimate kind.

Mrs. Bradley spent the evening of the 15th of July at Merlin's Cave, where after supping with some company in the garden, she went into the house, at the request of Cutler (as she says), to hear some women sing. The company went away about half past twelve; and all of them parted at the Cold-bath in Cold-bath-fields, except one lady, who went with Mr. Cutler and Mrs. Bradley to Brook-street, Holborn, where she likewise left them. Cutler now asked Mrs. Bradley to drink a glass of wine: she refused; but they went to her house, out of their regular road near half a mile: he followed her into the house; and a woman, who was attending Mrs. Bradley's children, then went away, and left the parties together.

Mrs. Bradley deposed, that, when the woman was gone, Cutler effected his purpose, by committing

ting an absolute rape on her in the kitchen; that she threatened to acquaint her husband with what had passed, and insisted on his going out of the house immediately; that in the interim two of her children being crying in the bed, she went up to them, but then coming down, she went up again with some drink which Cutler advised her to give to the children. Cutler followed her *, locked the door, and a second time committed the fact for which he was indicted.

She further deposed, that he insisted with an oath, that she should go to bed, and helped to undress her; that he lay an hour and an half in the bed, and then went down stairs, and she thought he was going away; that she went down afterwards, found him in the kitchen, and informed him that she would acquaint her husband how ill she had been treated.

On the following morning, Mr. Hamley, a relation of her husband, called on her; but what was presumed to pass on this visit will best appear from an abstract of Hamley's evidence on the trial.

He deposed in substance, that he called on Mrs. Bradley on the 16th of July; that she said she was not well, but desired him to stay, as she had something particular to communicate. She told him she had been at Merlin's Cave on the preceding evening, and mentioned her company; told him that Cutler came home with her against her remonstrances to the contrary, and that he perpetrated the fact as abovementioned. That Hamley

---

* We must remember that this is *her* evidence. We shall see how far it was credited.

told her " if she would defer going to her husband
" till the afternoon, he should be glad to meet her
" on Blackfriars-bridge, and take a walk into St.
" George's Fields." They met accordingly. Hamley said his motive was " to see, if possible, whe-
" ther there had been any intimacy before;" that
he asked her whether they had ever been together
before, but that she declared she had been innocent from first to last.

Hamley and Mrs. Bradley took a walk to
John o'Grote's house*, in St. George's Fields,
whence they returned to London; and Hamley
then leaving her, called at her house about nine
o'clock the same evening, to see if Cutler was in
her company; but no Mr. Cutler was to be
found.

The prisoner declaring that he left his defence
to his counsel, Caroline Taylor, who used to sell
fruit at Merlin's Cave in the summer, deposed, that
she knew the prosecutrix, and had attended her as
a nurse to her child; that Mrs. Bradley came to
the Cave the evening after the rape was supposed
to have been committed, and asked her (Taylor)
if she had seen Mr. Cutler.

This witness deposed that Mrs. Bradley was a famous skittle-player; that she had frequently seen
her and Cutler play together; and that she would
challenge any one to play at skittles.

This witness deposed, that Mr. Hamley frequently visited Mrs. Bradley, and that he sometimes staid till late hours; and that a Mr. Robinson had slept in the house a whole night, in Mr.
Bradley's absence. Being asked if she thought

---

* A public-house, famous for selling ale.

Mrs. Bradley a modest or immodest woman, she replied, "she cannot be very modest, when at all "times she would go out and come home at all "hours when I was there, and sometimes very "much in liquor."

It was enquired if she had seen her with other men besides her husband. Her reply was, "Yes, "that I have, divers of times, when her husband "was not at home at all, and men have laid in the "house when he was not at home." Being farther asked if she thought Mrs. Bradley an immodest woman, she answered "I don't know what "you call a modest woman, if you call that one."

Sarah Cooke, who had been servant at Merlin's Cave, proved that Mrs. Bradley called at the house on the evening after the presumed rape, and enquired for Cutler, who, she said, had promised to meet her there.

Mr. John Bates gave evidence still more conclusive against the character of the prosecutrix. Being asked if he remembered, when he was in the room in the evening with Bradley and Cutler, that the former laid a wager about any thing, he replied in the following terms; "No; but I remember "another circumstance which is rather more singu"lar; this was, Cutler was asked to sing a song, "which he frequently did; so he begins and sings "a bit; *by G—— (says he) I can neither sing nor do* "*any thing else:*—she took notice of it; she goes "out, and takes him with her into the passage be"tween the two rooms, and she comes in again, "and said that Mr. Cutler was fineable for what "he had said."

Mr. Bates farther said, that the company desired the ladies, who were four in number, to withdraw, to bring in the verdict, and that they retired into
another

another room. On their return a *foreman* was fixed on; and Mrs. Bradley was this foreman, who delivered a verdict that Mr. Cutler was fineable a bottle of ale; and the ale was called for, and he paid for it, " because he was not incapable."

This cause was tried before Mr. justice Gould, who, after Mr. Bates had given his testimony, said, " Gentlemen of the jury, you have heard this evi-
" dence so far; if you desire it, I shall sum up the
" evidence." — The jury replied, " We will not
" trouble your lordship, we are *very well satisfied,*
" and immediately acquitted the prisoner."

The writer of this well remembers that, when the charge was first made against Cutler before the magistrates in Bow-street, no person gave credit to the testimony of Mrs. Bradley; but, as the charge was positive, the magistrates were under the necessity of committing Mr. Cutler.

The issue of the trial seems to prove, that the jury had good sense enough to distinguish between a criminal intimacy with the wife of another man, and the perpetration of so horrid a crime as a rape. Mr. Bradley had for some time a confidence in the innocence of his wife: and perhaps it would have been happier for all parties if that confidence had been well-founded.

From this tale let it be learnt, that fidelity to the marriage-bed is one of the first duties of those who are bound together by one of the most sacred of all bonds; a bond founded equally in nature, in sound policy, in reason, and in religion.

The man and woman, who, united in wedlock, desert each other, who make separate interests, and seek to be happy independent of the original object of their choice, generally bring down misery on on their own heads, becoming wretched by the very means they seek to make themseves happy.

Account of the Trial of Mr. JOHN HARRISON, who was convicted of Forgery, but afterwards received His Majesty's Pardon.

MR. Harrison was accountant to the London assurance corporation; and it was his peculiar misfortune to be acquainted with a Mr. Angus Mackey, a merchant in the city in an extensive way of trade, who, by urgent solicitations, prevailed upon the unsuspecting and good-natured man to lend him several sums belonging to the company, solemnly promising to return the money before he would have occasion to make up his accounts.

When the time appointed for the first payment arrived, instead of returning what he had already got into his possession, Mackey urged Harrison for a further supply, assuring him that he was in daily expectation of remittances, on the receipt of which he would return the whole sum that Harrison was deficient in his account with the company; adding that, if he met with a refusal, he must inevitably stop payment, which would necessarily occasion an exposure of Harrison's violation of the trust reposed in him by the company.

In this manner was the unfortunate man amused for several months, during which time he supplied Mackey with different sums, amounting in the whole to £.7550; and, to prevent detection, he inserted figures in the book containing the account
between

between the bank of England and the London assurance company, so that the bank appeared to be debtor for £.7550 more than had been paid there.

He sent a clerk with £.210 to the bank; and, when the book was returned to him, he put a figure of 3 before the 2, which made the sum appear £.3000 more than was really paid; and similar alterations were made in other parts of the book.

A committee of the company being appointed to meet on Wednesday the 9th of July, 1777, Mr. Harrison mentioned the circumstance to Mackey, and told him that he must be utterly ruined unless the deficiency in the company's cash was made good before that day: but, notwithstanding the life and reputation of his generous and imprudent friend were at stake, he neglected to return the money.

About eleven in the forenoon of the day on which the committee was to be held, Harrison placed several account-books on the table of the committee-room, and had some conversation with Alexander Aubert, Esquire, the deputy-governor. When the committee was about to be opened, Harrison absconded; and, in about ten minutes after, the following letter was received by Mr. George Hall, secretary to the company:

"Dear Sir,

"I am distressed beyond expression, having for-
"feited every thing that is dear to me, by an act
"of kindness to a friend who has deceived me: in-
"closed is a state of my account with the company,
"which tortures my very soul to think of it. I
"know

" know the treasury will not forgive me, therefore
" don't care what becomes of me, as I dare not see
" them any more. God Almighty knows what
" will become of me, or where I shall fly for suc-
" cour: indeed, Mr. Hall, I am one of the most mi-
" serable wretches living, but I have betrayed my
" trust, for which I never can forgive myself.
" When I parted with the money, it was but for a
" few days, or I would sooner have died than have
" parted with it; but, alas! I shall now severely
" pay by suffering myself to be drawn in to serve a
" friend, who knew it was not my own, and saw
" the distress of mind it cost me when I did it.
" Please to present my humble duty to the gentle-
" men; tell them I can meet any death after this,
" sooner than I can see them again, and am deter-
" mined not to survive the shame: I am, dear sir,
" a lost, unhappy being; I am so bewildered, that I
" scarce know what I am doing, but believe the in-
" closed account is not right, as I don't recollect
" that I am any way short of cash; but in truth
" I am not myself.

"J. H."

When Harrison absconded, he left upwards of £.1900 in his desk, and among his papers were found securities on behalf of the company to a great amount, besides a bond given to him by Mackey for £.7550.

Notice being given at the office that Harrison was at a friend's house at Wapping, Mr. Aubert went there in the evening, and found him in a state of mind little short of distraction. Mackey's bond was produced by Mr. Aubert, and Harrison assigned it over to him as a security on behalf of the company. He accompanied Mr. Aubert to the office,

office, where two persons were ordered to attend him and prevent his putting an end to his life, which there was sufficient reason to suppose he would attempt; and the next morning he was taken before Sir John Fielding, who committed him to Tothill-fields bridewell. He was re-examined the following Wednesday, and committed to Newgate in preparation for his trial.

Harrison was tried at the Old Bailey in the September sessions, 1777, on an indictment for forgery, consisting of twenty-four counts, on twelve of which the jury pronounced him guilty. The prisoner's counsel objected to judgment being passed, on account of a supposed inaccuracy in the indictment, and the matter was left to be argued by the judges.

Having remained in Newgate some months after his trial, Mr. Harrison petitioned for the judges to meet; and that he might be heard by counsel. He was advised by an illustrious personage to waive the plea on which his petition was founded, and in consequence thereof the petition was immediately withdrawn. In a few days a messenger came to Newgate, and delivered Mr. Harrison the agreeable news that his Majesty had been graciously pleased to grant him an unconditional pardon; and the same evening an order was delivered to Mr. Akerman for his immediate enlargement.

Mr. Harrison was brought up in a merchant's counting-house, and soon after the expiration of his apprenticeship he began business on his own account, and had a lime and a coal wharf at Limehouse, where he carried on an extensive trade; but failing in that business, he engaged himself as a clerk to Mr. Smithen, previous to that gentleman's undertaking to construct the Eddiston light-house, and was entrusted with the care and management of all the money employed in that important work. His conduct under Mr. Smithen was in every respect unexceptionable; and that gentleman and many other respectable persons used their interest to procure him the office of accountant to the London assurance company, in whose service he would in all probability have continued till his death, but for his unhappy connexion with Mackey.

Harrison had been accountant to the London assurance company nineteen years and a half, when it was discovered that he had betrayed the confidence reposed in him; and till that period his character was without a blemish, and he was held in the highest esteem by all his acquaintance.

It is beyond dispute that Harrison entertained not the least intention to defraud, and that he meant to replace the money. He is still living, and finds the loss of a handsome income, reputation, and health (which, was greatly impaired during his confinement) a severe punishment for one act of indiscretion in which all the misfortunes of his life have their origin.

May the case of this man prove a warning to others who are employed in offices of trust. Let them remember, that in such men as can be guilty of persuading them to violate the confidence reposed in them no reliance can with safety be placed; that if they once give reason for an impeachment of their integrity, they will be constantly under the tormenting apprehensions of a discovery, which, if they happen to escape an ignominious death, will reduce them to poverty and disgrace.

An Account of the Trial and Execution of the Reverend BENJAMIN RUSSEN, who was hanged for committing a Rape.

THIS man was master of the subscription charity-school at Bethnal-green, in which had been bred up a poor girl named Anne Mayne.

At the sessions held at the Old Bailey in October 1777, Benjamin Russen, clerk, was indicted for having committed a rape on the said Anne Mayne on the 18th of June preceding. The girl deposed, that when Mrs. Russen lay-in, the prisoner desired that she (Mayne) might stay below stairs with him, while he went to sleep after dinner, lest he should fall into the fire; and that he took this opportunity to perpetrate the fact with which he was charged, and, after it was committed said that if she told her mother, sister, or any body of it, he would flog her severely.

She proved a second commission of a similar fact, during which he looked out at the door, in apprehension that somebody was coming; but this did not happen to be the case. It appeared, likewise, that the crime was committed a third time; but it would be indelicate in the highest degree to recount the particulars of a fact of this nature.

A surgeon, who was present when Mr. Russen was carried before Justice Wilmot, deposed that, on examination of the girl, he did not discover that any absolute violence had been committed.

There were three other indictments against Russen of a similar nature, but he was acquitted of them all. He now proceeded to call several persons to his character, who spoke well of him as far as they knew.

In his defence he denied the fact, and pleaded the malice of his enemies, who, he said, had charged him with those offences to deprive him of his place. He urged the favourable representation of the surgeon, who had sworn that the child had not been materially injured; and insisted that the time the fact was charged to have been committed he was so ill as to keep his chamber.

By endeavouring to prove this he proved too much; for the witness swore that he kept his chamber two months successively, contrary to the tenor of all the other witnesses; so that the jury were induced to think that he had not kept his chamber even one month.

The counsel for the prisoner laboured hard to adduce some proofs of his innocence; but the jury brought in a verdict that the prisoner was guilty, in consequence of which he received sentence of death.

After conviction, the behaviour of Mr. Russen was exceedingly proper for a man in his unhappy situation. No very extraordinary exertions were made to obtain a pardon for him, because it was presumed it would not have been granted.

On the morning of execution Mr. Russen was taken from Newgate to Tyburn in a mourning-coach. Just before he left the prison, seeing a number of people about him, he made use of this emphatical expression, " Stand clear, look to your- " selves; I am the first Hypocrite in Sion." The parting scene between himself and his son was extremely affecting.

He was attended in the coach by the Ordinary of Newgate, the Reverend Mr. Hughes, a sheriff's officer, and an undertaker who had engaged to take care of the funeral.

At the place of execution Ruffen seemed to have a proper sense of his past wicked life; but in regard to the crime for which he suffered, he thought himself ill-treated, as he always asserted that he had never been guilty of a rape, though he acknowledged, a day or two before his death, that he had taken liberties with the child which were highly unbecoming. Previous to the prayers commonly made at the place of execution, he made a long extempore prayer, and earnestly exhorted the surrounding multitude to take warning by his fate. He likewise censured the indecency of the people who stood near the gallows with their hats on, and with apparent unconcern, during the time of prayer; and observed, that the place where unhappy victims are to suffer the sentence of the law should be held as sacred as a church. He therefore requested the spectators to be uncovered, and to join in their supplications for him to Almighty God, which accordingly several of them complied with; and after having prayed for his wife and helpless children, he once more recommended his soul to the mercy of God, and was then launched into eternity.

On the way to execution the mob insulted Ruffen, but the propriety of his behaviour at the fatal tree had an evident effect on the spectators; and when his body was cut down, it was put into a hearse, and delivered to his friends for interment.

Benjamin Ruffen was executed at Tyburn on the 12th of December, 1777.

It is with pain that the pen of delicacy touches a subject of this nature; and this pain is increased, when we consider that the object of our remarks was in a line of life that ought to have induced him to set the best example to others. A clergyman who is a schoolmaster is bound by a double tie to

exhibit

exhibit every mark of his attention to the duties of religion and, morality; and, when he fails of this duty, his example is presumed to have a worse influence than that of a man in another line of life.

Mr. Russen had a wife and six children, which was no slight aggravation of his crime. Soon after his execution, some benevolent gentlemen caused advertisements to be inserted in the news-papers, soliciting charity for the unhappy widow, to enable her to get into some way of business. How far this succeeded is uncertain; but some subscriptions were raised for their immediate use.

From this sad tale the necessity of keeping a constant guard over our passions is obviously enforced; and we hope those may be actuated by it, on whom the superior obligations of religion might fail to have their proper weight.

A compleat Account of the Life, Trial, Conviction, and Execution, of Thomas Sherwood, *who suffered for Forgery.*

THOMAS SHERWOOD was the son of very worthy and respectable parents, and born at Newbury in Berkshire about the year 1735. From his infancy till he attained the age of fourteen years, he was distinguished by the gentleness of his disposition, and the complacency of his manners.

At the age above-mentioned he was sent to London, and apprenticed to Mr. Sanderson, a salesman in Houndsditch. He served his time with a degree of diligence and fidelity, that should furnish an example to other servants.

After

After his time was expired he succeeded his master in the business, which he carried on with the highest degree of reputation till within a year of the time of his fatal exit. Perhaps Mr. Sherwood thought himself sure of continued success; for he embarked in a scheme of building, which involved him in distress, and led, with certain and rapid steps, to his ruin.

A commission of bankrupt being issued against Mr. Sherwood in the beginning of December, 1777, he absconded, and went to Dover, with a view of escaping to France, conscious, as it was presumed, that his papers would lead to a discovery of the forgery: but a description of his person having been given at Sir John Fielding's office, he was followed to Dover by Mr. Clarke, who met with him waiting for the sailing of a vessel, and brought him to town on the 22d of the month, and he was committed, after a private examination.

On the 27th he was re-examined before Sir John Fielding, when it seemed to appear that, by means of a forged letter of attorney in the joint names of the Reverend Messrs. Myonnet and French, he had sold out stock in the three per cent. bank consolidated annuities, to the amount of 700 *l*. and in the south sea house 800 *l*. under the same forged power. Some other circumstances arose in the course of this examination, which will more fully appear in the following narrative of his trial.

Sherwood being committed to Newgate, was indicted at the sessions held at the Old Bailey in February, 1778, for feloniously forging and counterfeiting a deed with the names of John Myonnet, D. D. and James French, thereunto subscribed, purporting to be a letter of attorney, bearing date the 3d day of April, 1777, &c.

As we have not had an opportunity in the course of this work, of recording an instrument of this kind, we give the following as a specimen;—a specimen not to be *copied*, but *avoided*.

"Know all men, by these presents, that we, the Reverend John Myonnet, of Coney-court, Gray's-Inn, D. D. and the Reverend James French, of Bow, do make, constitute, and appoint, Thomas Sherwood, of Houndsditch, Draper, our true and lawful attorney, for us, in our names, and on our behalf, to sell, assign, and transfer, all, or any part of seven hundred pounds; being all our joint interest, or share, in the capital, or joint stock of three per cent. annuities, erected by an act of parliament of the 25th year of the reign of his Majesty King George II. intitled, an act for converting the several annuities therein mentioned into several joint-stocks of annuities, transferrable at the bank of England, to be charged on the sinking fund, and by several subsequent acts; also to receive the consideration money, and give a receipt, or receipts, for the same; and to do all lawful acts requisite for effecting the premises; hereby ratifying and confirming all that our said attorney shall do therein, by virtue thereof. In witness whereof we have hereunto set our hands and seals, the 3d day of April, in the year of our Lord one thousand seven hundred and seventy-seven.

John Myonnet, D. D. (L. S.)
James French,———— (L. S.)

"Signed, sealed, and delivered (the paper being first duly stamped) in the presence of us,
"*Thomas Hewlett*, Salesman, Houndsditch.
"*Francis Sherwood*, Salesman, Houndsditch."

Mr. Silvester, of counsel for the prosecution, having opened the indictment, Counsellor Wallace proceeded, and enlarged on the business, stating to the jury, that the prisoner married the daughter of a Mr. Thomas Hewlett, who lived at Westham, in Essex; that, in the year 1768, Mr. Hewlett having agreed on a marriage with a Mrs. Drathgate, and she being possessed of consolidated three per cent. annuities, and also three per cent. reduced annuities, it was agreed, previous to the marriage, that her interests in these stocks should be settled upon certain trusts, and conveyed to Dr. Myonnet and Mr. French, as trustees.

Mrs. Drathgate having conveyed the said stock in trust to the gentlemen above-mentioned, the marriage took place; and the trustees afterwards made out a letter of attorney, to enable Mr. Sherwood to receive the dividends, and to apply it to the use of the trusts.

Mr. Hewlett dying about three years before Sherwood's misfortunes, the latter received the dividends for the use of the widow. At length, to accommodate Mr. Sherwood, she agreed to sell out the reduced annuities; and the two trustees executed a letter of attorney, to enable him so to do. When Sherwood became a bankrupt, suspicions arose that he had likewise sold out the consolidated bank annuities; and when Mr. French enquired at the bank, he found that the said annuities had been transferred.

It appeared that the prisoner had applied to Mr. Nesbit, a broker, to sell the stock under the forged letter of attorney; and that the subscribing witnesses were Thomas Hewlett, Salesman, of Houndsditch, and Francis Sherwood, Salesman, of Houndsditch.

How thefe fubfcriptions were obtained to the lette of attorney will hereafter appear.

The fact is this: the fubfcribers were both of them related to, and lived with, the prifoner, who defired them to fet their names as witneffes to the letter of attorney, though in truth they had neither of them feen it executed by Dr. Myonnet or Mr. French. There is not the leaft probability that the fubfcribers believed they were doing a wrong thing; they figned it as a matter of courfe.

The transferring of the ftock was proved by Mr. Stonehoufe, an accountant at the bank. Mr. Nefbit, the Stock-broker, proved the felling it, and paying the money to Mr. Sherwood; and likewife proved that he faw the prifoner make the transfer; and the inftrument, being produced, was proved to be that under which Mr. Sherwood acted as attorney.

The counfel for the crown calling for the evidence of the rev. Mr. French, the prifoner's counfel objected to his examination, as he was an interefted witnefs; on which Mr. Robert Lewin, fecretary to the bank, began to read from the minute-book of the court of directors as follows:—
" At a court of directors, at the bank, on Thurf-
" day the 15th of January, 1778, Mr. Governor
" acquainted the court that"—

Here the prifoner's counfel objected to the reading the minute, as it was intended to be read for the purpofe of fhewing that Mr. French was a difinterefted witnefs, by proving that the court of directors had replaced the ftock, fo that it was indifferent to Mr. French whether the inftrument was valid, or a forged one.

This objection was over-ruled by the court, on the principle, that, if the prifoner fhould be convicted
of

of the forgery, the bank could never have the money back again, and therefore the company were in the strongest degree proving against their own interests.

On this Mr. Lewin proceeded to read the remainder of the minute, in the following words — " that " the committee of treasury have power to make good " to the said Dr. Myonnet and the reverend Mr. " French the said sum of 700*l*. consolidated three " *per cent*. annuities."

There was a variety of concurrent evidence unhappily combining to prove the guilt of the prisoner, who, being asked if he would say any thing in his defence, replied " I refer it to my counsel."

On this his advocate said, " I wish him to be in- " formed that the counsel cannot speak for him. " If Mr. Sherwood will urge what he has to say " for himself, if that furnishes a hint for his " counsel, they will pursue it."

The prisoner then spoke as follows. " The " power of attorney for selling 700*l*. three *per* " *cent*. reduced annuities, was signed by Mr. " French at a butcher's shop in Whitechapel; " there was nobody present but him and me at " the time he signed: that upon reading it over, " he said *this should be witnessed at the time of* " *signing*. I told him I supposed that was nothing " but matter of form; I would get it signed; he " said nothing more, and departed."

A number of witnesses were present, to prove, if it had been necessary, the general good character of the prisoner: but this was needless; it could have no weight in a case of this nature against such positive testimony, and was still the less necessary, because no tradesman, no merchant in London, ever bore a fairer character than the unhappy Sherwood, till this fatal deviation from the rule of duty.

Mr. Justice Ashurst having summed up the evidence to the Jury, they retired for a short time, and then returned with a verdict that he was "guilty of uttering and publishing the letter of attorney knowing it to be forged."

On the last day of the sessions Mr. Sherwood was put to the bar, and received sentence of death. His behaviour, both before and after conviction, was exemplary in the highest degree: — decent, modest, pious, and resigned. The assignees under the commission of bankruptcy attended in Newgate, where he made a full and ample disclosure of his estate and effects, with a degree of candour that was spoken of at the time in terms of the highest praise.

Mr. Sherwood was indulged with a mourning coach to the place of execution; and, when he came within sight of the fatal tree, he said, "this is the method God hath taken to bring me to himself." After hanging the usual time, his body was delivered to his friends; and he was interred, two days afterwards, in the burial-ground in Bunhill-fields.

Thomas Sherwood was executed at Tyburn on the 22d of May, 1778.

This unhappy man left a wife and six children. We are told that he was a liveryman of the Drapers company; and that one of their alms-houses near Tower Hill was soon afterwards bestowed on the widow, which affords her an humble subsistance.

From this melancholy tale we should learn to admire the wisdom of those laws which have been framed for the protection of property: but, at the

the same time, we should consider that no one has a right to invade the property of another.

There was not a man in England who bore a more unblemished character than Sherwood till distress of money urged him to commit the crime which ended so fatally. A resolution, therefore, to abide by the laws of rigid honesty, in all contingencies, is the great lesson to be learnt from the above affecting narrative.

A Narrative of the Trial of PETER CEPPI, otherwise SCIPIO, who was convicted of maliciously shooting at HENRIETTA KNIGHTLEY.

AT the sessions held at the Old Bailey in February, 1778, Peter Ceppi, otherwise Scipio, was indicted for maliciously, &c. shooting at Henrietta Knightley, with a pistol loaded with gunpowder and a leaden bullet, in the dwelling-house of James Draper, &c.

The prisoner, being a foreigner, was allowed a jury of half Foreigners and half Englishmen; and, not perfectly understanding our language, an interpreter was sworn.

Henrietta Knightley deposed, that the prisoner came to her lodgings between ten and eleven in the morning of the 18th of January, and entering her room, while she was in bed, said, *he was come to do her business*, or words to that effect. He desired her to get out of bed:—she did so; he pulled two pistols from his pocket, but returned one; she went towards the door, with a view to get out. He stood with his back to the door: she asked him to go out, and eat some breakfast with her: he answered, *he would have no breakfast, he would give her a good one.* She then called to Mrs. Robinson, who was in care of the house, and told her that the man had a pistol. The prisoner immediately cocked his pistol, which the prosecutrix desired him to put away, for if any one saw it he would be hanged. She then drew as close to the curtain as she could. The prisoner running towards her fired the pistol; she was sensible of the stroke of the ball, and fell against the wainscot. The prisoner then threw himself on the bed; and she heard another pistol go off, but did not see it in his hand. On this a washerwoman came up, and, breaking the lower pannel of the bed-chamber door, dragged her through the aperture; and the prisoner, following by the same way, quitted the house.

Sarah Collings deposed, that she lived in the house; that she saw Mrs. Knightley standing at the chamber-door; that her breast was naked; that the blood was running down; and that she helped her to a chair.

Elizabeth Robinson proved that she had the care of Mr. Draper's house; that the prisoner came thither, and, running to Mrs. Knightley's bed-chamber, fastened the door; that, finding the door fast, she tried to open it, but, not being able, called to the prisoner to do so; but that he answered *he would not, for she was his wife.*

After reciting other particulars, she deposed, that she saw Mrs. Knightley on the landing-place, who exclaimed " See how the villain has murder-" ed me!"—Mrs. Robinson deposed, that, on Mrs. Knightley's opening her handkerchief, she saw the blood running down.

Mr. Williams, a surgeon, deposed, that he found the lady sitting in a chair with a wound in her breast; that it looked like a gun-shot wound; that the ball passed through the cavity of the thorax, and lodged about eight inches distant in the side; that he presumed it missed the lungs, and he found it lodged in the integuments; and that making an incision, and extracting the ball, he found some linen or wadding after enlarging the wound.

The prisoner, in his defence, said, that he had lived ten months with the prosecutrix in the house of Mrs. Cross, and that she had promised him marriage: but that she moved from her lodgings and cohabited with a Jew; that in her last lodgings she promised him marriage the day before the unfortunate affair took place:—that she had frequently supplied him with money; and that he went to her lodgings, with a view to kill himself rather than her; and he even appealed to her for the truth of this circumstance.

The prosecutrix being interrogated as to this particular, she said, " she did not know what he " meant to do, but that he shot her with a pistol." Being asked if she believed he came with intent to kill himself, she said " she did not know whether " he might, or might not, with the other pistol."

Louisa Cross proved that the prisoner and the prosecutrix lodged together in her house; that they cohabited till within a month of the unfortunate transaction; and that Mrs. Knightley had spoken to the prisoner, in her house, only two days before the affair happened. She added, that she understood they were married, and knew not to the contrary till the prosecutrix informed her so, after they had left her house.

On consideration of the whole matter, the jury gave a verdict of guilty, and the prisoner received sentence of death.

Peter Ceppi was executed at Tyburn on the 22d of May, 1778.

The crime of this man, though very enormous, appears in a light of mitigation when we consider him as actuated by the madness of ungovernable passion. He certainly loved the prosecutrix to distraction, and found his life a burden without the possession of her.

From this tale then, beyond almost any one in our book, we are taught the necessity of keeping a strict governance over our passions, as we would wish to pass through life agreeable to the laws of religion and virtue.

> To temperate wishes, just desires,
>   Is happiness confin'd,
> And, deaf to folly's call, attends
>   The music of the mind.

An Account of that remarkable Offender, GEORGE BARRINGTON, who was convicted of stealing a Metal Watch from the Person of Elizabeth Ironmonger, on the 15th of March, 1778.

BARRINGTON was convicted of stealing a watch from a lady in the pit of one of the theatres, and sentenced to labour three years on the Thames. When about a year of the time had expired, he procured a petition to be presented to the court, praying that the remaining part of his sentence

Dodd delin. Pollard sculp.

The **CONVICTS** *taking Water near Black Friars Bridge, in order for their being conveyed to* **WOOLWICH**.

been concealed in Barrington's hair, and dropped on the floor when he took off his hat. She attended the examination of the prisoner, and, having sworn that the watch produced by Payne was her property, was bound over to prosecute.

Upon his trial, Barrington made a long, an artful, and a plausible defence. He said that, upon leaving the church, he perceived the watch mentioned in the indictment laying upon the ground, and took it up, intending to advertise it the next day; that he was followed to Snow-hill by Payne and another constable, who apprehended him, and had, in all probability, seen him take up the watch. "I reflected (said he) that how innocently "soever I might have obtained the article in ques- "tion, yet it might cause some censure; and no "man would wonder, considering the unhappy pre- "dicament I stood in *, that I should conceal it as "much as possible."

The jury having pronounced the prisoner guilty, he addressed the court, earnestly supplicating that he might be permitted to enter into his majesty's service, and promising to discharge his trust with fidelity and attention; or, if he could not be indulged in that request, he wished that his sentence might be banishment for life from his majesty's dominions. The court informed him, that, by an application to the throne, he might obtain a mitigation of his sentence, if his case was attended by such circumstances of extenuation as would justify him in humbly petitioning to be considered as an object of the royal favour. He requested that the money and bank-note might be returned. Hereupon the court observed, that, in consequence of

---

* Alluding to his former conviction.

his conviction, the property found on him when he was apprehended became vested in the hands of the sheriffs of the city of London, who had discretionary power either to comply with, or reject, his request.

George Barrington was convicted to labour on the Thames for the space of five years, on Tuesday the 5th of April, 1778.

Barrington was by profession a surgeon; and his education, abilities, and address, were such, that, had they been properly employed, would certainly have introduced him to a genteel competency, and a reputable station in life. He was early attached to dissipation and extravagance, to which the earnings of honest industry proving greatly unequal, he had recourse to felonious practices, for the means of indulging his insatiable desire of engaging in scenes of gaiety and fashionable amusement. Barrington seems to have had a natural taste for dress, in which particular he was never beneath gentility, but frequently bordering upon elegance. His appearance gained him ready admission to the most respectable public assemblies; and he was a frequent visitor in the galleries of both houses of parliament.

Count Orlow, the Russian minister, being in one of the boxes of Drury-lane play-house, was robbed of a gold snuff-box set with diamonds, estimated to be worth an immense sum; and one of the count's attendants, suspecting Barrington, seized him, and found the snuff-box in his possession. He was examined by Sir John Fielding; but the count, being in a foreign country, was influenced by motives of delicacy to decline a prosecution.

Some time after the above circumstance, a gentleman observed Barrington in the house of lords, and pointed him out to Philip Quarme Esquire, deputy usher of the black rod, who insisted upon his immediately quitting the house, assuring him that his attendance in parliament would, for the future, be dispensed with. We have not heard that he disputed Mr. Quarme's power of expulsion, or that, after the disgrace he sustained from the strong arm of authority, he made any attempt to gain a seat in either house. Barrington was long an accomplice of the famous Miss West, whose memoirs we have recorded in the preceding pages.

How strange is it that, after having experienced the intolerable severities to which offenders sentenced to labour on the Thames are exposed, Barrington should return to his former illegal courses! The horror he expressed upon being subjected to the same kind of punishment for a longer time, we hope will deter others from following his iniquitous example. To be deprived of all the comforts, conveniences, and almost, the very necessaries of life — to be cut off from all communication with the rest of mankind — to be condemned to hard, and almost incessant labour — to be exposed, in the most degrading situation, to which human nature can possibly be reduced, to public curiosity and public reproach — is a punishment of such extreme severity, that the dread of feeling its complicated miseries we should think sufficient to enforce a due obedience to the laws.

The Case of FRANCIS LEWIS, otherwise GRIMISON, who was convicted of a Burglary in the House of Thomas Edmondes, Esquire.

AT the sessions held at the Old Bailey in April, 1778, Francis Lewis, otherwise Grimison, was indicted for breaking and entering the dwelling-house of Thomas Edmondes, Esquire, on the night of the 14th of March preceding, and stealing a gold ring set with diamonds, value 40*l.* and a variety of plate and other valuable articles, to a very large amount.

The fact is this. The prisoner was butler in the family, his master was out of town, and had discharged the footman before he went. Grimison and three maids were all the servants that were left in the house with Mrs. Edmondes. The prisoner, who was a married man, had asked for permission to go and see his wife. He returned about ten at night. Mary Giles, the cook, fastened the door of the area a little before one in the morning. The prisoner slept in the pantry; so that she went to bed, and left him in the kitchen.

About three in the morning, as the watchman was passing, he heard a pistol fired in Mr. Edmondes's house, on which he rattled with his stick against the iron bars of the area near which the prisoner lay; but receiving no answer, he cried the hour, and at half past three, as he was going his rounds, he heard the prisoner cry out, *O Lord! I shall be dead!* The watchman called out to know what was the matter; and the prisoner answered, "there were "rogues, villains, in the house, and he should be "dead." The watchman then asked why he did

not

not open the door? He said, "he could not, for he was tied."

On this the watchman knocked till two servant-maids came down, who found the prisoner tied in his bed, both his hands being tied to his ancles. He said that the house had been broken open; that "there were three men came in; that the age of two of them was from thirty to six and thirty, and the other from twenty to four and twenty, that they had great coats on, and flapped hats; that one held a knife to him, and stood over him all the time, while the other two robbed the house."

Mary Robson, one of the above-mentioned servant-maids, deposed, that the prisoner said, "three men came in, and he fired a pistol at one; and then they tied his hands and legs, and asked where his mistress's jewels were, and where his mistress lay? that then they took the plate out of the closet." She farther deposed, "that he said that the plate was all carried away; that they insisted on having the key, and he gave it to them out of his pocket; that they doubled a silver tea-board together, tied it up in a table-cloth, and carried it away."

Information of this transaction having been given at Bow-street, three persons were apprehended, supposed to be those that the prisoner had described; but they were discharged, on his saying they were not the men who robbed his master.

On the day after the robbery was committed, Mr. Clarke went from Sir John Fielding's office, to examine how the burglary had been committed. When he came to Mr. Edmondes's house, he saw the prisoner sitting by the fire, and having two marks, as if cut with a knife. Mr. Clarke took him

him to the area, on the outside of which was a brick a little broken, on which the robbers were supposed to have stepped. Clarke desired the cook to put up the shutters as they were on the preceding night. She did so: he asked if they were bolted or barred: she said both. He demanded if she would swear before a magistrate that they were bolted and barred: she said, she would not swear that she bolted the place, but would swear that she barred it.

Clarke observed that the bar was a little broke, and that it went into a tenter-hook, which must have been wrenched if the place had been forced open: but the most remarkable circumstance was this: a pane of glass was broken, on the inside of which was a cobweb, which was in such a direction, that it must have been carried away if any one had come through the window.

Clarke now examined the door, and finding that all the force which had been used was on the inside, he had no doubt but that the robbery had been committed by some person within the house; on which he told Mr. and Mrs. Edmondes his opinion of the affair; but the latter seemed very unwilling to admit even a suspicion to the prejudice of the prisoner.

Mr. Clarke then shewed the lady the place, and asked her if she had given the prisoner leave to go out on the preceding night. She said she had permitted him to go and see his wife. Clarke finding that he was married, said, " depend on it the " things are at his wife's;" and having obtained a direction where she had lodged, he dispatched Charles Jealous and another person to the house of a grocer in Gofwell-street. There they learnt that she was removed to Holywell-street, Clare-market,

where

where they found her, having in her poffeffion a large trunk, with a quantity of plate and cloaths in it.

The woman, being taken before Sir John Fielding, acknowledged that fhe was wife to the prifoner; that they were his lodgings, and that he himfelf had taken them.

In the interim the husband was taken into cuftody by Clarke, who defired him to acquaint him where the reft of the plate was, that no imputation might lay againft the characters of the other fervants. On this he acknowledged that he had thrown it into the ciftern of his mafter's houfe. Hereupon Clarke went to the houfe, and found the plate at the bottom of the ciftern; and among other articles a large waiter bent double.

This and many other pieces of plate were produced in court, and fworn to by the profecutor; on which the jury gave a verdict that the prifoner was guilty of ftealing the goods in the dwellinghoufe; and at the clofe of the feffions he received fentence of death.

Of the behaviour of this malefactor after conviction no particular account is tranfmitted us: not any endeavours were exerted to fave him, becaufe it was juftly prefumed that he was unworthy of the royal mercy.

Francis Lewis, otherwife Grimifon, was executed at Tyburn on the 24th of June, 1778.

Breach of truft in fervants is one of the moft atrocious crimes that can be committed; and we feldom find that the fervant who is bafe enough to rob his mafter and benefactor obtains a pardon; nor indeed ought he. Almoft unlimited is the confidence which is placed in many fervants, and very facred fhould the truft be held.

One

One principal circumstance that led to the discovery of the offender in this robbery, was the passing of a cobweb across the window. Hence let us learn to admire the wisdom of Providence, which, from the most seeming trifles, frequently produces the most important events!

Account of the Trial, Conviction, and Execution, of WILLIAM TURNER, JOSEPH DAVIS, and HENRY JORDAN, who were convicted of Burglary.

THESE fellows, who were part of a most desperate gang of villains that had long infested London and its neighbourhood, were indicted at the sessions held at the Old Bailey in April, 1778, for breaking the dwelling-house of Eleanor Errington, widow, about two in the morning of the 26th of December preceding, and stealing plate, gold rings, a watch, silk gowns, and other wearing-apparel, to a considerable amount; together with fifty guineas in money.

Mrs. Errington was a widow woman who kept a public house called Copenhagen House, in the fields near Islington. Her family consisted of a man and maid-servant, and her daughter, a little girl. The waiter had secured the outer-doors; and Mrs. Errington had fastened the door at the bottom of the stair-case with two bolts on the inside. Hearing a noise, and finding that several people were in the house, she called as to her servants, by several fictitious names, to give the intruders an idea that she had a large family.

The villains having forced the door of the stair-case, and forced the lock of that of her room, one of them appeared with a black face, or a crape over it, and a round frock over his cloaths; the second had a handkerchief tied up to his eyes, and the third carried a dark lanthorn. Mrs. Errington having fire-arms in her room, they seized them, broke open her bureau, and took her linen and other cloaths. On the first alarm she concealed a purse, containing her money, between the bed and the sacking; and she threw a wainscot desk, containing her plate, under the bed, that it might escape their search. One of them, who was called *Captain*, said he was certain that she had plate; and in her fright she was obliged to tell them where it was. They took the plate, and going down stairs, they soon returned, and demanded her money, telling her that they were well informed she was in possession of cash; and at this instant she heard a fourth voice on the stairs, saying, "Don't ask her any questions; cut her throat." They threatened to dash out the brains of her little daughter, who lay with her; and at length terrified her so that she told them where her money was, which they took, together with her watch, which hung at the head of her bed. They likewise took money from her pocket, and some that lay loose in the drawer.

This being done, they went down stairs, sung songs, drank three bottles of wine, and ate some buttock of beef, and cold minced pies. Soon afterwards, Mrs. Errington heard one of them on the stairs, asking how she did, and saying that the beef was exceeding good, and that they should call again in half an hour.

They now quitted the house; the report of a pistol was heard, and one of the villains said, "You did not think it was me when you shot; I am wounded; I am afraid I shall be lame." From their entering the house to their quitting it was near three hours.

Henry Davis, the waiter, being sworn, deposed to the following effect; that he made the doors and windows fast on the preceding night; that he was awakened by his mistress's calling; that two men entered his room, asked him who was in the house, and said they would blow his brains out if he did not tell the truth. They then went into the maid's room, saying "they would cut her to "pieces;" but she had escaped to an upper room, where she concealed herself through terror. The villains commanding her to come down, she was obliged to obey, and get into her bed; and then they tied Davis into his bed, and left him bound.

On the first alarm, before they came up into his room, Davis put a gun out at his window, and threatened to fire, on which one of the robbers said "D—n you, fire away! if you don't, I will;" and immediately a pistol was fired, and the rogues ran up stairs. On examination the following morning, it appeared that swan-shot and cut lead were sticking in the chimney-piece, the contents, as supposed, of the pistol abovementioned.

Andrew Carleton, one of the accomplices, having been admitted evidence, swore, that the prisoners were concerned with him in committing the burglary; that they met in Southwark in the morning, and in the evening, at his lodgings in Feather-bed-lane, Cold-bath-fields; and that they went the back way to Copenhagen-house, and committed the robbery as above related; but there are some particulars in Carleton's evidence that will render it neceſſary to recite a part of it in the very words in which he delivered it:—" Turner had the crow; Davis and I broke the kitchen window; Turner and Jordan got in firſt; then a man called out from the houſe that he would fire. Davis ſaid, " if you don't put your head in I will ſhoot you." They who were got in called to us without to come in: I jumped with my two hands upon the window in order to get in, and in ſo doing an old horſe-piſtol I had in my hand went off and burſt, and cut my finger ſadly.—I ſuppoſe the ſtair-foot-door, which had been bolted on the inſide, muſt have been forced before I got in; for we found no impediment; we all got in: Turner forced a pannel of the miſtreſs's room. Turner bid me *ſtay there and take care of her, and to ſhoot her if ſhe offered to move.* I objected to going higher up ſtairs, becauſe the waiter knew me; therefore I was left in the room while they went up and ſecured the waiter. Turner opened the doors; I and Davis had waggoners frocks on; I had a handkerchief acroſs my face: I think Davis had a dark lanthorn; we found a box under the bed. Turner ſaid, take the things out one by one; I anſwered, *Yes Captain, I will.*"

This evidence depoſed to a variety of other circumſtances, correſponding with what has been already written; and then Frances Benſon ſwore that ſhe kept a public-houſe in Red-croſs-ſtreet in the Borough, and bought three gowns of the priſoners for three guineas, and had a pair of buckles into the bargain. She ſaid that the priſoners had uſed her houſe before, that they ſeemed to be acquainted, and had the appearance of ſmugglers.

Jane

Jane Blundell (sister to the last witness) swore, that she was present when the bargain for the gowns was made, and that all the prisoners were in the house, if not in the room, at the time.

John Clarke produced the gowns and buckles, which he received from Benson and her sister; and Mrs. Errington swore that they were her property.

Percival Phillips proved, that, when the prisoners were apprehended, there were five loaded pistols by their bed-side, and two crows, a dark lanthorn, and some gunpowder in the room. He farther said that the landlord of the house delivered him a blunderbuss, which Turner afterwards claimed as his property.

The defence made by the prisoners amounted to almost nothing. Turner endeavoured to impeach the credibility of Carleton, the evidence, asserting that he had been sworn to by four people, as having been concerned in robberies at Finchley. To this the judge said, " his credit the jury will de-
" termine upon, when they compare his testimony
" with the rest of the evidence."

After a short consultation, the jury gave a verdict, that all the prisoners were guilty; in consequence of which, they received sentence of death.

After conviction, there was nothing of extraordinary penitence in their conduct: though young men, they had been old offenders; and as they lived wickedly, they died almost unpitied.

Turner, Davis, and Jordan, were executed at Tyburn on the 24th of June, 1778.

These men had pursued a rapid course of iniquity: but justice failed not to overtake them, and they were but properly punished. Their exit should furnish an example to youth, and teach them that the ways of wickedness evermore lead to destruction.

Narrative

Narrative of the daring Robbery committed in the House of Mr. DANIEL CLEWEN, Farmer, at Finchley, with an Account of the Trial and Execution of the Offenders.

ABOUT one o'clock in the night between the 1st and the 2d of March, 1778, Thomas Horner, James Fryer, Henry Jordan *, and two other villains, forced the bolts and locks of the back-door of Mr. Clewen's house, which they entered and robbed of twenty-two guineas, a twenty and a thirty-pound bank-note, a quantity of plate, several gold-rings, a silver watch, and other property, to a considerable amount. They were a long time in the house, and, though they had disguised themselves, several of the family so exactly described their persons, that Sir John Fielding's officers readily concluded by whom the robbery was committed, and pursued speedy and successful measures for their apprehension.

A the first sessions held at the Old Bailey, after the commission of the robbery, the prisoners were brought to trial; and, at their request, the witnesses were examined apart.

William Quick, servant to Mr. Clewen, swore, that between twelve and one o'clock at night between the 1st and 2d of March, he and the other men servants were alarmed by the maid, calling " William Carter, for God's sake, get up!" that he heard a noise upon the stairs, and leaped out

---

* This man was convicted, with Turner and Davis, for the burglary at Copenhagen-house.

Engraved for The Malefactor's Register.

John Hartley, Ja.ᵈ Deane, and their accomplices in the House of Mʳ. CLEWIN, at FINCHLEY, where they committed a Burglary.

of bed, when four or five armed men rushed into the room; and by threats of instant death compelled them all to cover their heads with the bed-cloaths; that for some time after he heard the voices of two men, who remained in the room to watch them (as they supposed), while the others rifled the house; and that, when these men went away, they said they were going for some victuals, and should return in a quarter of an hour.

Richard Clewen deposed, that, hearing a terrible noise in the house, he rose from his bed, almost at which instant three men entered his room, and having thrown the cloaths over his head, one of them struck him on the back with something which he supposed to be an iron-bar; that the villains then went into all the other rooms on the same floor, after which two of them forced him to get out of bed, and to hold his hands before his eyes, while they conducted him to his father's bed in an adjoining room; that, after laying about half an hour, during which time he believed his father and himself were watched by two of the men, he was told, he might return to his own bed, and that " he need not hold his hands before his eyes, " as there was no person present whom they were " afraid of his seeing;" that, upon returning to his own bed, he saw a man in the passage, whom he believed to be Fryer, who had a handkerchief tied across his face, but not so as entirely to conceal his features. This deponent added that a man, whom he believed to be Horner, afterwards came to his bed-side, and said that, if he would declare where the money was concealed, his watch, which had been taken from under his pillow, and laid on a chair, should not be taken from him; that,

about

about a quarter of an hour after the villains were gone, he went down stairs, and found the door at the foot of the stairs fastened by a staple being driven over the latch; that this door being forced open by himself and the servants, they discovered that the robbers had entered by the back door, the staple for receiving the bolt of which had been forced off, and was laying at some distance from the door.

Anne Clewen deposed, that three men entered her room, and obliged her to cover her head with the bed-cloaths, and that Jordan was one of them; and Elizabeth Goodman, Mr. Clewen's maid-servant, who lay on the first floor, in the room where her mistress slept, confirmed that young lady's evidence as to the number of the men, and the threats they used; and she positively swore to the person of Condon.

This witness further said, that, being alarmed by an uncommon noise in the house, she went out of the chamber, and saw three men rushing up stairs; upon which she called to the men-servants who lay in the garret.

John Parsons deposed, that he and three other men servants to Mr. Clewen lay in the fore-garret, which was entered by five men, who threatened to murder them if they attempted resistance; and that Condon struck William Quick on the head, saying, "lie still, you bloody thief," and covered him over with the bed-cloaths.

William Carter and Thomas Gregory, the other servants, swore, that five men entered the room; the former was positive that Fryer and Condon were two of the villains; and the other swore to the person of Condon only.

Mr.

Mr. Clewen's daughter and maid saw only three of the robbers: but his son and all the men-servants saw five *.

John Bardolph swore that on the general fast, two days preceding that on which Mr. Clewen's house was broke open, he saw Fryer at a public-house near Finchley church, and that he asked several questions concerning Mr. Clewen's family and circumstances; and Robert Dodd deposed, that he saw the last witness and Fryer in conversation on the fast-day at the public-house near the church; and that the next evening he saw Fryer in company with another man upon Finchley-common.

Fryer occupied a small house in the city-road, where he was apprehended; and in the house were found a number of pick-lock-keys, and a hanger. Horner was taken at his lodgings in Perkin's Rents, Westminster, and a cutlass was found concealed in his bed. In the room where Jordan was apprehended, at an inn in the Borough, were found two hangers. Condon was taken at an ale-house in King-street, Gravel-lane, but nothing was found upon him of a suspicious nature.

The prisoners, in general terms, declared themselves innocent of the charge alledged against them: but the jury brought in their verdict " guilty." Jordan received sentence of death for the burglary at Copenhagen-house, and the others for that at Mr. Clewen's. Upon the sacrament being administered to Horner and Fryer, they declared that

---

* The reader will hereafter find that the other villain, concerned in this daring robbery, was apprehended after the trial of the above offenders.

Condon was not concerned with them in the fact of which they had been convicted, and therefore a respite was granted him on the evening preceding the day appointed for his execution.

On Wednesday the 24th of June, 1778, James Fryer and Thomas Horner were executed at Tyburn.

Considering the great number of executions for house-breaking, and the few instances of the perpetrators of that offence escaping the vengeance of the law, it is really astonishing that men should be so desperately resolved upon their own destruction as to be guilty of a crime which daily experience should convince them that they cannot reasonably expect to commit with impunity. We have had frequent occasion to remark on cases of this kind in the preceding pages, and shall, therefore, be more concise in the present instance. National policy requires that the man who breaks in upon the silent hour of night with a felonious purpose, should be removed from that society of which he has rendered himself an unworthy member; and religion sanctifies the decree that consigns him to the grave who has presumed to act in direct violation of the express command of the Almighty.

An Account of the Trial of MICHAEL CASHMIN, for escaping from on board the Lighter on the Thames.

FROM the nature of this trial it must be very short, since there was little else to be done than to identify the person of the prisoner.

Michael

Michael Cashmin having been tried in the April sessions preceding, convicted, and sentenced to labour on the Thames seven years, was accordingly sent on board the ballast-lighter, whence, in a very short time, he found means to escape.

On this his second trial, the record of his former conviction was read; and then John Marshall, the mate of the hulk, proved that the prisoner had been confined on board that vessel.

John Evans, a constable, being sworn, deposed that, either on the 16th or 17th of April, he found the prisoner concealed in a loft, near Tottenham-court-road; and that he had a bazzle (which is part of a fetter) on each of his legs.

The prisoner, by way of defence, spoke as follows:—" I was almost starved to death when I was " there; there is never a man there but would es- " cape from that place if he could: I would rather " be hanged than be there."

This short evidence being gone through, the jury could have no doubt but that Cashmin was the very person that had been sentenced to the ballast-heaving, and had escaped.

Hereupon they brought in a verdict that he was guilty; the consequence of which was, that, on the last day of the sessions, he was sentenced to work on the Thames for fourteen years, being double the term of his former sentence, agreeable to the act of parliament passed for the more effectual punishment of those who presume to escape.

The consequence of this sentence was, that he was again sent on board the lighter, where he now remains *.

---

* In March, 1779.

We have the rather given a little narrative of this particular case, because we would wish to impress on the minds of our readers in general, and our younger readers in particular, the almost absolute impossibility of a man's escaping the justice of his country. Laws would be framed in vain if there were not officers to see that they were carried into execution. These officers are perpetually on the search after those who have violated, or endeavoured to evade, the punishment of the laws: so that an absolute escape is scarce ever effected.

The inferences we would draw from this subject are, that all persons ought to reverence the laws of the land, and those of honesty: but if, unhappily, a man should, in one instance, be tempted to violate them, and punishment should ensue, he ought to submit patently to that punishment, and not, by seeking to avoid it, draw down farther vengeance on his head.

The Trial of ALEXANDER SCOTT, for publishing false News.

AT the sessions held at the Old Bailey in June, 1778, "Alexander Scott was indicted for "that he, on the 23d of April last, unlawfully, "wickedly, and maliciously, did publish false news, "whereby discord, or occasion of discord, might "grow between our lord the king and his people, "or the great men of the realm, by publishing a "certain printed paper, containing such false news; "which said printed paper is of the tenor fol- "lowing:

"In

"In purfuance of his majefty's order in council
"to me directed, Thefe are to give public notice,
"that war with France will be *proclaimed* on Fri-
"day next, the 24th inftant, at the palace royal,
"St. James's, at one of the clock, of which all
"heralds and purfuivants at arms are to take
"notice, and give their attendance accordingly.
"Given under my hand this 22d day of April,
"1778.

"EFFINGHAM, D. M."

We infert this trial merely as a matter of curiofity, and not to caft the flighteft imputation on the character of the prifoner, who was certainly impofed on by the artifices of fome man who wifhed to take advantage of the credulity of the good people of England.

The ftory is this: Scott is by profeffion a bill-fticker. Between ten and eleven o'clock on the night of the 22d of April, a perfon muffled up in a great coat, and having his hat flapped, went to the prifoner, and told him he came from Mr. Strahan, the king's printer, faying " you ftick up bills " for him?" Scott anfwered in the affirmative. The man faid he wanted him to ftick up fome bills in the morning; faying he muft ftick fome round the 'Change, and one at Wood-ftreet, where war was to be proclaimed; and he demanded what Scott was to have for his trouble. The latter enquired how many bills he had, and the ftranger faid only a dozen. Scott faid he would not charge Mr. Strahan any thing: but the other faid he defired he fhould be paid, and afked if five fhillings would do. Scott faid it was too much, but his employer infifted on his taking the money, faying it was a thing that did not happen every day.

In the morning Scott stuck up nine of the bills about the Royal exchange, and one at the end of Wood-street; and as he is an engine-keeper as well as a bill-sticker, he went afterwards before justice Girdler, to make affidavit respecting a fire that had happened.

In the mean time the town was alarmed by the supposed extraordinary news; stocks fell one per cent.*, and the circumstance coming to the knowledge of the lord mayor, he sent to the west end of the town to enquire into the truth of the affair, and found it was all an imposition.

In the mean time, Richard Willis having seen Scott stick up some bills at the Royal exchange, and Thomas Thorn, one of the 'Change keepers, having taken them down, by order of the lord mayor, Joseph Gates, an officer, traced Scott to the Golden cross, a public-house opposite justice Girdler's, and told him he must go before the lord-mayor, for he had been guilty of high-treason. Scott said, " I hope not, I have a family of children." Scott said, on his trial, that he had read the proclamation, and did not know but that it was true; and that he had never seen his employer since the time.

On the trial, the earl of Effingham, deputy marshal of England, under the duke of Norfolk, deposed, that the paper was not printed by his direction: that he knew nothing of it till after it was stuck up, nor gave any authority to any person to print or publish such a paper.

---

* Perhaps this is a sum greatly inferior to what the inventor of the scheme supposed they would have fallen.

Mr. Kirby, keeper of Wood-street compter, deposed to the prisoner being put into his custody by a constable; that he (Kirby) was present at his examination at the mansion house, when he owned that he had stuck up the bills, which were brought him the preceding night by a person wrapped in a great coat, who asked him if he could stick them up, to which Scott replied, " Certainly, it is my " business."

Mr. John Dench, a broker, proved that he had bought stock one per cent. cheaper that day than the day before, owing to the alarm that was spread through the city, by the pasting up of the abovementioned paper.

George Pattison deposed, that he worked with Mr. Strahan, and at that time the prisoner used to stick up bills, such as declarations and proclamations; but they were printed in a different manner, having, particularly, a large king's arms at the top. Mr. Pattison being asked if the difference of the usual bills and that in question was so great that the prisoner must have known it to have been a forgery, he replied, " I do not think he knew it." Being asked what marks of forgery there were in it, he said, " I do not know any: in proclamations, " *Effingham, deputy marshal*, is generally at length : " this is D. M. for deputy marshal."

Lord Effingham now generously spoke as follows: " The prisoner's witness has said that it is " a mark of forgery, the paper not having deputy " marshal at full length, as they say it generally is " in proclamations. I mention it for the prisoner; " they mistake it, for that is not the way of sign- " ing them neither."

Josiah Roe, a victualler, deposed, that Scott came to his house at half past ten at night on the

22d of April, and, pulling out one of the bills, said, "What do you think of the war now? I have bills to stick up; it is to be proclaimed on Friday." Mr. Roe said, "Sure nobody has deceived you!" Scott said, "No, they came from Mr. Strahan's;" and the next morning he put up one of the bills in Roe's house: and Mr. Roe was of opinion that he did not know his employer.

William House deposed that he was at justice Girdler's when Scott gave that magistrate one of the papers, and said he had been sticking up bills about war.

The jury did not hesitate to give a verdict that the prisoner was *not guilty*.

Whoever has given an attentive perusal to the preceding account, will see that the whole was a mere scheme to affect the price of stock, if it was not something worse; a scheme of our insidious enemies, the French, to dupe, for some political purpose, the unsuspecting people of this country.

Be this as it may, there was a double artifice made use of, which seems to mark the depth of the plan: the word *proclaimed* was used instead of *declared*; whereas every man of common-sense knows that peace is *proclaimed*, and war *declared*. It is likewise observable that the deputy marshal's signature was not in the regular form.

These contrivances seem to have been intended to screen the original offender from punishment, if he had happened to have been discovered: for our laws would have declared that a *proclamation* was not a *declaration* of war; and even the simple alteration from the usual mode of the earl marshal's signing his name, would have acquitted the prisoner.

It is to be lamented that so strict is the attention to the *letter* of the law, that the *intention* of it is but too frequently evaded.

An Account of the Trial, Conviction, and Sentence of MARY WEST, otherwise Groves.

AT the sessions held at the Old Bailey, in July 1778, Mary West, otherwise Groves, was indicted for stealing a silk purse, two crown pieces, and four shillings and six-pence, the property of John Bastin.

The fact was this. Mrs. Bastin was the wife of a glover in the Strand. Curiosity had led her among the croud that had assembled to see the late Earl of Chatham lie in state. On the 8th of June, about four in the afternoon, she was in Old Palace-yard, when the prisoner, and a woman whom she called her aunt, stood near her. The prisoner offered her assistance in her getting in, to see his lordship lying in state; but Mrs. Bastin said she had been there on the preceding day *. Almost immediately she felt the prisoner's hand in her pocket, and could have seized it in that situation; but that waiting to pull off her glove, Miss West had in the mean time conveyed away her purse. She was charged with the robbery, but denied it.

Mr. Lucas, high constable of Westminster, who well knew Miss West, came up at this juncture, and enquired what was the matter. Mrs Bastin told him that the prisoner had got her purse; on which he secured her, and took her to the Lobby, where Mrs. Bastin saw her put the purse on a ledge, whence Mr. Lucas took it, and the prosecutrix claimed it as her property, mentioned the mo-

---

* Does not this circumstance strongly mark the curiosity of the people of England? If Mrs. Bastin had been there on the preceding day, what business could she have to revisit the croud?

ney that was in it, and likewise that it contained a baker's bill for bread for the family for a week.

On this Miss West was taken into custody, and lodged in prison till the succeeding Wednesday, when she was conveyed to the Office in Bow-street, where the purse was produced, the facts were sworn to, and the offender was committed for trial.

At the Old Bailey Mrs. Bastin positively swore to a crown-piece which had a particular cut in it, and which she had carried in her pocket several years.

Mr. Lucas proved that he saw the prisoner lay the purse containing the pieces of money on a corner of a kind of ledge, at a door-way that leads into the Board of Works: that he immediately seized the prisoner, whom he had before seen in the painted chamber where Lord Chatham lay in state. He likewise said that he had told her she had no business there, and desired the officer to turn her out; and farther, that if she came there any more he should order the officer to take her into custody. He added, that upon hearing a contest between the prosecutrix and the prisoner, he took the latter into a corner, that she might not get near any person till the officer came.

The prisoner denied that she laid the purse on the ledge, or even ever had it in her hand; and said, that she had a material witness who was not come to town: but no credit could be given to any thing that she averred; her character was notorious; the evidence against her was conclusive, and the jury gave a verdict that she was guilty; in consequence of which, at the close of the sessions, she received sentence to be branded, and imprisoned two years; and she is at this time * in confinement.

---

* In March, 1779.

Miss West is one of the most notorious and artful pickpockets that modern times have produced. She used to go by the name of Elizabeth, though, on her last commitment, she chose that of Mary, and called herself Groves, when she was examined at Bow-street, which occasioned the *alias* to her sur-name; for she was too well known to be permitted to go to trial with Groves as her *first* name.

This woman has long been an atrocious offender: her usual places of plying for business were the play-houses, where she was amazingly successful; and though often apprehended, and conveyed to Sir John Fielding's office, she was repeatedly discharged, because, as she generally stole money only, the injured parties would not swear to their property.

She had been repeatedly tried at the Old Bailey, and acquitted, in defect of such evidence as could convince the jury of her guilt: and it was a very short time before she picked Mrs. Bastin's pocket that she was discharged from Newgate, after six months confinement for another offence; during which she was delivered of a child in the prison.

Miss West has long reigned the principal female pickpocket in London: but she is so perfectly well known; her crimes have been so numerous, and her character is so totally lost, that when the term of her present imprisonment expires, she must expect still less favour than even branding, and a two years imprisonment, if she be again convicted of preying on the property of unoffending individuals.

It may possibly be of some service to give a description of this offender, as it may prevent her artifices from taking effect in particular instances. She is of the middle size, genteely grown, her countenance is of the oval form, and rather ruddy;

her hair of a moderate brown, her eyes hazle-coloured, and her nose inclined to the aquiline; but she is best to be distinguished by a remarkably broad west-country accent, which she cannot disguise. She dresses gay, and is about thirty-five years of age; but looks rather younger.

Persons who may see such a woman crouding into the playhouse, or may happen to sit next her in the gallery, will do well to be cautious, or the pocket will be picked before any suspicion can arise. She will look a man hard in the face, ask him some unmeaning question, and ease him of his cash in an instant.—We have inserted this caution in the hope that it may be useful.

Particulars of the Trial of JOHN HOLT, JOHN DAVIS, ANDREW CARLETON, and ALEXANDER CARLETON, for Burglary.

AT the sessions held at the Old Bailey, in July, 1778, these malefactors were indicted for breaking and entering the dwelling-house of Robert Jobling, (the White Horse Inn at Cripplegate) and stealing sixteen silver dishes, value 110l. sixty-six silver plates, value 285l. with a great variety of other plate, (in the whole to the amount of about 2000l). the property of Thomas Stapleton, Esq;

George Parvin, the prosecutor's butler, swore that he packed up the plate mentioned in the indictment, and delivered it to Bartholomew Cooper, a carman, directing him to convey it to the White Horse, Cripplegate, whence it was to be taken in the waggon to Mr. Stapleton's house in Yorkshire;
and

and Bartholomew Cooper proved that he conveyed the plate received from Parvin to the White Horse Inn, and delivered it to Thomas Crompton, bookkeeper to the York waggon.

Crompton deposed, that on the 4th of June he received a quantity of plate, directed to Thomas Stapleton, Esquire, in Yorkshire, which he put into the warehouse, and that it remained there when he, as usual, secured the door with two locks, a short time previous to his going to bed; that about five the next morning he was alarmed by the ostler, who told him, that the warehouse had been broke open, in consequence of which he went to the warehouse, when he perceived that a burglary had been effected, marks of chissels appearing on different parts of the door post, the bar of the door being much bent, the padlock forced off, and lying on the ground, and three packages being broke open, and therefrom a great quantity of plate stolen. He added, that some time afterwards a bricklayer came to the inn, and gave information that a great quantity of plate found upon suspicious persons was secured in Cripplegate watch-house.

The evidence of John Negus, a constable and patrole of Cripplegate ward, was to the following effect: that about two in the morning between the 4th and 5th of June, he was informed by a watchman that some suspicious persons were in the neighbourhood, on which he went into Paul's alley, leading from Redcross-street to Aldersgate-street, where two men passed him; that presently after, a watchman, named William Phillips, came to speak to him, and that while they were in conversation, the prisoner Davis came up, whom, from the remarkable bulk of his pockets, they suspected to be a robber, and therefore seized him, when he let fall a bundle, containing several articles of plate, which they deposited in the watch-house, where they confined the prisoner and left him under a guard of constables.

William Phillips confirmed the evidence of Negus, adding that, after Davis was secured in the watch-house, he and Negus again went into Paul's-alley, where they presently secured Holt and Andrew Carleton; that they found upon Holt several articles of plate tied in a green cloth, and in the pockets of Carleton two silver candlesticks and a loaded pistol.

John Shepherd proved that he searched the house in which Andrew Carleton lodged, in Hare-court, adjoining to Paul's-alley, and found a hanger and a pistol loaded three fingers deep concealed in a cupboard, the key of which was delivered to him by Andrew Carleton; and John Kirby swore, that in an apartment occupied by Alexander Carleton in Cloth-fair he found between the bed and the mattrass a dozen of silver plates, half a dozen oval silver dishes, and a silver spoon, and a hanger, and a number of pick-lock keys concealed in the chimney.

The plate being produced, Parvin swore that the several articles were his master's property, and that he packed them up, and sent them to the Whitehorse-inn at Cripplegate.

The prisoners being called upon for their defence, Davis said, that passing through Old-street about two in the morning, with a returned post-chaise from Barnet, he found the plate which the watchman took from him in Paul's alley. Holt and Andrew Carleton said, that the plate they were accused of having stolen they found in an opening where drays stand near the bottom of Whitecross-street

street about two in the morning of the 5th of July. Alexander Carleton said, that besides his apartment in Cloth-fair, he had a room in the house where his brother lodged; that upon being informed by his brother's wife that she was fearful her husband was involved in trouble, he searched his apartment, and finding the cutlass and picklock-keys, took them to his lodging in Cloth-fair, and concealed them in the chimney, and that his brother's wife accompanied him with a bundle, the contents of which he then did not know, but had afterwards reason to believe the bundle contained the plate found secreted between the bed and the mattrass. The jury brought in a verdict of guilty against all the prisoners, and they were sentenced to suffer death.

John Holt and Andrew Carleton were executed at Tyburn, on the 19th of October 1778, the former evidencing the deepest marks of contrition [*].

The above malefactors had been almost entirely denied the advantages of education, and seemed to have but very imperfect notions of their religious duty.

It is to be lamented that greater care is not taken to instil the principles of virtue and religion into the minds of youth, who would thereby be rendered less liable to be seduced into the paths of vice. There are, comparatively but few among the violators of the law, who are not the offspring of the poorer classes of the people.

At the charity-schools, children are instructed in reading, writing, and arithmetic; but, we are sorry to say, very little attention is employed to

---

[*] Alexander Carleton died in Newgate; and it will be seen that Davis was hanged for the robbery at Copenhagen-house.

inspire

inspire them with just sentiments of religious and moral obligations. They are permitted to range the streets at all hours, and consequently are witnesses to scenes of infamy in all their horrid variety. Is it surprizing that, when their minds are most susceptible of impressions from outward objects, a familiarity with vicious examples should disqualify them for perceiving the abominable deformity of vice?

It is strange that political considerations have not prompted the legislature to adopt measures for more effectually defending the morals of the infant poor from corruption, which would tend towards ensuring obedience to the laws, and greatly encrease population, on which our national safety so materially depends.

" Princes and lords may flourish and may fade,
" A breath can make them, as a breath hath made;
" But a bold peasantry, their country's pride,
" When once destroy'd, can never be supplied;"
GOLDSMITH.

Proceedings on the Trial of WILLIAM FLINT, who was convicted of privately Stealing.

WE mention the case of this malefactor, not that there was any thing extraordinary in the robbery itself; but because the prisoner was an old criminal, and had offended after experiencing the royal mercy.

William Flint had been tried for a former offence, at the Old Bailey, and sentenced to three years labour on board the ballast-lighter, where he behaved so well for some months, that representations

tions were made to the king in his favour, and the remainder of his punishment was remitted.

At the sessions held at the Old Bailey in September, 1778, William Flint was indicted for stealing a silver watch, value 40s. the property of Aaron Coats, privily from the person of the said Aaron, on the 16th of August.

Mr. Coats deposed, that being at a fire in Nicholas-lane on the evening of the 16th of August, he staid about half an hour, from motives of curiosity; and that on coming from the fire, he felt for his watch in Lombard-street, and missed it; but he owned that he had not seen the prisoner at the fire.

Mr. Coats advertised his watch four days afterwards, and soon learnt that the prisoner was at Sir John Fielding's, charged with that and other offences; on which he went to Bow-street, where his watch was produced to him.

William Adley, a pawnbroker in Cow-cross, deposed, that the prisoner brought the watch to him, to offer it in pledge; that he asked him two guineas, that he lent him a guinea and a half on it; and Flint took a duplicate of it in his own name.

Moses Morant, one of Sir John Fielding's officers, deposed, that he went to apprehend Flint, two boys, and another person; that in Flint's parlour he found the duplicate of Mr. Coats's watch, and an old seal which had belonged to it; and the watch being produced was sworn to by the prosecutor.

The prisoner, by way of defence, said, that a person had given him the watch to pawn for him; but the jury gave no credit to this assertion, and found him " Guilty of stealing the watch, but not " guilty of stealing it privily from the person."

In consequence of this verdict, Flint was put t[o] the bar at the close of the sessions, to receive h[is] sentence, which was, that he should work on th[e] navigation (that is at ballast-heaving) for five years and he is now * undergoing his sentence; nor is [it] likely that he will receive any farther favour, bu[t] remain a prisoner, under the most ignominious ci[r]cumstances, during the whole time.

This Flint was a manufacturer, as we have bee[n] informed, in the silver branch, and lived in Quaker'[s] buildings, West-Smithfield. He had two appre[n]tices, whom he trained to the art of thieving, pri[n]cipally by picking of pockets.

At the sessions above-mentioned, Flint was i[n]dicted, together with William Boston, Thomas E[l]burn, and George Goodburn, for stealing a silv[er] pepper-castor and a table-spoon, the property [of] Jane Benham, mistress of the Catherine wheel-in[n] at Colnbrook; when they were all acquitted, excep[t] Goodburn (one of Flint's pupils), who was sent o[n] board the ballast-lighter for three years; and E[l]burn being tried on another indictment at the sam[e] sessions, and convicted, was sentenced to a simil[ar] punishment.

Hardness of heart is the characteristic of cont[i]nued villainy. Flint had experienced the roy[al] mercy, which was more than he deserved; but thi[s] appears to have had no influence on his futur[e] conduct: he was resolved to continue his depreda[tions on the public, though he was well capable o[f] supporting himself in a handsome manner by th[e] honest profits of his profession.

The master, who, as Flint did, sets an ill ex[-]ample to his servants, is deserving of the severe[st]

---

* In March 1779.

punishment; and one would almost lament, for the ake of the rising generation, that this fellow was not made an example of the utmost rigour the law can inflict.

Abstract of the Trials of THOMAS BRISTOWE and MORRIS BARNARD, who were convicted of a Conspiracy to cheat and defraud.

AT the sessions held at the Old Bailey in September, 1778, these offenders were indicted for a conspiracy to cheat and defraud one Thomas Orme, and for obtaining, by false pretences, five guineas, on the 28th of June preceding.

This case is inserted on account of its singularity, and to guard the unsuspecting against the artifices of the villainous. Thomas Orme of Castle Dunnington in Leicestershire, being somewhat embarrassed in his circumstances, was advised by a neighbour to apply to Bristowe, who had published the following extraordinary advertisement in the news-paper printed at Leicester:—" Whereas
" many persons, labouring under most grievous op-
" pressions from their defenceless situation, are
" constrained to silence and quiet submission to the
" atrocious robberies which are daily committed
" by the infamous appendages to the law:

" To remedy such evils as much as possible, a
" gentleman of known abilities and integrity,
" in conjunction with sundry able gentlemen
" of the law, proposes to give his assistance to
" such as wish to be extricated from intricate and
" perplexed embarrassment.

"The author is actuated by no other motives than those which tend to alleviate the affliction of the helpless, to relieve the unfortunate of every denomination, against the chicanery of pettyfogging (would-be) attornies; the shameful plunder and extortion of bailiffs and sheriffs brokers; and to prop up such as groan beneath opulent and intolerable tyranny.

"That unhappy species of debtors, who are amenable to the bankrupt laws, will assuredly meet with such able and friendly advice as will fortify them, not only against a prison, but most of those calamities attendant on bankrupts in general.

"The supporters and advisers of this address hope it will be received and esteemed to be what it really is, the dictates of benevolence, independent of any pecuniary views; as a proof of which, all persons in indigent circumstances will be entitled to every assistance free from expence.

"Apply to Mr. Thomas Bristowe, Cavendish-bridge, Leicestershire."

In consequence hereof Orme applied to Bristowe, who told him if he would go to London he would set him free; and if his creditor would not stay, he might tell him he would *treat him with the butt end of an act of parliament.* Orme enquired the expence; and Bristowe said, seven or eight pounds, and that they should be back in four or five days. They came to London with one Simon Norton, in like circumstances with Orme; and at the Swan-with-two-necks, in Lad-lane, they met with Barnard, who said to Bristowe, "We must swear one has been at Calais, and the other at another place," (which Orme could not recollect). Bristowe then wrote a paper for them to sign, and told

Norton he muſt pay Barnard five guineas: Norton heſitated, and wanted a receipt. Barnard aſked him, if he *diſputed his being a gentleman*. On this Norton paid the five guineas; and Briſtowe ſaid that Orme muſt pay Barnard a like ſum; which after ſome heſitation he complied with.

On a queſtion aſked, whether any thing was ſaid about croſſing the ſalt-water, Orme depoſed that ſomething was ſaid " about croſſing the ſalt-water " over a piſs-pot," or to that effect.

It ſeems that the proſecutors had a confuſed idea that they were to be diſcharged by the inſolvent act, but they did not underſtand the meaning of it.

Simon Norton depoſed that he met Barnard at the Swan-with-two-necks; that he and Briſtowe aſked for a private room, where Barnard pulled out a bag of writings, and ſaid to Briſtowe, " We " muſt fix them as fugitives." Briſtowe agreed, and the other began filling up the papers. Briſtowe likewiſe ſaid, that Barnard was an attorney, and that he was the man that was to do the buſineſs for them.

A paper being ſhewn to Orme in court, he ſaid, " that is the paper I ſigned, and all that was done " for five guineas."

William Payne (a conſtable) depoſed, that he apprehended the priſoners at the Paul's-head tavern: that he ſeized Barnard's bag, who ſaid, " let it " alone," and pulled out the two ſchedules. Payne aſked Barnard, if he had received any money of the men; he ſaid he never had: the two men declared they paid him ten guineas. He then confeſſed he had received that ſum, and given Briſtowe five guineas. The latter at firſt denied the receipt of them, but afterwards confeſſed it.

Briſtowe

Briftowe called three perfons, who gave him a good character; and Barnard endeavoured to exculpate himfelf, by faying that "he had nothing to do with the men; that Briftowe was to be his paymafter, and had told him they were to take the benefit of the act as fugitives, &c." with other circumftances to the like effect.

The jury gave full credit to the evidence againft the prifoners, and delivered a verdict that they were both guilty; in confequence of which, at the clofe of the feffions, they were fentenced to ftand in the pillory, and be imprifoned for a year; the latter part of which fentence they are now * undergoing.

As far as can be judged of this affair, it feems to have been an artful device of two villains to rob two unfufpecting countrymen of their property, under the moft fallacious pretences; and indeed the jury feemed to have been of the fame opinion, by the verdict that was given.

A Narrative of the Trials of FRANCES PEARCE, ANNE ARROGONY, and CATHERINE DAVIS, otherwife SIMPSON, for a Street-robbery.

AT the feffions held at the Old Bailey in † October, 1778, the prifoners were indicted for robbing Henry Kitchen, Efq; of a bank-note, value 15 £. two bills of exchange, the one for 350 £. and the other for 150 £. and feveral other bills, to a

---

* In March 1779.
† Mr. Kitchen was then lately elected to the office of fheriff of London and Middlefex.

confiderable

confiderable amount, on the night of the 15th of September.

As Mr. Kitchen was paffing near the New-church in the Strand, after ten at night, three women furrounded him, and took his pocket-book from him, which contained notes to the value or 14 or 1500£. He faw four hands held up: he cried *Watch*, and *Stop thief!* and inftantly fecured Pearce, but did not fee the pocket-book in her hand. The other women ran away.

Elizabeth Mills, an unhappy woman of the town, depofed that fhe faw Simpfon and Arrogony near Mr. Kitchen; that they were one on each fide of him. This deponent faw only thofe two women at that time. When Mr. Kitchen came near the New-church, Davis ran away, and the other fell down in attempting to run off. Mr. Kitchen cried out " Stop thief.—I am robbed." Five or fix women being ftanding near the church, he feized one of them, and faid, " I have got you; I have got " you."

On the crofs examination, this evidence faid that the woman had walked with Mr. Kitchen from St. Clement's church-yard, arm in arm; and that when he came near the New-church five or fix women were ftanding together; and he faid " I have got " you all."

To invalidate the teftimony of this witnefs, Samuel Price, a bailiff, was fworn, who depofed that he had known her ten years, and that he did not believe fhe was fuch a woman as deferved credit on her oath. Mary Hayes likewife depofed, that fhe was a very abandoned woman, that fhe had affumed feveral names, and ought not to be believed even under the fanction of an oath.

Amelia

Amelia Burchell swore, that she saw the prosecutor seize Pearce, and that he said he was robbed; and Elizabeth Thompson deposed, that she had likewise heard him say that he was robbed; that she saw Davis having hold of his arm; that Arrogony was four yards behind him, but at what distance Pearce was she did not know.

The jury, having considered the whole evidence, acquitted Arrogony and Davis, and found Pearce guilty of the charge, in consequence of which she received sentence to be imprisoned three years.

The notes thus stolen from Mr. Kitchen were passed into the hands of some Jews; but, by the diligence of the peace-officers, about half of them were recovered.

We have the rather mentioned this case, because women seldom commit street-robberies without the assistance of men. Women of the town are as usually attended by their bullies, as bailiffs by their followers. The men who reduce poor credulous girls to the necessity of plying to the casual passenger in the street, have much to answer for.

Even seduction, however, and its consequent distress, is no plea for acts of dishonesty, or for a continuance in the path of vice. London and Westminster abound with hospitals for the reception of the deceased or really unfortunate; and there is parish provision, at least, for all those who are utterly distressed; and any provision is preferable to a determined perseverance in the practice of wickedness.

An Account of the Trial, Conviction, and Execution, of James Bean, John Hartley, and Lambert Smith, who suffered for Burglary.

THESE men, though young in years, were old in offence, and therefore it becomes necessary to insert their story, that others may take warning from their fate.

At the sessions held at the Old Bailey in December, 1778, James Bean, John Hartley, and Lambert Smith, were indicted for breaking the dwelling-house of Levi Hart on the 20th of October, and stealing 68 silver watches, value 119*l*. 10*s*. a number of gold breast-shirt-buckles, set with pearls and garnets, some gold rings, and other valuable articles, the property of Abraham Davis.

The prosecutor is a travelling Jew, who carries goods through the country. He had a room on the first floor at Mr. Hart's, and saw all his things safe between six and seven in the evening, when he went to a coffee-house, and soon afterwards Hart fetched him home, informing him, that his apartment had been robbed. When he came home, he found two locks, and his jewellery boxes, broke, and missed all his property.

Levi Hart deposed, that he was landlord of the house; that some person knocking at the door, his wife opened it, and three men rushed in, who said " they had an information against the house." Mrs. Hart asked for what; when the candle was snatched from her, and two of them went up stairs, while the third staid below. Mr. Hart heard them break open the door, and when they had stolen Mr. Davis's property, they descended, threw the candlestick on the floor, and went away: but one of them held the door a-while, to prevent a pursuit; Mr. Hart deposed that he knew Smith, and could swear to him; but he could not swear to the other two.

Sarah Hart confirmed her husband's deposition; said that hearing a knocking at the door, she opened it, when the three men rushed in, and said they had an information against the house, against a young man, a lodger, who dealt in French silks; that on her asking if they had authority to come into her house, one of them produced a pistol to her husband, and said *if he stirred he was a dead man*; that she heard the closet broke open, and on her wanting to go up stairs, the villain who was below pushed her away twice, and seized her by the throat. She deposed that she knew all the prisoners, having looked in their faces as they entered the house; and she positively swore that Smith put a pistol to her husband's breast.

Information of this robbery having been given at Bow-street, Sir John Fielding's men soon traced the thieves; and, on the trial, Charles Jealous produced a watch, which he found on Lambert Smith, who said it was his own: but Richard Simpson proved that he made that very watch for Aaron Michael, who deposed that he left it, with two other watches, &c. in the care of the prosecutor.

Richard Ward swore that he bought forty-one watches of James Bean, all of which he had sold but one, and that proved to be Mr. Davis's property.

Bean, by way of defence, said that Smith knew nothing of the robbery; and that himself had the watches to sell for another man. Smith said that he he had a watch of Bean, to get a glass put in it; and Hartley denied being guilty of the charge: but the jury found all the prisoners guilty, and they received sentence of death.

It may be proper to mention that, at the same sessions, Hartley and Bean were tried for being concerned in breaking open the house of Mr. Daniel Clewin, of Finchley, on the 1st of March preceding, and were convicted on the fullest evidence: but, as we have already given an account of the other parties concerned in that atrocious burglary, it will be unnecessary to enter into particulars.

Of the behaviour of these criminals after conviction we have no favourable account. They were most daring and hardened offenders; and as they lived in constant violation of the laws, so they died almost unpitied.

James Bean, John Hartley, and Lambert Smith, were executed at Tyburn on the 12th of February, 1779.

Surely our younger readers cannot need the least caution to avoid treading in the steps which brought these young fellows to such a fatal and disgraceful end. It is but a very few years since Hartley was a mere child playing about the dirty allies adjoining to Water-lane, Fleet-street; but an attachment to bad company soon led him to the practice of every vice that his youth was capable of, and he fell an untimely victim to the insulted laws of God and his country.

> Learn hence, ye youths, those paths to shun
> Which quick to sure destruction run;
> And O! pursue that happier way
> That leads to realms of endless day.

An Account of the Trial of SAMUEL BONNER, who was convicted of writing a threatening Letter, with a Design of extorting Money from Mrs. SARAH TESHMAKER.

BONNER was born at Edmonton in Middlesex, in the neighbourhood of which place he had many years worked for different persons as a day-labourer, and bore the character of an honest, industrious, but simple man.

The following is a copy of the letter written by Bonner, and delivered by the penny-post to Mr. Francis Hardcastle, landlord of the Fox upon Winchmore-green, whom Mrs. Teshmaker had directed to receive her news-papers and letters, that the news carriers and post-men might not be put to the trouble of going out of the public road, from which her house stood at some distance.

" Ldy Tashmaker   Nov. 20th, 1778.

Wee dwo a blige You that you shall dwo this kindness of Charity to theas three people which wee menshon to you that his the Wheader Wakefield James Weave and Old Bonner & make each of them a preasant of one Gine & half to a Sift them in thear Distress. One Sunday Morning being the 22th of Nor. and send for them all three to your House be tween 11 and 12 & let one of you Sarvents give them thiss gift in a peas of paper & this leater neaver to be menshoned for the safty of your Self If you dwo not dwo a Corden to what this leater menshons you may expect that your Estate shall be Broght to ashes and Your Self to the Ground with a brase of marvels throu your C

It is not ondley you others shall be a blige to dwo the kindness of Chearity to the poor a-pon Winchmore

SAM.^L BONNER (under commitment for writing a threatening Letter to Mrs Teshmaker of Winchmore Hill) imploring assistance from M.^r DAY.

more hill as well as you wee are men that is well wishes to the poor near neabers a short life and a meary one

> This from your well wishers If you
> act a Corden to this Leater"

The prisoner was brought to trial at the Old Bailey in the sessions held in December, 1778. Mrs. Teshmaker produced the letter, and it was read, and found literally to correspond with the copy inserted in the indictment; the lady deposed, that on her return from a visit on the 21st of the preceding month, she found the letter lying on her dressing-table.

Francis Hardcastle swore that he received the letter from the penny-post man, and delivered it to John Draper, one of Mrs. Teshmaker's servants, who proved that the letter produced in court was that he received from Hardcastle.

Samuel Draper, clerk to Pearce Galliard, Esq; in the commission of the peace for the county of Middlesex, informed the court, that on Monday the 30th of November he, accompanied by Mr. Day, went to Clerkenwell bridewell, in order to postpone the re-examination of Bonner from Tuesday till Wednesday; and that when the prisoner was let into the yard between the gates, he ran towards them, and acknowledged that he had written the letter, saying it was the first offence he had committed, and earnestly supplicating that they would intercede in his favour.

Matthew Day deposed that, by the desire of Mr. Draper, he accompanied him to Clerkenwell bridewell on Monday the 30th of November, and stood in an obscure part of the yard during a short conversation between Draper and the prisoner, on the conclusion of which he was perceived by the prisoner,

soner, who ran to him, clasped him in his arms, and cried, "Pray, Sir, God bless you! Sir, be my "friend, and get me out of this dismal place; you "was always my friend;" that he asked him on what account he was confined; on which he said, "Oh, God knows! God bless you, Sir, get me "out of it; you will if you are my friend get me "out of it;" that in a whisper he acknowledged that his having written a threatening letter to the prosecutrix was the cause of his confinement, and said, "Oh, Sir, it was the devil, the devil, the "devil, and this leg (putting his hand to his leg, "on which he had some time before received a "wound) that induced me to do it. It is true I "did write this letter, but it is the first fact I ever "was guilty of."

Being called upon for his defence, the prisoner only said that what Mr. Day had related was truth; and upon the court asking him whether he had any person to appear on behalf of his character, he said, "only God and the gentleman."

The jury pronounced him guilty of the indictment, and he received judgment of death. The jury and the prosecutrix humbly recommended the prisoner to his Majesty's mercy, which he received.

If the law did not denounce very severe punishment against offenders convicted of writing threatening letters, neither life nor property would be any longer secure. Bonner's case was remarkable: there was great reason to suppose that, notwithstanding the violent threats in the letter, he would not have carried them into execution, had the lady refused her compliance, and declined pursuing measures for apprehending the writer; he was a man so remarkably deficient in point of intellect, that people were divided in opinion whether he did not

labour

labour under the infirmity of natural idiotism: on these considerations alone he was recommended to mercy.

In cases of forgery the punishment is the same, whether a fraud is or is not actually committed, the fact of forgery being sufficient to prove a fraudulent intention, and to constitute a breach of the law; and this doctrine holds good with regard to threatening letters.

Let it not be supposed that robberies may be committed with impunity by means of threatening letters, the writers of which are equally liable to an ignominious death with the perpetrators of the most desperate crimes of which human nature is capable.

Narrative of the singular Case of ROBERT MOODY, who was tried for a Rape, and acquitted.

ON Wednesday the 2d of December, 1778, Sarah Bethell charged Robert Moody, a waterman, with ravishing her in his boat, on his passage between Queenhith and Wandsworth, between seven and eight o'clock in the evening of the 10th of November preceding.

Though the evidence given on this occasion at Bow-street did not seem by any means conclusive against the prisoner, yet, as Mrs. Bethell swore positively to the perpetration of the fact, the magistrates thought themselves in duty bound to commit the prisoner for trial *.

At the sessions held at the Old Bailey in December, 1778, Robert Moody was indicted for ravishing

---

* This circumstance is worthy of remark.—Though a Justice of Peace, and a hundred persons who may be present, be

fully

ing Sarah, the wife of William Bethell, against her will.

The prosecutrix swore, that, having spent the day in London, she went to Queenhithe, where she saw the prisoner, whom she had known for some years; that she went with him into the boat, together with the beadle of Fulham, who finding the weather cold, landed at Westminster bridge, and said he would go by the stage; that she being now left alone with Moody, he stopped at the Spread-eagle at Mill-bank, where they drank some gin-hot together; that they again stopped at the King's-head at Chelsea, where the prisoner had a pint of beer, but she did not drink with him; that she was perfectly sober when they again got into the boat, and just before they got to Battersea-bridge, Moody said, " Mrs. Bethell, give us a " song;" which she declined to do, saying she was not so light-hearted.

Being asked what she meant by light-hearted, she said that her husband had been out of his mind, and discharged as incurable from a madhouse, which circumstance disturbed her mind. She deposed that, on her refusing to sing, he swore, " if she could not " sing, she should do the other thing," and that having pulled her down from the stern to the bottom of the boat, he said if she mentioned his name, or screamed out, he would throw her over. She farther deposed, that she made all possible resistance, notwithstanding which, he perpetrated the deed for which he was indicted, and that during her struggle, she received a bruise on her shoulder.

---

fully convinced of the innocence of an accused party, yet the magistrate is bound to commit, if the accuser positively swears to the charge. Hence we may learn how sacred and important is the power vested in our Juries.

She now threatened (according to her own account) to expose him; but he swore "he did not "mind being exposed." After this she said he rowed quietly to Wandsworth, without offering any farther violence; and that she went directly to the house of her brother, Mr. Firmage, and related to his wife what had passed.

Mary Firmage deposed, that she came to her house about half an hour after seven at night, and appeared to have been very much tumbled and *mousled* about; and seemed to be much agitated in her mind. The husband being in the shop, Mrs. Firmage took her sister-in-law into another room, and asked her what was the matter; to which she replied, that she had been used very ill by Robert Moody, who had committed a rape on her.

John Firmage, the father of Sarah Bethell, deposed, that he was sent for to his daughter, who said that Moody had used her very ill; on which this deponent said, he would make him suffer for it, and he should have what the law directed:— that on the following day, as he was going by his son's house, Moody came out, and said, "for God's "sake, have compassion upon me! consider my wife "and children."

Mr. Firmage and his daughter went to the Rotation-office in the Borough; but finding they had made application at an improper place, as the offence was presumed to have been committed on the Chelsea side of the river, they went to Sir John Fielding's, where they obtained a warrant; but this warrant was not served till the 27th of the month, in compassion, as was alledged, to the situation of the prisoner's wife, who lay-in at the time.

The prisoner, by way of defence, declared his total innocence of the fact; and, as it had been insinuated that he had absconded, in fear of being apprehended, he said he knew he had not offended.

On behalf of the prisoner, Martha Harrold was sworn, who gave a whimsical kind of evidence. She deposed, that Mrs. Firmage told her Bob Moody had committed a rape on Mrs. Bethell. Mrs. Harrold expressed her doubt of the fact, as they got twice out of the boat to drink: however, she went to Mrs. Firmage's, where she said, to use her own words, " how do you do now, after your *merry-bout?*" Being asked what was Mrs. Bethell's behaviour, she said, " she is a very *jokeus* merry woman, and not quite so sedate as some might be;" and that she had seen the hands of James Nicholls down her bosom. Being asked if she believed Mrs. Bethell to be a virtuous, modest woman; she replied, " I cannot pretend to say whether she is or not. I can only say, according to my belief, she is not so good as some may be; she is very vulgar in her speech." To this the court answered, " her behaviour does not appear to be so vulgar as your own."

Being asked, on her cross examination, if she thought it proper for a woman of decency to ask another " how she did after this *merry-bout*," and " whether she thought a rape was a *merry-bout*;" her answer was, " she is a *jokeus* woman—I only thought it a joke."

Elizabeth Wills, of the King's-head at Chelsea, deposed, that the prosecutrix and prisoner had drank together at her house, and appeared to be on very good terms; and that when they quitted the house they went out arm in arm; and on their leaving

leaving the tap-room, some men wished them good luck, because they saw them very sociable together. This witness farther deposed as follows: "He (the prisoner) called at our house on the "Friday after the rape was committed; he asked "me if I recollected his calling there on the Tues- "day? I said, I did. He had a man went in his "boat from our house that night."

A waterman being sworn, deposed, that he was on the water on the evening of the presumed rape: that Moody came within four or five boats length of him, and was very merry and singing:—that he did not hear any body scream out or make a noise; and that if there had been any noise, he must have heard it. He said that when he first saw Moody, he was rowing, and somebody was sitting upright at his backboard, but he could not tell whether it was a man or a woman.

William Pike, a waterman, gave the following evidence:—that he was putting his boat right when the prosecutrix and prisoner got into their boat from the King's-head: that he (this deponent) staid at the water-side five or six minutes; that he did not hear a screaming, outcry, or any noise, made by a woman;—and that the wind was in his favour to have heard any noise.

John Ingram, a youth of sixteen, remembered Mrs. Bethell landing with the prisoner on the night when the offence was alledged to have been committed. This witness swore, that he handed the prosecutrix out of the boat, and that she asked Moody if he would have any thing to drink? To which he answered, "no more to night, thank "you." They parted immediately, after they had mutually kissed each other; and she said, "God bless "you, good night." The counsel for the prosecution

cution asked Ingram, if it was not a dark night? He owned that it was, but there was light enough from the public house to enable him to see the parties. John Carter, master to the last witness, gave him an excellent character, saying he had never known him guilty of telling a lye.

The following persons appeared to the prisoner's character.—Elizabeth Benson had known him eight or nine years; had been in his boat late and early, and had never seen any thing amiss of him in her life: she had been after dark with him from London to Wandsworth, and averred that he was a sober, honest man, who did his best to maintain his family.

Mrs. Kenrick, who lived next door to him, had known him nine years, had been with him early and late by land and water, and deposed, that he bore an extraordinary good character.

Martha Leech had known him eighteen years: she said she had gone hundreds of times in his boat, at all hours, by night and by day; that he had never behaved immodestly to her in his life; and that he was an honest, civil man.

Esther Davis, who was only twenty-eight years of age, had known him eighteen years; had gone with him morning, noon, and evening, when he had always behaved with the greatest civility, and was an honest, industrious, sober man.

These testimonies of the women were confirmed by John Hodges, who had known him seven years; Ambrose Noswell, twenty-four; and Thomas Edmonds, fourteen; the latter of whom said, that he had a very good character, that he was willing to take care of his family, and he concluded by saying,

ing, " he is an indulgent husband, and as fond a
" father as can be."

After the evidence that has been recited, it is not to be wondered that the Jury brought in a verdict that the prisoner was *Not Guilty*.

We have been the more particular in the recounting of this trial, becaufe we think the acquittal of Moody does honour to his Jury. It is needlefs to fay that Juries fhould always take the favourable fide of the queftion, where there is any doubt of the guilt of the accufed party. It is to the credit of our Englifh Juries, that this is generally the cafe.

We do not mean, on this occafion, to affert that the profecutrix was perjured; but furely the evidence brought to criminate the prifoner was infufficient to fatisfy the mind of any reafonable man.

In cafes of rape particular caution ought to be ufed by thofe who are to be judges of the fact. A rape is one of the moft atrocious of crimes, and one of the moft difficult to be proved, as the proof of it muft generally depend on the fingle teftimony of the party fuppofed to be injured.

The violation of the will conftitutes the effence of the crime; for the perfonal injury is nothing, compared with the idea of a man's affuming the Bafhaw, and faying that a woman fhall be a flave to his luft.

In the courfe of this work we have hitherto concluded each trial with a ferious remark: We fhall finifh this with an anecdote.

In the reign of Queen Anne, a man * was apprehended, tried, and convicted, for committing a rape

---

* The name of the party is not mentioned in the printed accounts, or we fhould have given the trial in this work.

on a common woman of the town. Great intercession was made to save the convict, on account of the character, and situation in life, of the woman. At this juncture Dean Swift happened to be in England, and was in high favour with the ministry. In a letter to a friend in Ireland the Dean relates some of the particulars of the case, and says, "shall a woman be ravished because she is a whore? No, no, I'll take care of that;—the fellow shall be hanged, if I have any interest with the people in power:" and we are told that the man was hanged accordingly.

Particulars of the Trial of JOSEPH RELPH, who was indicted for Murder, and found guilty of Manslaughter.

AT the sessions held at the Old Bailey, in December, 1778, Joseph Relph, mariner, was indicted for the wilful murder of Andrew Schultz on the 26th of November preceding; and he likewise stood charged on the coroner's inquisition, for feloniously killing and slaying the said Andrew.

The prisoner was employed in the impress service, and the following is the state of the evidence adduced on the trial.—John Clear swore, that he was a beadle of Wapping; that Mr. James Stewart, a tallow-chandler, called him from the Mason's lodge, and told him a man was murdered: that he went to the sign of the Gibraltar, where he found the prisoner leaning down in a box, having the fingers of his left hand, which were bloody, tied in a handkerchief: that on this deponent's asking what was the matter, Relph said he had been used ill, and cut to pieces; that he went with him quietly to the Round-house, and the next day before a magistrate, who committed him to New prison.

John Hageman deposed, that he was a servant to Mr. Compton, sugar-baker, in Brewer's-lane; there were five of his companions, all of whom were going home to Mr. Compton's; that they were all on the foot-pavement, and the deceased was running before him: that he saw a woman with a lantern in her hand crossing the way, and a girl about eight years old with her; and that Hardwicke (one of the company) lifted up the woman's peticoats behind.

The counsel now interposed, and said he should prove that the woman and child were the wife and daughter of the prisoner.

Hageman proceeded, and said that the woman having walked a hundred yards, the prisoner overtook them; on which his wife pointed to Hardwicke, and said "This is the young man that laid "hold of my gown." The prisoner crossed to Hardwicke, and asked him what business he had to meddle with the woman's gown. Hardwicke made no reply; and one Kello coming up at the juncture, said to the lieutenant, (Relph) "Sir, I am your "prisoner, and will go with you where you like. This evidence farther deposed, that the lieutenant took Hardwicke by the neck, and pulled his hat off.

John Kello was now sworn; but not being perfect in the English language, an interpreter was sworn to deliver his evidence, which was to the following effect: that Andrew Schultz was one of the party, returning with his fellow-servants to Mr. Compton's; that he himself was sober, but

doubted

doubted if Hardwicke was not somewhat in liquor; that he did not see the prisoner, till he came and put a hanger to his breast; on which this deponent acknowledged himself his prisoner, and consented to go where he pleased; but that he thrust the hanger through his cloaths, and slightly wounded him in the breast.

When this deponent felt the sword hurt him, he jumped aside; and then Schultz said "You had "better put your sword by." After some struggling Kello took the hanger from the lieutenant, but did not observe whether Schultz was wounded or not; that the prisoner went to a public-house, and afterwards heard that Schultz was wounded; and that the lieutenant was cut in the hand.

Frederick Hardwicke, being sworn, acknowledged that he had touched the bottom of the woman's gown as he was passing her; owned he was a little disguised in liquor, and that, after he had touched the woman's gown, he received a blow from behind on his neck, and his hat fell off; but he could not tell by whom the blow was given. When he recovered himself, and got to his companions, he observed that Schultz was wounded, and that the lieutenant was going to the public house with a drawn hanger in his hand; he followed him, and staid there two minutes: he observed that the lieutenant's hand was bloody, and immediately went home to his own lodgings.

Sarah Hoskins, an oyster woman, wife of William Hoskins of Bell-dock, saw four young men in the highway, and observed the lieutenant collar Hardwicke, and likewise saw a woman on the other side of the way, whom she heard say "you dirty "fellow, how dare you meddle with my gown?" or petticoat, the deponent could not be sure which.

Her

Her husband, the lieutenant, then came up, and said "My dear, what is the matter?" to which she replied, "the dirty fellow has been pulling my "gown," or words to that purpose.

Mrs Hoskins then saw the lieutenant collar Frederick Hardwicke, and say "If you don't go "along with me, I will draw my sword and stab "you." They then struggled from the Bell alehouse door, till they got between a brazier's and tinshop, at the distance of nine or ten yards. In the mean time one of the men, who had a stick, hit the lieutenant on the back while Hardwicke and he were struggling. During this commotion the lieutenant's wife was hanging round his neck in the highway; but this deponent did not see the sword drawn, only heard the threat that it should be done: nor did she know whether the sword was drawn before or after the lieutenant was struck.

About five or six minutes after the lieutenant was struck with the stick, she heard somebody cry out, "Stop him, stop him, the young man is dead in "the tin-shop." The lieutenant then went into the ale-house.

This was the substance of the evidence; and the judge then said to the counsel for the prisoner, "Do you mean to make this less than manslaugh"ter?" To which the counsel replied in the following words: "No, my lord, we cannot make it "less than manslaughter. The lieutenant was "used very ill while his wife was hanging round "his neck to prevent any further fighting. She "was cut a-cross her neck, and the lieutenant had "his hand and his coat cut in two places, and was "beat all over his arm and shoulders."

The court now observing that, if the jury were satisfied, nothing farther need be heard, but if not they

they would proceed; the jury said, "My lord, we are all satisfied;" and soon afterwards they gave a verdict that the prisoner was "Not guilty of the murder, but guilty of manslaughter only;" on which he was branded and discharged.

We see that, in the instance before us, a life had been lost, yet the party accused could not be convicted of murder; and we have the rather inserted this trial, to caution people to avoid occasional quarrels in the streets, which can never be attended with any good consequences, and are frequently productive of the most fatal.

In the present case we find that the accused party was what is called a lieutenant of a press-gang; that is, the principal savage among savages. The custom of impressing, let counsellors plead, and senators debate till they are hoarse, is incompatible with every idea we can frame of the natural right to that freedom which God has bestowed equally on us all; and which, from the very nature of the donation, it appears to be every man's duty to support.

There is nothing very particular in the case before us which tends to prove any insolence on the part of the lieutenant; but these volumes are growing to a conclusion, and we could not think of putting a period to them, without entering our protest against a practice which opposes every sentiment of humanity, and militates against all the finer feelings of the soul.

What! because a man has served his country faithfully for a series of years by sea, and has at length retired in the fond hope of enjoying the sweets of domestic felicity, shall he be dragged from the fond wife, and the helpless innocents, when he wishes not again to tempt the danger of

Mode of punishment by BRANDING, or burning on the HAND, at the New Sessions House.

the seas? Honour, common honesty, plain sense, humanity, and even law, reprobate the idea!

We have had of late two or three instances of freemen of London being impressed; but they have been discharged: the hardiest, the most callous of our lawyers dare not bring the matter to a legal issue: they know that sound sense and the laws of the realm are against the practice; they therefore fly from the subject, and, like the Parthians, conquer in retreat.

Setting aside all moral considerations, and permitting even humanity to sleep on this subject, sound policy forbids this infernal practice. The British tars are full free to serve their country. Let proper bounties be offered, let proper encouragements be held forth, and the navy will never want a man. It will be said that the giving high bounties to sailors will occasion an increase of those taxes which are already nearly insupportable. No doubt but our taxes are very burthensome; but let our pensioners be reduced in number and in pay, and we shall not want a sum to reward our daring sailors. Besides, the bounties given to these men, politically considered, cost nothing. Every man knows that a seaman carries nothing abroad with him but his jacket, his trowsers, and his valour. He spends his bounty-money where he receives it; and the cash circulates among those who gave it.

Let BRITISH GENEROSITY vie with BRITISH VALOUR, and we may bid DEFIANCE to the WORLD!

Account of the Trial of HENRY BALL, THOMAS OSBORNE, and WILLIAM HILSDON, for a Burglary in an unhabited House at Hendon in Middlesex, whence they stole a Quantity of Household Furniture, some Linen, Wearing Apparel, and other Articles, the Property of BENJAMIN WOOD.

EERLY in the month of November, 1778, Mr. Wood and his family moved from Hendon to his house in town, for the winter season. About two o'clock in the morning of the 18th of December, John Fuller, a watchman at Hampstead, observed a cart passing through that town heavily laden, and attended by two men on horseback; and, stepping into the road, he asked, what was in the cart? To which no answer was given; but the horse being whipped, the cart was driven against the corner of a broker's shop, and overturned; when the horsemen rode off at full speed. Ball then came up, and being questioned by Fuller, denied that he belonged to the cart, and struck him with his fist on the neck; whereupon Fuller drew a hanger, threatening to put him to instant death, if he attempted any further resistance. Ball, having surrendered, Fuller delivered him into the charge of two constables; and then went to the cart, and gave that and the goods it contained and the horses into the custody of a constable, named Muddocks, who had just found a man's hat in the road, which was supposed to have been lost by one of the prisoner's accomplices.

About noon Mr. Wood received information that his house at Hendon had been broke open and robbed; and Mrs. Wood immediately set out to examine what loss was sustained. She found that the

the house was almost intirely stripped of the furniture; that the cellar had been broke open, and liquor of different sorts stolen, and from some rum being left in a tea-cup, she supposed the robbers had drank while they were in the house.

On the trial of the above offenders, Simon Edwards swore, that he searched Ball soon after his apprehension, and found in his possession an iron crow, a chissel, three common keys, and a number of pick-lock keys.

Samuel Muddocks deposed, that he had tried the three keys taken from Ball, and found them exactly to fit the locks to which Mrs. Wood had informed him they belonged; and that he had tried the pick-locks, and found that one of them would open the lock of the front door. This witness further said, that he tried the chissel and the crow, and that they fitted the marks in the door and other parts of the house that were broken; that it appeared as if the villains had entered by the front door, and broke open the back door, for the purpose of moving the goods with the greater secrecy; and that he had traced the marks made by a cart and one horse from the back-door into the road.

Dennis M'Donnald swore, that in consequence of an information exhibited before the bench of magistrates sitting at the Rotation-office in Litchfield-street, he went to the house of a Mr. Davis in Fetter-lane, and in a room on the second floor found Osborne and Hilsdon lying on a bed in their cloaths, and that their shoes were intirely covered with country dirt; that he found a towel with Mrs. Wood's mark on it lying upon the bed, and took two keys from Hilsdon, who was attempting to throw them away, and the next day went to Hendon, and found that the keys exactly fitted the

locks

locks belonging to the two closets in Mr. Wood's fore parlour; that he found an iron crow concealed in the chimney; and that Davis's wife told him Osborne and Hilsdon came in about five o'clock in the morning. Charles Grubb and James Hide confirmed the evidence of M'Donald; and Grubb produced the iron crow and the towel, which latter Mrs. Wood swore to be her property.

Thomas Boyce deposed, that on his way to London he stopped at Hampstead, and heard a report, that a robbery had been committed; that when he reached Battle-bridge, he observed a man walking in the road without a hat, and having a handkerchief tied upon his head, and remarked his person very particularly, as he entertained a suspicion of him from the circumstance of his being without a hat at that severe season of the year, and the recollection that a hat had been left on the road at Hampstead by one of the supposed robbers. Boyce said he could not positively swear to the person of Hilsdon, but believed him to be the man he had seen without a hat at Battle-bridge.

John Fletcher, clerk in the public-office in Litchfield-street, being sworn, said, that when Ball was brought before the magistracy for examination, he requested to be an evidence for the crown, which being refused, on account of the notoriety of his character, he voluntarily acknowledged his guilt, and mentioned the parties who were concerned with him in the robbery, in consequence of which officers were dispatched to Davis's house in order to apprehend them.

Boyce was called a second time, and questioned as to the dress of the man he had mentioned seeing at Battle-bridge; and he described him as being dressed

dressed in a sailor's jacket much worn. Grubb swore, that the description given by Boyce exactly corresponded with the appearance of Hilsdon at the time of his being apprehended.

Mary Davis appeared on behalf of Hilsdon, and positively denied having told M'Donald, Grubb, and Hide, that Osborne and Hilsdon came to her house about five in the morning of the 18th of December, but swore that she let Hilsdon in about eight o'clock in the evening of the 17th; that he went up to his own apartment, and that she saw him no more till about six the next evening, soon after which the officers came to apprehend him. Richard Davis said Hilsdon had lodged in his house about a year and three quarters, and that he had always believed him to be an honest man. William Hall and Joseph Loe also gave him a good character; and Loe swore that Osborne declared to him in the prison, that Hilsdon was not concerned in the burglary at Hendon. Mr. Lay, master of a coal-wharf, said, he had employed Hilsdon as a carman twelve years, during which time he had acted as an honest, sober, and industrious man, and that he had considered him as a very valuable servant; adding that he was in his business on the 17th, but not on the 18th of December. After some consultation, the jury declared the prisoners to be guilty, and they received sentence of death.

Henry Ball and Thomas Osborne were executed at Tyburn on Friday the 9th of February, 1779 *.

Ball was one of the villains concerned in the daring robbery at Mr. Clewen's at Finchley; his character had been long notorious as a house-

---

* Hilsdon was reprieved.

breaker, and he had been more than once admitted an evidence for the crown; he was a man of a remarkably stout make, and of an active spirit in exploits of villainy, where the danger did not seem great; but his companions frequently upbraided him for cowardice, on account of the terror by which he appeared to be affected when he supposed the officers of justice to be in search of him. Osborne had also been concerned in a great number of daring robberies, and was considered as a most dangerous nuisance to society. A few days before his execution he told a man of his acquaintance, that "he expected to die at the gallows; but "that he did not believe the hemp was then spun "that was to form the rope by which his body was "destined to be suspended."

What felicity can that man promise himself who infringes the laws instituted for the regulation and good order of society? He declares war against mankind, who, in order to provide for their own safety, unite in a common interest to expel him that community of which he has rendered himself a dangerous and disgraceful member. If we had no desires to satisfy, we should have no motive to activity; and a perpetual supineness and want of variety would render life insupportably tedious. If gratification is obtained by unjustifiable means, it must be slight and transitory; for the pains of a wounded conscience will admit of no intermission in the hours of solitude, and in those of hilarity they will only subside to return with aggravating poignancy. Let us teach ourselves to think with the excellent Rousseau: "When delivered from "the illusions of our bodies and senses, we shall "enjoy the contemplation of the Supreme Being, "and the eternal truths of which he is the source:
"when

"when the beauty of order shall strike all the
"powers of our souls, and we are only employed
"in comparing what we have done with what we
"ought to have done, then the voice of conscience
"will recover its empire; then the pure will, which
"springs from self-content, and the bitter regret of
"having disgraced ourselves, will distinguish, by
"inexhaustible sentiments, the lot which every one
"has prepared for himself."

Account of the Trials of WILLIAM COOPER, and THOMAS LEWINGTON, who were convicted of robbing a Waggon.

WE insert this case because the robbery of Waggons has become so frequent, within the last two years, as to render it necessary for the legislature to interpose, to provide a more effectual punishment for a crime which has increased to a most alarming magnitude, and which renders it unsafe for our traders to trust their property by the common mode of conveyance.

At the sessions held at the Old Bailey in December, 1778, William Cooper and Thomas Lewington were indicted for stealing seventy pounds weight of raw silk, value seventy pounds, the property of Edward Hewitt, on the first of the same month.

Robert Joblin, book-keeper at the White-horse Inn, Cripplegate, deposed, that on the 30th of November, one Atkins, porter to Mr. Hewit, a silk-mercer in Wood-street, brought four or five boxes to go by the waggon to Glasgow; that there was raw silk in some of them; and that they were loaded in the waggon, which waggon was afterwards robbed of a box directed to Brown, Burn, and Company, at Paisley.

William Stocker, warehouse-man to Mr. Hewit, proved the packing up five boxes to go by the Newcastle waggon *, and that they were sent to the inn, directed as mentioned by the preceding witness. The book-keeper went to Mr. Stocker the following day, and told him that the waggon was robbed of one of the boxes, and desired him to attend at Bow-street, where two men and a woman were in custody, on whom had been found a quantity of silk. Mr. Stocker went accordingly, and saw a box, to the direction of which he could positively swear. He likewise observed a mark on the silk, which the dyers put on to distinguish one person's silk from that of another; and he said the weight of the silk produced at Sir John Fielding' corresponded with that in the box; but, for his own part, he did not know the silk-dyer's mark.

George Durant, a silk-dyer, gave a very clear and conclusive evidence. He said, that he sent to Mr. Hewitt 400 lb. weight of such silk as that produced on the trial. He farther deposed, that it was morally impossible to swear to silk after it was out of his hands, unless it had his private mark on it; that he went with Mr. Stocker to the Brown Bear in Bow-street, opposite Sir John Fielding's, where he was shewn the silk, the whole of which he looked through, and found two, and only two, of his private marks. Before he looked at this silk he shewed

---

* From this evidence, compared with the former, it should seem as if the Newcastle waggon went to Glasgow, or that there is a waggon between one town and the other.

the officers the mark which should be on it, if it was the same that he dyed for Mr. Hewit. His custom was to tie a particular kind of knot to distinguish one man's silk from that of another; and he said, that as far as any private mark could identify any property, he could swear that the silk in question was the property of Mr. Hewit.

The court, observing that he had only found two marks on the silk, asked Mr. Durant how many there ought to have been? To which he replied in the following words;" "I do not know that it ought to
" have more; we seldom put more than two marks
" if it is 70 lb. weight; we divide certain quanti-
" ties into certain parcels; we seldom put less than
" 30 lb. in a parcel, sometimes five, six, or seven
" and thirty; we put a mark upon each; there-
" fore, I apprehend, this could have but two marks
" upon it. We often boil forty men's silk toge-
" ther; we have a different mark for every man's
" silk. This mark has been Mr. Hewit's as long
" as I have been in this way, which is ten years
" and upwards."

William Lee deposed, that he was a watchman in Kingsland road; that between eight and nine at night he saw the two prisoners and another man following the Newcastle waggon; that they were at the distance of about four lamps from the waggon; that he had some suspicion of them; that the porter went out of London a little way with the waggon, and when he returned he told him of these men following the waggon. On the following morning the waggoner acquainted him with the robbery, and asked him to shew him where the parties lived.

Lee being asked if he knew the parties, replied in the affirmative, and said, that he bad them good night on their return, and that Cooper bad him good night. This deponent went with the waggoner to a house at Hoxton, where they found the prisoners, and another man, who got away from them: he said that he secured Cooper, and his companion took Lewington into custody; and on searching their room the two bags of silk were found.

George Sturton, one of Sir John Fielding's men, deposed, that he was present when the room was entered, and Lewington was found asleep with his head on the table; and that he observed a trunk, the lock of which was taken off; that the porter opened the trunk, and said there was some of the property. This deponent going into another room, saw Cooper and Woodey (a supposed accomplice) both asleep with their cloaths on: Woody was on the bed, and Cooper on the ground with some of the property under him. Lewington rose up, and was seized, but Woody slipped aside, and made his escape. Sturton said, that the watchman seized Cooper as he was going down stairs. A constable was sent for; the room was searched, and two bags of silk, and other things were found. This deponent swore to the bags, which had never been out of his custody.

John Read deposed, that he was the driver of the Newcastle waggon, and that when he came to Hertford, about seven o'clock in the morning, he found that the ropes had been cut, that the sheet was rent to the length of about a foot, and that he missed three boxes. He said that an old gentlewoman, a passenger from the inn, was in the waggon all night, but that she was at such a distance, that the boxes might easily be taken out without her knowing it.

The driver saying that he had either walked or rode by the waggon all night, and that the ropes were cut on the off-side *; the jury asked him if he had not stopped to drink? To which he replied that he had drank a pint of beer at the Ship at Tottenham, but had not stayed a minute.

Cooper made an indifferent defence, and called four witnesses, who gave him a good character; but Lewington did not pretend to set up the slightest justification of his conduct.

The jury found a verdict of guilty; the prisoners were sentenced to work three years at ballast-heaving, and they are now † undergoing the sentence on board the lighter off Woolwich.

Perhaps if we had a law to make the offence of robbing a waggon equally capital with a common robbery on the highway, we should have few instances of such crimes being committed. As matters now stand, not a week passes but we hear of robberies of this kind: the dairy-man cannot send his butter, nor the farmer and grazier their meat to market, but some lurking villains are on the road, ready to cut the ropes. The packages fall unknown to the driver, owing to the noise made by the horses and carriage: some accomplices are behind with a light cart to pick up the goods thus dropped, and when they have them in possession, they turn about, and go into London by some other road.

Within a few months past these villains have gone as far as ten or a dozen miles out of London,

---

* This is always the case in robbing of waggons. The thieves constantly cut the ropes on the opposite side from the driver; and the noise of the carriage prevents his knowing what is transacted.

† In March, 1779.

to commit their felonies: but they have sometimes ventured on the early waggons after they have been on the stones of London.

It has been known that fifty pounds worth of provisions have been thus stolen, in one morning, from waggons coming to Newgate-market only; and some countrymen have lost as much in a week as the profits of three months could not repay.

We know that dogs of particular breed may be trained to any duty. The docility of these animals is amazing. Would it not be good policy in the owners of waggons to have one strong dog constantly in the carriage, and another walking under it? The dogs would certainly discharge their duty, and the property would be preserved. There are hundreds of villains who will rob and plunder their fellow-creatures, who would tremble at the idea of encountering a dog. We cannot conclude these observations more properly than by saying, *A word to the wise is enough.*

A Narrative of the Trials of GEORGE ROACH, ROBERT ELLIOT, and JONAS PARKER, who were convicted, the two first of stealing, and the other of receiving Part of a leaden Coffin *.

AT the sessions held at the Old Bailey in April, 1778, these men were indicted, the two former for stealing a leaden Coffin, of three hundred

---

* The trials of these men are inserted a little out of their proper order, at the request of a subscriber, who obligingly sent us a drawing for the print corresponding thereto.

Geo. Roach, Robt. Elliott, & Jas. Gould, stealing the LEADEN COFFIN of W. T. ASTON, Esqr. in the Vault of Aldermanbury Church.

pounds weight, value 5 £. the property of William Thornton Aston, Esq; and Parker was indicted for receiving fifty pounds weight of the lead, value 5 s. knowing the same to have been stolen. The second count † in the indictment laid the lead to be the property of the parishioners of Aldermanbury, and stolen by Roach and Elliott; and the third count charged Jonas Parker with receiving it, being the property of the parishioners of Aldermanbury, well knowing it to have been stolen.

William Thornton Aston, Esq; deposed, that, on the first of January preceding, his brother was interred in a leaden coffin, in the church of Aldermanbury; that the coffin was stolen out of the church, and was missed on the seventh of March.

James Gould, who had been admitted an evidence, deposed that Roach, Elliot, and himself, were journeymen carpenters, working under Mr. Augurs in the repair of the church. He said that on Friday the 6th of March he and Roach went into the vault, and unscrewed all the screws of Mr. Thornton's coffin except two, after which they returned to their work; and that, afterwards, themselves and Elliot agreed to work again on the coffin.

On the Saturday morning they went to the church, and about five o'clock a watchman followed them in, and desired a board to be planed, which was done by Gould. The accomplices then loosened the other screws, and turned the coffins bottom upwards, taking off the outside coffin, and

---

† We have not yet had occasion to mention the practice of laying different *counts* in an indictment. This seems to be intended to prevent, by every possible method, villains escaping the justice of their country.

leaving

leaving only the shell. They then cut the leaden coffin in pieces, and replacing the other coffin on the shell, screwed it down again.

These transactions lasted them till near eight in the morning, when they took the pieces of the coffin, and having concealed them under the childrens gallery, they conferred on selling what they had stolen; when Elliott mentioned Parker, in Grubb-street, as a likely purchaser.

The lead being in two pieces, Gould put one of them in a bag, and took it away, and the other was put in a basket, and carried by one of the accomplices. When they got to London-wall, Elliot beckoned Gould, and they went to a shop where they offered the lead to sale, to a person who refused to be the purchaser. They then went to Parker's, who weighed the lead, without asking them any questions, said it was forty-two pounds, and paid them three shillings and six-pence for it, being at the rate of a penny a pound. When they were going away with the empty bag, Mr. Augurs's apprentice came in and seized on Gould, desiring Parker, who was a constable, to assist in conveying him and Elliot to Mr. Augurs's. Parker said " You had better go to your master, and try to " make the matter up." They went, and were all charged with the felony. Parker said, " Give " them a *trevalle* for it."

Gould, being asked what he understood by that term, said he did not exactly know what it meant; but supposed it was a hint to attempt making their escape; on which they *made a run for it* (to use his own words), and Parker likewise ran away; but they were stopped and taken into custody, before they had got to any considerable distance.

John Brotherous, apprentice to Mr. Augurs, confirmed so much of the former testimony as related to himself. He said, that passing by London-wall about eight in the morning, he saw Roach coming down Wood-street, with a basket on his back, and that Roach seeing him, crossed over the street. Brotherous demanded what he had with him: he said his tools, and turned round, as if to prevent his looking in his basket; but he did look in, and saw there was lead; on which he seized Roach, and sent for a constable to take him into custody. This was the occasion of his going to the house of Parker, whom he knew to be a constable. On his arrival at Parker's, he met with Gould and Elliot coming out of the house with empty sacks, on which he supposed they had sold something there.

He charged Parker with the prisoners; but he said " You had bettter go to your master quietly, " and make the affair up." Brotherous informed his master what had passed; and he caused all the prisoners to be apprehended, who endeavoured to make their escape as the proper officer was conveying them to the Compter.

Mr. Reynolds, an undertaker, deposed that he buried Mr. Thornton in a leaden coffin: that he surveyed the vault on the 7th of March, when the coffin was missing: that he compared the pieces that were found at Parker's with the rest of the coffin that was found under the gallery of the church; and when all were beaten together into the same form, they made out the shape and quantity * of Mr. Thornton's coffin; the plate, with Mr. Thornton's name on it, was found in Roach's

---

* This seems to be a very conclusive kind of evidence.

chest; the lead, to the weight of fifty-two pounds, was found under the counter in Parker's shop; and this deponent added that it was a sort of lead worked in a fashion peculiar to coffins, and that people in the trade knew very well that it was coffin lead.

Isaac Mather deposed, that old lead was worth about thirteen shillings and sixpence the hundred weight, or three half-pence the pound.

By way of defence, Roach said, that Gould put the lead into his basket, but that he knew nothing of its being stolen. Elliot likewise denied all knowledge of the stealing the lead, and said he never received any money or other thing on account thereof, but was in Parker's shop, buying a hinge for his own use; but was astonished when he saw Gould there, and still more at his master's apprentice giving charge of him.

Parker's plea of defence was, that the evidence came into his shop to sell some lead, which he did not know was stolen; that when he had weighed, and was paying for it, Mr. Augurs's apprentice entered, and gave him charge of the prisoners; and that, when at the master's house, he charged him likewise; but that he immediately mentioned where the two pieces were which he had bought, in consequence of which they were found.

All the prisoners called persons who gave them good characters: but the jury, having fully considered the nature of the evidence, gave a verdict "That they were guilty;" in consequence of which, at the close of the sessions, Roach and Elliot were sentenced to labour three years on the Thames, and Parker to be imprisoned for a like term of time.

The robbing of churches has ever been deemed sacrilegious by all who have professed any veneration for the duties and obligations of religion. The idea of disturbing the ashes of the dead has something in it abhorrent to the feelings of human nature, to the dictates of christian piety. When the clay cold body is committed to the tomb, we presume that it is to rest in peace till the final renovation of all things; nor can the surviving friends and relations easily pardon those who violate the mansions of the dead, and make a jest of the rites of sepulture.

The solemn funeral once closed, we take a temporary farewel, in the hope of meeting in a glorious eternity; but, while the frailties of mortality surround us, it is impossible not to look with abhorrence on those who can commit a theft attended with every circumstance of horror!

Supposing our friends to repose in peace, we comfort ourselves that they have only drawn the inevitable lot; that they are gone but a short stage forward on that road whither we must soon follow them; and in this consideration we can chearfully say, with the poet,

Why should we mourn departing friends,
 Or shake at death's alarms?
'Tis but the voice that Jesus sends
 To call us to his arms.

Account of the Trial of Doctor BARTHOLOMEW DOMINICETTI, who was indicted for a pretended Forgery in altering the principal Sum of a Promissory-note, payable to MICHAEL PARYS, from 16£. to 20£. with Intention to defraud ANTONIO RAMPONI.

RAMPONI being desirous of opening a tavern, consulted doctor Dominicetti, with whom he had been some years acquainted, as to the measures he should pursue for entering into business with the most favourable prospect of success; and the doctor recommended him to Mr. Andrees, secretary to the Venetian ambassador; and through the joint interest of that gentleman and the doctor, Ramponi was enabled to open a handsome house in Panton-square.

Ramponi's business not proving so advantageous as was expected, he became involved in pecuniary difficulties; and his creditors being exceedingly importunate for their respective demands, the doctor offered him an asylum in his house at Chelsea. At this period, a settlement of all money transactions was proposed by the doctor, who then declared, that if Ramponi would pay him 100£. he would give him an acquittance of his whole debt, amounting to upwards of 340£. and John Dodsworth was employed to draw out the account current between the parties. Thus were matters situated when the circumstance took place which gave rise to the trial, the particulars of which we shall now relate.

Mr. Michael Parys, of the hotel in Suffolk-street, deposed, that in January, 1777, he received a note of hand for 16£. and 8£. 14s. 6d. in cash, of doctor Dominicetti, in discharge of a book-debt contracted by Ramponi to his brother-in-law, Mr. Harris of Bath; and being shewn the altered note on which the indictment was founded, proved that it was the identical note he had received from the doctor for 16£. and paid away for the same sum to Mr. Vickers.

The note being shewn to Mr. Thomas Vickers, he swore that he received it of Mr. Parys; and that when it became due he presented it to Messrs Stevenson and Gentel, to whom it was directed for payment; and that Mr. Gentel gave him in exchange for the note sixteen pounds in cash.

Mr. John Henry Gentel swore, that doctor Dominicetti authorized him to pay his note of hand for 16£. and that the note produced in court was the same he received from Mr. Vickers, and returned to the doctor as a note for 16£. in which state it was presented for payment.

The next witness examined was John Dodsworth, who deposed, that he was employed by doctor Dominicetti to draw out an account current between him and Antonio Ramponi; that he attended at the Doctor's house at Chelsea, and produced the account, which was examined and approved by both parties, who ordered him to cast up the several sums, and strike the balance; that, while he was casting up the account, Ramponi went out of the room, when the Doctor said, "Hold, Dodsworth, I recollect to have a note, the amount of which I paid to Mr. Parys for Ramponi;" that he produced a note for 20£. and ordered him to charge that sum to his account against Ramponi, which he did accordingly; that presently after Ramponi returned, and the account current was

signed

signed by both parties. Being asked if he knew Mr. Craigh, the Governor Advocate of Gibraltar, he replied, "Yes, to my mortification I do." He confessed that he had committed an offence for which that judge had sentenced him to be executed; and said that "since his enlargement he had endeavoured to act the part of an honest man." Upon the cross examination of this accomplished villain, the calm and determined manner in which he perjured himself, his shocking ingratitude, and a thousand instances of most abominable villainy, struck the court with astonishment and horror. He was brought to acknowledge, that doctor Dominicetti's son was present at the settlement of the account, though he had before sworn to the contrary; and that an alteration of four pounds which appeared in the account current was made by himself, in order to make the sum total correspond with the alteration made in the principal sum of the note.

The court and the jury, clearly perceiving with how iniquitous a view the prosecution was instituted, refused to hear further evidence, and honourably acquitted the Doctor; advising him to prosecute the delinquents under a bill of indictment, which had been already found by the grand jury against Ramponi and Dodsworth for a conspiracy.

Ramponi and Dodsworth had experienced innumerable instances of benevolence from Doctor Dominicetti, who supplied Ramponi with several considerable sums merely on his personal security; and even gave the note of hand for 16£. on which the prosecution was founded, when he knew Ramponi to be in desperate circumstances, and had so little hope of recovering that or any former sums advanced

vanced for his use, that he offered to accept 100£. for his whole demand.

The deplorable situation of Dodsworth excited the compassion of the Doctor, who took him under his protection, and allowed him a handsome maintenance for regulating his accounts, and some other little services for which he was qualified. He committed several forgeries upon the Doctor for small sums, and was guilty of many other acts of delinquency, which, at length, induced his generous benefactor to withdraw his patronage.

In return for the singular benevolence and liberality of the doctor, they entered into a diabolical combination to exhibit against him a felonious accusation, to which the life of a worthy man would have been sacrificed, but for those excellent laws which are equally framed for the protection of the innocent, and the punishment of the guilty.

Ramponi's view was evidently to free himself from a claim of upwards of 340£. and the promise of a trifling gratification prevailed upon Dodsworth to join in the infernal conspiracy.

The villainy of these men was so enormous, that to dwell on the subject would perhaps be thought impertinent, because it would be to anticipate those sentiments which a perusal of the above narrative must necessarily suggest to our readers. That species of ingratitude, which consists merely in neglecting a proper acknowledgement of benefits received is justly numbered among the vices most degrading to human nature: but what terms of reprobation can convey an adequate idea of the abhorrence that every man, not wholly abandoned to all the principles allied to virtue, must entertain for those characters that aggravate the sin of ingratitude by deliberately concerted schemes to involve in affliction and ignominy such as by repeated acts of beneficence have entitled themselves to the warm effusions of grateful acknowledgement!

Narrative of the extraordinary Case of ROWLAND RIDGLEY, who was convicted of having in his Possession a Puncheon, on which was impressed the Figure of the Head-side of a Shilling.

AT the sessions held at the Old Bailey in December, 1788, Rowland Ridgeley was indicted " for that he, not being a person employed
" in, or for, the mint, knowingly, feloniously,
" and traiterously, had in his custody and posses-
" sion, a puncheon made of iron and steel, in and
" upon which was made and impressed the figure,
" resemblance, and similitude, of the head-side of
" a shilling, without any lawful authority or suffi-
" cient excuse for that purpose, against the duty of
" his allegiance, and against the statute, &c. on the
" 19th of June *."

The first witness called was John Clarke, who deposed, that he went to the house of one Ball in Bunhill-row; that he knew the room belonged to the prisoner, by the cloaths that were found there, which very cloaths he had seen the prisoner wear; and that after he was apprehended, and taken before a

---

* He was likewise indicted for having in his possession a puncheon, upon which was impressed, &c. the figure of a guinea.

magistrate

The BELL-MAN at St Sepulchre's, speaking the admonitory Words to the Malefactor's going to Execution.

magistrate, he acknowledged that the lodgings belonged to him, and that the cloaths were his property.

Moses Morant testified, that he went with Clarke to Bunhill-row, where they broke open the door in presence of Ball:—that he found under the chest of drawers a quantity of halfpence, and, among some litter, a leaden pot containing a parcel of puncheons and halfpence; and that under the drawers he found some shillings; and some half-crowns on the tester of the bed.

Clarke said farther, that there were some bad guineas in the pot, and that the puncheons which were found were completely finished; that it might have been proper to have had a tail-side made; but that would have been attended with more trouble and expence, and therefore only the head-side was represented. Clarke would not undertake to swear that the impression on the counterfeit shillings was made from the puncheons found, but that it had all the appearance of being so.

Thomas Ball, landlord of the house, deposed, that the prisoner had lodged with him about a week; that he had the key of he room in his own possession; and that he never heard him make a noise with any instruments, which he thought must have been the case if the prisoner had used any. This deponent was present when the articles above-mentioned were found.

John Dixon swore, that he apprehended the prisoner on the 8th of October, but found not any counterfeit money on him; however, he found a paper writing, dated the 30th of September, which imported to be a notice from him of his intention to surrender.

Mr. Pingo was next sworn.—To afford a clear idea of the force of his evidence, it will be necessary to give it in his own words:—" I am an en-
" graver of the Mint; the prisoner is not employ-
" ed by the Mint; the puncheon makes the dye,
" and the counter-puncheon is the dye when it is
" made; the machines produced are puncheons,
" but not puncheons made at the Mint. The me-
" thod by which these are made is, that they first
" take a true shilling, and cut it away to the out-
" line of the head; when they have done that,
" they take a piece of steel, on which they fix this
" outline; and then they file or cut the steel close
" away to that outline, till the steel is exactly the
" shape of the head, and that is what is called a
" puncheon; these particular puncheons are all
" ready for use, for they are all hardened, and they
" never are hardened till they are ready for use;
" that is the last operation they go through. It is
" impossible to say positively whether the shillings
" found in the prisoner's lodgings were made from
" these puncheons, because they are so imperfect,
" but they have all the appearance of it. In a new
" dye, or counter-puncheon, the letters are always
" engraved in the counter-puncheon after it is
" struck; there is no occasion to have any letters
" on old coin, it will pass without. The letters are
" put on afterwards, and a puncheon is complete
" without any letters at all; a puncheon may have
" letters made upon it, but they never use such
" puncheons at the Mint, from the inconvenience
" of them, because they would be so liable to
" break, and would require so much nicety to re-
" present all the little angles and corners of the
" letters; that is the very reason that we engrave
" the letters afterwards upon the counter-pun-
" cheon;

"cheon; but for making base shillings nothing
"else is necessary but this puncheon; these pun-
"cheons which are produced, barely as you see
"them, though they might be for the making base
"shillings, yet they may be made use of for other
"purposes; namely, for making seals, buttons,
"medals, or other things, where such impressions
"are wanted."

Ann Goodman deposed, that she was a servant to the landlord of the house where the prisoner lodged; that she went frequently up into the room next Ridgley's apartment, and his door was never locked.

Several persons deposed, that he was a bookbinder by trade, that he had worked for them, and bore the character of an honest man; nor did they know any thing to impeach that character, till the present accusation against him.

The jury having considered of the whole of the evidence, gave a verdict, "That the prisoner was "guilty;" but judgment against him was respited for the opinion of the judges; which opinion was delivered at the sessions held in February, 1779, and imported, that his case was within the meaning of the act of parliament; in consequence of which, at the close of the sessions, he received sentence of death.

Of the behaviour of this malefactor after conviction we have nothing very favourable to say. He did not seem properly affected by the dreadful situation in which he stood.

It is remarkable of Ridgley, that he had made himself so sure of acquittal, that, just before he was put on his trial, he told some persons who attended him that he should be discharged in a few minutes.

We have been informed that he had been many years a notorious coiner, and a chief inftructor of feveral of thofe who came to the gallows before him:—a dreadful trade! how horrid to think of bringing up youths to the moft certain fate of ignominy!

On the morning of execution, this man behaved, on his quitting Newgate, and on his way to the fatal tree, with the greateft appearance of unconcern, repeatedly fmiling, and fhaking hands with his acquaintance as he paffed; yet he evidently ftruggled to conceal an anguifh of mind that could *not* be concealed.

When the bell-man at St. Sepulchre's church was fpeaking the admonitory words, Ridgley, who had belonged to a club with him, faid, " Remember me at the club to night."

When he arrived at the place of execution, his behaviour took a different turn; he acknowledged the juftice of his fentence, and died a penitent.

Rowland Ridgley was executed at Tyburn on the 31ft of March, 1779, and the body delivered to his friends for interment.

After all that has been faid on the fubject of coining, it will be unneceffary to add a fingle remark; for furely no man can think of practifing this dangerous trade, who is not refolutely bent on his own deftruction!

Particu-

Particulars of the Trial, Conviction, and Execution, of FREDERICK JOHN EUSTACE; and likewise of the Trial and Acquittal of HENRY LANGHAM, for Housebreaking.

EUSTACE had been a servant to lord Clarendon, but had quitted his lordship's service some months before the commission of the fact of which he was accused.

At the sessions held at the Old Bailey in February, 1779, Frederick John Eustace was indicted for breaking and entering the dwelling-house of the right honourable Thomas earl of Clarendon on the night of the 23d of January, and stealing ten shirts, eight neckcloths, four guineas in money, and other effects, the property of Henry Johnson, in the same dwelling-house.

Mr. Johnson deposed, that he was second coachman to lord Clarendon, with whom the prisoner had lived as the upper coachman, but had quitted his service in the preceding summer; that his fellow-servant, John Cowen, had fastened the doors of the coach-house, which were broke open between eight and nine o'clock on the night mentioned in the indictment, when the above-recited articles and others were taken away: that he did not observe any marks of violence, but that a person who was with him thought he saw the mark of a stick which had been put in to force open the door; and he added, that the persons who committed the fact went up stairs into the room, over the stable, where he slept, and took his box, which contained four guineas, and several other articles.

This box was found on the following morning in Hyde-park, and within it was a smaller box, which contained the money; whereupon Eustace was suspected, and both the prisoners were taken into custody. When he visited them in prison, he found one of his shirts on Eustace, who likewise wore a pair of his stockings; and in his pocket was found a letter directed to a woman, to go to New-street, Carnaby-market, to fetch some linen, some of which was found at the house of his washerwoman. This deponent being asked, if the coach-house and the rooms where the things were was behind the house, answered in the affirmative; but said it was connected with it by walls, and that there was a passage ran from it to the dwelling-house *.

John Cowen (upper coachman) swore, that he fastened the coach-house door at eight o'clock; that he was to fetch his lord from the Opera-house at ten o'clock; and that he fastened the door with a bar across it, and an iron rail over the bar, as was usually done when the coach was to go out again: he added, that it was so fastened that it could not be opened with the hand, but might be by a stick, or a long knife; that after it was fastened, he and the other coachman, and the postilion, went to a public-house to drink; and that, on his return, the back-door was open.

Sarah Betney deposed, that she was a washerwoman employed by both the prisoners; that she received from Henry Langham two pair of stockings belonging to the prosecutor: that the prisoners asked her permission to leave some clean linen of

---

* On this circumstance the event of the trial seems to have turned. The connexion of the buildings made the coach-house (in a *legal* light) a part of the dwelling-house.

their own on the Sunday morning, and took it away on the following day.

She added, that an inventory was taken of the linen by the desire of both the prisoners, and in their presence, by Mr. Rozea, with whom this woman lived. This inventory was produced, as drawn by Rozea, and signed by the washerwoman.

John Dixon deposed, that he apprehended the prisoners for a different fact than that alledged in the indictment; that he went to the washerwoman's and saw the linen, and found the inventory in Langham's pocket.

By way of defence, Eustace said that he had bought the effects in Monmouth-street, and that meeting Langham in Compton-street, he told him he had better leave them at the washer-woman's for safety: in reply to which Dixon said that the prisoner had declared, when before the justice of peace, that he had bought them of a Jew, and that on the justice enquiring what Jew, he said, " it might be a Turk for what he knew."

Hereupon Eustace declared that he had bought them of a Jew woman for two guineas and a half, and that Langham was innocent: and the defence of Langham was that he never saw Eustace till he met him in Compton-street, when they drank a pint of purl, and then went together to the washer-woman's.

In behalf of Langham appeared his brother, who deposed, that he had never known him guilty of any act of dishonesty; that he was never out of his house later than ten at night; though, in other respects, his conduct had not been so regular as might have been wished.—Andrew Paterson, who had known Langham eighteen months; Mr. Dudley,

ley, who had known him two years; and Mr. Jones, one year; combined to give him a good character.

The jury, after a short consideration, found Eustace not guilty of the burglary, but guilty of stealing in the dwelling-house, and he received sentence of death; but Langham was acquitted.

The deportment of Eustace after conviction was exceedingly well adapted to his unhappy circumstances. He behaved with decent resignation, and exemplary piety. He was executed at the same time with Rowland Ridgley, mentioned in the preceding narrative. On his way to the place of execution he employed himself incessantly in singing psalms, or in other acts of devotion. At the fatal tree he confessed, that an attachment to abandoned women of the town had led to his ruin; but he died, to all appearance, a sincere penitent.

Frederick John Eustace was executed at Tyburn on the 31st of March, 1779.

From the fate of this man servants will see the danger, and they should reflect on the crime, of robbing the houses of their masters and benefactors. Eustace was not in the immediate service of Lord Clarendon when he committed the robbery:—but his crime was not the less; for he was seeking to injure an old fellow-servant, who was under the immediate protection of his late master.

Servants who perform their duty with fidelity are generally as happy as any rank of people in the community; while those who fail of it are commonly as miserable as they ought to be.

An Account of the remarkable Crime and Trial of James Donally, who was convicted of a Robbery on the Highway.

THIS prisoner was examined at Bow-street, on a charge of having extorted money, under the vilest of all insinuations, from the Honourable Charles Fielding, second son of the Earl of Denbigh; and the magistrates, deeming that the offence amounted to a robbery on the highway, committed him for trial; and Lord Denbigh was bound to prosecute on behalf of his son, who was under age.

James Donally, alias Patrick Donally, was indicted, at the sessions held at the Old Bailey, in February, 1779, "for that he, in the king's high- "highway, in and upon the Honourable Charles "Fielding did make an assault, putting him in "corporal fear and danger of his life, and stealing "from his person, and against his will, half a gui- "nea, on the 18th of January;" and there was a second count in the indictment for robbing the same gentleman of a guinea on the 20th of the same month.

This fact was so atrocious in its nature, and so clearly proved, that it will not be necessary to state the evidence in detail as it arose on the trial, but to give the story by way of narrative.

Between six and seven in the evening of the 18th of January, Mr. Charles Fielding was going from the house of a lady with whom he had dined to Covent Garden theatre, when he was accosted in Soho-square by Donally, who desired he would give him some money. Mr. Fielding, astonished at this address, asked him for what? Donally said he had better comply, or he would take him before a magiſtrate, and accuſe him of an attempt to commit an unnatural crime.

Terrified by this inſinuation, the young gentleman gave him half a guinea, which was all the money he had about him; and, returning to the houſe where he had dined, borrowed half a guinea of the ſervant, with an intention of going to the play.

Two days afterwards he again met the priſoner in Oxford-road, when he repeated his threats of carrying him before a magiſtrate, and to priſon; ſaying that he knew very well what had paſſed in Soho-ſquare the other night; and, unleſs he would give him ſome more money, he would take him before a magiſtrate, and accuſe him of the ſame attempt which he had threatened on the other day. He added, that it would go hard with him, unleſs he could prove an *alibi*.

Terrified by theſe threatenings, Mr. Fielding went to Mr. Waters, a grocer in Bond-ſtreet, to whom, under the immediate impreſſions of his fear, he gave a guinea, to give to the priſoner.

It happened, providentially, that on Saturday the 12th of February, Lord Fielding was going up Hay-hill; when Donally, owing to the great perſonal likeneſs to his brother, accoſted him in words which he did not rightly underſtand. His Lordſhip ſaid he believed he had miſtaken him for ſome other perſon, for he did not know his face. Donally ſaid he believed he muſt know him, and aſked if he did not remember giving him half a guinea in Soho-ſquare? He likewiſe mentioned the money given him at the grocer's; a knowledge of which his Lordſhip, as well he might, utterly denied.

The priſoner again aſking if he did not recollect having given him any money, his Lordſhip aſked him

him what was his present demand? and desiring him to explain himself, some farther altercation ensued; on which Lord Fielding desired the prisoner to go before a magistrate, with which he seemed to comply, but at length stopped, and said, he would not go. During this contest his lordship was something terrified; and scarcely knowing what kind of charge to make against the prisoner, he was, as he owned on the trial, " weak enough " to loose his collar, and let him go." Donally then turned about, addressed him by the title of " My Lord," and said, " he should hear from him " again."

On the Tuesday following, as Lord Fielding was walking near the same spot, he heard a voice over his shoulder, saying, " Sir, I have met you again," or some such expression. His Lordship, recollecting his voice, turned round, and seized him by the collar. Donally complained that he had used him very ill the last time he saw him. The other replied, " that he had used him too well, for he had " let him go; but he would take care to do better " this time."

Donally now desired to be treated like a *gentleman*, saying, he would not be dragged, but would go quietly. Lord Fielding, not seeing any person that was likely to assist him, and apprehending a rescue, told him, that if he would walk along quietly to the next coffee-house, he would not drag him. They walked down Dover-street together; but the prisoner increasing his pace, Lord Fielding followed, and seized him. He fell down twice, but was again seized as soon as he arose.

By this time a croud was assembled: Major Hartley and two other gentlemen happened to come by. The prisoner was seized, and conveyed to

Bow-street, where the magistrates, on hearing the evidence, thought that the crime amounted to a highway-robbery, and committed the prisoner for trial accordingly *.

Donally, in his defence, acknowledged that he had met lord Fielding twice; that he had addressed him with decency, and desired him to hear something respecting his brother; and that Sir John Fielding had made the honourable Charles Fielding carry on the prosecution. He did not deny the receipt of the guinea at the grocer's in Bond-street: but averred that he did not deserve death on account of the charge against him.

Mr. Fielding swore, that he had given the same account at Bow street as on the trial; and the jury, having considered the whole evidence, brought in a verdict of "Guilty;" but Mr. Justice Buller, before whom the offender was tried, reserved the case for the opinion of the judges; and Donally yet † awaits their awful determination.

We wish to avoid saying much on this subject, because the fate of the convict is yet undetermined, and it would be unfair to prejudge; but with regard to the crime itself, we cannot but remark that there is *only one* greater. The attempt to extort money, on the pretence of making a charge of an abominable crime, can be exceeded only by the commission of the crime itself. That every reader of this work may be incapable of such atrocious baseness, is the fervent wish of the Compiler!

---

* There have been three, and only three, instances of conviction for crimes of this nature before the present.
† On the 2d of April, 1779, when this concluding narrative was written.

PRISONERS stopping at the Baptist's Head in St John's Lane, on the day of removal from the NEW-PRISON to NEWGATE.

Concluding Note, by the Editor.

THUS have we endeavoured, and we hope not unsuccessfully, to compleat this work, in conformity to the proposals originally offered to the public. We trust we have not omitted any trials of great importance, nor inserted many of a trifling nature.

Those who wish well to Society will be pleased to see vice exposed in every shape, and reprobated under all the variety of forms it may assume. Too much cannot be said to discountenance its propagation, or to enhance the charms of true religion and virtue.

To advance these important purposes should be the aim and end of every publication. The book that does not tend to make people wiser and better is a nuisance to society, and a disgrace to the press.

As the reformation of prisoners, rather than the punishment of them, should be the great aim of our legislators, we beg leave to submit to our readers some extracts from letters written by a gentleman to a Member of Parliament, both of them of the most amiable private characters, and both of them zealous promoters of every public good.

Jonas Hanway, Esq; in a letter to Sir Charles Bunbury, says, " In the general view of our prisons, I
" beg leave to make a few remarks, which to those
" who have not considered the subject may carry
" some degree of information. Of all the abuses
" which ever crept into civil society, professing
" Christianity, considering the evil propensities of
" the common run of our malefactors, the *tap-house*
" seems to stand in a distinguished rank. What re-
" formation

" formation can be expected, where it is the interest
" of the keeper of a prison to promote inebriety and
" dissipation of thought? If he is suffered to sell
" strong liquors for his own emolument, he will be
" tempted to shut his gates against every one who
" would relieve the real crying wants of those who
" are in need, and open them wide to all such as
" will supply the means of drunkenness. There can
" be no good reason for an indulgence, which, scat-
" tering the thoughts, will create a desperate re-
" pugnance to the calls of heaven. When the soul
" ought to tremble, as being on the verge of eter-
" nity, such a conduct is abominable beyond all
" expression.

" Doth not the magistrate prostitute his authority,
" in granting licences, on the puerile presump-
" tion that he shall increase the revenue? Or is it
" that knowing how scanty the allowance is to the
" keepers of prisons, he gives them a liberty which
" he knows cannot be used without the most deadly
" consequences, even that of promoting the very
" temper and disposition which encouraged the
" malefactor to commit the crime for which he is
" imprisoned! This conduct is reproachable in the
" highest degree. The magistrate ought rather to
" refuse the licence, and represent the necessity of
" allowing keepers of prisons salaries suitable to
" the importance of their office.

" The conversion of a house, which ought to
" be a scene of sorrow and repentance, into jollity,
" and carelessness to all events, is one of the chief
" causes of the evil with which we are so sorely
" afflicted. If this is not remedied, can any expe-
" dient restore good discipline and true œconomy
" in prisons? If some prisoners should be thus de-
" prived of a comfort they might be entitled to, it
" would

"would be far better than granting an indulgence,
"so pregnant with mischief to the generality."

"By an act of the third of his present majesty,
"no jailor in Ireland is to sell ale, beer, or any
"other liquor, by himself or any other person,
"under the penalty of 5 £. for every offence; and
"I am assured it operates happily in preventing
"the ordinary bad effects. With us the case is dif-
"ferent; for every capital prison is a public-
"house; and though spirituous liquors, commonly
"so called, are prohibited, yet, under the name
"of cordials, I am told they pass; or at least that
"by the force of wine, and malt liquor, all the
"bad effects of intoxication are continued.

"Among the several grievances which rise in
"judgment against us, are the fees demanded of
"malefactors, now softened, but not abolished.
"The want of medical assistance—the deficiency
"of baths—inattention to cleanliness—foul air for
"want of ventilation—want of a change of clean-
"washed and well-dried garments, with a regular
"change of linen—where these are wanting, death
"must be a familiar guest to a prisoner. Even
"the regular washing of hands and feet is of con-
"sequence. A proper regard to diet, according
"to the apparent wants of prisoners, is necessary
"to the preservation of life in prisons, more than
"in other places; and the defect often operates
"like a plague."

That a reform in the management of our prisons is necessary, no man of common sense can doubt; and it remains with the wisdom of legislature to provide a remedy for the evil.

Perhaps the keeping prisoners separate from each other, and totally denying all the means of intemperance,

perance, would go far towards effecting that reformation which is so much wanted.

As matters now stand, the man charged with felony is repeatedly visited by the most abandoned of his acquaintance, and they mutually harden each other in vice. These visits should be very unfrequent, and never permitted but in the presence of the keeper or his deputy, who should be people of the most unexceptionable character, and take care that not an improper word is uttered.

To drop, however, this subject, let us conclude these volumes by a fervent wish that the readers of them may carefully and steadily avoid every vice therein recorded, every folly therein exposed. Let honesty be the prevailing, the ruling, principle among us; let us be humbly content in the situation which Providence hath allotted us; not seeking to possess ourselves of the property of others; and paying a devout reverence to that divine command, the authority of which no one will deny:

"Thou shalt not covet thy neighbour's house,
"thou shalt not covet thy neighbour's wife,
"nor his man-servant, nor his maid-servant,
"nor his ox, nor his ass, nor ANY THING that
"is his."

A correct List of all the capital Convictions at the Old Bailey, &c. since the Commencement of the present Century; which will be of the highest Use to refer to on many Occasions:—— together with the Volumes and Pages in which they occur in this work.

	Vol.	Page.
ADAMS, Mary, Privately Stealing.	i	58
Adams, William, Forgery.	iv	103
Adler, Lydia, Murder.	iv	186
Adshead, John, House-breaking.	v	97
Alexander, Moses, Forgery.	iv	366
Allpress, Joseph, Robbing the Mail.	v	91
Alsworth, Benjamin, House-breaking.	v	97
Andrews, John, Forgery.	iii	378
Andrews, Thomas, Sodomy.	iv	203
Angier, Humphrey, Robbery.	i	357
Annesly, James, Murder.	iii	70
Ansel, James, Murder.	i	362
Aram, Eugene, Murder.	iv	131
Arragony, Anne, Street Robbery.	v	302
Athoe, Thomas, Senior, Murder.	i	341
Athoe, Thomas, Junior, Murder.	i	341
Ayliffe, John Esq; Forgery.	iv	147

B

Bacchus, Thomas, High Treason.	v	77
Baker, William, Forgery.	iii	294
Balfour, Alexander, Murder.	iv	49
Ball, Henry, Burglary.	v	324
Balmerino, Lord, High Treason.	iii	119

Baltimore,

	Vol.	Page
Baltimore, Frederick, Lord, Rape.	iv	330
Barnard, Morris, Conspiracy to cheat and defraud.	v	299
Baretti, Murder.	iv	376
Barkwith, Thomas, Highway Robbery.	ii	369
Barrington, George, Picking a Pocket.	v	264
Barwick, John, High Treason.	iii	136
Bates, Benjamin, Burglary.	v	200
Bean, James, Burglary.	v	305
Beddingfield, Anne, Petit Treason.	iv	246
Bellamy, Edward, Burglary.	ii	142
Berghen, Catherine Van, } Berghen, Michael Van, } Murder.	i	10
Berry, John, Perjury.	iv	90
Berry, Thomas, Murder.	ii	84
Bigg, John, Altering a Bank Note.	i	176
Bigg, Jepthah, Sending a Threatning Letter.	ii	206
Billings, Thomas, Murder.	ii	99
Birch, Edward, Forgery.	v	25
Bird, Edward, Murder.	i	242
Blake, Daniel, Murder.	iv	239
Blake, Joseph, Burglary.	i	387
Blandy, Mary, Murder.	iv	10
Blastock, Edward, Highway-robbery.	ii	305
Blewit, William, Murder.	ii	84
Blood, Andrew, High Treason.	iii	141
Bodkin, John, } Bodkin, Dominick, } Murder.	iii	67
Bolland, James, Forgery.	v	38
Bolton, John, Murder.	v	149
Bonner, Samuel, Writing a Threatening Letter.	v	308
Bourke, Patrick, Killing Sheep.	iv	188
Bowen, William, Highway-robbery.	iii	231
Branch, Elizabeth, } Branch, Mary, } Murder.	iii	9
Brett, John, Forgery.	iv	198
Brian, John Herman, Robbing and Firing a House.	i	95
Brightwell, Francis, } Brightwell, Benjamin, } Highway-robbery.	i	382
Brinsden, Matthias, Murder.	i	301
Bristowe, Thomas, Conspiracy to cheat and Defraud.	v	299
Britain, Jonathan, Forgery.	v	59
Brown, Nicol, Murder.	iv	70
Brownrigg, Elizabeth, Murder.	iv	308
Bunce, Stephen, Burglary.	i	104
Burk, William, Robberies.	i	322

	Vol.	Page
Burnworth, Edward, Murder.	ii	84
Burridge, William, Horse-stealing.	i	272
Butler, James, Robbery.	i	353
Butler, Richard, Forgery.	iii	302
Butler, Thomas, Esq; Highway-robbery.	i	252
Butloge, Thomas, Felony.	i	298
Butterfield, Jane, Murder.	v	153

C

	Vol.	Page
Caddell, George, Murder.	i	19
Cameron, Dr. Archibald, High Treason.	iv	44
Campbell, Mungo, Murder.	iv	385
Canning, Elizabeth, Perjury.	iv	64
Cannon, Luke, Burglary.	v	13
Caldclough, James, Robbery.	ii	352
Carleton, Alexander, Burglary.	v	292
Carleton, Andrew, Burglary.	v	292
Carnegie, James, Esq; Murder.	ii	157
Carnwarth, Robert, Earl of, High Treason.	i	185
Carr, John, Forgery.	iii	284
Carrol, Barney, Maiming and Defacing: — tried on the Coventry Act.	iv	275
Carter, William, Murder.	iii	192
Cashmin, Michael, Escaping from on board the Ballast Lighter.	v	282
Ceppi, Peter, Maliciously shooting.	v	261
Chadwick, Thomas, High Treason.	iii	141
Charteris, Colonel Francis, Rape.	ii	209
Chandler, William, Perjury.	iii	359
Chetwynd, William, Murder.	iii	79
Chivers, Elizabeth, Murder.	i	138
Churchill, Deborah, Murder.	i	116
Clarke, Mathew, Murder.	i	261
Cluff, James, Murder.	ii	177
Cobby, John, Murder.	iii	188
Cock, George, Privately Stealing.	iii	161
Coleman, Richard, Murder.	iii	210
Colley, Thomas, Murder.	iii	365
Collington, John, Firing a Barn.	iii	202
Conner, Terence, High Treason.	iii	180
Conway, Peter, Murder.	v	1
Cook, Henry, Highway robbery.	iii	46
Cook, Thomas, Murder.	i	72
Cooke, Arundel, Esq; Cutting and Maiming.	i	275
Cooper, James, Murder.	iii	249

	Vol.	Page.
Cooper, Joseph, House-breaking.	v	110
Cooper, William, Robbing a Waggon.	v	329
Corbett, William, Murder.	iv	264
Cowland, John, Murder.	i	36
Coyle, Richard, Piracy and Murder.	ii	78
Cox, William, Stealing Bank Notes.	v	128
Cromartie, Earl of, High Treason.	iii	119
Cutler, Ralph, Rape.	v	241

D.

	Vol.	Page.
Damaree, Daniel, High Treason.	i	125
Darking, Isaac, Highway-robbery.	iv	191
Davis, Joseph, Burglary.	v	273
Davis, John, Burglary.	v	292
Davis, Catherine, Street-robbery.	v	302
Davis, Vincent, Murder.	i	413
Dawson, Hugh, Robbery.	iii	227
Dawson, James, High Treason.	ii	137
Day, Alexander, Defrauding.	i	326
Deacon, Thomas, High Treason.	iii	141
Deitz, Barnard Christian de Nassaw, Misdemeanour.	v	204
Derwentwater, James, Earl of, High Treason.	i	185
Dickenson, Emanuel, Murder.	ii	84
Dickson, Margaret, Murder.	ii	153
Dignan, David Brown, Fraud.	v	235
Diver, Jenny, otherwise Mary Young, Privately Stealing.	ii	382
Dodd, Dr. William, Forgery.	v	207
Dominicetti, Dr. Bartholomew, Forgery.	v	340
Donally, James, Highway-robbery.	v	353
Dowdell, Joseph, Street-robbery.	iii	350
Dorrell, John, High Treason.	i	205
Douglas, Thomas, Murder, by Stabbing.	i	171
Dramatti, John Peter, Murder.	i	66
Drew, Charles, Murder.	iii	3
Dromelius, Gerrard, Murder.	i	10
Drury, Anthony, Highway-robbery.	ii	129
Duce, William, Robbery.	i	353

E

	Vol.	Page.
Edmonson, Mary, Murder.	iv	128
Egan, James, Perjury.	iv	90
Elby, William, Housebreaking and Murder.	i	83

	Vol.	Page.
Elliot, Edward, Murder.	i	362
Elliot, Robert, Stealing a Leaden Coffin.	v	334
Ellis, George, Killing Sheep.	iv	188
Estrick, Thomas, House-breaking.	i	63
Eustace, John Frederick, House-breaking.	v	349
Evans, Walter, Murder.	iv	395
Everett, John, Highway Robbery.	ii	160
Everett, John, Privately Stealing.	iii	290

F.

	Vol.	Page.
Fairall, William, Breaking open the Custom-house at Poole.	iii	216
Ferrers, Laurence, Earl, Murder,	iv	159
Field, William, Highway Robbery,	v	121
Fisher, Margaret, Privately Stealing.	i	306
Fitz-Gerald, Gerald, Murder.	i	76
Fletcher, George, High Treason.	iii	140
Flint, William, Privately Stealing.	v	296
Flood, Matthew, Robbery.	i	311
Fontaine, Peter de la, Forgery.	iv	30
Fryer, James, Burglary.	v	278
Fuller, Robert, Shooting at a Person, — tried on the Black Act.	iv	183

G.

	Vol.	Page.
Gahagan, Usher, High Treason.	iii	180
Gammell, John, Robbery.	iii	227
Gansel, General William, Firing a Pistol at a Sheriff's Officer.	v	124
Gardelle, Theodore, Murder.	iv	175
Gardener, Stephen, Burglary.	i	375
Gascoign, Richard, High Treason	i	207
Gibson, James, Forgery.	iv	325
Gidley, George, Piracy and Murder.	iv	287
Gonzalez, Bli, Privately Stealing.	iv	99
Goodman, James, Horse-stealing.	i	224
Goodere, Captain Samuel, Murder.	iii	36
Gordon, John, High Treason.	i	205
Gow, John, Piracy.	ii	181
Gray, Arthur, Burglary.	i	266
Gregory, James, Murder.	ii	133
Gregg, William, High Treason.	i	110
Green, John, Burglary.	v	200
Griffiths, George, Privately Stealing.	i	23

	Vol.	Page
Griffenburg, Elizabeth, Acceſſary to a Rape.	iv	330
Griffiths, William, Highway Robbery.	v	105
Gueſt, William, High Treaſon.	iv	318
Guyant, Joseph, Robbing the Mail.	v	91

H.

	Vol.	Page
Hall, John, Burglary,	i	99
Hall, John, Eſquire, High Treaſon	i	214
Hall, James, Petit Treaſon	iii	41
Hallam, Robert, Murder.	ii	219
Hamilton, Colonel John, Murder.	i	140
Hamilton, John, Eſquire, Beheaded for Murder	i	221
Hamilton, John, Eſquire, High Treaſon	iii	147
Hammond, John, Murder.	iii	189
Harpham, Robert, Coining.	ii	10
Harriſon, John, Forgery.	v	246
Harrow, William, Houſe-breaking,	iv	242
Hartley, John, Robbery.	i	281
Hartley, John, Burglary.	v	305
Harvey, Margaret, Privately Stealing.	iii	246
Harvey, Anne, Acceſſary to a Rape.	iv	330
Hawes, Nathaniel, Robbery.	i	268
Hawke, William, Highway Robbery.	v	132
Hawkins, John, Robbing the Mail	i	283
Hawkſworth, William, Murder.	i	337
Henderſon, Matthew, Petit Treaſon.	iii	90
Henſey, Doctor Florence, High Treaſon.	iv	121
Higgs, John, Murder,	ii	84
Hill, Samuel, Murder.	iii	375
Hill, James, otherwiſe James Ackſan, commonly called John the Painter, ſetting Fire to the Dock-yard, at Portſmouth.	v	228
Hilſdon, William, Burglary.	v	324
Hogan, John, Murder.	iii	67
Holt, John, Burglary.	v	292
Horner, Thomas, Burglary.	v	278
Horne, William Andrew, Eſquire, Murder.	iv	151
Houſden, Jane, Murder.	i	145
Houſſart, Lewis, Murder.	ii	3
Hughes, Richard, Forgery.	iv	103
Hunter, Thomas, Murder.	i	29
Hutchinſon, Amy, Petit Treaſon.	iii	277

J.

	Vol.	Page.
Jackson, William, Murder.	iii	189
Jackson, Nathaniel, Robbery.	i	295
Jefferies, Edward, Murder.	i	87
Jefferies, Elizabeth, Murder.	iv	3
Johnson, William, Murder.	i	145
Johnson, Joseph, Privately Stealing.	ii	314
Johnson, Christopher, Murder.	iv	50
Joines, Edward, Murder.	ii	377
Jones, Catherine, Bigamy.	i	247
Jones, Thomas, Murder.	iii	371
Jones, Robert, Sodomy.	v	102
Jordan, Henry, Burglary	v	273

K.

	Vol.	Page.
Keele, Richard, Murder.	i	166
Kello, John, } Forgery. Kello, Joseph, } Forgery.	iv	232
Kenmure, William Viscount, High Treason.	i	185
Kerr, William, High Treason.	i	205
Kidd, John, Piracy.	i	39
Kidden Joshua, Highway Robbery.	iv	56
Kilmarnock, Earl of, High Treason.	iii	119
Kingshell, Robert, Murder.	i	362
Kingsmill, Thomas, Breaking open the Custom-house at Poole.	iii	216
King, William, Maiming and Defacing—tried on the Coventry Act.	iv	275
Kingston, Elizabeth, Dutchess of, Bigamy.	v	186

L.

	Vol.	Page.
Lancaster, George, Forgery.	iii	151
Lancaster, John, House-breaking.	iii	166
Lancy, Captain John, Burning a ship.	iv	59
Langham, Henry, House-breaking.	v	349
Langley, Gilbert, Highway robbery.	iii	15
Layer, Christopher, Esq; High Treason.	i	316
Lazarus, Jacob, Robbery and Murder.	v	17
Legee, John, Murder.	ii	84
Leonard, John, Rape.	v	115

Levee

	Vol.	Page.
Levee, John, Robbery	i	311
Lewis, Paul, Shooting at a Person on the Highway.	iv	257
Lewis, Francis, Burglary.	v	269
Lewington, Thomas, Robbing a Waggon.	v	329
Llewellin, David, Murder.	iv	395
Lincoln, James, Murder.	i	308
Lovat, Lord, High Treason.	iii	119
Low, Richard, Burglary.	i	104
Lowen, Roger, Murder.	i	92
Lowry, Captain James, Murder.	iii	387
Lowther, William, Murder.	i	166

M.

	Vol.	Page.
Macklane, James, Highway Robbery.	iii	264
M'Cloud, Peter, House-breaking.	v	87
M'Daniel, Stephen, Perjury.	iv	90
M'Kinlie, Peter, Piracy and Murder.	iv	287
M'Naughton John, Esquire, Murder.	iv	213
Mahony, Matthew, Murder.	iii	36
Malcolm, Sarah, Murder.	ii	251
Marshall, Henry, Murder.	i	362
Martin, John Andrew, Burglary.	iv	362
Martin, Matthew, Forgery.	v	25
Mason, Elizabeth, Murder.	i	135
Massey, John, Piracy.	i	346
Matthews, John, High Treason.	i	249
Meff, John, Returning from Transportation.	i	263
Merchant, William, Murder.	ii	133
Merritt, Amos, House-breaking.	v	146
Metyard, Sarah, } Metyard, Sarah Morgan, } Murder.	iv	219
Milksop, Thomas, Murder.	i	308
Mills, Charles, Footpad Robbery.	v	135
Mills, John, Murder.	iii	223
Mills, Richard, Senior, } Mills, Richard, Junior, } Murder.	iii	190
Montgomery, William, Defrauding his Creditors.	iv	37
Moody, Robert, Rape.	v	311
Morgan, Charles, Murder.	iv	395
Morgan, David, Murder.	iv	395
Morgan, David, Esquire, High Treason.	iii	142
Morgan, Richard, Privately Stealing.	v	82
Morgridge, John, Murder.	i	106

	Vol.	Page
Morris, William, Murder.	iv	395
Mullins, Darby, Piracy.	i	46

N.

	Vol.	Page
Nairn, Catherine, Incest and Murder.	iv	279
Nairn, William, Lord, High Treason.	i	185
Neale, Thomas, Highway-Robbery.	iii	231
Neale, Benjamin, Housebreaking.	iii	242
Newington, William, Forgery.	ii	319
Nicholson, James, High Treason.	iii	145
Nithisdale, William, Earl of, High Treason.	i	185
Noble, Richard, Murder.	i	151
Nowland, Martin, Enlisting men into the French service.	iii	63

O.

	Vol.	Page
Oaky, Richard, Robbery.	i	311
Ogilvie, Walter, High Treason.	iii	145
Ogilvie, Patrick, Incest and Murder.	iv	279
O'Hara, Felix, High Treason.	i	182
Oneby, Major John, Murder.	ii	168
Orton, Samuel, Forgery.	iv	300
Osborne, Thomas, Burglary.	v	324
Oxburgh, Colonel Henry, High Treason.	i	206

P.

	Vol.	Page
Packer, Thomas, Highway-robbery.	i	411
Page, William, Highway-robbery.	iv	107
Paleotti, Ferdinando, Marquis de, Murder.	i	229
Parker, Jonas, receiving stolen lead.	v	334
Parkes, John, Forgery.	iii	158
Parkhurst, Nathaniel, Murder.	i	173
Parsons, Wm. Esq; returning from Transportation.	iii	306
Parvin, Richard, Murder.	i	362
Paul, Rev. William, High-treason.	i	208
Pearce, Frances, Street-robbery.	v	302
Penlez, Bosavern, Rioting.	iii	236
Perreau, Robert, Perreau, Daniel, Forgery.	v	161
Perin, Richard, Breaking open the custom-house at Poole.	iii	216
Perrott, John, Concealing effects under a commission of Bankrupt.	iv	206

	Vol.	Page
Phillips, Thomas, Highway-robbery.	i	255
Picken, Joseph, Highway-robbery.	i	411
Pink, Edward, } Murder. Pink, John,	i	362
Placket, John, Robbery.	iv	227
Pledge, Sarah, Murder	iv	27
Plunkett, Henry, Murder.	i	169
Porteous, Capt. John, Murder.	ii	264
Porter, Solomon, Robbery and murder.	v	17
Powel, Robert, Forgery.	v	33
Powel, Henry, Highway-robbery.	i	178
Power, John, Piracy and murder.	iv	322
Powis, Joseph, Burglary.	ii	232
Poulter, John, Highway-robbery.	iv	74
Price, John, Murder.	i	239
Price, George, Murder.	ii	323
Priddon, Sarah, Assault.	i	333
Pugh, John, Footpad-robbery.	v	135
Purchase, George, High-treason.	i	125

Q.

| Quin, Thomas, Street-robbery. | iii | 352 |

R.

Ramsey, Robert, House-breaking.	iii	45
Rann, John, Highway-robbery.	v	138
Ratcliffe, Charles, Esq; High-treason.	iii	133
Rebels, in the year 1715.	i	181
Rebels, in 1745.	iii	103
Redding, Joseph, Murder.	iii	70
Reeves, Thomas, Robbery.	i	281
Relph, Joseph, Murder.	v	318
Rice, John, Forgery.	iv	252
Richardson, John, Piracy and murder.	ii	278
Richardson, Michael, murder.	v	1
Richardson, Elizabeth, murder,	iv	358
Ridgley, Rowland, a coiner.	v	344
Ringe, Richard, Petit-treason.	iv	246
Roach, George, stealing a leaden coffin.	v	334
Roberts, David, High-treason.	ii	359
Roberts, Samuel, High-treason.	v	77
Roche, Philip, Piracy.	i	349
Rosa, Anthony de, Murder.	iii	382

	Vol.	Page.
Ross, Norman, Murder.	iii	279
Rudd, Margaret Caroline, Forgery.	v	181
Russen, Benjamin, Rape.	v	251

S.

	Vol.	Page.
Salmon, James, Perjury.	iv	90
Sampson, James, Robbing a house.	iv	354
Savage, Richard, Murder.	ii	133
Scott, Alexander, Publishing false News.	v	284
Seymour, Bryan, Murder.	iii	198
Sharp, Thomas, Murder.	i	78
Shelton, William, Highway Robbery.	ii	224
Sheppard, James, High Treason.	i	232
Sheppard, John, Burglary.	i	392
Sherwood, Thomas, Forgery.	v	254
Siday, John, Burglary.	v	13
Simpson, George, Robbing the Mail.	i	283
Simpson, John, House-breaking.	i	15
Simms, Henry, Highway Robbery.	iii	95
Slanghterford, Christopher, Murder.	i	118
Smith, John, Highway Robbery.	i	80
Smith, John, alias Half-hanged Smith, Burglary.	i	89
Smith, Lambert, Burglary.	v	305
Smith, William, Forgery.	iii	258
Smythee, Henry, Esquire, Murder.	iii	31
Spencer, Barbara, High Treason.	i	258
Spiggot, William, Highway Robbery.	i	255
Spiggot, William, Murder.	iv	395
Squires, Mary, Robbery.	iv	64
Stanley, John, murder.	i	367
Still, Joseph, murder.	i	227
Stirn, Francis David, Murder.	iv	170
Stockdale, John, Murder.	iv	50
Stone, John, Firing a barn.	iii	202
Stretton, John, Robbing the Mail.	v	7
St. Quintin, Richard, Piracy and Murder.	iv	287
Strodtman, Herman, Murder.	i	48
Stroud, William, Fraud.	iii	395
Sullivan, Joseph, High Treason.	i	182
Swan, John, Murder.	iv	3
Syddall, Thomas, High Treason.	iii	140
Swift, Richard, Receiving stolen goods.	iv	296

T

	Vol.	Page.
Talbot, Thomas, Street-robbery.	iii	350
Tapner, Benjamin, Murder.	iii	188

	Vol.	Page
Taunton, William, Murder.	iv	37
Thompson, Thomas, Horse-stealing.	iii	175
Thornhill, Richard, Murder.	i	13
Torshell, Elizabeth, Murder.	i	8
Totterdale, John, Murder.	ii	274
Toton, John, Highway-robbery.	ii	30
Townly, Colonel Francis, High Treason.	iii	139
Town, Richard, Defrauding his Creditors.	i	147
Tracey, Martha, Street-robbery.	iii	86
Tripp, Grace, Murder.	i	125
Tucker, Reginald, Murder.	v	157
Turner, William, Burglary.	v	275
Turpin, Richard, Horse-stealing.	ii	331

U

Udall, William, Highway Robbery.	ii	296

V

Vicars, John, Murder.	iii	280

W

Waltham Blacks, An Account of them.	i	362
Weil, Asher, Weil, Levi, } Robbery and Murder.	v	17
Welch, James, Murder.	iii	371
Wells, Abraham, Horse-stealing.	ii	349
Wesket, John, Burglary.	iv	268
West, Mary, Picking a pocket.	v	289
Whale, Anne, Petit Treason.	iv	27
White, Charles, Murder.	iii	36
Whitty, Robert, High Treason.	i	182
Whurrier, William, Murder.	iii	155
Widdrington, William, Lord, High Treason.	i	185
Wilford, Thomas, Murder.	iv	23
Wild, Jonathan, Receiving stolen goods.	ii	13
Willis, Francis, High Treason.	i	125
Wilkinson, Robert, Murder.	i	308
Williamson, John, Murder.	iv	304
Winton, George, Earl of, High Treason.	i	185
Woodburne, John, Cutting and Maiming.	i	275
Wood, Thomas, Murder.	ii	99

Y

	Vol.	Page.
Youell, Hosea, murder.	iii	149
Young, John, Forgery.	iii	174
Young, Mary, Privately Stealing.	ii	382

Z

Zekerman, Andrew, Piracy and murder.	iv	287

Directions to the Binder for placing the Cuts.

VOL. I.

Frontispiece to face the Title.
A new plan for the punishment of Highwaymen by hard labour on the Roads } to face the preface — 6
Thomas Hunter murdering his pupils — 29
John Smith cut down at Tyburn — 89
William Johnson shooting Mr. Spurling — 145
Execution of John Hamilton Esq; by the machine called the Maiden — 221

Jack

	Page.
Jack Ketch arrested	241
The punishment formerly inflicted on those who refused pleading to an indictment	255
The Mail robbed near Colnbrook by Hawkins and Simpson	283
View of Hounslow Heath, with the Gibbets	295
Jack Sheppard in the Room called the Castle in Newgate	392

VOL. II.

FRONTISPIECE—View of New Prison, Clerkenwell, and of Tothill-fields Bridewell	
Lewis Houssart cutting his Wife's throat	3
The manner of burning a Woman convicted of Treason	124
A Pirate hanged at Execution-dock	204
Richard Turpin shooting a man near his Cave on Epping Forest	331

VOL. III.

FRONTISPIECE—View of the Public office in Bow-street.	
Charles Drew shooting his own Father	3
The Smugglers throwing stones on the body of Daniel Chater	188
The Dead body of William Galley	193
Kenith Hossack flogged and murdered by James Lowry	387

VOL. IV.

FRONTISPIECE. The New Sessions House, and New Gaol of Newgate.	
Surgeon Forbes visiting Mr. Jeffries at Walthamstow.	3
Miss Blandy at the Place of Execution.	10
Christopher Johnson robbing a Postman, while John Stockdale shoots him.	50
William Page leaving his Phaeton, while he robs a Gentleman near Putney.	107
Mr. Johnson, Steward to the Earl of Ferrers, shot by his Lordship.	159

	Page.
The Body of a Murderer exposed in the Theatre of Surgeons Hall.	169
Samuel Orton committing Forgery on the Bank of England.	300
John Williamson's cruel Treatment of his Wife.	304
Mrs. Brownrigg in the Cell, Newgate.	308
The Skeleton of Mrs. Brownrigg.	317
William Guest drawn on a Sledge to Tyburn.	318

VOL. V.

	Page.
FRONTISPIECE. A man publicly whipped in the Sessions House Yard.	
Peter Conway and Michael Richardson shooting Mr. Venables.	1
Levi Weil preventing Hyam Lazarus from shooting Mrs. Hutchins of Chelsea.	17
James Bolland executed for Forgery.	38
William Cox, in the Press Yard, Newgate.	128
Hawke robs Captain Cunningham and Mr. Hart on the Highway	132
William Hawke, in the Press Yard, Newgate.	134
Margaret Caroline Rudd, on her Trial.	181
Doctor Dodd, at the Place of Execution.	207
View of the Justitia Hulk, with the Convicts at Work, to face Dignam's Trial.	235
The Convicts taking Water near Black Friars Bridge.	264
John Hartley, &c. in the House of Mr. Clewin, at Finchley.	278
Samuel Bonner imploring Assistance from Mr. Day.	308
Mode of Punishment by Branding, &c.	322
Roach, Elliot, and Gould, stealing the Leaden Coffin of William Aston, from the Vault of Aldermanbury Church.	334
The Bellman at St. Sepulchre's, to face Rowland Ridgeley's Trial.	344
The Prisoners stopping at the Baptist's Head, St. John's lane,—to face the Concluding Note by the Editor.	357

FINIS.

This Day is published,

Price ONLY EIGHTEEN-PENCE,

Embellished with an entire NEW FRONTISPIECE, Adapted to the various Subjects of this very useful

FAMILY BOOK,

THE

FARMER's WIFE;

OR, THE COMPLETE

COUNTRY HOUSEWIFE.

CONTAINING

Full and ample *Directions* for the Breeding and Management of *Turkies, Fowls, Geese, Ducks, Pigeons*, &c.

Instructions for fattening *Hogs*, pickling of *Pork*, and curing of *Bacon*.

How to make *Sausages, Hogs-Puddings*, &c.

Full *Instructions* for making *Wines* from various Kinds of English Fruit, and from Smyrna Raisins.

The *Method* of making *Cyder, Perry, Mead, Mum, Cherry-Brandy*, &c.

Directions respecting the *Dairy*, containing the best Way of making *Butter*, and likewise *Gloucestershire, Cheshire, Stilton, Sage*, and *Cream Cheese*.

How to pickle common English *Fruits* and *Vegetables*, with other useful Receipts for the Country *House-keeper*.

Full *Instructions* how to brew *Beer* and *Ale*, of all the various Kinds made in this Kingdom.

Ample *Directions* respecting the Management of *Bees*, with an Account of the Use of *Honey*.

To which is added,

The Art of Breeding and Managing SONG BIRDS;

LIKEWISE

A Variety of RECEIPTS in COOKERY,

And other Particulars, well worthy the Attention of Women of all Ranks residing in the COUNTRY.

Instructions, full and plain, we give,
 To teach the Farmer's Wife,
With Satisfaction, how to live
 The happy Country Life.

LONDON:

Printed for ALEX. HOGG, in PATERNOSTER-Row, and sold by all Booksellers, &c. in Town and Country.

SUPPLEMENT.

In Order to maintain the distinguished Reputation of THE MALEFACTOR'S REGISTER, or NEW NEWGATE AND TYBURN CALENDAR, (which has been rendered in the Course of the Publication far superior to any Old Work of the Kind) the EDITOR has presented the Public with the following Particulars, and intends in future to continue this useful and entertaining Work, by adding the most remarkable Trials as they occur, together with a genuine Account of each notorious Offender.

An authentic Account of the Reverend Mr. JAMES HACKMAN, *who suffered for the Murder of Miss* REAY.

IT was a just observation of Solomon, "that there is nothing new under the sun;" and yet there are some events of so sudden, so striking a nature, that when they happen in our own time, and within the compass of our observation, they affect us more than when we read of them in antient authors; such is the case before us, and an affecting one it is.

Mr. James Hackman was born at Gosport in Hampshire, and originally designed for trade; but he was too volatile in disposition to submit to the drudgery of the shop or counting-house. His parents, willing to promote his interest as far as lay in their power, purchased him an ensign's commission in the sixty-eighth regiment of foot. He had not been long in the army when he was sent to command a recruiting party, and being at Huntingdon,

Huntingdon, he was frequently invited to dine with a noble Earl, well known in the political world. Here it was that he first became acquainted with Miss Reay, who lived under the protection of that nobleman.

This Lady was the daughter of a stay-maker in Covent-Garden, and served her apprenticeship to a mantua-maker in George's-Court, St. John's-Lane, Clerkenwell. She was bound when only thirteen, and in 1760, when she was eighteen, her apprenticeship being expired, she was discharged with a fair character. She was soon after taken notice of by the nobleman above-mentioned, who took her under his protection, and treated her with every mark of tenderness. No sooner had Mr. Hackman seen her than he became enamoured of her, and finding he could not obtain preferment in the army, he turned his thoughts to the church, and entered into orders. Soon after he entered into orders, he obtained the living of Wiverton in Norfolk, which was only about Christmas last, so that it may be said he never enjoyed it.

It is probable that Mr. Hackman imagined that there was a mutual passion, that Miss Reay had the same regard for him as he had for her. Love and madness are often little better than synonymous terms, for had Mr. Hackman not been blinded by a bewitching passion, he could never have imagined that Miss Reay would have left the family of a noble Lord at the head of one of the highest departments of the state, in order to live in an humble station. Those who have been long accustomed to affluence, and even profusion, seldom chuse to lower their flags. However, he was still tormented by this unhappy, irregular, and ungovernable passion, which in an unhappy

moment

moment led him to commit the crime for which he suffered.

Miss Reay was extremely fond of musick, and as her noble protector was in an high rank, we need not be surprized to find that frequent concerts were performed both in London and at Hinchinbrook; at the latter place Mr. Hackman was generally of the party, and his attention to her at those times was very great. How long he had been in London previous to this affair is not certainly known, but at that time he lodged in Duke's-Court, St. Martin's-Lane. On the morning of the 7th of April, 1779, he sat some time in his closet, reading Dr. Blair's sermons; but in the evening he took a walk to the Admiralty, where he saw Miss Reay go into the coach along with Signiora Galli, who attended her. The coach drove to Covent-Garden theatre, where she staid to see Love in a Village acted. Mr. Hackman went into the theatre at the same time, but not being able to contain the violence of his passion, he went home to his lodgings, and having loaded two pistols returned to the play-house, where he waited till the play was over: seeing Miss Reay ready to step into the coach, he took a pistol in each hand, one of which he discharged against her, which killed her on the spot, and the other at himself, which however did not take effect.

The moment she fell, Mr. M'Namara, a gentleman who was going to hand her into the coach, laid hold of her, thinking she had fallen into a fit by the report of the pistol; but he was soon convinced of his mistake when he found himself bloody, and so sick that he was not able to stay any longer than to see the body carried into the Shakespeare tavern, where it lay till the coroner's inquest was taken.

In the mean time Mr. Hackman's wounds were dressed, and he was committed by Sir John Fielding to Tothill-fields Bridewell, and then to Newgate, where a person was appointed to attend him, lest he should have laid violent hands on himself. In Newgate, as he knew he had no favour to expect, he prepared himself for the awful change he was about to make. He had dined with his sister on the day the murder was committed, and in the afternoon wrote a letter to her husband, Mr. Booth, an eminent attorney, acquainting him of his resolution of destroying himself, desiring him to sell what effects he should leave behind him to pay a small debt; but this letter was not sent, for it was found in his pocket.

His trial came on before Judge Blackstone, and he was found guilty upon the clearest evidence. In his defence he made use of the common plea of insanity, or at least of having no intention to murder Miss Reay, but that could avail him nothing, seeing he had two loaded pistols. He heard the dreadful sentence pronounced with more fortitude than could have been expected, and being conducted back to Newgate, behaved with a becoming decency under his unhappy circumstances. On the morning of his execution he got up a little after five, dressed himself, and spent some time in private meditation. About seven he was visited by Mr. Boswell, and some other friends, with whom he went to the chapel and received the sacrament. When he came out of the chapel and was haltered, he seemed to be much shocked, which is not much to be wondered at. The reverend Dr. Porter, and Mr. Villette, the Ordinary, went into the coach along with him, accompanied by Mr. Brent, the sheriff's officer.

During

During the whole of the procession he seemed much affected, and said but little; and when he arrived at Tyburn and got out of the coach, and mounted the cart, he took leave of Dr. Porter and the Ordinary. After some time spent in prayer he was turned off, and having hung the usual time, his body was carried to Surgeons-Hall.

Such was the end of a young gentleman, who might have been an ornament to his country, the delight of his friends, and a comfort to his relations, had he not been led away by the influence of an unhappy passion.

He was executed on the 19th of April, 1779.

As the letter, intended for his brother-in-law, and his Defence, are of an interesting nature, and will serve to throw some light on the causes which produced his unhappy end, we shall present our readers with the following genuine copies.

LETTER.

"My dear Frederick,

"When this reaches you I shall be no more, but do not let my unhappy fate distress you too much; I have strove against it as long as possible, but it now overpowers me. You well know where my affections were placed; my having by some means or other lost her's (an idea which I could not support) has driven me to madness. The world will condemn me, but your good heart will pity me. God bless you my dear Fred. Would I had a sum to leave you, to convince you of my great regard: you was my only friend. I have hid one circumstance from you, which gives me great pain. I owe Mr. Knight, of Gosport, 100*l.* for which he has the writings of my houses;

but I hope in God, when they are fold, and all other matters collected, there will be nearly enough to settle our account. May Almighty God bless you and yours with comfort and happiness; and may you ever be a stranger to the pangs I now feel. May heaven protect my beloved woman, and forgive this act, which alone could relieve me from a world of misery I have long endured. Oh! if it should ever be in your power to do her an act of friendship, remember your faithful friend,

J. HACKMAN."

DEFENCE.

I should not have troubled the court with the examination of witnesses to support the charge against me, had I not thought that the pleading guilty to the indictment gave an indication of contemning death, not suitable to my present condition, and was, in some measure, being accessary to a second peril of my life; and I likewise thought, that the justice of my country ought to be satisfied by suffering my offence to be proved, and the fact established by evidence.

I stand here this day the most wretched of human beings, and confess myself criminal in a high degree; yet while I acknowledge with shame and repentance, that my determination against my own life was formal and complete, I protest, with that regard to truth which becomes my situation, that the will to destroy her who was ever dearer to me than life, was never mine till a momentary phrensy overcame me, and induced me to commit the deed I now deplore. The letter, which I meant for my brother-in-law after my decease, will have its due weight as to this point with good men.

Before this dreadful act, I trust nothing will be found in the tenor of my life, which the common

charity

charity of mankind will not excuse. I have no wish to avoid the punishment which the laws of my country appoint for my crime; but being already too unhappy to feel a punishment in death, or a satisfaction in life, I submit myself with penitence and patience to the disposal and judgment of Almighty God, and to the consequences of this enquiry into my conduct and intention.

Account of THOMAS HILLIARD *tried for setting Fire to his House, and acquitted on a Point of Law.*

THE case of this man being not only recent, but likewise singular, merits a place in this Work, although the person accused was not found guilty. Thomas Hilliard had been several years a Porter at the Royal Exchange Assurance Office, and likewise went on errands for Bankers, Merchants, and Tradesmen in that neighbourhood. He was Parish Clerk of St. Mildred in the Poultry, and the Rev. Mr. Bromley employed him to collect his Tithes for him—Had he not been considered as a man of integrity, he would never have been intrusted with an office upon which the support of a Clergyman depended, and so far as it appears, he kept his accounts regular, without injuring any one. However, be that as it will, on March 16th 1779, while he lived in Bird-in-Hand Court, Cheapside, his house was discovered to be on fire, and he himself went to the watch-house and gave information of it to Mr. Washington, the constable of the night. Hilliard, who was himself a constable, at the same time, seemed much frightened, and begged that an engine might be sent for. Mr. Washington, and one Mr. Bagwell, went to view the premises, and found there

was

PUBLISHER'S NOTE

pp.24-63 are missing.

was much smoke on the stairs, but could not discover any fire. Upon further enquiry it was discovered that there was a pitch barrel in a closet, which had been set on fire, so that there arose some suspicion that it had been done by Hilliard himself; upon this he was apprehended, and carried before Alderman Hart at Guildhall, where in some respects he behaved like one subject to temporary fits of insanity; for he wanted to confess more than he was charged with. Every thing of this nature, whether real or imputed, raises an indignation in the minds of the people; and to enhance the guilt of the prisoner it was given out that he had a considerable sum of money in the funds, and that he had set fire to his house in order to defraud the Assurance Office.—All this, however, turned out to be false, for he was not worth a shilling, having spent what trifle he had by gambling in the lottery. All the circumstances alledged against him were proved on the trial; but here the glory and humanity of the English laws stood in his defence.—It is a maxim in law, that when the life of a man is at stake, every error, every trifling circumstance that seems to create a doubt, shall be construed in his favour.—This is not done to encourage guilt, but to preserve the persons of whose guilt there may be some doubt. Thus it was proved that the closet where the fire was discovered, did not make part of the dwelling house, according to Stat. Hen. VIII. Cap. 1. Sect. 3. so that he was acquitted. From some circumstances that came out in the evidence, it would appear that this man laboured under some sort of religious melancholy; but from what motives he really acted must be left to unerring wisdom to determine—As the law has acquitted, let the charge against him be forgotten. He was tried at the Old Bailey April 17th, 1779.

Account of JOSHUA CROMPTON, *who was tried and executed for a Forgery on the Bank of* England.

ON Friday, July 31, 1778, his trial came on at Guildford, for the above-mentioned crime. There were two charges of Forgery laid in the indictment, viz. " For forging a 2ol. bank note, dated May 5, 1773, No. 56, marked K payable to Thomas Harris, Esq; or bearer, on demand, purporting to be a bank note, signed by the governor and co. of the bank of England, and subscribed Thomas Grant." It was also stated as " a promissory note from the governor and co."

A great number of witnesses were examined on this occasion; after which, and the evidence being closed, the jury found him guilty; in consequence of which, he was executed at Gangley-green, near Guildford, in the county of Surry. After his arrival at the place of execution, he behaved steadily and penitent, acknowledging his crime, and owning his guilt, continually praying to God to forgive the person who artfully drew him over to England after he had made his escape from the New-Gaol in the Borough, and was the means of hanging him for ten guineas, after he had assisted him in his escape.

Thus this person fell a victim to an inordinate thirst for money, which instigated him to commit a crime extremely injurious to public credit and private property, and which could only be expiated by an ignominious death.

He was executed Aug. 20, 1778.

A brief Account of THOMAS BOULTER, *the noted Highwayman.*

THIS man had for a considerable time infested the western counties, where he had committed several daring robberies; but was at length apprehended near London, and committed to New Prison, Clerkenwell, from whence he found means to make his escape, and renew his depredations on the public. He committed several robberies in Hampshire, and was become the dread of that part of the kingdom; so that Sir J. Fielding thought proper to send some of his men in pursuit of him, who took him, July the 4th, 1778, at the Greyhound inn at Bridport in Dorsetshire. He was afterwards tried and convicted at Winchester, and found guilty on two indictments. The audacity of this adventurer was so great, even after his above-mentioned escape from prison, as

d

to

to prompt him to go low down into the weſt, where he was univerſally known, and rob many people; which gives room to reflect, that iniquitous practices, ſooner or later, meet with the worſt of wages; and villainy, tho' it may prove ſucceſsful for a time, yet ſeldom fails to involve the perpetrators in certain ruin; for notwithſtanding the judge, to the ſurprize every perſon in court, recommended him to mercy,

He was executed at Wincheſter, Aug. 15. 1778.

An authentic Relation of JAMES MATHISON, *who was tried at the Old Bailey, for a Forgery upon the Bank of* England.

HE was tried on Thurſday, the 20th of May 1779.—— There perhaps never appeared in any court of juſtice ſo capital nor ſo ingenious a man in his ſtyle as this perſon. His practice for ſome time paſt had been to go to the Bank, and take out a note: this he counterfeited, paſſed the copy, and after ſome time returned the original. His frequent applications at length exciting ſuſpicions, which were increaſed by his appearance in life and other circumſtances, he was taken up. When brought before juſtice Fielding, he was there known to be the perſon charged with forgeries upon the bank at Darlington. The particular forgery now charged on him, was, for making and uttering a note for payment of 20l. with intent to defraud Mr. Mann of Coventry and the Bank of England. The note was produced in court, and witneſſes were brought to prove its having been negociated by him.

This fact being eſtabliſhed, the next circumſtance in conſideration was, to prove that the note was abſolutely a counterfeit one. This his proſecutors were totally unable to do, by any teſtimony they could adduce; ſo minutely and ſo dexterouſly had he feigned all the different marks. The note itſelf was not only ſo made as to render it altogether impoſſible for any human optic to perceive a difference, but the very hands of the caſhier and the entering clerk were alſo ſo counterfeited, as entirely to preclude a poſitive diſcrimination, even by theſe men themſelves. The water mark too, namely, Bank of England, which the bankers have conſidered as an infallible criterion of fair notes, a mark which could not be reſembled by any poſſible means, was alſo hit off by this man, ſo as to put it out of the power of the moſt exact obſerver to perceive a difference. Several paper-makers were of opinion that this mark muſt have been put on in the making of the

paper;

paper; but Mathifon declared that he put it on afterwards by a peculiar method, and known only to himfelf.—The extreme fimilitude of the fair and falfe notes had fuch an effect upon the judge and jury, that the prifoner would certainly have been difcharged for want of evidence to prove the counterfeit, if his own information, taken at Fielding's, had not been produced againft him; which immediately turned the fcale, and he was found guilty.

He was executed at Tyburn, purfuant to his fentence, on July 28th, 1779. At the place of execution, he made a fpeech, which took up fome minutes; wherein he acknowledged his guilt, and hoped for forgivenefs from the Almighty. He alfo warned others to avoid the crime for which he fuffered, and forgave his profecutors.

Such was the fatal and untimely end of a man, who, if his talents had been laudably employed, might have proved an ornament and ufe to fociety; but which being abufed to the bafe and illegal purpofes of fraud and injuftice, made him obnoxious to that fevere punifhment which the laws of his country affix to a crime fo highly detrimental to the public and individuals. Which inftance, with many others of a fimilar kind, prove the truth of the obfervation in fcripture, that "a little which the righteous poffeffeth, is better than all the riches of the ungodly."

Some Particulars of JOHN SPENCER, *who was executed at* Nottingham *for the wilful Murder of* William Yeadon, *Toll-collector, and his Mother, at* Scrooby Turnpike.

THE commiffion of this horrid crime being proved upon him, it will be fufficent to add, that he confeffed, on the morning of his execution, that the two perfons he had accufed as accomplices were intirely innocent of the fact, and that *he* only committed the fhocking murders for which he was going to fuffer:—That he was at the turnpike early in the evening on which he committed the fact; went away from thence and wandered about the common till late, when he returned and knocked at the turnpike-houfe, pretending he had fome beafts to go through; and as foon as William Yeadon opened the door, he knocked him down with a hedge-ftake, and repeated his blows till he was nearly dead; he then went in, took his watch; went up ftairs, where the mother was in bed and afleep, and with the fame weapon killed her alfo.

For this atrocious deed, detestable both to God and man, and which always cries to heaven for vengeance, he was

Executed at Scrooby turnpike, and hung in chains near the spot.

A short Account of Miss ELIZ. WATKINS, *for the Murder of her own Child.*

SHE was charged with the murder of her natural child, and tried for the same at the sessions in the Old Bailey, September 1779; but the evidence produced by the witnesses to prove the fact not being sufficiently strong to criminate her,

She was acquitted.

Account of JOHN BENFIELD, WILLIAM TURLEY, *and* MARY WILLIAMS, *for Coining.*

INdictments being found against these offenders, they were tried, Jan. 14, 1780, for feloniously and treasonably coining and counterfeiting the current silver of this realm, called shillings, sixpences, and half crowns, at a house in White's-alley, Chancery-lane — The two men pleaded innocence, pretending to have been decoyed into the house; and said, if they suffered, it would be as innocent persons. However, as there was no doubt that the sentence was just, they were all condemned; the two men to be hanged, and the woman to be burnt, after having been previously strangled.

As scarce any crime can be attended with greater inconvenience to the community in general, and many individuals of the lower class, than this; so none calls for a more exemplary punishment. Idleness and profligacy are the common forerunners of this and most other heinous crimes, which, if continued in, are sure to be followed, sooner or later, with destruction and shame; to both which, the want of moral honesty, and a disregard to salutary laws, expose multitudes of unthinking mortals, most of whom ascribe their ruin to one or both of the above causes, and an unhappy fondness for vice and vicious company.

John Benfield and William Turley were executed Jan. 12, 1780; but Mary Williams was reprieved, and pardoned.

Authentic

Authentic Account of ELIZABETH BUTCHILL, *who murdered her Female Bastard Child.*

THIS unfortunate young woman was a native of Saffron Walden in Essex, born of honest and industrious parents, and had lived for a considerable time with her aunt, who was a bed-maker belonging to Trinity college. Till the unhappy affair which brought her to so ignominious an end, she was generally esteemed for the decency and modesty of her conduct; and it is much to be lamented, that a mistaken fear of shame should have induced her to commit an action at which nature shudders, the destruction of her own offspring.

The following are the particulars of the shocking murder perpetrated by this malefactor, as they appeared on the coroner's inquest, and on the trial.

On Friday the 7th of January, 1780, about 11 in the morning, the body of a new-born female infant was found in the river near Trinity college bogs; which was immediately taken out, and a coroner's jury summoned to sit on the body.

Mr. Bond, a surgeon, deposed, that he examined the body, when he found the head swelled and bruised, the scull fractured in several places; that on opening the body, the lungs appeared distended, and were on trial specifically lighter than water; and that he was of opinion the child was born alive, and received its death by the wounds in the head.

Esther Hall, the wife of William Hall, brewer to Trinity college, whose dwelling-house was within the college gates, at no great distance from the place where the child was found, deposed, That her niece Elizabeth Butchill, had lived about three years with her in the capacity of a bed maker in the said college: that about three o'clock in the morning of the 6th inst. she heard her niece groan very much, and, getting up to inquire into the cause, found her complaining of a violent cholic; that she heated some peppermint-water, &c. and gave to her, with some hot flannels, which seemed to give her ease; that about six in the morning the said Esther Hall went to college, leaving her niece in bed, where she found her on her return about ten o'clock.

William Hall, husband to the said witness, hearing a child had been found, suspected the said Eliz Butchill, and sent for a surgeon to examine her. In her voluntary confession, taken before the mayor and Dr. Ewin, and read to the jury, she confessed that she was delivered of a female child on Thursday morning about half past six o'clock, by herself; that the child cried some little time after its birth; and that in about twenty

minutes

minutes after, she herself threw the said infant down one of the holes of the necessary into the river, and buried the placenta, &c. in the dunghill near the house. Upon this evidence the jury brought in their verdict Wilful Murder, but did not charge the said Elizabeth Butchill as the mother; she was therefore committed to the castle on her own confession, as soon as she could be removed with safety.

On Wednesday morning she was tried before judge Buller, when her voluntary confession being produced, and many corroborating circumstances appearing in evidence, the jury found her guilty, and the judge passed sentence on her in a very pathetic and affecting manner. When the unhappy culprit, in extreme agony, solicited mercy, his lordship told her, that as she had been deaf to the cries of the innocent, and, stifling the strong ties of maternal affection, had been the murderer of her child, it was impossible for mercy to be extended to her in this world; he therefore exhorted her to seek for a sincere repentance, and sentenced her to be executed the succeeding Friday, and her body to be anatomized.

From the time of her commitment she was in a bad state of health; but her behaviour was modest, patient, and penitent. A worthy clergyman visited her daily, and administered the sacrament to her, when she was perfectly resigned to her fate, and acknowledged the justice of her sentence. In the evening before her death, she took an affectionate leave of her friends, and passed the night tolerably composed, except at intervals, when she seemed to be deprived of her senses.

In the morning of the fatal day the before-mentioned clergyman attended her to the place of execution, where her behaviour was firm, resigned, and exemplary. She joined with the minister in prayer, and sung the Lamentation of a sinner, with marks of a sincere penitent, declaring she had made her peace with God, and was reconciled to her fate. Desiring her example might be a warning to all thoughtless young women, and calling on Jesus Christ for mercy, she was launched into eternity amidst thousands of commiserating spectators, who, tho' they abhorred the crime, shed tears of pity for the unhappy criminal.

She was a decent plain young woman, about 22 years of age, and, before this unfortunate affair, bore a good character for her modest behaviour.

The murder of infants born in bastardy has of late years become so general in this kingdom, as to be a disgrace to humanity. Many instances there doubtless are where this horrid crime has been committed without suspicion, and the

murder

murder is known only to the perpetrator, and to the Almighty; and too frequently it happened, that where the crime has been discovered, from a deficiency in the evidence the criminal has escaped.

May the melancholy end of Elizabeth Butchill be an example, an awful example, to deter all mothers, in the like unfortunate circumstances, from being the secret murderers of their children; to teach unthinking females to be on their guard against the possible consequences of unlawful love; and, where they have been unfortunately deluded, not to add crime to crime, by suppressing the tender feelings of a mother, and, instead of the protector, become the murderer of the helpless innocent.—If her untimely end shall prevent a similar crime, or bring one hardened sinner to repentance, she will not have died in vain.

She was executed at Cambridge, March 17, 1780.

Account of JAMES BURNET, *for Murder.*

HE was one of those violators of the laws in being, who, contrary to the statute in that case made and provided, presume to destroy and take the Game in different parts of the kingdom. Being detected in this unlawful practice by Thomas Hewitt, game-keeper to the duke of Richmond, and ordered to deliver up his gun, he refused, and, on the duke's servant approaching to take it away, he shot him dead on the spot. This happened at Goodwood in Essex, in Dec. 1779. Burnet was then in company with one Dilloway, who not being concerned in the murder, escaped punishment. Burnet was tried for the wilful murder of the said person, Mar. 20, 1780; but some circumstances appearing in his favour, from the suddenness of the fact, he was found guilty of manslaughter, sentenced to be burnt in the hand, and imprisoned 12 months in Horsham gaol.

Tho' his punishment for this crying sin has been thus mitigated in an earthly court, yet as a more awful indictment at the bar of divine justice stands out against every such offender, it is hoped sincere repentance will be granted, lest a worse punishment, without the least mercy, fall upon them; for, whatever men may think, the day is approaching, when every secret and open sin, unatoned for and unrepented of, shall undergo a strict and impartial scrutiny at that awful bar

"Where the bad meet punishment, the good reward."

Account

Account of JOHN KNIGHT, for Murder.

AS crimes which affect the property of the community in general have been the peculiar object of the British legislature, who have from time to time enacted wholesome laws, and inflicted severe punishments against the perpetrators thereof; so none can come more properly under this denomination than that of smuggling, or dealing in uncustomed goods, inasmuch as it is extremely detrimental to the fair trader, as well as to his Majesty's revenue. This practice Knight had been carrying on for some time; and on the 26th of Feb. 1780, having, with some other smugglers, met two dragoons at Whitstable, near Canterbury, he assisted in shooting them. Being apprehended, on the 16th of March following he was tried at Maidstone assizes for the fact, found guilty, and afterwards executed on Pennington Heath.

Thus we find, in this and numberless other instances, that " the wages of sin is death;" and that evil company and examples plunge many inconsiderate mortals into destruction; whilst, on the contrary, the happiness and tranquillity which a life of sobriety and industry affords to others, prove to a demonstration, that ' honesty is the best policy,' and ' virtue is its own reward.'

An authentic Account of the dreadful Riots *which happened in the Beginning of the Month of* June 1780, *and the destructive Effects thereof.*

WERE it not that facts put the matter beyond a doubt, it would seem almost incredible that such horrid devastation, which we shall here give some account of, could be committed by a gang of lawless miscreants, and also increase for several days together, in the very heart of the kingdom, and its capital, to the terror of all ranks and orders of people.

This alarming commotion took its rise from a resolution of the Protestant Association, of which lord George Gordon was president, to address the parliament, by petition, in order to obtain a repeal of the act lately made in favour of the Roman catholics; which petition was agreed to be accompanied to the parliament-house by the whole body of subscribers. Accordingly on the 2d of June they assembled in St. George's Fields in four divisions, to the amount of at least fifty thousand; and proceeded from thence to the house of parliament, where

where having waited till the members came, some of them were very roughly treated by them; particularly the abp. of York, the lord president, lords Mansfield and Stormont, bp. of Lincoln, Welbore Ellis, Esq; Mr. Strahan, &c. The rabble even attempted to force their way into the house of commons, so that the members could scarcely get in or out. Lord Geo. Gordon endeavoured to disperse them, by telling them, their gracious king would give them relief, and that their petition would be heard on Tuesday.

The mob now formed themselves into parties, some going to the Romish chapel in Duke-street, Lincoln's inn-fields, and others to that in Warwick-street, Golden-square, both which buildings they in a great measure soon demolished. Thirteen of the rioters were taken and lodged in prison, and the tumult for the present subsided.

On Sunday afternoon the rioters attacked the chapel and dwelling-houses of the Roman catholics in Ropemakers-alley, Moorfields, the furniture and fittings up of which they burnt. They now declared their resolution of releasing the people confined in Newgate for the violence committed at the Sardinian and Warwick-street chapels.

On Monday, the mob growing more formidable, the chapels in Virginia-lane, Wapping, and Nightingale-lane, East-smithfield, were destroyed by several parties. Mr. Rainsforth, of Stanhope-street, and Mr. Maberly, of Long-acre, who had given evidence against those who had been taken, had their houses stripped, and the contents committed to the flames; and the house of Sir Geo. Savile shared a like fate.

On Tuesday the military were ordered upon duty at both houses of parliament, St. James's, the Tower, &c. Notwithstanding which, the earl of Sandwich, in his way to the house of lords, was dragged from his carriage, and with difficulty rescued by the soldiers. Lord G. Gordon afterwards desiring the people to disperse, they took the horses from his carriage, and dragged his lordship to his house in Welbeck-street.

After destroying the house of justice Hyde, near Leicester-fields, a party of the rioters broke into Newgate, set fire to Mr. Akerman's furniture, which they had thrown into the street; and afterwards burnt the gaol itself, which had lately been erected at an immense expence, the walls being only left standing; and released about three hundred prisoners.

The same night, a party of these desperate ruffians set fire to earl Mansfield's house in Bloomsbury-square, which was intirely consumed, with a collection of very valuable pictures, and (an irreparable loss to the present age and posterity) 300 manuscript

script volumes of notes on great law cases, and the constitution of England and privileges of parliament (the last of which his lordship had just transcribed for the press), after having been collected with unremitting assiduity by this great law luminary, and also many very scarce manuscripts, were sacrificed to the fury of an ungovernable mob! The military did not arrive in time to prevent the mischief, but, in dispersing the mob, killed six men and a woman, and wounded many others. The house of justice Cox in Great Queen-street, and of Sir John Fielding in Bow-street, they also destroyed, and set at liberty all the prisoners in New Prison, Clerkenwell.

At the close of Wednesday was exhibited one of the most awful and dreadful spectacles ever seen in the metropolis; for they destroyed by fire the King's Bench and Fleet Prisons, the toll-house on Blackfriers bridge, two houses of Mr. Langdale an eminent distiller in Holborn, one at the bottom, and the other near the Bars, besides several dwellings of Roman catholics, so that the inhabitants were terrified at the sight of many different fires (some say twelve or upwards) burning at the same time in the middle of the night, and the streets were crouded with persons moving their goods, scarcely knowing where to go for safety. The insurgents had likewise declared their determination of destroying the Bank, Gray's Inn, Lincoln's inn, the Temple, the grand arsenal at Woolwich, the royal palaces, &c. &c. It now became necessary to exert the royal prerogative, and give the military discretionary power.

For the protection of the Bank, guards were stationed before that building, and within the Royal Exchange, St. Paul's church, inns of court, &c. and at the water-works belonging to the New River company and London-bridge, both which last had been threatened with destruction. The rioters made two attacks upon the Bank, and one upon the Pay office; in which attempts, many persons were killed and wounded by the soldiers. Two men and a boy were shot in the Fleet-market, three men were shot dead upon Blackfriars bridge, numbers killed themselves by excessively drinking non-rectified spirits at Mr. Langdale's distilleries, others burnt to death or buried in the ruins, from which about 20 of these wretches were dragged out, many of them being dead. The same scenes of shocking intemperance happened at several other places, and were attended with the like dreadful effects.

Some disturbances happened in the Borough, where several individuals suffered considerably in their property; but the rioters were soon dispersed by the military; as they also were at lord Mansfield's fine seat at Caen-wood, Hampstead.

The

The following is a general view of the trials of the rioters, under a special commission, granted for that purpose: In London and Middlesex—Tried, 84; found guilty, 34; respited, 15; executed, 19; acquitted, 50. In Southwark—Tried, 50; found guilty, 24; respited, 18; executed, 7; acquitted, 26.——Besides the above who were executed, the return published of those who were killed by the soldiers, amounted to 210, and 75 died in hospitals; in all, 285; and upwards of 2000 were set at liberty from the several gaols.

The sessions at the Old Bailey, at which the London rioters were tried, began June 29th, and ended on the 11th of July following, when 34 were capitally convicted.——At St. Margaret's hill sittings, held by special commission, and which ended July 20th, 50 persons were tried as rioters, of whom 24 were capitally convicted.

It is necessary to observe, that there was not one man of character or condition, of any description, who abetted the rioters in the commission of such dreadful enormities; nor any man among the associated protestants, who was either tried or taken up on suspicion, except the imprudent young nobleman (afterwards tried and acquitted), whose intemperate zeal precipitated him into measures which he was far from imagining would be productive of those dreadful consequences by which the whole metropolis, and its environs were thrown into a state of convulsion unparalleled in the annals of history.

We must here observe, that the enormous outrages committed by these abandoned wretches were so numerous and terrifying, and the further mischiefs dreaded from their menaces were so tremendous, that (as was remarked of one of the cruel Roman emperors) one would almost think Divine Providence had suffered them to run such shocking lengths, to shew what horrid excesses the human mind is capable of when left to its own evil bias, without restraint.—But the punishment due to such heinous crimes soon overtook many of them, tho' it is to be feared not all of the most guilty; since many imprudent and over-curious persons, by mixing with the principal actors, had involved themselves in the same punishment. But however, the sufferings of some of the most notorious offenders, at the same time that it may serve as an example of terror to evil doers, sufficiently proves, that how daringly soever wickedness may triumph for a season, it will draw after it the punishment justly due to the transgression of human laws, and, without repentance, an obnoxiousness hereafter to the vengeance of the Almighty.

The names of the malefactors, with the times and places of their execution, are as follow:

William Macdonald, Charlotte Gardiner, and Mary Roberts, were executed July 11th, at Tower-hill; Wm. Brown, in Bishopsgate street; and William Bateman, in Coleman-street.——On the 12th, Tho. Taplin and Richard Roberts, in Bow-street; and James Henry, on Holborn-hill.——On the 13th, Enoch Fleming, in Oxford-Road.——On the 20th, John Gamble, at Bethnal Green; Sam. Solomons, in Whitechapel; and James Jackson, in the Old Bailey.——On the 21st, Tho. Price, James Burn, and Benjamin Waters, in Old-street; and George Staples and Jonathan Stacey in Moorfields.——On the 22d, Charles Kent and John Grey, in Bloomsbury-square.

Borough rioters executed Aug. 9, 1780, in St. George's-fields: Robert Lovell, Mary Cook, Edw. Dorman, Olive Johnson, Eliz. Collings, Henry Penny, and John Bridport, who all behaved in a very becoming manner.

Account of ABRAHAM DARNFORD *and* WILLIAM NEWTON, *for assaulting* James Watts, *the Bankers' Clerk.*

THIS extraordinary affair happened Aug. 5, 1780, at No. 21, in Water-lane, Black Friars, which house Darnford and Newton hired, after it had been empty for some time. A note payable at this house, and which became due on the above day, had been previously left with Mess. Smith, Wright, and Gray, bankers, in Lombard-street. Their clerk, a young man about 18 years of age, came to the house for the money: they opened the door, and on his entering collared him, attempted to gag him, and drag him down into the cellar. Finding their intention was to murder him, by an extraordinary effort he got from them, and ran to the street-door; this being locked, they again seized him and attempted to drag him back, having previously barricadoed the cellar windows, and fixed double doors on the stairs, so as to prevent the hearing the cries of any person put therein. But his screams being providentially heard by Mrs. Boucher, who kept the Glasiers Arms on the opposite side of the way, she ran over to his relief, and thundered at the door; which being fast, she burst open the lower sash window and got so far in as to see the transaction in the passage, and to seize and secure Darnford. Newton jumped out of a one pair of stairs

stairs window, but, being immediately pursued, was overtaken and brought back.

There have been several instances of bankers' clerks being missing, who have been supposed to abscond with the property entrusted to them; but it is more than probable that they have met with a fate similar to that which had so nearly befallen the above-mentioned clerk.

They were tried at the Old Bailey, Sept. 17th, for the assault on the said clerk, and robbing him of a pocket-book containing notes and bills to the amount of about 4000 l. and were condemned chiefly on the evidence of Mrs. Boucher, as Mr. Watts, being a quaker, refused to give evidence on oath.

As Darnford had defrauded many people in a very singular manner, and as the method which he took to do it was not only very injurious to the parties respecting their property, but also productive of much confusion and distrust between the country and London correspondents; it may not be improper, for the satisfaction of our readers, and detecting the like practice in future, to give a few particulars of the means he made use of for carrying his villainous designs into execution. In a paper delivered to the ordinary at the place of execution, he informed the public as follows:

"The method I chiefly put in practice, was, forging the post-mark of different towns, which I put on a piece of paper made up as a letter, and then went to the inns where the coaches came, and heard the parcels called over; then went to a neighbouring public-house, and wrote the direction on the letter the same as was on the parcel I had fixed on. The book-keepers seeing the direction the same, and the post-mark on it, usually gave me what I asked for, on paying their demand." He then gives the following instance, among several others:

"In Sept. 1777 I obtained a parcel from Norwich, directed to Mess. Smith, Wright, and Gray, which contained bills to the amount of 500 l. and upwards; one of them, for 216 l. 5 s. was drawn on Mr. Gaussen, in St. Helen's; which I carried for acceptance, and prevailed on him to give me the cash for, allowing him the discount; I wrote John Watkins on the bill, and likewise on the draft, which Mr. Gaussen paid me; the amount I received in cash at the bank of England. Two more of the bills I left for acceptance, and the others I destroyed."

He had also been concerned in taking from carriages, inns, &c. boxes, trunks, portmanteaus, &c. which if on opening he he found contained no cash, or materials worth keeping, he always sent according to the directions. By these means he was enabled to purchase several houses, which produced an income of about 120l. per annum.—He denied having had the least thought or intention to murder the clerk; and that he never divulged his intentions concerning the fact to Newton; who also, in a paper delivered to the minister before execution, solemnly declared he was only employed by Darnford on pretence of confining an evidence for an hour or two, that he might not appear on a trial against him.

They were both executed at Tyburn Nov. 22, 1780.

Authentic Particulars of JOHN DONELLAN, *Esq; who was executed for the Murder of Sir* Theodosius Boughton, *Bart.*

CAPT. Donellan entered very young into his Majesty's service; and in 1757 went to Madras in the E. Indies, where he was a subaltern in the 39th regiment commanded by capt. Aldercorn. He continued in the service here till 1759, when he and some other officers were dismissed, pursuant to the sentence of a court martial, for seizing and retaining the effects belonging to the garrison and black merchants of Mazulipatam the capital of Golconda, after they had capitulated. This disgraceful sentence putting an end to his military character, he embarked for England, to obtain a reversal of it; but without effect.

After his return to England, being unhappily under the controul of irregular propensities, his fortune soon became greatly injured; but he still reserved a sum sufficient to purchase a share or two in the Pantheon, which, his embarrassments increasing, he was obliged to sell under great disadvantages. Play and gallantry, the ultimate subterfuges of dissipation, wholly engrossed his time and thoughts. His universal intercourse with polite prostitutes was well known, and tended to increase his consequence: his connection with a married lady was also the subject of much conversation, her house, table, servants, and carriages being at his command. He was a great, but generally an unsuccessful gamester.

He first met with lady Boughton and her daughter at the Pantheon in London. The young lady being in possession of a handsome fortune, attracted his notice, and occasioned him to shew the most unremitting assiduities and attention to the ladies, till having at length made an impression on the daughter not unfavourable to his wishes, they agreed to make each other

other happy by an elopement and clandestine marriage. This affair exasperated the lady's relations for some time, till, by his decent behaviour, and unwearied efforts to conciliate the esteem of the family, he so far succeeded as to obtain an invitation to Lawford Hall, the seat of the Boughtons, where he soon acquired an ascendency over every branch of the family; no arrangement being made, nor alteration admitted in the domestic œconomy, without his advice and participation; his orders were as punctually obeyed as though he had been the owner of the mansion.

He was tried at Warwick assizes Mar. 30. 1781. By lady Boughton's evidence it appeared, that her son was 20 years old; his fortune, when at age, would have been about 2000l. a year, most of which, at his death, was to descend to his sister, Mrs. Donellan: that Sir Theodosius being under cure at Lawford-hall for a venereal complaint, the witnesses alledged, Mr. Donellan found means to mix laurel-water (a strong poison, of his own distilling) with Sir T.'s physic. This being innocently administered by his mother, lady Boughton, threw him into convulsions, and in about 10 minutes after he expired, Aug. 30. 1780. Captain Donellan, seeing what had happened, immediately washed and rinced the bottles, for which her ladyship blamed him. This circumstance, and his hastily burying the body to prevent inspection—the coroner's charge of Wilful Murder—the physician's evidence, from viewing the body when taken up—and the evidence of a number of witnesses, who were of opinion that Sir. T.'s death was occasioned by poison prepared by capt. Donellan—these testimonies concurring to criminate him, the jury declared him guilty, and the judge pronounced sentence of death upon him.

At the place of execution, he solemnly declared, as he was shortly to appear before God, that he was innocent, and that he fell a sacrifice to the malice of his prosecutors.

In this unhappy man's case and lamentable catastrophe, we have a striking proof of the dreadful consequences of a life of vicious pleasure and gaiety, which too frequently impel their votaries to use base and illicit means for acquiring money to support extravagant expence: these pursuits tend to harden the conscience, and exclude all thoughts of morality and religion, the only road to true pleasure; forasmuch as profaneness and debauchery lead the unwary to the chambers of death.

He was executed near Warwick city, April 3, 1781.

Account

Account of the Trial, &c. of WM. MEYER, *Esq; for Murder.*

ON the 18th of Oct. 1780, Joseph Spinke, a bailiff's follower, had been left with Mr. Meyer, after he had been arrested, till next morning, when the bailiff was to go to Kirkhammerton, the seat of the prisoner's father, for bail or money to pay the debt. About ten at night, after the prisoner and his wife had whispered together, she went out and brought in a pair of pistols under her apron, and gave them to her husband, saying, "There are your pistols, to fulfill your foolish humour." He ordered them to leave the room; which they refusing to do, he fired and shot Spinke in the neck, the ball went thro' the windpipe. Thomas Meyer instantly said, "Now, Mr. Meyer, you have done for yourself." The servant-maid, on hearing the pistol, ran up-stairs and met her mistress, who exclaimed, "By the Lord God, here is a man killed." Meyer was secured; Spinke died in a few hours, forgave the prisoner and his wife, but laid his death to their charge.

They were both tried for this fact at York assizes, Mar. 20, 1781. when Wm. Meyer, Esq; was sentenced to die for the same on the 22d of the same month: but afterwards obtained a respite, which did not avail him long.

His behaviour at the last was very unsuitable to his awful situation: he severely accused his wife, and thought his sentence hard; nor had he such an affecting sense of his crime as to repent of it as became him, but wasted his few remaining moments in a light and trifling manner.

It is our hearty and sincere wish, that a due and timely reflection on the denunciations of the Almighty against this and other heinous crimes, and the ignominious punishments inflicted on those who are guilty of them, may deter men from such evil practices; and that, instead of attacking the lives and property of others, sobriety and industry may take place, and every laudable pursuit render them valuable and useful members of the community.

He was executed at York April 6, 1781, having been respited from March 22d till that time.

F I N I S.

N. B. *The public are requested to observe, That these supplementary pages were written on purpose, and delivered gratis, for* The Malefactors' Register, *or* New Newgate and Tyburn Calender, *printed only for* Alex. Hogg, *No.* 16, Paternoster-Row, London.

CONTINUATION OF THE SUPPLEMENT TO THE NEW NEWGATE CALENDAR.

Printed for ALEX. HOGG, at No. 16, Pater-noster-Row, LONDON.

Some authentic Particulars of FRANCIS HENRY DE LA MOTTE, *who was tried, convicted, and executed for High Treason.*

THIS gentleman was indicted for procuring, with the assistance of his agent Lutterloh, an accurate narrative of the general situation of the British navy, and sending the same to the French, by which information they were enabled to counteract and defeat the measures concerted in the British cabinet. The discovery of the fact was made in January 1781, when the papers in his possession, leading thereto, were seized at his lodgings in Bond-street.

He was tried for the above crime on the 14th of July following, when it appearing, upon the evidence of a variety of witnesses, but more especially from his own papers which had been seized, that under disguised appellations he had given intelligence to the enemy of the names, strength, number, time of sailing, destination, &c. of the several fleets and ships belonging to the British Navy, and other particulars relative to the state of the politics in this country;—the Jury, after withdrawing for a few minutes, returned, and pronounced him guilty of High Treason.

Treason and rebellion are crimes offensive to God, and injurious to mankind. The king is God's vicegerent, whom we we are exhorted to honour as such. If we wish to be happily and quietly governed, we should revere and pray for the sovereign. If we are true patriots, we shall use our utmost endeavours to promote the welfare and prosperity of the State, which may be termed our political parent.

On the 27th of July he was conveyed on a sledge from the Tower to Tyburn, where he was executed pursuant to his sentence.

An Account of GEORGE WESTON, *otherwise* SAMUEL WATSON, *and* JOSEPH WESTON, *otherwise* JOSEPH WILLIAM WESTON, *otherwise* WILLIAM JOHNSON, *who were tried for robbing the Mail, and taking thereout several Bank Bills and a Lottery Ticket.* George Weston *and* Joseph Weston *were acquitted. But*

GEORGE WESTON was likewise indicted for forging the acceptance of a bank-post bill in the name of a clerk in the bank; and the fact being proved on the evidence of an officer in the bank, and others, he was found guilty.

Joseph Weston, the other accomplice in the above robbery, was tried for firing a loaded pistol at John Davis, and wounding him in the face and neck, as he was attempting to apprehend him for breaking out of Newgate. The Jury brought him in guilty of the charge.

Robberies of this kind are confessedly very hurtful to trade, as well as individuals; and are generally ventured upon by the most daring and abandoned. The other crimes these men embarked in, and for which they suffered, evince the spreading nature of vice, which sooner or later plunges its votaries into irretrievable misery and ruin.

They were both executed at Tyburn, September 4, 1782.

An authentic Summary of the Trial of JOHN *and* JANE GRAHAM, *for Forgery.*

THE crime of which these persons were accused, was, the altering a 15l. bank note to 50l. by means of a stamp cut in wood.

They were apprehended by the servant of the governor of Tothill-fields Bridewell, at the Coach and Horses at Southampton; and brought up to London to take their Trials at the

the Old Bailey; where the crime being fully proved against them, they were both condemned.

Craft and deceit are indications of a corrupt and debased heart, of which forgery is the degenerate offspring. The danger of this practice being no less great in itself, than injurious to society, the authors of it frequently reap the bitter fruit of their misimployed talents, by the just severity of the law against them.

John Graham was executed for this forgery on October 16, 1782. But Jane Graham, his wife, was respited, and afterwards obtained a free pardon.

A brief Account of JOHN EDMONDS *and* CHARLOTTE GOODALL, *for a House Robbery.*

THEY robbed the house of Mrs. Frances Fortescue. Goodall was a servant in the house, and had several times robbed her mistress; to conceal which, she had procured Edmonds and two other men to commit the robbery. But it being suspected that she was an accomplice, the fact was soon after proved on the trial, chiefly by the evidence of her fellow-servant, Eliz. Sterne. Edmonds and Goodall accordingly received sentence of death for the same, and were executed at Tyburn, Oct. 16, 1782.

Unfaithfulness to those, whom it is our duty conscientiously to serve and obey, is a heinous sin. But this affords a true picture of the heart of man, which is " deceitful ABOVE ALL THINGS, and desperately wicked." An enemy without the walls may be guarded against and repelled; but an enemy within the citadel, being less suspected, is on that account the more dangerous and offensive.

An Account of JOSEPH CADDIE *and* JOHN STUNNEL, *for a Robbery, attended with Circumstances of Cruelty.*

THEY were tried and cast on the evidence of Milbourne, an accomplice. They robbed some passengers in a post-chaise and pair below the Turnpike near Battle-bridge, and wounded a gentleman in the hand in a desperate manner with a cutlass.

Wanton and unprovoked cruelty gives some men a near resemblance to the devil, who was a murderer from the beginning, and who now, as a roaring lion, goeth about, seeking whom he may devour.

They were both executed at Tyburn, Sept. 16, 1782, the Monday after their condemnation.

Relation of FRANCIS GRAY, *for Murder.*

THIS man, in company with William Milbourne, Joseph Caddie, and John Stunnel, mentioned in the preceding account, was apprehended and tried for attacking three men and a boy near Iflington, one of whom Gray shot with a piftol. He was convicted upon the evidence of Milbourne, an accomplice in the robbery, who proved, to the fatisfaction of the court, that Gray committted the murder as above-mentioned. He denied having an intention to kill the deceafed, and perfifted to the laft moment, that the piftol went off by accident. The Jury, however, found him guilty.

Men who go on in a mad career of wickednefs, are like a heavy ftone rolling down a fteep hill, which it is impoffible to ftop; in like manner they who enter upon bad courfes, begin with fmaller crimes, till the hardened heart drives them on to greater; thus, in the above inftance, robbery led to murder, when death and deftruction finally clofed the dreadful fcene.

He was executed at Tyburn, Oct 12, 1782.—His behaviour was ftupid, nor did he give himfelf the leaft concern for his fituation.

An Account of DANIEL MACGENNIS, *for Murder.*

HE was tried and convicted, at the Old Bailey, for the murder of Mr. Hardy, of Newgate-Street, in whofe houfe he lodged. This melancholy affair was occafioned by Macgennis throwing fome foul water out of his window upon the fkylight over the room where Mr Hardy was fitting at tea. This imprudent act giving offence to Mr. Hardy, he went up ftairs to Macgennis, and reproved him for it; whereupon the latter, being incenfed, drew a knife out of his pocket, and thruft it into Mr. Hardy's left fide, of which wound he immediately expired upon the ftairs. The Jury pronounced him guilty, principally on the evidence of the two fervants, Mary Decrow, and Adey Lancafhire.

In

In this cafe we fee the dire effects of paffion, which often changes men of the moft amiable qualities into devils. How ought fuch men to watch over their own fpirits, to be open to reproof, and not render evil for evil! "Watch and pray, (fays our Saviour) left ye fall into temptation."

He was fentenced to be executed on Monday, Jan. 29, 1783; but in confideration of the excellent character given him, by feveral reputable noblemen and gentlemen, for charity, humanity, and good nature, he received a refpite for fourteen days, and afterwards a pardon on condition of being imprifoned in the King's Bench for two years.

An authentic Relation of WILLIAM WYNNE RYLAND, *for Forgery.*

HE was tried at the Old Bailey, and found guilty of forging and uttering a bill upon the Eaft India Company for 210l. The fervants of the Company not producing fufficient proof of his having uttered the bill, he was convicted by feveral circumftances which the Jury and Court adjudged fufficient to fix the fact upon him. The cafe of this gentleman was the more unhappy, as he informed the Court, in his defence, that he was able to pay 20l. for every 20s. he owed, poffeffed 7000l. in the Liverpoole water-works, 10,000l. ftock in trade, had 200l. per annum penfion from the king, and made 2000l. a year by his profeffion, which was that of an engraver. On his being apprehended, he cut his throat, but the wound did not prove mortal.

What pity is it that the gift of ingenuity, which fome men are amply endowed with, fhould be proftituted to the bafeft and moft nefarious purpofes! It is a juft remark of Montaigne, "If men would take half the pains to be honeft, which they employ to be knaves, they might enjoy the comforts of life with fafety and reputation." This man's affluent circumftances greatly aggravated the criminality of his offence; and fhews us, that a life of pleafure and prodigality, if perfifted in, will unavoidably terminate in poverty and difgrace.

He was executed the 29th of Auguft, 1783, and was the laft criminal that fuffered at Tyburn.

An Account of JOHN BURKE, for Robbery.

HE was tried for robbing Thomas Fellowes, Esq. a justice of peace, as he was returning in his carriage from the County-hall in Clerkenwell-Green, to his house at Uxbridge: the robbery was committed by Burke and two others at a place called Brent Bridge. The person of Burke being positively sworn to by the prosecutor, he was capitally convicted.

This unhappy man afforded one instance, among a number of others, of the pernicious and fatal effects of evil company and bad examples, both which unite together in drowning multitudes in destruction and perdition.

This malefactor was executed Dec. 9, 1783, with nine others, who were the first that suffered on the new gallows before Newgate.

An Account of JOHN CLARKE, for Murder.

THIS unhappy wretch was found guilty of the murder of one Johnson, at the Hoop and Bunch of Grapes public-house in Ratcliff-Highway. It appeared, on the trial, that on the 5th of November, at nine o'clock, Clarke went into the tap-room of the said house, reached across the table, and run a knife into the belly of the deceased, who died in the hospital of the wound, after lingering two days. This melancholy deed seemed to be the effect of liquor, and the dreadful consequence of a quarrel that had previously subsisted between the parties.

Idleness and intemperance are twin vices, and prove to many the high road to destruction. The former paves the way to dishonesty and dissipation; while the latter renders them the willing slaves of the devil and their own furious and disorderly passions and lusts.

He was executed Dec. 22, 1783.

Some authentic Particulars of JOHN ASH, for Forgery.

THIS young man was tried for personating Tho. Eaton, a silversmith in Salisbury-court, Fleet-street, in whose name he sold 572l. 16s. 3d. four per cent. Bank-stock, the property of the said Mr. Eaton. He was convicted chiefly on on the evidence of Mr. Benjamin Hatwell, the broker whom he employed to transfer the stock.

In this person's case, as in that of many others, the observation in scripture was verified, namely, that "the (inordinate) love of money is the root of all evil," by coveting to obtain which in an unlawful manner, some men have pierced themselves through with many sorrows, and have at length ended their lives with misery and shame.

He was executed on the 4th of March, 1784.

An Account of THOMAS WHITE, *for a Robbery.*

HE was in the service of Lady Forrester, in Portland-street, whose house he caused to be robbed of plate and other valuables, early in the morning of Sunday the 9th of May. In order to conceal his being a party in this piece of villainy, he suffered himself to be tied hand and foot, in which condition the watchman found him, when he entered the house. Being taken up on suspicion, and examined, he was on the trial fully proved to be a principal in this atrocious affair. He made no defence.

There cannot be a greater token of a depraved heart, than when men betray the trust and confidence reposed in them. Such are the most dangerous members of society; for, as "ingratitude is worse than the sin of witchcraft," consequently when that odious quality is complicated with a specious of villainy injurious to a friend, benefactor, master, or mistress, they form a character too detestable to be described, and which is justly deemed punishable to the utmost rigour of the law.

He was executed July 27, 1784.

An Account of JOHN BRANTON *and* CHARLES GANLEY, *for Robbery.*

THESE men were tried for robbing the house of Mr. Thompson, at Islington, into which they rushed, after pretending to be sent with a letter to one Miss Young. There were five or six in the gang, one of whom, named Haskey, turned evidence. John Branton was found guilty, and received sentence of death, and Charles Ganley was acquitted.

Wrong

Wrong and robbery are two sore evils, and if not timely relinquished by repentance and amendment, will infallibly lead the perpetrators of them to the chambers of death. The salutary advice of scripture is, "Let him that stole, steal no more, but rather let him work with his hands the thing that is good."

John Branton was executed July 27, 1784.

An Account of WILLIAM HOLMES *and* JOHN MASH, *for a Burglary.*

ON the 23d of June they broke into the house of Mr. Hamilton, an innkeeper at Endfield, and stole plate and other things of value. They were detected by William Pratt, the servant, whose room they entered when he was awake. He immediately alarmed his fellow-servants, and Holmes was taken not far from the house. Mash was afterwards apprehended by one of Justice Wilmot's men. Holmes was pronounced Guilty, Death; Mash, Not guilty.

House-breaking is a most desperate species of robbery. Those who engage in it may fitly be compared to Satan, who in an inauspicious hour broke into the garden of Eden, stripped our first parents of their innocence, and filled the world with violence and rapine. Thieves and robbers, therefore, are of their father the devil, and the works of their father they will do; but all such enjoy short and unsatisfying pleasure, to which long woe frequently succeeds.

Holmes was executed on the first of September, 1784.

Account of RICHARD EDWARDS, ROBERT MOORE, JOHN SHELLY, *and* JAMES NAPIER, *for Robberies, &c.*

RICHARD EDWARDS was capitally convicted for assaulting the Hon. Keith Elphinston, near the theatre in the Haymarket, and forcibly taking from him a gold watch, gold seal, &c. Robert alias John Moore, for assaulting Mrs. Arabella Jeffreys, near St. James's gate, and snatching from her head-dress a cluster-diamond pin. John Codd, for a street-robbery on Samuel Ellison. John Shelly, for being concerned, with others, in rescuing and carrying away 350lb. which had been seized by an excise officer. James Napier, for robbing Albina Hobart, near the opera-house, of a diamond ear-ring, by tearing the same from her ear, but which, slipping out of his hand, fell into her hankerchief. These unhappy men joined the ordinary in fervent devotion, who recommended them to the divine mercy, which if they had before sought diligently, they would have escaped their dreadful doom.

They were executed at Newgate, with William Holmes, before-mentioned, 1st of Sept. 1784.

HENRY MORGAN, *for a Murder and Robbery.*

THIS unfortunate malefactor was found guilty of robbing Mr. Charles Linton, on the highway, in the parish of St. Martin in the Fields, and afterwards stabbing him in the belly with a case knife. The judge, before pronouncing sentence, told him, among other things, " You have deprived the wife of her husband, the " children of a father, and both of their protector: you have reduced " an innocent family to misery and distress, and deprived them of " that support, or forced them to seek it from the public, which they " derived from the honest industry of the deceased." Soon after the ordinary quitted the scaffold, this wretched criminal continued to repeat, in an impassioned tone of voice, " Oh my God, forgive " all my sins ; Lord have mercy upon me; Christ Jesus receive my " soul." And while uttering these ejaculations, soon, after a few convulsive struggles, became motionless. He was a melancholy instance, among others, of those who, having respectable relatives and friends, pursue such destructive courses as compel the justice of the laws to cut them off as corrupt members of society, and disturbers of the public tranquillity.

He was executed on Sept. 20, 1784.

SAMUEL HARRIS *and* JOHN NORTH, *for Piracy.*

HARRIS was formerly a porter at a tavern near Temple-bar, and recommended as a waiter to a public house at Margate, where he unhappily got connected with some smugglers, and entered

tered into their fraternity. North, alias Norton, was a native of Donnegal in Ireland, and bred to the sea. They were afterwards hung in chains at Deal.

Harris and North suffered at Execution-Dock, on Nov. 13, 1784.

The following Criminals suffered Death for divers Robberies, &c. namely,

JAMES LYDE, alias William Johnson, for assuming the name and character of Edward Stokes, late a seaman on board the Lively sloop, in order to receive Stokes's wages. William Hogborn, for stealing two geldings and a cow, the property of divers persons, from Putney common. William Rellions, for robbing William Rough of 5s. 1d. on the highway. William Collop, for robbing James Fergus of a pair of studs, and a pair of knee-buckles. James Forbester, for a burglary in the dwelling-house of Daniel Andrews. George Drummond, for stealing from the person of the earl of Clermont a gold watch, steel chain, and two seals. Peter Le Roche, for stealing a quantity of apparel, the property of James Martin. Joseph Hulet, for privately stealing in the house of Mr. Priestman, a pawnbroker in Bloomsbury, to whom he was apprentice, watches, rings, &c. to the value of 350l. Kyran Ryan, for forging the will of John Welch, deceased. Hulet, a slim lad, about 18, kicked and struggled surprisingly, and continued so to do for several minutes after his fellow-sufferers were dead. Such was the unhappy fate of nine men, who, it is probable, owed their ruin to idleness, bad company, and pernicious examples, the bane of thousands.

They were executed Nov. 17, 1784.

Account of the six Malefactors executed Dec. 20, 1784; viz.

WILLIAM RYAN, for personating the brother of John Harrison, late of his Majesty's ship Isis, and administering to a counterfeit will, with intent to defraud said Harrison. James alias Joseph Treble, and George Hands, for robbing Edward Rutter on the highway, of a watch and five shillings. William Coombes, for being at large before the expiration of the time for which he had been transported. Henry Moore and Richard Dodd, for assaulting John Cotton, near Poplar, and robbing him of a silk purse, two guineas, and half a crown. They manifested every appearance of sincere repentance. More and Dodd died with hands closely clasped together, which did not separate for some time after their bodies were motionless. Happy had they united heart and hand in practising virtuous actions, instead of walking in the paths of vice, which lead to the chambers of death!

GEORGE OWEN, for Forgery.

THIS unhappy young man was condemned for forging, and publishing as true, a certain order to the assay-master of the goldsmiths' company, for the delivery of certain silver goods, left for the assaying and marking, with intent to defraud. He was ordered for execution with the six last mentioned; but obtained a respite after he had been haltered, and was preparing for execution; and the moment he received the welcome tidings, he dropt on his knees, and with great fervency returned thanks to the Almighty for his goodness. However, the respite being expired, he was again ordered for execution; but was nevertheless prepossessed with a notion, even to the last moment of his existence, that he should receive the royal mercy. He had a week before the first order been perfectly reconciled to his sentence, and often declared, he should have felt no regret on leaving the world at that period: but his unexpected respite, and the sum left him by his father (near 700l. and a freehold of 52l. per annum) recalled all his affections for sublunary enjoyments. On leaving his cell, he said, "Surely God will grant me a longer life;" and intreated the sheriffs to wait for some "good news." They very humanely postponed the poor creature's execution till near two hours after the usual time. He desired leave to give the signal, by dropping a handkerchief, but continuing near half an hour without making that sign, the executioner was ordered to drop the scaffold. How flattering and deceitful are those hopes which are founded on any thing short of integrity and virtue!

He was executed Jan. 6, 1785.

Execution of Twenty Criminals for Robberies, Burglaries, &c.

THE names of these unhappy men, and the crimes for which they suffered, were as follows: John Hamilton, William Astel, John Kelsey, William Finder, William Steward, and Melvin Simmonds, for different burglaries. George Goldsmith, Richard Hobson, Lawrence and John Jones, for a burglary at the Black Dog in Shoreditch. Edward Johnson and John Evans, for privately stealing in separate dwelling-houses. James Dunn, for publishing a forged seaman's will. William Abbot, for publishing a counterfeit bill of sale with intent to defraud the owners of the Warren Hastings Indiaman. Allen Williams, for assaulting and robbing a passenger at Shepherd's Bush. John Shaw, Thomas Tabbs, Geo. Harris, Thomas Battledore, and John Moody, for assaulting Tho. Francis, near Bagnigge Wells.

This day exhibited indeed a very awful spectacle to sober minds; but yet, alas! not sufficiently so to alarm hardened profligates, and deter them from committing further depredations on the public, and acting in defiance of the laws, till disgrace and destruction overtake them!

They were executed on the 2d of Feb. 1785.

EDWARD PAYNE, JOHN PRICE, JOHN BROWN, SAMUEL DAVIS, and WILLIAM HUNT, *for Highway Robberies, &c.*

PRICE declared in the most solemn manner, after he was ordered for execution, and on the scaffold, that he and another man, then in custody, were the persons who robbed Mr. Alderman Kitchen, about two years ago, on the highway near Hornsey, for which Peter Airey and —— Davis were capitally convicted, but received a respite, and were a short time ago transported to the British Settlements in Africa. And, previous to his execution, William Hurt confessed to the ordinary of Newgate, and to Mr. Akerman, that he, and another man then confined in a county gaol, were the persons who robbed Sir Thomas Davenport and his lady in October last; for which Thomas Wood and George Brown were tried and acquitted at the December sessions.

The above were executed on the 2d of March, 1785.

An Account of the Execution of Nineteen capital Convicts; viz.

JAMES Wiggan and James Russel, for footpad robberies. Joseph Hitchcock and James Gray, for stealing on board the ship Elbe, Joel Goddard master, in the Thames, 3 casks and 2 boxes, containing 10,000 dollars and 20 watches. John Lucas, John Waters, and Richard Summers, alias Smith, for stealing out of the dwelling-house of Thomas Knott, in King-street, Covent garden, a large quantity of black and white lace, ribbon, and other things, value 700l. and upwards. James Cowan, William Bland, Jasper Robins, Robert Roberts, for divers burglaries. Charles Peyton, Robert Mott, and Thomas West, for returning from transportation. James Coyle, and John Johnson, alias Bandy, for street-robberies. Michael Johnson, alias M'Mahone, for forging a seaman's will. Holland Palmer, alias Farmer, convicted of feloniously uttering and vending certain forged receipts for payment of money, with certain stamps thereon, resembling the stamps provided by the late act. Oh that men were wise, that they would consider and amend their ways, and thereby attain a peaceable, instead of an ignominious latter-end!

They were executed on the 23d of April, 1785.

JOHN THOMPSON, *alias* WRINKLE, *for Burglary.*

HE was convicted fo breaking into the house of Henry Wells, in Thames street, violently throwing down Mrs. Wells, and

other

other outrage, with intent to rob the house; and for this fact, executed on April 26, 1785.

GEORGE WARD, Thomas Scott, Thomas Conner, Henry Wood, Thomas Bateman, alias Parker, and John Hughes, for divers robberies; Patrick Dudley, for private theft; George Mawley, for escaping a second time from the hulks; William Harding and James Haywood, for burglaries; were executed on the 4th of June, 1785.

JOHN IVENAY, John Honey, for highway robberies; Peter Shaw, for stealing in the dwelling house of Edwin Francis Stanhope, Esq. in Curzon Street, May-Fair, two gold boxes, six watches, &c. Joseph Brown, for a burglary; and Robert Jackson, for forging a seaman's letter of attorney; were executed before Newgate, on the 6th of July, 1785.

On the 18th of August, 1785, were executed in the Old Bailey,

JOHN REBOULT, alias Prescott, John Morris, and James Guthrie, for highway robberies; Martin Taylor, and Elizabeth Taylor his sister, for a burglary; and James Lockhart, for theft.

On the 10th of Nov. 1785, the following Malefactors were executed before Newgate, viz.

JAMES ROWE, for sheep-stealing; John Hayes, George Reynolds, James Lewis, and William Beer, for privately stealing; James Masdell, Thomas Browning, Thomas Winderbank, William Barnes, and Richard Silvester, alias Jack the Gardener, for highway and street-robberies; Amos Rowsell, Benjamin Howell, and William Moore, for burglaries; Joseph Banning, for forging a draught in the name of George Prescott, Esq. on Mess. Prescott and Co. bankers; John Ashbourn, and Joseph Wood, for house-breaking; John Lloyd, alias Jones, for horse-stealing; and James Connel, for house-breaking. Thus eighteen unhappy wretches are, for their felonious practices, justly cut off from society, who by virtuous courses might have proved honourable and useful members of it.

The following nine Criminals were capitally convicted in October Sessions; viz.

MICHAEL SMITH and James Nesbit, for burglaries; John Isaacs, for a highway robbery; William Powley, for horse-stealing; William Vandeput, James Beaman, Francis Storer, and

Daniel

Daniel East, for breaking into the dwelling house and warehouse of Lewis Teffier, Esq. of Old Bond-Street, and stealing a bale of silk, value upwards of 200l.; George Manning, alias Francis Hill, for house-breaking. They were executed, pursuant to their sentence, on Dec. 1, 1785.

John Hogan, a Mulatto, for Murder.

THE circumstances of this horrid act were as follow: Mr. Orrell, an attorney, in Charlotte-street, Rathbone-place, went out with his wife, at three o'clock on Sunday afternoon, June 29, 1785, leaving their maid in the house. They returned within the hour; when the servant not answering the door, they concluded that she had slipped out; and they went away again for a short time; upon their second return, the same difficulty occurring, it was determined to enter the back part of the house, by getting over a wall; when the girl was discovered upon the kitchen floor, weltering in blood, a most shocking spectacle. From the various marks of violence, she must have made strong resistance. Her head appeared to have been struck at with a poker; her throat effectually cut through the wind-pipe; two fingers nearly cut off; a deep gash on one breast, and otherwise dreadfully mangled. She was yet alive, and made signs; but was unable to speak; she was conveyed to the Middlesex hospital, and expired about one in the morning. The house was found to be robbed of spoons, and some other plate that lay about. The murderer had visited the girl two or three preceding Sundays, which caused a suspicion of his guilt.

A short time before the murder, he had brought home some chairs to Mr. Orrell's, and a person answering his description having been seen in the neighbourhood that day, suspicion fell on him, and he was twice taken up, and twice discharged for want of evidence. On being afterwards taken to the body of the deceased, he appeared not in the least agitated; but putting his hand on her breast, he said, "My dear Nanny, I do remember you well; I never did you any harm in my life!" These expressions very forcibly added to the suspicions of his guilt, because her face was so exceedingly cut and mangled, that Mr. Orrell declared he could not possibly have known her. Two other circumstances which tended to criminate him, were a spot of blood on a waistcoat which he wore, and some slight marks of blood on one of the sleeves of his coat; which coat had been washed, though the blood on the sleeve remained; and an effort seemed to have been made, but in vain, to rub out the spot of blood from the waistcoat.

Hogan having been afterwards tried for a larceny, and Mr. Orrell reading his trial in the sessions-paper, it occurred to him to search at the pawn-broker's, where he had pawned the property stolen, for which he was so tried, to see if any of his property, which was stolen at the time of the murder, had been lodged with that

that pawnbroker:—there he found a cloak of his wife's, pawned the morning after the murder, by the woman with whom the prisoner co-habited, who was also the principal evidence against him. She deposed, that he brought her home a cloak, which he said he had bought, on condition of paying for it at the rate of so much a week. The cloak was produced in court, and Mrs. Orrell swore to it as her property. The deponent said, that after Hogan had been twice taken before a magistrate, he, at intervals, appeared to be very uneasy; that particularly he could not sleep in bed; that she said to him one night, "For God's sake, what is the matter with you? surely you are not guilty of what you have been taken up for?" that his answer was, "Yes, I am,—I am guilty,—I did it." She then was much troubled in mind, and apprehended fatal consequences to herself, particularly as he said to her, "You must say nothing, you must be quiet: for if I be hanged, you will be hanged with me;" and on her asking him, why he had murdered the young woman, he answered, because he wanted to be great with her, and she resisted him." He said, in his defence, "I am innocent; and if any body takes away my life, I will never forgive them." Such are the dire effects of ignorance and obduracy! He was executed on a gibbet opposite Mr. Orrell's house, Jan. 16, 1786.

On April 13, 1786, twelve Malefactors were executed before Newgate.

THE morning preceding the execution, Major Arabin called at Newgate on Thomas Burdett, (who was to be executed next day, for breaking open the house of Mr. Chancellor, at Holywell Mount,) and asked whether he knew any thing of the robbery of his house, on the 7th of March last. To this Burdett answered in the affirmative. The Major then desired to know if he had any accomplices, and if they were still at large; to which Burdett replied, "You, Major, I suppose, call yourself a man of honour."—"Yes."—"So do I."—"Have you any hopes of a pardon?"—"No; nor would I make the desired discovery to procure it, and my immediate enlargement: I have long been a wicked man; I deserve the punishment I am going to suffer, and am perfectly resigned." Thus did this son of violence awfully retain his attachment to his companions in wickedness, and thereby, with a hardened conscience, countenance their vile practices, even to the last!

ON *June* 21, 1786, JONATHAN HARWOOD, for assaulting Mr. Drummond on the highway, and obtaining money from him, by threats of charging him with an odious crime; and Phœbe Harris (who was burnt,) for counterfeiting shillings; with four other malefactors, were executed before Newgate.

Account of MICHAEL WALKER, RICHARD PAYNE, *and* JOHN COX, *for Murder.*

ON December 22, 1786, Twenty-three prisoners received sentence of death. Michael Walker, Richard Payne, and John Cox, were tried in this sessions; the first as principal, for the murder of Mr. Duncan Robinson, near Stuart's Buildings, Holborn, by cutting him down the face and shoulder, and stabbing him in different parts of his arm, of which he died in three days; and the other two for being present, aiding and assisting in the said murder. One of the prisoners had picked the pocket of a Mr. Hunt, who was walking in company with the deceased: Mr. Hunt apprehended the prisoner, on which a scuffle ensued, in which Mr. Hunt knocked down his antagonist twice, when Payne attacked him, and Mr. Robinson coming to his assistance, received the dreadful wound that occasioned his death. Mr. Baron Hotham, at the close of his charge to the Jury, made some excellent observations on the law, tending to prove, that when several partners are in pursuit of an illegal action, and a murder ensues, all are equally involved in the guilt. They were executed on Monday the 18th, near the spot where the murder was commited.

An Account of ELIZABETH SEDGWICK, *the Incendiary.*

THIS unhappy woman was convicted of setting fire, at different times, to two barns, and one stable, belonging to her master, Mr. John Taylor, at Feltham-Hill, Middlesex. It appeared, on her examination, and confessions, that the first fire (on Sunday, Dec. 10.) was merely accidental; as she had then gone into the barn to examine the hens, and that, on returning to the beams on which they roosted, she had fallen on the straw, and, as she thought, put out the candle; but discovering the flames, as she returned to the house, had invented an excuse, by pretending to see a man in the yard with a lantern. But the remaining part of her confession was perhaps the most extraordinary that ever marked the waywardness of the human mind: she said, that on Sunday, the 17th of January, the day of the second fire, as she was making the toast for tea, the thought struck her, that she would go out, and set the other barn on fire; and that when her business was done, she had taken out a candle and candlestick, and placed them in such a situation as to effect her strange purpose in a few minutes. She declared that she did this without any motive whatsoever, and no motive could in fact be assigned, but that of absolute insanity, or inveterate resentment; but, on a strict examination of the evidence, that she had never given the smallest occasion to doubt the sanity of her intellects, and that so far was she from being displeased with her master or mistress, that she always spoke of them in terms of the highest praise.

She was executed on April 27, 1787, before Newgate, with fourteen other malefactors.

An Account of Henrietta Radbourn, *otherwise* Gibson, *for Murder.*

THIS unhappy person was apprehended, and tried at the Old Bailey the latter end of July, for the murder of her mistress, Hannah Morgan, by wounding and stabbing her in the head, while asleep in her bed: she was indicted, in one count, for petty treason, and for wilful murder. The Jury acquitted her of the former, and found her guilty of the latter. But her judgment having been respited, for the opinion of the judges, she was, on the 9th of Dec. 1787, set to the bar of the Old Bailey, and acquainted, that their lordships had confirmed the verdict of the jury; whereupon she was sentenced to be executed on the morrow, and afterwards to be dissected. She was accordingly executed Dec. 10, 1787.

At the same sessions in July, came on the remarkable trial of James Elliott, for shooting at Miss Boydell, now Mrs. Nicol, of Pall-Mall, niece to Mr. Alderman Boydell. It appeared, that as Miss Boydell, and Mr. Nicol, bookseller to the King, were walking up Prince's-street, Leicester-fields, a person came behind them, and suddenly fired a pair of pistols so close to the lady's side, as to set fire to her cloak; yet she happily received no other hurt than a slight contusion on her shoulder. Mr. Nicol instantly seized the assailant; and the pistols (fast bound together with a cord) were picked up by a servant that was passing by at the instant, and who saw them discharged. The person who fired them, being carried before a magistrate, appeared to be Dr. Elliott, well known among the literati.

Dr. Simmons, physician to St. Luke's hospital, and other witnesses, were called to prove the insanity of the prisoner, which, however, could not be established to the satisfaction of the court. The prisoner, nevertheless, was acquitted; because he had been indicted for shooting at the prosecutrix with a pistol and ball; and the jury were satisfied that there was no ball in the pistol. He was then remanded to Newgate, in order to take his trial for an assault: but the feelings of the unhappy man, it is supposed, were insupportable, for he died a few days after; and the coroner's jury brought in their verdict, "That he died by the visitation of God."

W. Everett *and* S. Dawson, *for an Assault.*

WILLIAM EVERETT, and Samuel Dawson, two boys, about fourteen years old, were tried at the Guildhall, in Westminster, for feloniously assaulting Frances Gilson, with intent to burn and destroy her cloaths, by maliciously throwing upon her apparel a certain quantity of oil of vitriol. This offence is made transportation by stat. 6 Geo. I. subject to the exercise of a discretionary

tionary power in the court to moderate the punishment according to the circumstances of the case.

The prosecutrix deposed, that as she was passing about her lawful business, the prisoners being together, one of them came up to her, and said to the other, "Do it," and that instantly they threw something upon her clothes, which very much burnt them.

The prisoners made no defence; but an apothecary in Oxendon-street, their master, gave them a good character. They were both found guilty of this offence, and of a similar one against Sophia Burnham.

After Mr. Mainwaring had consulted with the other magistrates, he addressed the prisoners as follows:

"William Everett and Samuel Dawson,

"You have been convicted of a crime the most dangerous to the "community at large, since no persons, who have occasion to walk "the streets, would be safe either by day or night, were offences of "this description to be committed, without the most exemplary "punishment. It is as wicked in it's intention, as mischievous in "it's consequences; for there is no knowing where it might end. "The legislature, therefore, has justly annexed to a crime of such mag-"nitude, the greatest punishment short of that of death, namely trans-"portation. It is not without much difficulty that the court have "forborne to sentence you to the most rigorous punishment the law "will allow. It is the consideration of your tender years, that in-"clines them to mercy. With sorrow, however, I observe, that you "appear totally unconcerned in your present unfortunate situation. "Every person in court seems to feel for you more than you do for "yourselves. Unhappy youths! the depravity of your minds ap-"pears but too evident; I hope, however, the sentence I am about to "pronounce, will lead you to that salutary reflection and compunc-"tion of heart that may work a change in your future life, and "induce you to become useful, instead of injurious to society."

Mr. Mainwaring then pronounced the sentence, "that the "prisoners be confined in prison for the assault on Frances Gilson, "three months, and be whipped in gaol; and for the assault on "Sophia Burnham, the further term of three months, and be also "whipped in the said gaol." The second imprisonment to commence from the expiration of the first. They were tried on the 18th of Oct. 1788.

It is equally astonishing and painful to a serious and sensible mind, to perceive at what an early period the seeds of vice grow up to maturity, and shew their baneful effects; and to what a pitch of malicious wickedness the evil propensities of youth impel them, even sometimes without the least prospect of advantage to them-selves! which may for the most part be justly ascribed to the want of proper instructions, example, and restraint in their tender years, from their parents or guardians.

Account of the Murder of MARY PATERSON, *by her Husband.*

THE particulars of this extraordinary case for deliberate cruelty, &c. is not paralleled even in that of Williamson, who was executed in Moorfields in 1767. It seems, the deceased had been married to the prisoner upwards of thirteen years; but that he had cohabited with another woman, in the same house, for a considerable time past; and that the former being delivered of a child about five weeks since (i. e. Christmas 1788), was confined to an empty back garret, though previously lame of a white swelling in the knee; and, notwithstanding the inclemency of the weather, had neither fire nor bed, except some straw, and scarce any covering, nor any attendant but her own daughter, about 12 years of age, who acknowledged, upon the examination before the magistrates at the Rotation-Office, that she used to be sent up to the deceased with bread, water, potatoe parings, &c. since her lying-in; but that sometimes she was not sent with any thing for two or three days together. From this cruel treatment, it appeared, the young child died a day or two after it's birth; and, what was more shocking to humanity, was taken away by it's unnatural parent, and sold to a surgeon for four shillings; and who, expecting the death of it's mother, had also procured a coach to take away her body for the same purpose the evening he was apprehended. The barbarous usage of his wife had been discovered a few days before her death, by a woman that came as a lodger into the next garret to which the deceased lay, by her groans; and on the former going into the room imploring for water, which being heard by the woman the prisoner cohabited with, the other was forcibly turned out. This occasioning an alarm among the neighbours, several of them were so abused by the prisoner on insisting to see the woman and child, that their suspicions were communicated to the churchwardens; who, much to their credit, came immediately to the house, and apprehended the man and woman. The corpse was found in a manner too shocking to be described, nearly overgrown with hair, and burnt in several places, occasioned by the prisoner's setting fire to the straw on which she lay after her decease. The deceased bore the character of a person perfectly quiet and inoffensive, had lived in good circumstances, and is said to have been formerly stolen by the prisoner from a boarding-school.

Some circumstances appearing in the prisoner's favour, he was acquitted of an intention to murder.

Some Account of Nine capital Convicts.

WILLIAM COLLARD, Charles Messenger, Treadway Pocock, John Norrington, and John Craig, for burglary; James Grace, Joseph Walker, for making counterfeits of two pieces of base metal, so as to resemble shillings; Hugh Murphy and Christian Murphy,

Murphy, alias Bowman, for making counterfeits of divers pieces of base metal, so as to resemble shillings and sixpences; were executed before Newgate, on the 19th of March, 1789. Christian Murphy, the woman, was, after strangling, burnt to ashes at the stake.

Henry Lloyd, and Hugh Partington.

HENRY LLOYD, for a burglary; and Hugh Partington, for a footpad robbery, and cutting and wounding Mr. Debney, in a cruel manner; were executed in the Old Bailey, on Dec. 9, 1789.

Account of John Dyer, for Forgery.

HE was indicted for uttering, on the 7th of May, 1789, a forged acceptance to a bill of exchange, knowing it to be forged.

The circumstances of the case were shortly these: The prisoner, on the 7th of May, called at the shop of Mr. Scott, a wax-chandler in Old Bond-street. He applied to the porter for 36lb. of candles, which he said were for Sir William Hamilton, and produced a bill of exchange for ten guineas, in these words:

"£ 10 10   No. 25.

"Richmond, Surry, April 22, 1790.

"Fourteen days after date please to pay William Smith, or
"Order, the sum of Ten Pounds Ten Shillings, Value received, as
"advised.

"To Messrs Hankeys,   CHARLES THOMAS.
"bankers, in London.

"Accepted for Self and Co.
"JOSEPH CHAPMAN HANKEY."

This bill was immediately discovered to be a forgery; in consequence of which Dyer was secured, tried, and found guilty.

In his defence he said, that he had received the bill from his master, whose name was Kelsy, and that he desired him to put the name of William Miller upon it; that he was ignorant of the consequence of so doing, and that in the whole of this transaction he had acted in the capacity of a servant.

He was of reputable parents, and had been brought up at a merchant's compting-house, was originally educated at Westminster-school, and was scarce 19 years of age. Several reputable persons appeared to his character. He was however clearly found guilty.

He was executed opposite the Debtors' door, Newgate, Aug. 5, 1790.

Particulars relating to the Trial and Conviction of George Barrington.

HE was indicted for feloniously stealing, on the 1st of Sept. at Endfield races, a gold watch, valued at 20 guineas; a chain
likewise

George Barrington,
As He appear'd at the Bar of the Old Bai[ley]
Drawn by an Artist during the Trial.

likewife of gold, valued at 40s. and a feal alfo valued at 40s. the property of Henry Hare Townfend, Efq.

Mr. Townfend, the profecutor, being firft examined, depofed, that on the 1ft of Sept. having entered a horfe for the races at Endfield, he accordingly went there at one o'clock in the afternoon: he put his watch in his waiftcoat pocket, as much for the convenience of looking at it, as to prevent the chain from foiling his breeches, which were of leather. About a quarter paft two he felt his watch in his waiftcoat pocket. As he was leading the horfe, which was to run, up to the ftarting poft, a perfon dreffed in a light coloured coat, rudely rufhed in from behind him, and pufhed againft the arm which had hold of the horfe: the fame perfon again repeated his pufh, but in a more violent manner.

Mr. Townfend further depofed, that, from the reiterated apparent infult offered to him, he, accompanied with an oath, afked Barrington what he wanted? to which he returned no anfwer, but obferved the prifoner looked much confufed. The conduct on the part of Barrington appeared very odd; but he entertained no fufpicion of having been robbed, until Mr. Blades came up to him, and afked him, if he had not been robbed? On feeling his pocket, he found his watch was gone. Mr. Blades informed him that Barrington was upon the courfe, and he verily believed that he was the thief. After this, they had agreed to fay nothing about the matter, until they had found the fuppofed offender. They then walked about in fearch of Barrington, and at laft faw him on the oppofite fide of the courfe: this was at the very moment when the horfes were going to ftart. Nothing occurred till after the horfes were paft; after which they went up to him; and Mr. Townfend, going behind him, feized him by the collar, and faid, "You rafcal, "you have robbed me of my watch." No fooner had Mr. Townfend faid the words, but he again laid hold of him faft by one hand and arm, and Mr. Blades took hold of the other, and conducted him to a booth.

Buxton Kendrick affirmed, that after he had been about a minute in the booth, he heard fomething rattle, and, looking down, he faw the watch fall rather between his legs. John Waldeck, Mr. Townfend's coachman, alfo declared, that he heard the watch jingle as it fell from the prifoner: that Barrington attempted to kick the watch further behind him; but that he picked it up, and gave it to lady Lake, in the next booth, who was a relation of Mr. Townfend.

William Blades, the principal witnefs, depofed, that he faw Barrington at the races, he was near the ftand, and clofe to Mr. Townfend: that he obferved no converfation at the time paffing between the profecutor and prifoner. Soon after this, he afked Mr. Townfend, if he recollected a tall thin man, in a light coloured coat, ftanding by him; which he faid he did, but knew nothing of him. Blades after this informed Mr. Townfend, that

he

he supposed he was robbed, which appearing to be the fact, they both went in search of the prisoner, whom they apprehended, as above related.

Mary Dandy deposed, that she was standing in the next booth, and saw the prisoner drop the watch out of his hand; after this, she looked him full in the face, and consequently could not tell whether he kicked it, or not. She at the same time accused him of throwing the watch down, but was immediately pulled back by some person near her.

Barrington made a long and specious defence, and, among other things, charged the evidence with being imperfect, inconsistent, and in some respects unsafe, especially that of Mary Dandy.

Lord chief baron Eyre, having summed up the evidence in a clear and circumstantial manner, observed, that the prosecutor had demonstrated his lenity, by making the indictment only for single felony, when it might have been made capital.—The jury, after a short deliberation, found the prisoner guilty,—Transportation for seven years.

The chief baron then addressed Barrington in a far different style from that he used before: his lordship observed, that he must consider himself as peculiarly fortunate in the lenity of his prosecutor: he said, that he had had many warnings, not only from the fate of others, but the many narrow escapes he himself had had; and he regretted that talents like his should be employed in a manner so truly disgraceful to him; and (said his lordship), notwithstanding your life is now saved, I fear that these wicked habits are so far rooted in you, that your existence will still terminate in a *shameful spectacle*.

Among other things said by Barrington in his address to the court, the following is not unworthy notice:

"The world has given me credit for much greater abilities than I am conscious of possessing: the world should also consider, that the greatest abilities may be so obstructed by the ill nature of some unfeeling minds, as to render them nearly useless to the possessor. And where was the generous and powerful man to come forward, and say, you have some abilities which may be of service to yourself and the public, but you have much obstruction—I feel for your situation, and shall place you in a condition to try the sincerity of your intentions; and as long as you act with diligence and integrity, you shall not want for countenance and relief?"

"My Lord, the die is now cast; I am prepared to meet the sentence of the court with respectful resignation, and the hard fate that awaits me with becoming resolution."

The prisoner then made a low bow, and retired from the bar.

Barrington was sent off from Newgate, Feb. 2, 1791, to embark for Botany Bay.

FRANCIS

FRANCIS FONTON, for Forgery on the Bank of England.

HE was a clerk of the Bank, and was charged with having signed a receipt for 47l. 12s. 6d. with the name of J. Pearce subscribed to it, and the date of which was May 8, 1789. It appeared to be a stock receipt, which the seller of stock, when he receives his money for it, gives to the buyer.

The indictment charged this offence upon the prisoner, as done with an intent to defraud William Papps. Another count, or way of charging it, was, that the receipt was forged with a view to defraud the Governor and Company of the Bank of England.

He was also charged with uttering and publishing this forged receipt, knowing it to have been forged with a view to defraud the said parties.

There were four other indictments against the prisoner, though he was only tried upon the first. The jury found the prisoner Guilty.

The recorder, previous to passing sentence, thus observed to him: "Fraud, which strikes at the credit and security of the bank of England, has never passed unpunished. The policy of the state requires that the punishment, in a case of that sort, should be the most severe. A servant, for transgressing, can expect no mercy. I must therefore hope, prisoner, that your example will convince others disposed to offend in like manner, that no art nor cunning, no experience nor knowledge of the subject, no character, how imposing soever by that gravity which is supposed to attach on old age, will cover fraud from detection; and that sooner or later dishonest acts will lead to that disgraceful end which you are about to suffer."

He was executed before Newgate, at the same time with Storey, for a highway robbery; William Burbridge, James Sullivan, Joseph Page, Thomas Dunklin, for house breaking; Thomas Tyler, the noted Swindler, for forging and uttering as true, the acceptance of William Fielder to a bill of exchange drawn on John Lindsey, No. 25, Gun-street. Spitalfields, value 10l. to John Philips, Esq. or order, dated Bristol, June 20, with an intent to defraud Mrs. Cockburn, of Stoke Newington; Edward Ivory, James Smith, and James Royer, for counterfeiting six-pences; viz. on the 24th of Nov. 1790.

The fate of F. Fonton will, we sincerely hope, be a caution to other men in respectable situations, not to pursue the baneful and illegal practice of insurance in the lottery, by which, it is said, he sunk 3000l. When once a person embarks in it, he is urged on in hopes of retrieving his losses, and in the end plunges himself into difficulties, beyond the possibility of recovery. How many lives have fallen a sacrifice to this destructive passion for gaming, either by self-murder, or by public justice: and yet the evil seems every year increasing!

Account of EDWARD LOWE, *and* WILLIAM JOBBINS, *the Incendiaries.*

EDWARD LOWE and William Jobbins were tried for feloniously and wickedly, on the 16th of May 1790, setting fire to the house of Francis Gilding, in Aldersgate-street; in consequence of which, that and many others adjoining were consumed.

Flindall, the accomplice, said he had been acquainted with Lowe eight years, and with Jobbins nine months; on Sunday the 16th of May last, he was at the fire; the prisoners at the bar, with two other persons and himself, set fire to the premises. It was proposed to effect their purpose on the 12th, at Lowe's house, in Hartshorn court, Golden lane; Jobbins said, he had fixed upon Mr. Gilding's house to fire, rob, and plunder. They met at the Swan in Cow Cross the next evening, Barnard was there; the witness and Jobbins went to shew Barnard the house. They went through the inn yard, and there was a cart unloading clover into a hay-loft, which Barnard pitched upon as the place to fire.

On Saturday, the witness met Barnard at the Sun, and proposed to set the house on fire that night. At five Jobbins came to the Sun, and Lowe came to them at eight, and at ten they went to Lowe's, when the wife brought in some spirits of turpentine; this they mixed with rags, which, with some matches, were put into a glove; Jobbins and the witness took some turpentine wood in their pockets.

They ordered Mrs. Lowe not to go to bed, lest she should be wanted to help to take away the plunder. They went to the Nag's Head public house, where they staid till past twelve, and went out each with a lighted pipe, in order to fire the matches. They went down Carthusian-street, when two pipes were broken; they then went to the back gates of the Red-lion-inn yard; Jobbins got over the gates, but broke his pipe; the witness followed, when finding the pipe extinguished, he put it through a hole in the gate to Lowe, who was without; and in the mean time Jobbins went down the yard, and found a ladder, which he placed against the hay loft door. Lowe then returned with the lighted pipe, and put it through the gate. The witness went down the yard with the pipe, and gave it to Jobbins with the matches, who went up the ladder with the pipe in his mouth, and the matches in his hand, which he lighted, and set fire to the combustibles placed amongst the clover. It soon blazed up; they got over the gate, and found Lowe waiting, who directed him to go and fetch Mrs. Lowe, which he did, and found her lying down in her cloaths. When they returned, the fire was burning rapidly. They found Lowe in the inn-yard bringing out boxes. They went into Mr. Gilding's room, and took a case, containing 24 silver spoons, threw the case away, and putting the spoons into a handkerchief, carried them to the house of Lowe, and put them in a cupboard under the stairs. The witness went to call Barnard, who came with him to the fire; when he saw the goods, he he said, This is something like indeed! Both of them went to get a cart, but could not get one. Lowe carried the drawers away upon his head towards Barnard's house, and desired the witness to follow, which he did into St. John's-street, where Barnard lifted them from Lowe's head to the witness's head; and in New Prison Walk he was taken into custody by Lucie, a patrole, with the drawers upon his head. Barnard walked off. When Lucie had secured the witness in New Prison, he went out, and took Lowe into custody.

The witness was tried and convicted of stealing the drawers; and when in New Prison, got a man in the same ward to write a letter to Alderman Skinner, promising, on certain conditions, to discover the whole of this most horrid transaction; which being complied with, and his pardon obtained, and pleaded in court, he was admitted an evidence against his accomplices.

The evidence of Flindal was confirmed in circumstances by Samuels, a Jew, in Houndsditch, and his wife, to the former of whom Lowe had confessed his guilt. Being found guilty, they were both executed near the spot where Mr. Gilding's house stood, in Aldersgate-street, Nov. 20, 1790. Jobbins had been educated at St. Paul's school, was bred a surgeon, and only 19 years of age when he suffered. Lowe was about 23 years of age.

EDWARD WELSH, *for the Murder of his Wife.*

IT appeared in the course of the trial, that the prisoner and his wife had lodgings near Dyott-street, St. Giles's.

That on Saturday the 4th of December, a quarrel arose between them, relative to some money. Many foul words passed between them, when Welsh, who was an Irishman, swore if she did not hold her tongue, he would soon find a way to make her. Unhappily she still continued to aggravate him in the most abusive manner. Upon this, he ran up to her, and giving her several blows, she fell. Whilst upon the ground, she screamed out Murder! in a violent manner. Enraged at this, almost to a pitch of madness, he drew his knife, and swore she should cry Murder for something. He then ran up to her, and jobbing the knife into the lower part of her belly, ripped her up a considerable way.

By this time, the noise had drawn together several of the neighbours. Some of them attempted to go into the room, but he brandished his knife, and swore he would butcher the first who entered. Finding nothing but violence would do, they knocked him down with a bludgeon, and he was secured. A surgeon was immediately sent for, but proved of no use, the poor woman being dead. The facts being plain, and the prisoner having little to say in his defence, the jury found him guilty.

This criminal was born in the kingdom of Ireland, and got his living as a porter in Covent Garden market.

On Monday morning, Dec. 13, 1790, he was executed, in the presence of a number of spectators, calling upon the Lord to have mercy upon him, and receive his soul. His dead body was taken to Surgeons Hall.

Account of RYNWICK WILLIAMS, *otherwise called the Monster.*

THE indictment charged, that he, Rynwick Williams, on Jan. 18, 1790, with force and arms, at the parish of St. James, Westminster, in the king's highway, and in a certain public street, did unlawfully, wilfully, and maliciously, make an assault upon Ann Porter. The indictment further charged, that on the same day, and at the parish aforesaid, the prisoner at the bar did unlawfully, wilfully, and maliciously, tear, spoil, cut, and deface, the garments and clothes, to wit, the cloak, gown, and petticoat of the said Ann Porter, contrary to the statute, and against the king's peace.

The chief evidence, on this trial, was that of Miss Ann Porter, the injured lady, who was not chargeable with the smallest degree of inconsistency even on her cross-examination. Her evidence was also confirmed by that of her sister Miss Sarah Porter. After which, Mr. Tomkins the surgeon proved, that the wound which Miss Porter received was a very dangerous one indeed; that it was between nine and ten inches in length, and in the middle between three and four inches deep—at the ends only just through the skin; and, but for her stays, must have penetrated the abdomen: she must have been cut with a sharp instrument.

After a full and impartial hearing, the jury found the prisoner guilty.

Mr. Justice Buller then ordered the judgment in this case, and the recognizances of the persons bound to prosecute, to be respited till Dec. sessions. All the witnesses were examined separately.

At the commencement of the sessions at the Old Bailey, on the 10th of Dec. judge Ashurst addressed the prisoner nearly in the following terms: " You have been capitally convicted under the stat. 6 Geo. I. of maliciously tearing, cutting, spoiling, and defacing the garments of Ann Porter, on the 18th of Jan. last. Judgment has been arrested upon two points—one, that the indictment is informal; the other, that the act of parliament does not reach the crime. Upon solemn consideration, the judges are of opinion, that both the objections are well founded; but although you are discharged from this indictment, yet you are within the purview of the common law. You are therefore to be remanded to be tried for a misdemeanor."

He was accordingly, on the 13th of the same Dec. tried at Hicks's Hall, for a misdemeanor, in making an assault on Miss Ann Porter. The trial lasted 16 hours: there were three counts in the indictment, viz. for assaulting with intent to kill, for assaulting and wounding, and for a common assault.

The charge was, that he, on the 18th of Jan. 1790, made an assault on Ann Porter, and with a certain knife inflicted on her person a wound nine inches long, and in the middle part of it four inches deep.

The same witnesses were then called, in support of the charge, as appeared on the trial at the Old Bailey: they gave a very clear, correct, and circumstantial evidence, positively swearing to the person of the prisoner.

The facts proved were nearly the same, with very little variation indeed, with those which were given in evidence, on his trial for the felony at the Old Bailey; for which reason we forbear to enter more fully on the trial.

The prisoner produced two witnesses, Miss Amet and Mr. Michelle, who attempted to prove a clear *alibi*, and the credit of their testimony was not impeached by any contradiction. The question therefore was, to which the jury would give credit, for the evidence was on both sides equally fair and unexceptionable.

The chairman made a most excellent summing up; the jury retired, and at half past two o'clock the next morning, returned a verdict of Guilty.

The prisoner was again put to the bar at 10 o'clock the same morning, and tried on the remaining indictments, on three of which he was found Guilty; when the court sentenced him to two years imprisonment in Newgate for each, and at the expiration of the time to find security for his good behaviour, himself in 200*l*. and two sureties in 100*l*. each.

Account of the Trial of LORD VISCOUNT DUNGARVAN, *Son to the Earl of Cork.*

THE indictment charged his lordship with the capital offence of stealing privately from the person of Eliz. Weldon, three guineas and an half, on the evening of Wedn. Jan. 13, 1791.

The prosecutrix swore, that she was at the play on Wednesday night, and was handed out by a gentleman to a hackney coach. When about half way home, she felt his hand at her pocket; and discovering her loss, charged the gentleman with having picked her pocket. When they got out of the coach, she said, that, on accusing him with the theft, he offered her a guinea to let him go. She answered, he should not; and if he offered to go, she would call out, Stop thief! That he then ran off; she pursued him, called out, Watch! and stop thief; in consequence of which he was taken to the watch house, where she charged him with the felony in question.

William Whitebroke and Robert Boyce proved, that the prosecutrix had lodged in their houses; and that she was a woman of such a loose and disorderly character, that they were obliged to get rid of her.

Many other witnesses were called in behalf of his lordship, who invalidated the facts sworn to by the prosecutrix. Among these were the link-man and the coachman, who invalidated the evidence of the prosecutrix in very material points, and rendered her testimony of no avail.

Mr. Sheppard, the attorney for the defendant, also gave his evidence as to what passed in the parlour of the magistrate, and also contradicted the testimony of the prosecutrix. Mr. King the barrister confirmed this. The testimony of several other witnesses left not the smallest doubt upon any person in court, of the abandoned character of the prosecutrix, of the iniquity of the prosecution, and the innocence and honour of the noble lord.

A great many of the first characters in the kingdom also attended, among whom were his Grace of Devonshire, duke of Portland, &c. to give the defendant the most amiable and honourable character, if the case should require it.

The jury, clearly perceiving the complexion of the prosecution, and being convinced of the perfect innocence of the defendant, pronounced him Not Guilty.

The learned judge addressed his lordship in these words:

"My lord Dungarvan,

"It is but justice to you to say, it is impossible you can go away from this bar with the smallest imputation on your character. Of your imprudence in this business, you seem to be already very sensible."

The trial lasted near six hours. When the defendant was found Not Guilty, there was an universal shout of approbation, and the prosecutrix was hissed out of court, and with great difficulty escaped feeling the effects of the people's resentment.

BARTHOLOMEW QUAIN, *for Murder, in the Isle of Ely.*

HE was tried and convicted at the last assizes for the Isle of Ely, Cambridgeshire, for the wilful murder of Ann his wife. He was brought from the King's Bench prison, and placed at the bar, when Mr. Plumtree, Counsel for the Crown, stated the circumstances of the case, and contended that the fact, of which the prisoner had been found guilty, amounted to the crime of wilful murder. He said that the Jury, under the direction of the Chief Judge of Ely, had found a Special Verdict, in order to take the opinion of the Court of King's Bench upon the following question, viz. "whether the facts found by the Jury amounted to murder, or only to manslaughter?" The circumstances of the case, as proved upon the trial, were these:—The prisoner and his wife came out of a house together in the Isle of Ely. They appeared to have been quarrelling. The prisoner had one of his children in his arms. His wife sat herself upon the ground, and then rose and walked. The prisoner followed her, and gave her two

two or three kicks, upon which she shrieked out and ran away; he pursued, and kicked her again; in consequence of which she fell upon the ground: he then retired a few paces, returned to her again, and, while she lay on the ground, he gave her several more kicks; she then got up, when he kicked her down again; the deceased then said, "You have killed me." A woman, hearing her shrieks, remonstrated with the prisoner against his conduct; upon which he said he would serve her the same. The deceased then arose, struggled, fell down, and died. The prisoner, upon finding she was dead, expressed great sorrow. It appeared that her spleen had burst, and the indictment stated that of this she died, and that it was occasioned by the kicks and blows given her by the prisoner. The whole lasted near half an hour.

Mr. Plumtree cited a number of cases to prove that the offence of which the prisoner had been convicted amounted to wilful murder. To constitute murder, the law said, there must be malice expressed or implied. Barbarity always implied malice. If one man cruelly beat another without provocation, although he did not intend to kill, yet the law would imply a malicious purpose, and if the party died it would be murder. He made many apposite remarks upon the case in question, and contended that it clearly amounted to murder, according to the opinions of Lord Hale, Mr. Justice Forster, and other great legal authorities.

The Court were clearly of opinion that the facts proved against the prisoner amounted to murder. There appeared to be no provocation on the part of the deceased, and no man had a right even to inflict chastisement without a just provocation. It was not necessary to prove express malice, to constitute murder. If one person provoked another to chastise him, it must be done with moderation, and with a proper instrument, otherwise the law would infer malice.

He was executed at Kennington, on Feb. 7, 1791.

JOHN ETHERINGTON, and JOHN RANDALL, *for Robberies, &c.*

JOHN ETHERINGTON was indicted for feloniously returning from transportation, before the term for which he was transported was expired, and being seen at large within this kingdom.

On the part of the Crown it was proved, that the prisoner had been sentenced to be transported for seven years, from the year 1787. The record of his conviction being produced, and his person identified by one of the persons belonging to Newgate; he was therefore found guilty.

He was again indicted for breaking and entering the dwelling-house of the Baron Wenzel, in Sackville-street, on the first of December, and stealing therein a counterpane and a silk cloak, value 5l.

The Baron being in France, the prisoner, in company with another man, genteelly dressed, came to the house on the first of December, under pretence of taking it, and went up stairs with the house-keeper, to view the different rooms.

On their coming to the garret, she missed the other person who came with the prisoner, which raised her suspicion; and, on their coming down stairs, the parlour-door, which she had left open, was shut, and the street-door half open. The house-keeper immediately seized the prisoner, and shutting the street-door, insisted on his giving an account of the other man who had come with him; on which a scuffle ensued; and the prisoner, in order to effect his escape, struck her several times, and cut her in a desperate manner.

She cried out murder, and alarmed the neighbourhood, when two servants from the next house came to her assistance, and secured the prisoner.

These facts being fully proved by the housekeeper, the Jury without hesitation, brought in their verdict guilty.

This criminal was born of reputable parents, who gave him a decent education, and placed him as an apprentice to a saddletree-maker. Being out of his time, he fell into bad company, and committed a felony, in which being detected, he was sentenced to be transported. Finding means to return, he renewed his depredations, which brought him to the gallows.

Whilst under sentence of death, he behaved in a penitent manner, having little hopes of mercy, as the Judge, immediately after his conviction, bid him prepare to die, as his crimes were enormous.

He was a decent looking man, about 30 years of age.

JOHN RANDALL was cast for breaking into the house of George Telfer, and stealing a pair of cotton stockings, a cotton petticoat, a muslin handkerchief, half a crown, some halfpence, &c.

On the trial, the facts were plainly proved against the prisoner, who being an old offender, was ordered for execution.

During the time he lay under sentence of death, he behaved in a very penitent manner.

He had received but a very indifferent education, and was under the necessity of requesting his fellow prisoners, and others, to read to and pray with him, for which he appeared exceedingly thankful.

Particularly did he desire every one to take warning by his unhappy fate, to avoid drinking and Sabbath-breaking, shun bad company, fear God, and obey their parents.

These two malefactors were executed on Feb. 23, 1791.

As Soze de Souza and Thomas Herbert were to have been executed with the above, but were respited; and tho' their fate was not determined when this account went to press, it may not be improper to give some particulars concerning them.

SOZE

SOZE DE SOUZA, a Portuguese Jew, was capitally convicted of privately stealing, in the dwelling-house of Gregory Lucy, twenty-four guineas, a crown-piece, and a silver watch, his property.

This criminal was born in the kingdom of Portugal, and had followed a seafaring life, till he came to England, where he committed the fact for which he was condemned. While under sentence of death, he behaved in a very reserved manner, yet appeared in general greatly shocked when he reflected on his awful situation. Being of the Roman catholic religion, he was attended during his confinement, and in prospect of a speedy execution, by one of the priests of that persuasion. He owned he was guilty of the crime for which he expected to suffer death; and confessed, that from his youth he had been addicted to pilfering.

This unhappy man affords an instructive caution to other young people, that are thievishly inclined, not on any account to invade and purloin the property of others; inasmuch as one bad action, how small soever, commonly tends to harden the conscience, and lead unthinking mortals to greater, till destruction closes the fatal and melancholy scene. The following useful lesson, therefore, well learnt, and deeply impressed on the mind, will be an effectual preservative against all dishonest practices, namely, " Avoid the least appearance of evil."

THOMAS HERBERT was cast for burglariously entering the dwelling-house of Dennis Dolan, and John Magaurin, and stealing a metal candlestick, value 3 s.

This malefactor was born of honest parents, who did every thing in their power to induce him to walk in the path of virtue; but his own evil propensities rendered all their endeavours ineffectual. He was not bred to any business, but had lived in several places, having been employed to look after horses, &c. He had so little fear of dying for the crime he had committed, that, previous to his trial, he entertained the greatest hopes of being acquitted.

While under sentence of death, he behaved in a decent manner, but was rather too chearful for one in his dreadful situation. He continued for some time confident of receiving a respite: but when the dead warrant came down, and he found himself ordered for execution, it is impossible to express the horror of his mind. But the night before he was to be executed, his Majesty extended his royal clemency to him by a respite; and should his life be spared, it is hoped a serious reflection on the destructive consequences he had experienced from pursuing evil courses, will prove a means of his reformation in the future part of his life. He was only about 21 years of age, and being low in stature, had a boyish look.

Relation

Relation of WILLIAM BAKER, *the Murderer, at Pancras.*

AN account has been received from Portsmouth, that William Baker, alias King, being taken ill, has confessed, when in Hasler Hospital, that he was the person who, about a twelvemonth ago, so cruelly murdered the woman near St. Pancras.

We are told, that this unhappy man was lately a sailor on board one of his Majesty's ships, where his behaviour was so singular, that all his shipmates noticed it. In the day-time he was full of jollity, skipping about the deck in the highest glee; but when night came on, his mind was so agitated, that the continued noise he made disturbed all the ship's company.

At length he became so bad, that when the ship was at Spithead he was sent to Hasler Hospital, and being likely to die, he sent for two clergymen, viz. Dr. Bruce, and Dr. Walker, and made the following confession to them:

"Finding, by the justice of God, that I can have no rest, by night or by day, I do confess, to ease my sin-sick soul, that I, and only I, committed that shocking murder, upon the body of the woman near Pancras, about a twelvemonth since. I then went to sea, that I might fly from justice, but have found it all in vain; for no sooner did I lay down upon my hammock, than the ghost of the deceased woman appeared before me, pointing to her bleeding wounds, and demanding my life as a forfeit for the horrid crime.

"Tormented in this dreadful manner, I was determined to make a full confession of my offence, which I now do, in the presence of the Rev. gentlemen above-mentioned.

"I do not desire to live, but wish to die; yet hope, by the blood of Jesus Christ, and a sincere repentance, that a wicked offence may meet with heaven's pardon.

"I desire the prayers of these gentlemen, and all christians; am in my perfect senses, and make this confession freely and voluntarily, to ease my soul.

"In witness whereof I have signed my name, the twelfth of February, 1791.

"WILLIAM BAKER."

The unhappy wretch, since this confession, is considerably recovered, and is, of course, kept under a strict guard.

When able to be tried, he will be brought to town, and, undoubtedly, if found guilty, receive the just reward of his crime.

www.ingramcontent.com/pod-product-compliance
Lightning Source LLC
Chambersburg PA
CBHW080919180426
43192CB00040B/2467